Poltergeists

Poltergeists

Alan Gauld and A.D. Cornell

www.whitecrowbooks.com

Poltergeists

Original copyright © 1979 by Alan Gauld and A. D. Cornell.
This edition: Copyright © 2017 by Alan Gauld and
A. D. Cornell. All rights reserved.

Published and printed in the United States of America and the United Kingdom by White Crow Books; an imprint of White Crow Productions Ltd.

The right of Alan Gauld and A. D. Cornell to be identified as the author of this work has been asserted by them in accordance with the Copyright, Design and Patents act 1988.

No part of this book may be reproduced, copied or used in any form or manner whatsoever without written permission, except in the case of brief quotations in reviews and critical articles.

For information, contact White Crow Books
at 3 Hova Villas, Hove, BN3 3DH United Kingdom,
or e-mail info@whitecrowbooks.com.

Cover Design by Astrid@Astridpaints.com
Interior design by Velin@Perseus-Design.com

Paperback ISBN 978-1-78677-039-4
eBook   ISBN 978-1-78677-040-0

Non Fiction / Body, Mind & Spirit / Death & Dying / Parapsychology

www.whitecrowbooks.com

Disclaimer: White Crow Productions Ltd. and its directors, employees, distributors, retailers, wholesalers and assignees disclaim any liability or responsibility for the author's statements, words, ideas, criticisms or observations. White Crow Productions Ltd. assumes no responsibility for errors, inaccuracies, or omissions.

Contents

Errors from the previous publication [vi]
Preface [ix]
Acknowledgments [xi]

Part I Survey and sampling of cases by Alan Gauld [1]
  1 Introduction [3]
  2 Three sixteenth-century cases [22]
  3 Poltergeists and witches [40]
  4 Poltergeist people [67]
  5 Destructive poltergeists [85]
  6 Fantastical poltergeists [98]
  7 Poltergeist assaults [116]
  8 Poltergeists and the dead [143]
  9 Poltergeists and daemons [158]
  10 Hauntings [176]
  11 Some intermediate cases [208]
  12 Poltergeists and the computer [224]

Part II Some personal investigations and conclusions by Alan Gauld and A. D. Cornell [241]
  13 Explaining away the poltergeist [243]
  14 Some poltergeist cases [263]
  15 Some cases of haunting [283]
  16 Some unusual cases [295]
  17 The forces at work [319]
  18 Are poltergeists living or are they dead? [339]
  Appendix to Part I Chronological list of 500 cases, with sources and case characteristics [363]

  Index of cases [399]
  Index of names [403]

Errors from the previous publication

Case 208. Immediately before 'Spicer' should read: 2, 2 (0.2044, 0.1103)

Case 262. At the end should read: 6, 4;   1   5   7   8   9   22   24   27   54

Case 276. at the end should read: 4, 5:   1   6   9   16   22   23   24   54

Cases 227 and 245. Case 245 seems to be a misdated and somewhat garbled version of case 227. It should not be there.

Illustrations

Between pages 180 and 181

1. Melchior Joller and his family (*By courtesy of Martin Gyr Verlag, Baden-bei-Zürich*)
2. Melchior Joller's house in Stans (*By courtesy of Martin Gyr Verlag, Baden-bei-Zürich*)
3. Title-page of the North Aston pamphlet (*By courtesy of the British Library*)
4. The Gerstmanns' house at Dortmund (*By courtesy of the British Library*)
5. The poltergeist house at Newbury, Massachusetts
6. Swinging lamps in the Rosenheim case (*By courtesy of Prof. H. Bender and Elek Science*)
7. Title-page of the Sandfeldt pamphlet (*By courtesy of the Staats- und Universitätsbibliothek, Hamburg*)
8. Eleonora Zugun, with scratch-marks on face (*By courtesy of the Harry Price Library, University of London*)
9. Hand of Eleonora Zugun, showing bite-mark (*By courtesy of the Harry Price Library, University of London*)
10. The 'haunted house' at Cheltenham (*By courtesy of the Harry Price Library, University of London*)
11. 'Beth-oni', Tackley, Oxon., view from garden (*By courtesy of the Harry Price Library, University of London*)
12. Willington Mill about 1890
13. The 'haunted house' on Canvey Island towards the end of last century (*By courtesy of the British Library*)
14. The dressing-table which was overturned by the 'East Midlands' poltergeist
15. Hannath Hall
16. The 'house-shaking apparatus'

Preface

This book is intended more for the general reader interested in the stranger side of nature than for the professional parapsychologist, though we hope the latter may find things in it to interest him. Part I, by AG, is a survey of representative cases of poltergeists and hauntings. It tries whenever possible to illustrate the different kinds of case with instances which, though relatively well-authenticated, are little known. It concludes with a statistical analysis of the characteristics of 500 sample cases from the literature. As a result of this analysis, some tentative proposals are made as to the groups or classes into which cases of poltergeists and of hauntings fall.

In Part II, by AG and ADC, we describe various of our own case investigations, and take up some of the issues raised in Part I in the light of our experiences. The last two chapters touch on the main theoretical problems raised by reports of poltergeist phenomena – the problem of the nature of the physical forces involved, and the problem of whether the 'intelligence' so often manifested in poltergeist phenomena is that of a living human being or of a discarnate entity of some little understood kind.

There are no formal footnotes or bibliography, but every attempt has been made to enable readers to follow up any case of which they desire further details. A certain amount of bibliographical information has been included in the text, and at the end is an appendix containing a chronological list of the 500 sample cases mentioned above, with the sources for them. Cases are referred to in the text by the year and the place of the first phenomenon. This may sometimes obscure the fact that a well-known case is being referred to – e.g. the case of Eleonora Zugun, the 'poltergeist girl' from Talpa, Rumania, appears in the text as Buhai (1925) or Buhai (1925–7) – but in general it will facilitate location of a case in the chronological list. All but a very few of the cases mentioned will be found in the chronological list.

Acknowledgments

During the writing of this book many persons and institutions have been kind enough to help us in one way or another. Many of our printed sources have come from the fine collections in the Library of the Society for Psychical Research (the 'SPR'), and in the Harry Price Library, Senate House, University of London, and we are indebted to Miss Eleanor O'Keeffe and Mrs I. M. Barry of the former, and to Mr A. H. Wesencraft of the latter, for much help and numerous kindnesses. We are also much indebted to Glenis Pickering of the University Library, Nottingham, Dr F. H. Stubbings, the Librarian of Emmanuel College, Cambridge, Mr K. C. Newton of the Essex Record Office, Mr R. Wilson of the Cambridge and County Folk Museum, Miss M. Sheldon-Williams and Mr W. Andrews of the Bodleian Library, and Alison M. Gee of the British Library. Various rare works were supplied, in original or photocopy, by the University Library, Cambridge, the Deutsche Bibliothek, Frankfurt, the Deutsche Staatsbibliothek, Berlin, the Wissenschaftliche Allgemeinbibliothek, Erfurt, and the Staats- und Universitätsbibliothek, Hamburg. For information, references, or help in other ways we have to thank Helen Dent, Sheila Gauld, Howard Wilkinson, Martin Chamberlain, Trude Cornell, Eleonore Speirs, the Rev. T. G. Williamson, Pat Howarth, the late Mr L. F. Newman, the late Professor E. M. Wilson, Denys Parsons, Mr Raymond Bayless, the Rev. G. Wrayford, Carl Sargent, Bernard Carr, Mrs D. L. Gauld, Dr E. J. Dingwall, Mrs C. C. Baines, Diana Broom and Dr G. de Boni. Last, we must express our special gratitude to Michael Henstock and Doreen Newham, our very patient linguistic consultants, and to Hugh Smith and Roger Henry, whose expertise and advice made possible the computer analysis of data described in chapter 12. In the preparation of the illustrations we have been much indebted to the skill and kindness of Sam Grainger.

For permission to use or quote from copyright material we have to thank the editor of the *Journal of the SPR*, the editor of the *Journal of the American SPR*, the editor of *Light*, Professor

J. G. Pratt, and the Harry Price Library. For permission to print the letters and diary of John Mompesson we are indebted to the President and Fellows of Corpus Christi College, Oxford. For permission to quote from an unpublished case report by the late Mr H. M. Popham we have to thank Mrs M. Popham. For permission to reproduce photographic material we are indebted to the British Library, the Harry Price Library, the Staats- und Universitätsbibliothek, Hamburg, Professor H. Bender and Elek Science and Martin Gyr Verlag of Baden-bei-Zürich.

Part I Survey and sampling of cases

by Alan Gauld

1 Introduction

In his *Disquisitionum Magicarum* (1599), Martin Del Rio, a learned Jesuit, distinguishes (Book II, Question 27, section 2) eighteen different kinds of demon or demonic apparition. The sixteenth kind are

> those spectres which in certain times and places or homes are wont to occasion various commotions and annoyances. I shall pass over examples, since the thing is exceedingly well known, and instances can be read in older and more recent authors. Sometimes they are content just to annoy and disturb, doing no bodily harm, like that throwing spirit of which William of Paris writes, which disturbed his slumbers with clattering of pots and hurling of stones, and, having pulled away his mattress, turned him out of bed, and that Salamancan fiend of Torquemada, which indiscriminately attacked people with large stones, striking them, nevertheless, with an empty and harmless blow. Which Marcus Magus in Psellus says to be characteristic of the subterranean demons of which we shall next treat. By what arrangement demons can throw stones and perform other things of kinds which seem to require hands and bodily instruments, the Scholastics dispute. I agree with those who hold these things to be done by a demon substantially present in that place and moving the air next the stone by a command of will.

Demons of this class differ from those of Del Rio's other seventeen classes in one important respect: they are still with us. Whereas nowadays we hear little or nothing about subterranean demons, demons which guard treasure, demons which shun the light, about demons of earth, air, fire and water, about sphinxes, lamias and Kobolds, we still hear plenty of 'poltergeist' stories.

'Poltergeist' is an old German word meaning 'noisy spirit', and it is an appropriate one because, as Del Rio indicates, the phenomena in question often consist in or result in the generation of noise. Another German word of equal antiquity is 'Rumpelgeist' ('jolting' or 'rumbling' spirit), but 'poltergeist' has become more or less standard English. Curiously enough, it seems to be little used nowadays by Germans, who prefer the term 'Spuk'. Perhaps 'poltergeist' has for them the same sort of connotations as 'goblin' has for the English, 'lutin' for the French, 'folletto' for the Italians, and 'trasgo' for Spaniards, so that it is hardly possible for them to introduce the word in more or less serious discussion. Modern parapsychologists, particularly American ones, often use the impressive term 'RSPK' ('recurrent spontaneous psychokinesis') instead of 'poltergeist', which they think has undesirable overtones of primitive animism. Personally I am not happy with this innovation. We do not know sufficient about psychokinesis (literally 'mind-movement') as investigated in certain sorts of laboratory experiments to say whether or not it has any kinship with poltergeist phenomena. And we must not slip into thinking that because we have applied to the phenomena a scientific-sounding rubric like 'RSPK' we are somehow nearer to explaining them. At least it should be clear to everyone that labelling certain obscure phenomena 'poltergeist' phenomena no more explains them than would calling them 'goblin' phenomena or 'gremlins'.

The phenomena that have been and are laid at the door of the poltergeist make up a pretty motley collection. The two commonest major classes are perhaps those of percussive sounds – raps, taps, thumps, thuds, crashes, bangs and bombinations – and those of object movements – the tilting, displacement, movement, lifting, and hurling of objects, generally small objects, but sometimes ones weighing several hundredweight. Other sorts of phenomena which have been attributed to poltergeists include communication by means of a code of raps; inundations of water; mysterious outbreaks of fire; interference with electrical equipment; the playing of musical instruments; cutting or tearing of clothes or soft furnishings; frightening of or interference with animals; imitation of sounds, including the sound of the human voice; arrangement of objects into patterns; the appearance of lights, luminosities, misty figures, phantasms, etc., including the phantasms of animals; and the beating, wounding or biting of particular individuals. About all that these various kinds of alleged happening have in common is that they are localized in a place or around a person, are for the most part physical, and are not susceptible of any immediately obvious explanation. The chief justification for lumping them together under the same general heading is their frequent association with each other, and their even more frequent association with the two especially common sorts of 'poltergeist' phenomena which I mentioned first of all, namely percussive sounds and object movements. It must be borne in mind, however, that lumping them together in this way may be a mistake.

It may be objected at this point that I am beginning to treat these preposterous phenomena seriously. Why should they not all be consigned to the realm of superstition, like the doings of Del Rio's other seventeen kinds of demons? The answer is, of course, that whereas we do not have many first-hand accounts from sane persons who have encountered demons of the other seventeen sorts, we do have quite a lot of eyewitness accounts of poltergeist phenomena. Some of these accounts are not easy to dismiss as nonsense, and they raise a number of problems. It will be convenient to introduce these problems in the context of an actual case.

For this purpose I shall take a fairly old Swiss example, the Stans case of 1860–2. This case has the advantages of being *prima facie* fairly strong – the principal witness was an educated and able man who kept a detailed diary of events – and of being relatively little-known to English readers. It also has the advantage, for immediate purposes, of not being so strong as to offer no purchase at all to some standard sceptical objections.

The 'principal witness' to whom I referred a moment ago was a distinguished Swiss lawyer, journalist and member of the National Council, named Melchior Joller (1818–65). The afflicted house was his own, in Stans, near Lake Lucerne, and our chief source of information about the happenings there is his own pamphlet *Darstellung selbsterlebter mystischer Erscheinungen* (Narrative of personally experienced strange phenomena) published at Zürich in 1863. This scarce pamphlet is conveniently reprinted, with some additional documents, in Fanny Moser's *Spuk: Irrglaube oder Wahrglaube?* (Baden-bei-Zürich, 1950), which also supplies further details about Joller, his career, his family, and his descendants.

The dominant impression which one gains of Joller is of a methodical man, with ordered ways of thought and ordered ways of doing things – a man, too, with a fair share of the obstinacy which so often characterizes such persons. The story of the case is the story of how Joller's methodical approach to life first cracked and ultimately disintegrated under the pressure of the extraordinary happenings. In the end the wretched man, plagued by sightseers, ridiculed in the press, and assailed by political enemies, fled with his family from his ancestral house, to die three years later in Rome, an impoverished and embittered exile.

True to his methodical nature, Joller begins his pamphlet with a detailed account of his house and its locality. It seems to have been a cheerful and well-situated building in the old Swiss style. The ground floor had thick walls of brick or stone with few windows, and was divided into three main compartments, a cellar, a dairy, and a space known as the *Hütte*, which I think must have been used as a washing and general purposes area. Upon the solid walls of the ground floor rested the wooden walls of two further complete stories. The lower of these, to which access was ordinarily gained by an outside staircase, contained a porch, the kitchen and main living room, a little kitchen room, a bedroom, main corridor, and an unlit small corridor leading, apparently, to a toilet. The upper contained Joller's study, together with four bedrooms and a corridor. At the very top of the house, beneath the apex of the steeply sloping roof, were a second living room, known as the *Saal*, a drying room, a couple of small bedrooms, and some attic space.

In this house Joller lived in moderate affluence with his wife Karoline, their four sons Robert (b. 1843), Edward (b. 1851), Oscar (b. about 1852), and Alfred, and their three daughters, Emaline (b. 1845), Melanie (b. 1848) and Henriette (Henricka, b. 1850), and one or more maids. The family's style of living was simple and pious – they were sincere, and perhaps devout, Catholics.

The first rumblings of the coming storm were heard in the early autumn of 1860. The Jollers' then maid complained one morning that she had heard and felt clear knockings on her bedstead. A few weeks later, when Joller returned from a business trip, his wife told him that she and their daughter Melanie, sharing a bedroom, had been woken up the previous night by a quick knocking on their bedside table. While they were nervously discussing what it could have been, it began again, and gave about ten or fifteen quick blows, at first powerful, but becoming weaker. Though his wife and daughter were much frightened, Joller attached at the time no importance to their experiences.

The following summer saw a further outburst of odd incidents. About the beginning of June, little Oscar, then nine years old, failed to show up for supper. He was discovered lying unconscious in a little room used as a wood store. When he was able to speak again he said that soon after he had gone into the wood store three knocks had sounded on the door. Then the door had burst open, and a whitish, formless shape came in. Soon after this others of the children began to complain of hearing footsteps, raps, and other noises, and the youngest daughter, Henricka, was frightened by the phantasm of a small child. Towards autumn the maid complained of seeing grey shapes in the darkness of the *Hütte*, shapes which came close to her and then disappeared. One morning she said that in the night someone had climbed the stairs, gone past her room, and ascended towards the *Saal* (the attic living room). From the stairs her name was many times clearly called. The footsteps went up three times, and at last entered the *Saal*, from which, for a time, she heard profoundly disturbing sobs. Once again Joller brushed these stories aside, but he seems before long to have dismissed the maid, whom he regarded as a superstitious person; at any rate, in October 1861 she was replaced by a servant girl of thirteen. All was quiet thereafter until the summer of 1862, when trouble began in earnest.

On 15 August 1862 Joller set out for Lucerne at seven in the morning, with his wife and eldest son Robert, leaving the rest of the family alone with the servant girl. He did not return until late. Subsequently he pieced together from what his children told him the following complicated and dramatic story. During the morning Melanie (aged about fourteen) and the servant girl fell to discussing certain strange rappings which Henricka thought she had heard in the little dark corridor on the first floor. They proceeded down there. Henricka, who was about twelve, also arrived. Melanie, who was sceptical, called out in loud tones, 'In God's name, if there is anything to it, let it come and rap!' At once something began to rap as if with a knuckle. Shortly afterwards Oscar arrived and heard the tale. He repeated the challenge and received the same reply. As soon as the elder brother, Edward, heard of this wonder, he hurried to the spot, issued the same challenge, and was similarly answered.

Now they became frightened and rushed headlong out of the house. While they were sitting on the stone steps outside, taking stock of the situation, a pebble, almost fist-sized, fell between Melanie and the youngest boy, Alfred. When lunchtime came nearer they ventured into the house again to prepare a meal. They found all the house-doors and cupboard doors wide open. They closed them, and bolted some, but they began to open again, even the bolted ones. The children were further alarmed by the sound of a heavy tread coming down the staircase; and they shortly fled back to the garden.

At lunchtime the servant girl ventured into the kitchen again, but rashly peered out into the corridor and believed she saw coming towards her a shape somewhat like a sheet hung up by one corner. She called, 'Who is that outside?' and with a quick 'Wuh' the figure disappeared. The girl dashed from the house in terror, but when Joller's eldest daughter Emaline came up, she recovered sufficiently to go in and bring out the food. Doors and windows continued to fly open, and the children eventually took refuge in a barn, where some of Joller's labourers were at work. From this secure base they now and again crept towards the house to see what was happening. When they did this they almost always heard a noise. Once Edward and the servant girl ventured to the top of the steps, from which they could look in through two of the living room windows. They saw a chair slide of its own accord from its place, and then in an instant throw itself round, legs in the air. Those below heard the racket, and all sprang away in terror. Another time, standing before the house, they clearly heard through the open bedroom window a deep, groaning voice say, in tones of intolerable melancholy, 'Even if no-one is around!'

At last there arrived the wife of Joller's tenant, who lived in an outhouse with her husband and family. The children asked her to come into the house with them. There, on the floor in front of the grindstone, as if poured on, they discovered a little snow-white picture, no bigger than a small coin, so like a death's head in the smallest detail that an engraver could not have bettered it. They could not discover of what material this picture was made; and it shortly grew darker and lost its shape. Then further noises frightened them out again.

Between 4.00 p.m. and 5.00 p.m. they lit a fire in the *Hütte* to heat a kettle; and about 7.00 p.m. the maid lit the kitchen range to prepare supper. Suddenly it became light in the chimney, and, looking upwards she saw coming down it a sugar-loaf-shaped object with innumerable little blue flames. This object disintegrated inside the chimney, and in so doing dowsed the fire with an appreciable quantity of water. A piece of the object, however, fell into the adjoining chimney of the *Hütte*, at the bottom of which young Edward was playing with the kettle. At once Edward and the maid simultaneously cried out, 'The chimney is on fire!' The former found the kettle, the latter her jacket, covered with the thousand pointed rapidly running little flames that had a moment ago dissolved into water. At this they lost all courage, and when Frau Joller returned about 8.30 p.m. she found them in the outhouse, weeping with terror.

Next morning the children wanted to tell their father of these remarkable occurrences. Joller refused to listen, scolded them for their superstitious fear, and threatened them with the rod if he heard any more of such nonsense. They went off muttering. However, on Tuesday 19 August, Joller himself witnessed the phenomena, and from this date on we have his own record, in diary form, of what he observed. When he returned home in the evening his wife called him down to the corridor to hear the strange rappings on the wall. Rather unwillingly he obeyed and heard from the back wall of the little kitchen room

> a repeated peculiar rapping of 10–12 blows, which came very quickly towards the end, as if someone, tapping nervously on a door with his finger, demanded instant admission. The rappings were repeated many times after short pauses. I sought and found, with my ear to the wall, the precise location of the sounds, which, however, frequently moved. Thinking it must be a living creature, such as a rat, I hit the wall to frighten it away. Instead it more than once replied with the same sound, followed sometimes by one or two more powerful blows as if with a fist. I had a candle brought, went into the little room, and searched it with the greatest care in order to discover some trace of the disturbing agency. During this undertaking the rappings continued as before, and my investigation remained without result. Listening longer and more carefully, I now perceived the raps coming from other places in the corridor.

Stubborn in his opinion that there must be a natural explanation, he consoled his family with promises of a thorough investigation. At supper in the living room he read from an improving book a passage entitled 'The Power of Superstition'. This salutary procedure was interrupted by rappings from the floor, some of them very powerful. Finally came rappings on the room door as though someone wanted to come in. Taking a candle and a sharp stiletto, Joller descended to the ground floor and searched everywhere, including the cellar under the living room. The raps continued above his head, but he discovered nothing. He even extinguished the light and crept about very quietly to pounce on the culprit. When things became calmer he ordered the family to prayers and rest. The two eldest boys, Robert and Edward, went into an upstairs bedroom. The remaining children were so frightened that they betook themselves to the first-floor bedroom where the maid could guard them. Joller and his wife retired upstairs, but were at once brought down by the frightened cry that noises had begun in the childrens' room.

> A pause followed, and I lay down on the edge of the bed. Then it began to tap again in the western corner of the room, came nearer and nearer, thumped with strong and heavy blows on the footboard of my bedstead, and then upon the chair standing immediately next to me. I quickly struck a light, searched everywhere, in vain, and found doors and windows closed. A longer pause followed. I put the candle out and seated myself on the footboard of the bedstead. After a while the tapping on the wall began again, and the blows on the footboard, which I grasped with my left hand, were so strong that it shook powerfully together with the whole bedstead. None the less I felt nothing more than a light touch on the index finger of my left hand. The sounds repeated themselves while the candle was alight without my being able to see anything at all. At last, it must have been towards midnight, things grew quieter, and by and by I fell asleep.

The racketing began again at 6.00 a.m. next day, Wednesday 20 August, moving here and there all over the house. Joller searched the house from top to bottom while the sounds were in progress. He points out that he was born in the house and knew every finger's breadth of it; yet his search was in vain.

> Now my investigation narrowed down to the phenomenon itself, which resounded at short intervals especially upon the living room and lower bedroom doors, and on the floors of the rooms. I placed my hand sometimes from the inside and sometimes from the outside on the place in the upper half of the door around which the blows were perceptible without feeling anything on my hand, even a draught or disturbance of the air. I also held the door half-open, so as to observe it from both sides; the rapping occurred again without my perceiving any cause . . . . At last, such mighty thumps came upon the door between the bedroom and the kitchen that, being made of weak fir wood, it visibly bowed inwards each time from the weight of the blow. I placed myself, around ten o'clock in the morning, in the

bedroom, immediately beside the lock. I gently pulled back the bolt near the raised latch so that the door was only just held in the rabbet. My wife stood with a boy some 22 paces behind me, in such a position that, when the door opened, she had the kitchen window as the background to her view, whilst I only had the dark kitchen wall. After a little while the door was so powerfully struck that flying open it travelled to the wall. In that moment I saw with the fullest certainty some dark thing, although I could not precisely make out its shape against the unfavourable background. It shot with lightning speed from the door to the side of the chimney. However, before I, quickly hurrying after, could say a word, my wife and my lad called out that they had just clearly seen a dark-brown half armbone dart back from the door, and their assertions were so quick and simultaneous that I could not doubt this vision had passed before them . . . . I did not fail to institute the most stringent search of the chimney, but found it empty, with no mark on the fallen soot, nor any other clue.

The remainder of this day was marked by the exciting experiences of the servant girl, who kept being frightened out of the kitchen – once by footsteps on the stair, three times by a deep voice groaning, 'pity me', and once by a transparent, grey little cloud, which floated in through the partly open kitchen window, crossed the room, and pounded on the door to the bedroom. It was also enlivened by a visit from the priest, whose blessings availed little, since the racketing began again as strongly as ever in the late evening.

The next day, Thursday 21 August, marked the real beginning of Joller's downfall. Things began to get out of hand. He was no longer able to calm his family. Tongues were beginning to wag in the neighbourhood. His departure for court was delayed by phenomena of the utmost violence – blows came on the floor 'as powerful as a wooden mallet might make when swung with all the strength of a powerful arm', the massive walnut door of the living room burst open and slammed shut again with the greatest force, kitchen and bedroom doors were pounded upon with such power that Joller feared they would split. The noise was so great that the affair could not be kept from outsiders.

Yet again I investigated the matter with all possible coolness, checked the pressure by laying a hand on each side of the door, and felt not the slightest air-movement, whilst the force of the blows, like that of the most powerful fist, jerked the closed door two or three inches away from the rabbet. Once, when I came into the kitchen, I noticed that it struck the bottles, glasses and vessels on the table as if with a metal instrument. The blows in the different parts of the house followed each other so quickly that, if one wished to suppose the spook admitted of human agency, it would have taken at least four or five persons.

Joller's diary is too long to be taken *in toto*; though indeed towards the end, as conviction and despair alike overwhelmed him, the entries become very much shorter. He had a number of the most curious experiences. On the night of 23–24 August, he, his wife, and the servant girl, all resting in the first-floor bedroom, were separately touched on the head as if by a hand. Joller and his wife each grasped the hand, and found it to be small and warm, like a child's. On Thursday 11 September, he wrote as follows:

> During the morning it racketed now here, now there, on floors and walls. It was bright sunshine. Towards 9.00 a.m. the living room was empty. In the middle the massive walnut table stood longways as usual, against the walls, chairs and sofa. Everything being thus in order I left the room with my wife and two of my children (the others were away) and wanted to take them – they were very frightened – into the room above. The servant girl was busy in the kitchen. While we were on the stairs we heard on the wall of the corridor above a quick rapping in a dancing rhythm. Struck by a stirring in the living room, we rushed back to the door, off which I had never taken my eye, and listening a moment at it, we heard a sound as if a gathering of many people were dancing around in socks. The door was quickly opened; but all was still. The heavy table lay longways near the door, upside-down. To the left, and further into the room, two chairs lay likewise by the stool in front of the sofa. We scarcely credited our senses. A minute might have passed since we left the living room.

About 6.30 p.m. the same day, as it was growing dark, he saw float in through the partly open living room door something that appeared like a three-cornered little grey shawl. It floated across to the open cupboard of the corner buffet, and there vanished.

Perhaps the oddest of all Joller's experiences took place on Tuesday 16 September.

> Towards eight o'clock in the morning I witnessed the strange hopping around of an apple. It was thrown down from the upper part of the house, over the lower stairs, to the house-door, from which, with numerous jumps, it hopped past me, through the corridor and into the kitchen. The servant girl, who was in

there, busy at the hearth, took this battered apple and placed it on the kitchen table. From there, after a short rest, it again hastened with two or three jumps towards the corridor. The girl seized it, and threw it out of the kitchen window. In an instant it flew in again through the same window onto the kitchen table. From there, after a very short rest, it bounced with many jumps through the kitchen and the corridor, into the living room, and there, after another short rest, jumped into the sharp corner by the bedroom door, where it lay quietly on the floor.

In his diary Joller recorded not just his own experiences but the accounts of his family and friends. Their stories, being at second-hand, are of less interest than Joller's; none the less I have little doubt that he carefully and conscientiously set down what was told to him. Among the phenomena concerned were: a 'deep-groaning' voice, heard principally by the servant-girl; grey or white cloudy or cloth-like figures, sometimes seen to rap on doors; cold fingers and hands on faces and in hair; footsteps; noises imitating, for example, the sounds of money being counted, of wood being chopped, of sweeping with a birch broom, of a spinning wheel; chairs seen to move in bright light by more than one person; rooms found in disorder; showers of stones, usually outside the house, but sometimes in it; and the phantasm of a girl dressed in green.

As an example of the sort of thing reported by Joller's family, here is part of his diary entry for Wednesday 10 September:

> I left home about 7.30 a.m. and returned about the same hour in the evening . . . . When I arrived back I learned that shortly after my departure three quick and meaty thumps had come from below on the living room floor. My wife, who was in the bedroom, stepped, with our eldest daughter Emaline, through the living room door. In that moment both saw a chair in the living room . . . first of all slowly pushed from its place, and then of a sudden overturned with its legs in the air, and smashed so forcefully to the floor that it raised the dust from the crevices in the boards. At this the living room door slammed so powerfully into its catch that someone came running from a distant neighbourhood at the sound.
>
> About noon, my eldest daughter Emaline was in the garden in bright sunlight. Suddenly hearing a rustling sound in the trellis above, she looked up and saw the figure of a woman leaning out of the window near the little corridor and reaching up to the trellis. Convinced that it was the servant girl coveting grapes,

she watched her without exactly being afraid, and it struck her that contrary to her custom she had her hair smoothly parted, wore a hair-net and a dark neckcloth, and bowed her head in such a melancholy manner. She boldly called the servant girl's name, and the latter emerged from the cellar, whilst the figure vanished as if ducking under the leaves. Thorough investigation revealed nothing more.

On 6 October a very similar figure was seen on four occasions by a total of five persons. In 1938 Emaline, as a very old lady living in Italy, gave to Fanny Moser through Dr Emilio Servadio, a well-known Italian parapsychologist, a closely concordant account of the figure which she had seen leaning out of the window seventy-six years before.

When it began to dawn on Joller that his attempts to get to the bottom of the happenings would be fruitless and that tongues were starting to wag and rumours to circulate, he called in various outsiders; as much, perhaps, in the hope of exonerating himself and his family as in the expectation that the mystery would be solved. The police set watchers in the house; a specially appointed commission of enquiry took over the house for several days, during which the Joller family went elsewhere (there were no phenomena at the house in their absence); *savants* came with assorted apparatuses for the detection of electrical, magnetic, or volcanic forces; but all in vain. The poltergeist racketed on, and the agency behind it remained totally obscure.

Late in October 1862 Joller fled with his family to Zürich. His home had latterly been overrun with sightseers; gossip and malice had rendered his political situation untenable; no doubt his legal practice had diminished catastrophically. What, of course, one would very much like to know is whether the phenomena went with him to Zürich; for they certainly did not continue in Stans after his departure. In the 1930s Fanny Moser interviewed, or otherwise contacted, a number of Joller's descendants, partly in the hope of obtaining an answer to this question. Unfortunately the replies which she received were contradictory. The most authoritative answer came from Joller's eldest daughter Emaline, who stated that the phenomena did *not* follow the family to Zürich, but that when alone one night her father had an experience after which he said, 'Now I understand!' What this experience was he never revealed, or perhaps only revealed during a private audience with the Pope a little before his death.

Many issues arise in connection with this case. They are essentially the issues which arise in connection with most other reports of poltergeist cases, and several of them will receive more extended and more general discussion later in this book. They may be itemized as follows:

1 What is the status of the primary document in the case, namely Joller's diary as reproduced in his pamphlet? Could it be a fiction or a forgery? So far as I know the diary itself does not survive; but that it once existed and was transcribed, perhaps with improvements and amplifications, in Joller's pamphlet, hardly admits of doubt. There is ample independent evidence that in the autumn of 1862 Joller's house was the scene of exceedingly odd events; his daughter Emaline told Dr Servadio that she could remember him writing the daily shorthand entries in his diary; and we have no reason for doubting his own word that he did keep a journal. We must bear in mind, however, that the issue of forgery might be raised in regard to other cases.

2 Of course, even if we accept that Joller did keep and transcribe a diary, the issue of his own good faith still remains. Could he, for his own dark and devious reasons, have connived at or even assisted in the fraudulent production of the phenomena which he so carefully chronicles? I do not think that anyone who has carefully studied his diary will countenance this idea for a moment. It is a document of, at times, almost painful honesty. Furthermore there is no doubt that as a result of the poltergeist Joller was financially crippled and politically destroyed. No man in his senses would connive at his own ruination. But again it must be borne in mind that the possibility of connivance could arise in other cases.

3 Suppose, then, that Joller was an honest witness. Was he also a *good* witness? One might well propose that as witnesses go, he probably *was* good. He was initially sceptical, he was systematic in his attempts to pin down the causes of the phenomena, he remained calm when other men's bowels would have turned to water, he recorded promptly and methodically. And clearly he was no fool. He had risen to a position of fair eminence chiefly through his own endeavours and abilities, and,

so far as the poltergeist was concerned, he was alive to the likelihood of delusion and trickery, and to the possible relevance of seismic and geological factors. There still remains, however, the crucial question, how 'good' is even the best witness? Some writers, basing themselves upon data from the psychological investigation of the reliability of witness testimony, seem inclined to argue that so fallible is human testimony about dramatic happenings that one should hesitate before accepting any of it. For the moment we can only note this issue; it will be discussed again in chapter 13.

4 Good witness Joller may have been; but could some accomplished charlatan or trickster have deceived him? If we examine the diary carefully, can we find someone whose recorded movements make him a candidate for this role? The suspicions of the neighbourhood seem to have centred on Joller's eldest son Robert, who was credited with having learned certain magical arts from the gipsies, or with having set up some (unspecified) electrical apparatuses, and the servant girl, whom an anonymous correspondent of a local newspaper claimed to have detected making raps. But many phenomena took place when neither of these persons was in evidence, and, in general terms, one might well suppose that Joller would have been a hard man to deceive in a house every hand's breadth of which had, as he pointedly remarked, been known to him from childhood. For the hypothesis of trickery to appear plausible it has to be supplemented by the supposition, which we have already discussed, that Joller was either a hopelessly bad witness or else in on the act. It has also, of course, to be supplemented with some detailed proposals as to *how* the trickery might have been accomplished.

5 It is a commonplace of poltergeist stories that poltergeists tend to centre round particular persons, often adolescents, especially girls. These persons have often been termed poltergeist 'agents' or poltergeist 'mediums'. Some authorities seem to wish to make this feature one of the defining characteristics of 'poltergeists', and to distinguish poltergeists sharply from cases of what are commonly called 'hauntings'. In hauntings the focus of the disturbances is a place rather than a person. The phenomena are, it is supposed, mainly nocturnal, and consist in, for example, footsteps, voices (often indistinct), noises as if crockery or furniture were being smashed, raps, occasional small dis-

placements of objects or furniture, touches, and the appearance of phantasms. The further move is sometimes made of trying to assimilate cases of hauntings to cases of haunting ghosts, i.e. of recurrent localized apparitions, of which there are perhaps a few dozen first-hand records in the more reputable literature. It is widely held that in cases of recurrent localized apparitions, the figure which is repeatedly seen is hallucinatory, has no reality outside the minds of the perceivers. If this is so, there is no problem as to *what* the various witnesses saw – they did not see anything. The problem is rather why several different people should have similar hallucinations in the same locality. And it is certainly a difficult enough problem. Now if this view of haunting ghosts is correct (and I cannot go into the pros and cons of it at this juncture), the effect of assimilating cases of hauntings to cases of haunting ghosts is obviously to constrain us to regard the phenomena of hauntings – the footsteps, the raps, the crashes, the voices – as likewise hallucinatory. Any phenomena that solidly resist this interpretation – e.g. instances in which some object has undeniably been moved – are explained away ad hoc in terms of ordinary natural causes like rats or house subsidence. And then we can present the following simplified picture. *Poltergeists*, where not fraudulent, are outbreaks of spontaneous paranormal physical phenomena centring upon the organism of some particular individual. If apparitions are also seen, or voices heard, these are hallucinations consequent upon the upset nerves of uncomprehending persons frightened by the poltergeist phenomena. *Hauntings* are cases in which visitors to or residents in a particular locality are, for reasons which we do not yet understand, afflicted with concordant hallucinations; only instead of being, as in the classic cases of recurrent localized apparitions, chiefly visual hallucinations, they are primarily auditory or even tactual ones.

We can now ask whether, in these terms, the Stans case is a 'haunting' or a 'poltergeist'. And the answer is that it does not obviously belong in either of these categories as just defined. Some at least of the phenomena strongly resist any attempt to suppose them hallucinations – furniture was overturned, stones rained down and could be taken away as souvenirs, and so on. And yet there was no obvious person upon whom the phenomena focused, whose presence was essential to them. It is true that there were teenage children and a teenage servant girl in the house, and many poltergeist cases seem to focus around a teenager. It is true also that when the whole family vacated the house for several days in favour of the commission of enquiry, phenomena ceased altogether. But there was no one person whose immediate presence seemed essential to the phenomena, which sometimes took place in empty rooms and even when the house itself was ostensibly empty, and which do not seem to have occurred anywhere other than in just the one house. We must therefore ask, can a distinction in these terms between poltergeists and hauntings really be maintained?

6 If the phenomena which Joller and his family witnessed were genuine, what can we infer from them as to the nature of the physical forces involved? To this there is a simple answer: nothing. It is, however, perhaps worth noting that some of the primitive electrical, magnetic and volcanic (*sic*) apparatuses of the time were apparently tried out to no avail. Whether data from other poltergeist cases will yield any relevant information is a question which we shall have to discuss later.

7 How characteristic are the phenomena which Joller records? That is, can we find other cases of apparently paranormal physical happenings in which the phenomena, or aspects of them, were similar to those reported in the Stans case? Stories of inexplicable events or sets of events are obviously easier to accept if some parallels or analogies for them can be found. An unique oddity is an incredible oddity; though it does not follow from this that an oddity which is not unique is necessarily credible.

In fact, of course, substantial parts of this book will be devoted to showing that the Stans case, whether or not credible, is at least not unique. There are many records of poltergeist cases and of hauntings; and there are not a few such records which are as detailed as, or more detailed than, Joller's diary. Part of the aim of this survey will be to set these records in a comparative perspective, to compare current cases with cases long ago and with cases in other societies than our own. What is the value of doing this? First of all it might, I think, reasonably be argued that if poltergeist cases have exhibited the same or similar features in widely separated cultures and times, it marginally strengthens our grounds for regarding the phenomena as genuine. If, for example, apparently similar poltergeist phenomena have centred around children or young persons in Bologna in 1580, in Stockwell, England, in 1772, in Finland in 1885, in Java in 1892-3, and in Miami in 1966-7, we cannot reasonably suppose that all these young mischief-makers have had access to a common body of literature or tradition about the habits of poltergeists and have engineered their trickery accordingly. (Once, when reading a sixteenth-century account of poltergeist phenomena, I was interrupted by a phone call from a lady who told me of very similar phenomena taking place in her own home.) It might be replied here that there are plenty of examples of closely similar folk-tales springing up in different and apparently insulated cultures – the macabre theme of 'the grateful dead' discussed in G. H. Gerould's well-known monograph is perhaps an appropriate example. Why should we not suppose that the myth-making tendencies of the human mind run along lines which transcend cultural gulfs and barriers? We might then claim that poltergeist stories exemplify similar myth-making tendencies, with the difference that, instead of *telling* the stories, the young persons in whose minds the myths well up so to speak *enact* them. I do not find this proposal very convincing. To give weight to it we should have to unearth evidence for the poltergeist myth-making tendency other than factual accounts of poltergeist cases. Such evidence might take the form of, for example, widely distributed and unquestionably fictional folk-tales about poltergeists. So far as I know there is very little material of this kind.

In any case, a comparative analysis of poltergeist phenomena might in principle be of value in another and more important way. For suppose that, after examining a number of the best-attested poltergeist cases, we were to come to the conclusion that we really do have good evidence that these bizarre and currently inexplicable phenomena sometimes take place. Then from an examination of apparently comparable cases in remote times or remote cultures we might be able to determine which features of poltergeist phenomena are fundamental and which have simply reflected in one way or another the cultural settings within which the cases have taken place.

For example, poltergeists have in the past frequently thrown stones, rung the old-fashioned domestic bells on wire bell-pulls, and broken crockery. Does this reveal some fundamental affinity between the forces at work and certain kinds of materials;

or are we dealing with some very general kind of force which operates simply upon the materials most conveniently to hand? In the latter case we should expect modern electric bells to be affected as much as old wire bells, modern plastic objects as much as old porcelain ones, etc. Or again, in some few past cases the phenomena have presented the superficial appearance of being produced by demons. Do these appearances mirror some underlying reality, or do they reflect prevailing superstitions? Presumably, it is often said, the latter, since in the wake of modern Spiritualism demons have apparently been supplanted by the spirits of deceased persons. No doubt, on this view of things, we must shortly expect the first poltergeists which function as messengers from the occupants of UFOs.

If the following survey and sampling of poltergeist phenomena were aimed first and foremost at presenting the strongest possible evidence for their genuineness, it would no doubt have to concentrate upon cases which have been recently investigated by 'trained' parapsychologists – and as a matter of fact there are not a few such cases. However, since an important part of its aim is, for the reasons just given, to consider poltergeist phenomena in a cultural and historical perspective, I shall, whilst giving, I hope, a proper weight to recent investigations, also be presenting some very much older material. Now I would not like it to be thought that I regard these older cases as necessarily inferior in evidential quality to more modern ones. There are some parapsychologists who seem to think firstly that no, or very few, detailed accounts of poltergeist cases were set down prior to the inception of modern psychical research, and secondly that the people who investigated poltergeist cases in previous centuries were in all probability superstitious believers in witchcraft taken in by simple tricks. Moreover they had not had the chance of acquainting themselves with the insights and words of wisdom to be found in modern parapsychological literature. That the first of these ideas is to a considerable extent mistaken, I hope to show in the remainder of this survey. In fact, some at least of the early accounts are considerably more detailed than any published by either the British or the American Society for Psychical Research prior to the year 1909. As for the second, I would not, of course, wish to maintain that a study of the modern literature on poltergeists may not enlarge one's understanding of possible motives for deception and of possible means for perpetrating it.

But it is life rather than literature that one needs to know well to get to the bottom of fraudulent poltergeist phenomena, and no age has been short of persons with that qualification.

2 Three sixteenth-century cases

The comparative study of poltergeist phenomena will at any rate not founder from lack of material. The 500 cases of poltergeists and hauntings listed in the appendix, and analysed in chapter 12, probably represent just the tip of the iceberg. Even this no doubt fragmentary collection contains examples from quite early times and from cultures very unlike our own. It is hard to say which of the cases is culturally most remote – perhaps one from the China of around AD 900. The most remote in time, from the life of St Caesarius of Arles, is from the year AD 530. Some writers think that they have found even earlier instances. A favourite here has been the somewhat numerous 'showers of stones' stated by Livy to have been among the omens which affrighted the Romans during the Second Punic War (218 BC to 201 BC). However, these same showers of stones have been freely claimed by astronomers as fragmented meteorites, and it would be imprudent to make too much of them. (Incidentally, several writers on poltergeists misdate these stories of Livy's to the sixth century AD. This seems to have happened because William Howitt, the first person to propose a poltergeist interpretation of the showers of stones, used in his article – in *The Spiritual Magazine* for 1865 – the Roman rather than the Christian method of numbering years.)

More plausible candidates for the earliest known poltergeist cases are perhaps some happenings recorded by Flavius Josephus in his *Antiquities of the Jews*, written about AD 94. Josephus himself witnessed the performances before the emperor Vespasian of a Jew named Eleazar who was noted as an exorcist of possessed persons. It was Eleazar's custom to prove that the demon had really been driven from the sufferer's body by making him (the demon) overset a bowl of water standing some distance away. A similar tale is recorded, though not from personal observation, in Philostratus's life of Apollonius of Tyana (iv, xx). Apollonius lived in the first century AD. There does seem to be some overlap between poltergeist cases and cases of so-called possession, so perhaps it could be claimed that these are the earliest known ostensible poltergeist phenomena.

Little purpose would be served by discussing any of the poltergeist stories from the chroniclers and hagiographers of the period between the collapse of the Roman Empire and the beginning of the sixteenth century. In only a few cases do we have more than the most cursory accounts, and even these cases are not set down at any length. It is not until the sixteenth century that we find more detailed accounts of poltergeist cases, and in this chapter I shall outline and briefly discuss three of them. The first case is French, the second German, and the third English, so the enquiry begins, appropriately enough, on an international note.

The earliest of these is a French case of 1525–6. Our knowledge of it derives from a pamphlet by Adrian de Montalembert, almoner and preacher to Francis I of France. It was published at Paris in 1528, and is entitled *La merveilleuse histoire de l'esperit, qui depuis n'agueres s'est apparu au monastere des religieuses de Saint Pierre de Lyon* . . . (The wonderful history of the spirit which has lately appeared at the house of the Nuns of Saint Peter at Lyons). This little booklet was reprinted in N. Lenglet Dufresnoy's *Recueil de dissertations* (Volume I, Avignon, 1752), whence it was disinterred by Andrew Lang. Through Lang's deservedly popular *Cock Lane and Common-Sense* (London, 1894) the story has become fairly well known; though Lang, indeed, makes no mention of certain rather curious passages.

I have not been able to discover much about Adrian de Montalembert. I should suppose that he was a member of the famous French family of that name, but Saint-Allais' *Nobiliaire Universel de France* (Paris, 1875), which devotes a substantial section to this family, does not mention him, whilst the article on him in Michaud's *Biographie Universelle* tells us little more than can be gathered from the pamphlet. However, he occupied a position of modest eminence, and his pamphlet is lucid enough. It has sometimes been hinted that the affair was got up to dish the Lutherans, whose views on purgatory it appeared to controvert. De Montalembert does indeed proffer some remarks on that subject. But in general I concur with Lang, who says that 'the whole story in its pleasant old French, has an agreeable air of good faith'. Traditions about the affair lingered in the nunnery so late as 1630.

The nuns at the Abbey of St Pierre followed the rule of St Benedict, but it seems that prior to the year 1516, when reforms were instituted, a fairly lax state of affairs prevailed, and the nuns came and went as they wished, by day or by night. For one of them, a young woman named Alis de Telieux, the temptations thus made available proved too strong. She took advantage of her position as sacristan (keeper of relics and sacred objects) to depart for the big city with certain of the valuables belonging to the community. About eight years later, in 1524, unrecognizable from disease and privation, yet still praying to Heaven for forgiveness, she died, not, as had been her last and dearest wish, in the abbey where she had once lived, but abandoned by the world in the fields of a little village. There, as de Montalembert says in a passage of which I cannot bring myself to attempt a translation, she was wretchedly buried 'comme la plus méprisée créature du monde, sans obséques, ni funerailles, ni prieres, ni solennités quelconques, & par l'espace de deux ans a esté enterrée & consumée, sans que mémoire d'elle eust régné en la souvenance d'aucune créature du monde'.

In the abbey at this time there lived a young nun about eighteen years old, named Anthoinette de Grollée. She is described as wise for her age, of good family, and exceedingly religious. She had been in the nunnery since before 1516, and it seems that when sister Alis lay dying the latter had continually talked of her and called her name.

One night about the beginning of 1526, this sister Anthoinette, alone in her room, lay half asleep in bed. Suddenly someone lifted her veil, made the sign of the cross on her forehead, and kissed her tenderly. She woke up, astonished rather than terrified, but seeing no-one, dismissed the experience as a dream. However, a few days later she began to hear little raps beneath her feet, as though someone were knocking with the end of a stick underneath a tile or step. The noise seemed to come from a few inches underneath the ground. 'I have often heard it,' de Montalembert notes in an aside, 'and at my request it would rap as many blows as I demanded.' The sounds followed her everywhere, showing signs of great rejoicing during divine service; and they were never heard when she was not present.

The astonished nuns asked sister Anthoinette what she thought of these happenings. Anthoinette replied that she did not know what it could be unless it were sister Alis the sacristan, inasmuch as since the latter's death she had often dreamed of her. The rapping entity itself was then questioned, and the reply was received (through what code we are not informed) that it was indeed the spirit of sister Alis. It gave a clear token of its identity, but again we are unfortunately not told what the token was. The Abbess then instituted a search for the body of sister Alis. The spirit was asked whether it wished it buried in the abbey. It answered that it did. The remains were located, disinterred – not I imagine a very pleasant task – and brought to the abbey. As the body approached, the spirit made more and more noise, and when it reached the abbey, the rappings became positively frantic.

The nuns were, as can be imagined, a little out of their depth in this affair, and on 16 February 1526 the suffragan bishop of Lyons asked de Montalembert to look into the matter. Much of the rest of the pamphlet is concerned, in somewhat tedious detail, with the ecclesiastical activities which the latter set in motion for the benefit of the defunct sister Alis, and also with the measures taken to dispose of an intrusive evil spirit which transiently possessed one of the other sisters. The remains of the deceased were carried into the chapter-house of the abbey, and sister Alis was solemnly conjured to answer certain questions which the bishop read out to the waiting Anthoinette. These questions (which were answered by raps for 'yes' or 'no') concerned such matters as the good angel who accompanied and guided her, the existence and inhabitants of Purgatory, the pains inflicted there, whether they are respited on holy days, and how Alis could be delivered from them. A lengthy service was then held with the aim of promoting this deliverance; and during it sister Anthoinette seems to have *played the role of* the departed sister Alis in the most extraordinary way. For example, we are told that, immediately after a speech in which the bishop called upon the Abbess and nuns to forgive the errant Alis, Anthoinette stood up and 'in the person of the deceased' (*en la personne de la deffuncte*) went with great humility to kneel at the feet of the Abbess, and most piteously begged for mercy, saying, 'Reverend Mother, have mercy on me, for the sake of him who hung upon the Cross for our salvation, and be pleased to consent to my absolution'. These pious words so melted the hearts of all present that there was no-one who did not weep bitterly. Some of the events narrated could almost have taken place at a modern spiritualist seance; were it not, indeed, that a Catholic bishop had charge of them! At the end of the service a form of plenary absolution was pronounced.

On the third day after these events de Montalembert returned to the abbey to judge of the efficacy of the proceedings. His coming was known in advance to the spirit of sister Alis, which rapped incessantly, and raised sister Anthoinette into the air! De Montalembert asked sister Alis to rap nine times if she were free of the pains of Purgatory. The raps were duly given.

From then onwards the raps seem to have become fainter. On 20 March sister Anthoinette, alone in her room, saw a human figure which vanished into a corner. On reflection she thought it might have been sister Alis. Then in the small hours she was woken by a feeble voice which called her, announced itself as sister Alis, and stated that as a result of the prayers of the sisters the Creator had revoked his sentence of thirty-three years in Purgatory.

The final act of this little drama came, appropriately enough, on Saturday 21 March, 1526, the feast of St Benedict, patron of the nuns of St Pierre at Lyons. The nuns were at table, and a reading had begun, when thirty-three powerful blows were heard. These were held to signify that sister Alis's sentence had been reduced from thirty-three years in Purgatory to thirty-three days.

No purpose would be served by speculating about the phenomena reported in this case. De Montalembert does not go into sufficient detail about the rappings to enable one to form an opinion at this distance of time about whether or not they could have been fraudulently produced. He is less concerned about the genuineness of the phenomena (which he takes for granted) than about the ecclesiastical ceremonies which he arranged in consequence of them. The case is of interest chiefly as a precursor to, and early parallel for, later poltergeist cases in which communication has been held with a purported spirit by means of raps. Such cases have been (as we shall see) surprisingly numerous, and it was through one of them – at Hydesville in 1848 – that the modern Spiritualist movement began. At Hydesville the two young girls round whom the poltergeist phenomena centred became the first Spiritualist mediums. Had Anthoinette de Grollée lived at a later date and in a different setting she too might have become such another.

A case of communicative rappings in which a colleague and I personally witnessed the phenomena will be described in chapter 16. At the 1977 International Conference of the Society for Psychical Research in London, Dr Barrie Colvin described, and illustrated with tape recordings, a case of poltergeist phenomena, chiefly raps, centring round a twelve-year-old girl in Andover, Hampshire. The raps, which could not have been fraudulently produced, spelled out messages. The phenomena had a monthly periodicity, and ceased with the girl's first menstruation.

The second of our sixteenth-century cases took place at Töttelstedt (later Tuttelstadt) near Erfurt in the year 1581. Erfurt, now in East Germany, was at that time, though predominantly Lutheran, under the titular sovereignty of the Archbishop of Mainz. The case is described by a person who became involved in it, a certain Johann Körner, priest of the church of St Nicholas, and canon of (I presume) the cathedral at Erfurt, in a fairly substantial pamphlet *Warhaffte Beschreibung einer Wundergeschicht* . . . (Truthful narrative of a wondrous affair) published at Cologne in 1581. I have not been able to find out more about Herr Pfarrer und Kanonikus Körner, or about the case, than is contained in this pamphlet; but for almost every detail of Körner's account numerous parallels can be found, and I rate his honesty and his accuracy quite highly. It is clear that his account of the phenomena is based on what the witnesses themselves told him.

The *mise-en-scène* of this little drama was the cottage occupied by a peasant farmer named Hans Schiel, his wife Margareta, and their two sons, Hans (about sixteen) and Martin (about nine). Schiel and his wife are described as good but poor little people, who won their nourishment by the sweat of their faces. On Tuesday 28 February 1581, this worthy little family retired to bed between 7.00 p.m. and 8.00 p.m. However, rest was not to be theirs. Shortly there burst out around the room a sound of clattering and throwing so intense that they thought a thief had broken in. Father and elder son lit oil lamps and searched the whole house. Finding nothing, they returned to bed, leaving a lamp alight. No sooner had they done so, than they were all assailed with little lumps of earth, which also struck the lamp, the walls and the furniture. They did not see whence the pieces of earth came, but only noticed them just before they struck, something which has been reported in numerous other poltergeist cases. In terror the family fled into the lower room, but to no avail. The throwings lasted until early morning.

The next evening they asked some friends and relations to join them, without, however, saying anything about the spook. The company talked for a while. Then Thomas Schawer, Schiel's father-in-law, and the village's oldest inhabitant, was struck several times on his bald head with little pieces of earth. At first he took no notice; but after the third occasion he became angry. Then earth was thrown at the others present. Seventy-five little pieces were later picked up. Schiel's brother Erhardt brought in a fist-sized lump of wet clay to see if it too could be thrown. He laid it on the floor. It was not at once thrown, but suddenly they saw that it had been bitten as if by a dog with sharp teeth. The marks were smoothed away, but reappeared without visible cause. This was repeated a number of times, until eventually 'the monster' seized the clay and threw it at the heads of the watchers.

On the next evening Margareta Schiel and her younger son stayed elsewhere. A neighbour, one Peter Teschener, came to comfort the family. Perhaps he was one of those whose sympathy is not unmixed with less generous feelings. At any rate a heavy stone was at once thrown on his big toe so that the nail was crushed and split and the poor man ran howling and lamenting from the house. On 3 March, in addition to the usual pieces of earth, stones were thrown. These ranged in weight from ½ lb to 10 lb. Some came from the yard and some from the street. One could see the holes where they had been pulled out. The wretched occupants of the house were so bruised and swollen that they could hardly move. Schiel went to see his parish priest in Erfurt, but the latter obviously did not believe him, and sent him away with some pious platitudes about trusting in prayer. Meanwhile the poltergeist raged more furiously than before. Plates, spoons, dishes, shoes, jars and all kinds of household objects were thrown around.

On Saturday 4 March many people came by on their way to market in Erfurt and were treated to a first-class performance. The poltergeist raged, racketed and threw in daylight so frightfully that the people thought it would destroy the whole house. Shingles were torn out of the roof, and through the hole thus made stones were hurled all day. Perhaps because of this the priest, Johan Zimmer, began to take some notice. After mass on Sunday 5 March he went to the house with Johan Raumburger, the schoolmaster of Melchendorff. The priest was at once struck on the neck by a lump of earth; and both visitors were then bombarded with earth and stones. Impressed by this tangible evidence, Zimmer took Schiel into Erfurt where they were eventually admitted to see the suffragan bishop, Nicolao Elgart. The bishop counselled prayer, but also took the more practical step of sending Körner to investigate.

On 7 March Körner celebrated mass in the house and all was quiet until the evening of 11 March, when phenomena began again. A further visit from priests quietened things down for a couple of days, but on the 14th the nuisance broke out once more, with such violence that the family no longer felt sure of their lives. The Schiels' cattle (probably a cow and calf) were tormented, and the rope by which the calf was tied was several times bitten or cut through. (The *stallspuk*, the entity which frightens horses and cattle in their stalls, loosens and unloosens them, knots their manes and tails, etc., is a recurrent feature of continental spook stories. Such happenings are first mentioned, so far as I am aware, in William of Auvergne's *De Universo*, written about 1225.) On 15 March, no doubt at Körner's instigation, a highly placed government official visited the house, together with Körner himself, and a considerable retinue of clerks, soldiers, etc. The house was thoroughly searched, and inaccessible parts were poked with spears. Schiel and his family told their stories and were subjected to a strict cross-examination. They stood firm, and the conclusion was inescapable that the phenomena were the work of Satan rather than of wicked men or of magicians.

After this inquisition all was quiet until Easter Monday, 27 March. At three o'clock that morning stone-throwing started up again. The Schiels were struck around the head and neck by stones of 3–5 lb weight. When Margareta went to milk the cow a 2 lb stone smashed the milk jar which she had placed in a cupboard. Next day, 28 March, when she again went to milk the cow, she was knocked down, and her head cut, by a 3 lb stone, and her eldest son, who took up her work, was laid low by a 2 lb iron ball, apparently a cannonball picked up as a souvenir by Schiel many years before. At this Schiel set out for Erfurt again and succeeded in convincing the suffragan bishop that strong action was required. The bishop called together a council of priests, including Körner, and ordered them to make ready for the coming struggle by fasting and prayer, a preparation in which they were joined by various worthy and well-disposed citizens of Erfurt. Schiel was instructed to return home and remain there until battle was joined.

At his home the poltergeist phenomena continued. On the evening of 29 March an oil lamp was brought into the living room, and one of Schiel's brothers, known as 'little Hans', remarked that perhaps 'it' would put out the light. 'It' at once responded by knocking over the lamp with a mallet or cudgel. Before they could relight it, the tinder box was taken from the table. Then, in the darkness, 'it' seized Schiel's elder son and began to strangle him. When his father, with his two brothers, the boy's uncles, went to tear the lad free, he too was similarly attacked. Frau Schiel then brought in a burning light, which apparently saved the situation. They searched for the tinder box, but could not find it. However, when little Hans sat down beind the oven, the box was hurled past his head, with such force that it made a hole in the wall into which two fingers could be laid.

On Thursday 30 March Schiel and his wife and their elder son went to work in the fields. Their younger son went to a neighbour's. At midday they returned to feed the cattle. Two stones, each weighing 12 lb, were hurled down from the foliage surrounding the house. They struck the walls without hurting anyone. Körner says, 'I myself, along with others, have seen the holes the stones made, and also held the stones.'

In the evening it was very bothersome. Schiel went into the kitchen, perhaps to cook some vegetables, and locked the kitchen door behind him. However, this did not suffice to keep out the devil, who threw pots and lids and a pestle at him, so that he fled back to the living room to his wife and children. When he ventured into the kitchen again, a sharp-pointed axe was thrown past his head. The phenomena began to mount to a new crescendo of violence, and eventually the family ran out of the house, pelted with axes, hatchets, oven-forks and excrement. No-one was hurt. They stood outside, along with half the village. Bowls, baskets, benches, chairs, buckets, and other objects were hurled out of the house.

When Körner, with two priests and another helper, arrived at

6.00 p.m. he found the door shut, and the occupants and their neighbours standing in front of it. On the ground was a heap of things which had been thrown out. At Körner's request, Hans Schiel reluctantly opened the house again. Körner and his friends made the sign of the cross and, entering the house, fell on their knees. They said the seven penitential psalms, the Litany, and other powerful prayers. At this the people outside took heart, entered, and likewise knelt and prayed. The poltergeist remained quiet.

The night was spent in prayer, and in the morning mass was celebrated. This procedure was repeated for two further nights, without provoking a response from the unseen enemy. However, on the third night the living room door was rattled, and in the morning, while Körner was pronouncing the words *conjuro te, Diabole, ut dimittas locum hunc* ('I command you, Devil, to leave this spot'), the unclean spirit threw a little piece of earth, the size of a bean, through the window. It hit the assistant at mass on the arm.

Körner's narrative of these exciting events does not, it will readily be understood, minimize the drama of combat with the infernal powers. Those powers, indeed, appeared for the time being to have been subdued. However, on Friday 7 April, the poltergeist again caused disturbances, though it seemed to be not so strong as before. A further visit from the priests procured eight days of quiet. Thereafter there were some sporadic but weak phenomena, which were finally dispelled by a visit from the suffragan bishop himself on 28 April. The bishop, we are told, entered the house, flung himself face downwards on the living room floor and prayed to God for the beleaguered occupants. Then he caused an altar to be set up there and celebrated mass. From that day and hour onwards the devil was heard no more in the town of Töttelstedt.

Whether the activities of the bishop had anything to do with the cessation of the phenomena is a debatable issue. Poltergeist cases tend to die out anyway in the course of a few weeks. The spectacle, however, of a sixteenth-century bishop in full robes casting himself upon the floor of a peasant-farmer's cottage must have presented a notable contrast in styles of life.

A curious analogy to the Töttelstedt case presents itself from a totally different time and place. In 1923, the then Anglican bishop of Zanzibar, Frank Weston, caused a minor stir in the press when he recounted the following experience (a version of it is to be found in the biography of him by H. Maynard Smith). He went to a native hut from which, it was alleged, clods of earth were flung at approaching persons. Similar clods fell on people inside the house. As the bishop came towards the hut, he was struck between the shoulders by a great clod of earth. He went in alone. While he was inside pieces of earth were detached from the walls and thrown up at the ceiling. The house was surrounded at the time by a cordon of guards. The bishop exorcized the poltergeist, and the manifestations ceased.

Many modern parapsychologists would suspect that one or other of Hans Schiel's two sons must have been the poltergeist 'agent' at Töttelstedt. It is notorious that in many similar poltergeist cases the phenomena have undoubtedly centred around some young person, even to the extent of following that person from place to place. Hence, of course, the well-known 'naughty little girl' hypothesis of the origin of the phenomena. However, in the Töttelstedt case there is no clear evidence to inculpate the two boys either as agents or as tricksters. In fact during some of the phenomena they were not in the room, and during others not even in the house. Rather similarly, in the next case I shall describe, that at North Aston, Oxfordshire, in 1591-2, a young maidservant figures prominently in the story; but we cannot definitely say that she played an essential role, and there is, indeed, some evidence to the contrary.

The North Aston poltergeist is the first British case known to me of which we have a detailed account. That account is contained in an anonymous black letter pamphlet published in London in 1592 and entitled *A True Discourse of Such Straunge and Woonderfull Accidents, as hapned in the House of M. George Lee of North-Aston, in the Countie of Oxford* .... A copy of this pamphlet has recently been acquired by the British Library, and I am indebted to Dr E. J. Dingwall for putting me on its track. It is somewhat of the same *genre* as the English witchcraft pamphlets of the time, and must be assessed accordingly. To say this is not necessarily to cast doubts on its trustworthiness. Witchcraft pamphlets were of course written to catch the public eye; but none the less the more detailed ones have often proved quite accurate when it has been possible to compare them with other contemporary records. (On the reliability of witchcraft pam-

THREE SIXTEENTH-CENTURY CASES 33

phlets see A. Macfarlane's *Witchcraft in Tudor and Stuart England*, London, 1970, chapter 5, and pp. 345-6 of W. Notestein's *A History of Witchcraft in England*, new ed., New York, 1968.) With regard to the North Aston pamphlet, I have not been able to find any other reference to the events which it narrates. The case is not even mentioned by a very erudite local historian, W. Wing (author of *Annals of North Aston*, Oxford, 1867) who was very probably descended from one of the leading participants. There is, however, no doubt that the *dramatis personae* really existed. I have managed to locate contemporary references to several of them, and a more diligent search than I have had time for would no doubt bring further ones to light. Edward Giles, for example, was vicar of North Aston from 1585 to 1608; William Wing and John Yeomans figure in the North Aston Parish registers (now in the Bodleian Library, Oxford); and the Lee family, which was clearly of some consequence in the neighbourhood, is mentioned in *The Visitations of the County of Oxford* edited by W. H. Turner for the Harleian Society in 1871. From this last source we learn that Edward Lee had two children, George and Anne, that George was baptized on 1 March 1569 and was therefore twenty-one years old when the poltergeist phenomena began, and that Edward Lee was buried in London on 7 December 1594, more than two years after the pamphlet was published. Under these circumstances it is most improbable that the story was a fabrication. Indeed it seems from internal evidence more than likely that the anonymous author of the pamphlet derived much of his information from Edward Lee. We may note, too, that the pamphlet was entered in the registers at Stationer's Hall on 21 July, 1592, so that it must have been written within a few weeks of the cessation of the phenomena.

The pamphlet begins as follows:
Maister *George Lee* of North-Aston, son to M. *Edward Lee* of the same par[ish], perceiving on the 29. day of November 1591.
divers Stones of contrarie bignes, some weighing a pound, some two, some three[,] some foure, and some two and twentie pound, to fall verie straungely, or to bee violently flung (as it were) thorow the top or roofe of his Hall, not knowing how, or whence this strange accidents [*sic*] should happen: grewe into no little griefe of minde and amazement. For it is well knowen to the Honorable and worshipfull of Oxfordshire, and others of great credite that haue heard of, and seene these accidents, hee

made diligent search to find the cause heereof, and with ladders caused men to viewe everie place, both within and without his house, as if some thing had beene amisse in the Tiles or Slates, or whether any other sinister deceit were wrought, to raise matter of marueile, by false illusions: yet all this labour was to no purpose, the falling or flinging of the stones stil continued, the reason thereof unknowen, as also no man was able to coniecture whence they came, sauing they behelde them fall either thorow, or from the roofe of the Hall. And yet there could neuer bee seene anie place, either in the hall, or in anie other place in the flowre or seeling, through which they should be floung.

The apparent dropping or throwing of stones through a ceiling or roof is a phenomenon that has been reported in a number of poltergeist cases; I have notes of examples from (to take a few at random) Sumatra in 1903, Java in 1831, Bratislava in 1927, and Jamaica in 1931. In the case at Klopotiva in 1880, stones were seen to detach themselves from ceiling beams, which were boxed in with boards. No holes could be found through which the stones might have passed. Of course, that the stones passed *through* an undamaged ceiling is an inference made by the witnesses; some of whom, indeed, have been careful to state that they first caught sight of the stones immediately underneath it.

To return to the North Aston story: the unexplained stone-throwing in George Lee's farmhouse continued, it seems, with fair frequency through Christmas and into the new year. It was witnessed by various neighbours and workpeople, and also by Mr Giles the vicar, all of whom at various times were asked by George Lee to keep watch in the house. On some unspecified date the house was abandoned because of these inconveniences. The Lees seem to have stayed with the vicar, who was a relative. However, Edward Lee desired 'that some or other shuld stil remain there, and lie in the house, to be resolued when the falling of the stones should cease'. To this end he on one occasion rather unfeelingly sent his young daughter, Anne, together with a servant maid, Joan Measey, to pass a night there. However, when they drew near the gate of the house 'they might easily heare ye stones dash, smite, and ratle against the walles', which so dismayed them that they retreated. They were then provided with an escort of three of Lee's workmen, John Yeomans, John Wright, and George Wright.

when they were come into the little court before the doore, they heard the stones smite against the walles, with such violence, as before they had done, at which noise they were at the first somewhat amazed, yet by reason of the continuance, they grewe somewhat the bolder, yet the cause unknowen, *Iohn Yeomans* sayd: What Tiler or Sclator have we heere, in the name of God: and at these woordes he unlocked the hall doore, when they no sooner entred the hall, but they behelde the falling of the stones in the former most straunge manner, whereat *Iohn Yeomans*, more bold than the rest, thus spake: If thou bee a good fellowe doe us noe harme, for we come not hither to do thee any. So passing thorow the hal they went up the staires into the Gallerie, where they durst not abide long, but went into a midle chamber, when suddenly fell two stones, the one a pretie space after the other: the one lighting upon the postal at the entraunce of the chamber, the other on a Curteine rod of a bedde that standeth in the chamber causing it fal to the ground from of the hooks very violently.

It appears that by this time familiarity had bred in some people a certain contempt for the unseen stone-thrower. Thus *William Whing* and *Richard Hickes* commming [*sic*] into the Farme on S. *Iohns* day in the Christmas holidaies [i.e. December 27th], at their first entrance used very good and godly speeches: but hauing bene there a prettie whlie [*sic*], and seene nothing, *William Whing* fell to pleasant iesting tearmes, saying: Iacke, if thou bee a good fellow, fling us downe a quoit or two, that my companyon and I may go play at the quoits. Presently there fell down a thinne broad stone, in iust forme and proportion of a round quoite, such as commonly men use to play with all, as they walke in the fieldes or elsewhere. *William* seeing that, continued his iesting stil, saying: nay Iack, if thou be a good felow indeed, let us haue another, that each of us may haue one, and then immediatly fell an other like the first. Art thou such a good fellow? quoth the said *William*, then throw downe two more, that we may be prouided alike, or else we cannot make any sport. And then there dropt downe two more, one after another: the one of them had bene plaid withall on the Greene before the house, as was well perceived by some noted marke on the quoite, and beside it was green round about the edges with playing in the gras.

If this story be taken at face value it provides us with yet another example of a kind of communication with and response by a poltergeist; and such ostensible communication, it may be observed, is not uncommon among poltergeist cases. Almost any kind of poltergeist phenomenon can, as it were, be taken up and utilized for the purposes of the transaction.

The night after the episode of the quoits, the phenomena took new turns. Edward Lee himself went to pass the night at the farm, accompanied by two young men, William King and Thomas Churchill, and two servant maids, Joan Measey and Mary Alder. Towards two o'clock in the morning Edward Lee, thinking it was nearer day than it was, let the young men go home. He also sent Mary Alder out on an errand. Then he went back to sleep. Before very long he was woken up by Joan Measey crying out, 'The gown, the gown', to find that the cover beneath which he had been lying had been pulled from his bed. Joan began to tell him how, while he was asleep, she had been assailed with stones, when both heard the sound of footsteps from the rooms above. At daybreak they investigated. They found the window of one of the bedrooms open – a window which had previously been closed – and a sword, which had been lying on the bed, thrust through the window and hanging by the hilt.

The same morning they searched other roomes of the house, and they found where two bolsters were taken off the bed in the great parlor, and were throwen in the middest of the floore, which the maid *Ioane Measey* seeing, called her maister to beholde. Hee demanded how they came there? I know not (quoth the maid) but I am sure I laid them upon the bed, and so I left them there yester night: and to this agreed the other seruant maid, and M. *Lee* himselfe did knowe the same to be true, for he did marke the laying up of all things of purpose: Well said her maister, goe fetch me a peece of chalke, which when she had brought, hee made a circle therewith about the bolsters, in forme and manner as they lay, making it so iust and euen euerie way as he could, and then bad her lay them upon the bed againe, which boeing [*sic*] done, they departed out of the roome, to try if they should be throwen down againe. Soone after returning into the Parlor, he founde the circle of chalke to be wiped out, whereat meruayling, in respect nobody was in the house but he and the mayde, and neither of them was absent from eche others company in all this time: wherfore he tooke the chalke, and in the same place made the circle fresh to be seen againe. Then making fast the doore, the maide and he departed thence againe, and about halfe an hower space they both returned, when they found the chalke to be wyped out againe. Not knowing what to coniecture heereof, once more he would needs make triall of the same again, and hauing made the scores good and great, crossed them ouer from the one end to the other, not for any superstitious obseruation, but only to trie if so many chalkings euery way would be so easily wiped out again altogether, but at their return they found al ye chalking to continue, but hard by the chalking where the one bolster did lodge they found t[r?]aced a prety way into a floor of boords which had lien there for the space of thirtie yeeres, as it had beene the print or forme of a paw, resembling the paw of a yong Bear: which signe or print continueth there to this day to be seene: and adioyning to the chalking where the other bolster did lodg, they found as it had beene the print of an Haukes talent, which as yet remaineth to be seene also.

Edward Lee must certainly have been one of the first persons to have attempted to obtain poltergeist phenomena under controlled conditions.

The stone-throwing and other 'straunge accidents' continued to 6 January 1592, when they ceased for a while. But on 15 February the stone-throwings broke out again 'in more fierce and stranger manner than before'. Their fame ran abroad, and various gentlemen of the county, including Mr Cope, the High Sheriff, came to look into them. New happenings were reported – drops of blood appearing on the hall table (the author of the pamphlet tells us he has seen the stains); the whole house lit up as if by a fire; apparitions, or supposed apparitions, of strange or grotesque dogs or other animals (a not uncommon feature of poltergeist stories); and so on. The pamphlet concludes as follows:

> When Maister *George Lee* was in the house, then fell the stones in most violent sorte, and (as it were) followed him sometime. But in Maie last hee ended his life, and was buried the 22. of the same moneth, since when nothing at all hath beene heard or seene, but all is in as quiet sort, as heart can require.
>
> To iudge heereon I refraine, committing it onlie to God, who neuer sendeth such examples, but to prooue our patience, to exercise our faith, and to expresse his hatred against sinne, and to warne us to lead our lives in better regard than we doo.

What can we make of it all at this distance of time? Little enough perhaps, except in so far as we can find better attested parallels to the phenomena alleged to have happened so long ago. But, as I said before, I do not think the story has simply been invented. This curious little pamphlet, crudely written as it is, and badly printed, and containing occasional inconsistencies, has to me a certain ring of truth. It had, so far as I have discovered, no immediate predecessors. Its author got his story not from a pre-existing large body of comparable pamphlets, but from talking to eyewitnesses; and what those eyewitnesses told him conforms in a number of respects with what subsequent witnesses have also reported. If we accept that he has got his facts more or less right, then the problems of interpretation become quite complex. There was no one person whose presence was essential for the phenomena; in fact they appear to have continued inside locked rooms and even inside the locked and empty house. Thus there is no obvious candidate for the role of poltergeist agent or for that of juggler. We might perhaps suppose that, for reasons of which we have no inkling, the Lees' servants engaged in a complicated conspiracy against their employers. But I can see no clear indication of this.

These early poltergeist stories have, as I have tried to indicate here and there, more than a merely antiquarian interest. But it is time to leave the sixteenth century and to examine some cases of which we possess rather more detailed accounts. In selecting sample cases for examination I shall, for reasons on which I have already touched, attempt so far as is possible to combine diversity of cultural and historical background with evidential strength. What sort of evidence, it might well be demanded, is strong evidence where poltergeist cases are concerned? Some general questions to do with evidence will be discussed in chapter 13. But as a preliminary and *prima facie* reasonable move, I shall adopt the following principle. The strongest of all possible kinds of evidence that in some poltergeist cases inexplicable physical phenomena really do take place would be provided by instrumental recordings (video-tape, tape recordings, physical instruments, etc.) made under controlled conditions by qualified persons. Failing that, detailed notes made during or immediately after the phenomena by competent persons fully aware of the requirements of the situation would be the next best thing. Now we do not have a great deal of this sort of evidence even for modern poltergeist cases, though we do have some, and of course we have practically none for cases from other times and cultures than our own. There are, however, two kinds of sources of *fairly* detailed information about poltergeist cases from times and/or cultures other than our own. First of all, in a number of instances, persons confronted with poltergeist phenomena have thought them sufficiently interesting or important to make detailed and day by day diary notes of the occurrences (as, for instance, Melchior Joller did in the case discussed in chapter 1). Secondly, poltergeist cases have sometimes, for one reason and another, resulted in court cases or in the establishment of a committee of enquiry. In some instances the detailed evidence taken down in court or before a committee has come down to us. When, therefore, selecting for examination cases from times or from cultures outside the sphere of modern recording methods, it is principally for evidence from diaries or from court or similar proceedings that I shall look.

3 Poltergeists and witches

Diaries and court records relating to poltergeists, especially the former, are surprisingly common even from quite early times, and I have accumulated far more material than I can make use of in this survey. Some prominent members of the British Society for Psychical Research (the 'SPR') used to speak as though few if any detailed eyewitness accounts of poltergeist phenomena had been set down prior to the foundation of that august body in 1882. This is far from true, as even a perfunctory examination of the literature will quickly reveal. Take, for example, the sequence of German Lutheran diarists who, inspired perhaps by Luther's own accounts of conflicts with Satan, recorded their experiences at Annaberg (1691), Dortmund (1713), Gröben (1718) and Sandfeldt (1722). The diarist in the first of these cases, Pastor Enoch Zobel, gave a very full account of the events which transpired in his household; but he was himself a witness of only a few, and there is much to suggest that he was imposed upon. His efforts, however, directly inspired the Dortmund pamphlet, and indirectly no doubt the others.

The diarist at Dortmund was Florian Gerstmann, a member of a noted medical family, and his account, though it does not always give details one would like to have, is clear and clinical. One suspects that he was ordered to write it by his formidable father, whose lengthy comments, interspersed among the entries, mix, in an indiscriminate and almost lunatic fashion, reflections, self-justifications, bibliography, hymns, bad poetry, and theological twaddle. The case is notable as perhaps the most revolting on record. There was an initial phase of stone-throwing, but after this the phenomena had mostly to do with human excrement, which was taken from the 'necessarium' in the garden and thrown around or transported into the house in such quantities as might seem almost to exclude fraud. Occasionally, by way of a change, objects were transported from the house into the necessarium. Such cases are, I am glad to say, almost unheard-of today, perhaps because of more efficient sewage disposal. I must confess that if they were commoner my own enthusiasm for case investigation would at once evaporate. The Sandfeldt diary will be discussed later on (chapter 6), but the Gröben one, which was published at Jena in 1723, deserves a brief mention. The diarist, Jeremias Heinisch, was pastor of Gröben from 1714 to 1736, and an article by F. Lehman in the *Zeitschrift für Parapsychologie* in 1929 tells us that his manuscript was at that time preserved in the local *Pfarrarchiv*. Heinisch writes clearly and in some detail, and he keeps down the theological twaddle, which is separated from the actual diary. The phenomena, which went on for some weeks in the summer of 1718, consisted mainly of the throwing of stones and other missiles, at first outside Heinisch's house, but later on within it. Here is one of his more memorable observations:

> On August 1st, the throwing began early, and while I was lying in wait at a hidden place in the house to spot the perpetrator, I must between 6 and 7 in the morning have seen with my own eyes several stones rise up from the ground in the yard, where however a little before none had been, and strike the stable roof. And when I now paid very close and keen attention, I saw quite certainly that a number of stones flew out of the parsonage wall which lay opposite the stable across to the [afore-]mentioned roof, and yet one could observe no opening or chink in the wall; rather it remained quite uninjured and intact, as it had been before. What is more, I additionally saw how several stones came out of the passage by the orchard door and went around the corner of the barn. They were consequently carried along beside the barn in a semi-circle. Which remains impossible in a throw of a natural kind.

I have already remarked how frequent in poltergeist cases are reports of the apparent passage of matter through matter, e.g. of stones through a ceiling. Another of the kinds of phenomena noted by Heinisch is likewise often mentioned, namely the flight of objects through the air not as if they had been thrown but as if they had been carried. They move in curved or erratic paths, travel slowly, land gently, and so on. Other instances will be described later. However, it is not my purpose in this chapter to give a detailed account of these eighteenth-century diaries; my aim is rather to describe the very earliest court and diary records that I have been able to disinter.

Court cases have arisen over poltergeists for two principal reasons: either litigation has been instituted over the lease of a house which has been rendered uninhabitable by the spooks; or some unlucky person (usually the presumed poltergeist agent) has been suspected of producing the phenomena by natural or by occult means. Legal or official action against suspects seems to have been especially common in Germany, and things often went ill with the unfortunate persons concerned. In a case at Thorn (then in Prussia) in 1655 a maid was tortured, without, however, eliciting a confession. In a German case of 1789 another unfortunate girl suspected by the police was shown the rod and flogging block and threatened with a birching. Even Karl Wolter, the poltergeist agent in the case at Resau (1888), who was merely sentenced to an undeserved six weeks' detention, must have had an exceedingly unpleasant time.

Unlike diaries, court records seem to be somewhat thin on the ground prior to the nineteenth century. One or two of the numerous British pamphlets which describe witch trials – e.g. the trial of the Chelmsford witches (1579) and the trial of Joan Buts, the Ewell witch (1681) – mention happenings of a poltergeist kind. But of 'official' or semi-official records of trials or hearings I have only come across three prior to the year 1700 in which poltergeist phenomena figure prominently. Two of the cases concerned – the Tidworth (1662-3) and Newbury (1679) cases – will be treated later in this chapter. The third took place at Lolworth in Cambridgeshire in 1676-7, and the records were first published by a well-known local antiquary, Dr W. M. Palmer in the *Cambridge Standard* for 17 May 1935. They consist of transcripts of the examinations of the principal witnesses before local justices (one of whom was Roger Pepys, cousin of the diarist). It appears that about February 1676 Richard Curtis, of Lolworth, had had an argument with Robert Norton of the same village, and that Norton had threatened that 'he should never be at peace in his house'. He had also incautiously told another person that Curtis and his wife 'should have no peace unless they agreed with him'. Thereafter Curtis's house had been constantly disturbed at night by raps, noises and footsteps – in fact with the classic phenomena of a mild haunting (see chapter 10). In consequence a charge of witchcraft was brought against Norton. He was bound over by the justices to appear at the next assizes, but what the outcome was is not known.

Turning now to poltergeist diaries, we find a number of examples antedating the year 1700. In fact it seems likely that the pamphlet describing the famous case of the 'Divell of Mascon' (1612) was based upon a diary or upon contemporary notes. The first case I know of in which we have a record taking the actual form of a diary is the well-known one of 'The Just Divel of Woodstock' (1649). However, since the story is well-known, and since the provenance of the records is somewhat uncertain, I shall pass it by, recommending the interested reader to the useful analysis of the case in A. R. G. Owen's *Can we Explain the Poltergeist?* (New York, 1964). Next in chronological order comes the case of the 'Demon Drummer of Tedworth' (Tidworth, 1662–3). It too is very well-known, but it is none the less worth discussing, for there exist in connection with it contemporary manuscript materials, including a brief diary, which have not hitherto been published in full. I propose in the next few pages to give an account of the case based primarily on this manuscript material, using printed sources only to provide supplementary information.

The case took place in the house of John Mompesson at North Tidworth, Wiltshire. Mompesson, a Justice of the Peace, came of a well-known and well-connected family, but I have not been able to find out much more about him than is disclosed by the material set forth below. He matriculated at Wadham College, Oxford, on 8 June 1638, being then fourteen years old. He would therefore have been about thirty-eight at the time when the famous disturbances began. He was married, with several children, and although the pre-1700 Tidworth Church registers were, according to Hoare's *History of Wiltshire* (1812–21) missing even in the early nineteenth century, we know that he was still alive about 1690, for Richard Baxter's *Certainty of the Worlds of Spirits* (London, 1691) says that he 'is yet living, no Melancholy nor Conceited Man'. His death is not recorded in Musgrave's *Obituary*.

Mompesson's house seems to have been a largish timber framed structure with interior walls of board or boarded lath and plaster, and external weather boarding. Anyone who has been in a comparable building of that period will appreciate how perfectly suited it must have been to the inclinations of a rapping and drumming demon. The house itself no longer stands, having been replaced by a more recent building on the same site.

The story of the Demon Drummer has commonly been taken (as by Harry Price in *Poltergeist over England*, London, 1945, and by Sacheverell Sitwell in *Poltergeists*, London, 1940) from Joseph Glanvill's *Saducismus Triumphatus* (London, 1681). Glanvill (1636–80), who became rector of the Abbey Church, Bath, and chaplain-in-ordinary to Charles II, was a well-known writer on religious and theological subjects, and a fellow of the Royal Society. He held that the study of natural science, and the application of scientific method, could lend support to religious belief; and in *Saducismus* he turns with that aim to consider various narratives of spooks and witches. If one criticizes Glanvill from a modern point of view one can make him appear a most credulous individual; but from a standpoint in his own time he can be seen to have made serious attempts at the critical sifting and assessment of his materials. In the case, for example, of the Demon Drummer, which is the first story in his 'Collection of Relations', he talked and corresponded with witnesses, visited the spot, and himself observed various of the phenomena.

The *Saducismus* narrative was not Glanvill's first account of the Tidworth affair. A much racier version, probably drafted during 1663 (see M. H. Nicolson, ed., *Conway Letters*, Oxford, 1930, pp. 216, 219), was published in 1668, as an appendix to his *A Blow at Modern Sadducism; or Philosophical Considerations touching the Being of Witches and Witchcraft*. The early narrative is reprinted in J. Ashton's *The Devil in Britain and America* (London, 1896). I have, however, here used the slightly fuller *Saducismus* version.

The manuscript material consists of contemporary copies, by William Fulman (1632–88), a noted antiquary of the time, of three letters from John Mompesson to Dr William Creed (1614?–63), Regius Professor of Divinity at Oxford, who had married Mompesson's cousin. These letters, which are dated 6 December 1662, 26 December 1662, and 4 January 1662/3, are among the Corpus Christi Manuscripts in the Bodleian Library, as also are Fulman's copies of a journal kept by Mompesson from 10 January to 22 January 1662/3, and of a short letter of 6 January 1662/3 from William Maton to his nephew Francis Parry, of Corpus Christi College, Oxford (MA 1661). Two other copies of the letter of 6 December are known to exist. They differ from the one I shall utilize only in minor details. One of them is reproduced in Appendix A of Price's *Poltergeist over England*.

I shall now proceed to construct from this manuscript material, together with extracts from *Saducismus*, what will, I hope, be the fullest account of this famous case yet published. The advantages of thus basing oneself on the manuscript material are these:

1 Glanvill is a trifle vague, and sometimes inaccurate, on dates and chronology; we can improve the situation a little in this respect. Glanvill also makes one or two minor errors, e.g. over the adventures and whereabouts of William Drury, of Uffcott, Wilts, whose drum Mompesson confiscated at the start of the story.

2 Although Glanvill undoubtedly saw these letters, and follows them quite closely, he omits a few details and episodes which we can fill in.

3 We now have not a second-hand narrative, but Mompesson's own words, some of them contemporary with the happenings. Not only does this improve the evidential standing of the case; it helps us to form some opinion of Mompesson himself, clearly a crucial factor in one's assessment of the case.

I shall begin, then, with Mompesson's letter to Creed of 6 December 1662. Omitted passages (mostly of pious reflection, or of debate whether to leave the house) are indicated by dots. Interpolations by myself are in square brackets. In the interests of clarity I have taken some liberties over paragraphing.

> In the middle of March last being at a neighbour towne called Ludgarshall and at the Bailyff house, I heard a Drum beat, and inquired the occasion of it, the Bailyff told me they had been with the Drummer, who had been with the Constables to demand money, by virtue of a Passe which he produced but the Bailyffe thought was counterfeit, so I sent to the Constable to bring him from an Alehouse where he was, to the Bailyffes house to me, which accordingly was done. I then demanded of him by what authority he demanded money of the Kings Subjects, and how he durst menace them for not giving him money, he told me [he] had good authority and produced his Passe and a Warrant under Sir William Cawleys hand and Seale and Colonell Ayliffes, of Gretenham, persons I both knew well and was acquainted with their handwriting. I presently saw it was forged, I commanded him to put up his Drum, and told him I would seize that by my authority, and charged the Constable to carry him to the next Justice of Peace to be proceeded against. The fellow then confest that he had gotten it to be made, and beggd of me for his Drum. I told him, if I might understand from Colonell Ayliffe (whose Drummer he pretended to be) that

he had been formerly an honest man, he should have his Drum again, but whereas he pretended to have been a souldier for the King etc. I could give no credit to a man taken in a forgery. So I left the Drum at the Bailyffes, and the Drummer in the Constables hands, who upon much intreaty let him go.

About the middle of April the Drum was by the Bailyffe sent over to my house; I was then preparing for a London Journey: Upon the fourth day of May when I came home again from London, my wife told me that my house had been like to have been broken up, and they had been much affrighted in the night with thieves. I rejoiced with her at the deliverance, and after I had been at home three nights, it was come againe, so I arose and tooke some pistols in my hand, and went up and downe the house, and heard a strange noise and hollow sound, but could not see any thing: I must confesse I did at first doubt it to be what it proved to be, because I was confident no theives [sic] would adventure themselves in that manner. [Glanvill adds: 'When he was got back to bed, the noise was a Thumping and Drumming on the top of his House, which continued a good space, and then by degrees went off into the Air'.] So then it came oftner, five nights, and be absent three, and in such course that we could guesse when it would come, and thumpe very hard all in the outside of my house, and constantly came when we were going to sleep, whether early or late.

For a month it continued in the outside of my house, and then [about mid-May 1662] it came to the roome where the Drum lay, being my Mothers chamber, where he was thrown under a board, for my children did use to knock and play with it, and shee delighting their company caused it to be put there. There it would be foure or five nights in seven, and make very great hollow sounds, that the windowes would shake and the bedds, and come constantly within half an houre after we were in bed, and stay almost two houres, and when it came we could heare a perfect hurling in the aire over the house, and when it went away many times the Drum beat the same point of Warre that is usually beaten when guards breake up, as truely and sweetly as ever Drum beat in this world, and so continued in that roome for two months, I laying there all the time to observe it, and though I could take no rest at the fore part of the night, yet after two houres time (except it were now and then) it was all very quiet. We often tried what prayer would doe, and sometimes it would move a little way, and sometimes it would not.

After this it began [about mid-July 1662] to goe into other roomes over it, and keep the same noyse still though with some addition. Sometimes it would imitate the happering of pease upon boards, the shoing of horses, the Sawyers, and many others, but, God be praised, my Wife drawing neer her time of childbed, it came a litle that night she was in travaile, and forbore the house for three weekes untill shee had her strength againe, and this was indeed a great mercy.

We then hoped we had been free, but it returned [presumably about September 1662] with mighty violence and applied it self wholly to my youngest children, whose bed steeds it would beat, when there have been many strangers as well as ourselves present in the roome, that we did at every blow expect they would have fallen to pieces, and we hold our hands upon those bedsteeds all the while, and could feel no blows but feele them shake extremely, and for an houre together play the tune called Roundheads and Cuckolds goe digge, goe digge, and never misse one stroke, as sweetly as skillfully as any Drummer in the World can beat, and then the Tattoo, and severall other points of Warre. Then it will runne under the bed-teeke [i.e. tick, the bolster or mattress case] and scratch as if it had iron talons and heave up the children in the bed, and follow them from roome to roome and come to none else but them.

There being but one cock loft [attic] in the house where it was never observed to have been above stayres, I put those children there, and put them in bed whilst it was faire day light, and it came before they were covered in their beds.

The fift of November in the morning, it kept a mighty noise and one of my men observing in the roome where the children lay that there was two boards stood edge long and did seem to move, he said to it Give me that board, the board came within a yard of him, he said againe, Nay, Let me have it in my hand; it came home to his very foot, he shuft it back again to him, and so from one to another at least twenty times, but I forbad such familiarity, and that morning it left in that roome a sulphurous smell, which was very offensive, but staid not long: I must confesse I never doubted whether I should be able to stand my ground till that time, but I thank God, we have no more of those noysome smells.

At night Mr Cragge our minister [John Cragg, probably of Christ's College Cambridge, MA 1632] and many of my Neighbours came to me, we went to prayer by my Childrens bed sides, where it was very loud; it went at that time of Prayer into the cock loft, and when we came away it returned, and in our presence and sight the chaires did walk about, the childrens shooes were tost over our heads, and every loose thing throwne about the roome, a bed staffe was thrown at Mr Cragge and hit him in the legg, but so softly that a lock of wooll could not fall more softly.

I perceived it persecuted these little children so much [I] lodged them at a neighbours, and took my eldest daughter about ten yeares old into my chamber where it had not been in a month: as soon as shee was in bed, that was there too, and has continued so about three weekes, and still beats the Drumme, and let us knock at any time, it will hearken and knock the same presently, and play any tune of the drum that we bid it.

I was forc't the other night to bring my youngest children home, the people where they laid being full of strangers, and we could not remember that it had ever been in our parlour where we dine and sup, and therefore laid in some beds about the ground and lodged our children there, but the drum came, and they were pulled by their night geare and their hayre, each of them had a pluck and so away; I must I doubt remove them againe, for I see the devill has most malice where there is most innocency.

I have often after prayer followd it and conjur'd it in the name of God to appeare to me and declare the reason of its troubling this place so, but could never see any appearance neither any of my people.

Sir, you may imagine that I have reason enough to suspect this Drummer, by what hath been all ready said; and indeed I had prosecuted him ere this but that I was prevented for he layes now in Gloster Gaole for stealing of hoggs. [The Drummer, who had been at liberty since March 1662, was imprisoned about the end of November or beginning of December 1662, and remained in prison until April 1663.] When I inquired into his conversation, I found he had been in the Parliament Army foure years, and when he came home, he wrought a litle time at his trade, being a taylor, but continued not long at work, but went up and down the Countrey to shew Hocas pocas, feats of activity, dancing through hoops and such like devices, but as soon as he comes home I shall visit him, for I am informed that he spake words which if proved, it may goe hard with him.

Here have been many spectators as well Divines as others, persons of judgment, who doe all conclude it to be witchcraft, and the truth is, it doth so many anticke things impossible to relate, that there is no great question I think to be made of it. Yet I know we live in an uncharitable and censorious age, and many I suppose may be ready enough (and have been as I am told) to judge that this comes upon me for some enormous sin or other; for my own part I am far enough from justifying my self, I know I deserved far greater punishments at the hand of God then these have yet been, but had my conscience accused me of any such particular crying sin I should scarcely have indured this, for surely my own guilt would have driven me far enough from it, and men were best take heed how they censure others in these or the like cases, lest they prove themselves not so good as they should be, whilst they take others to be worse than they are. And sure the rule of Gods providence is no more revealed to these censurers than to others . . . .

I have often thought that if any learned man had made these observations that I have done, he might have discovered much of the nature of these spirits.

It has taken our servants up in their beds, bed and all, and lifted them up a great height, and layd them down softly again, and layes often on their feet with a great weight. Sometimes the candles will not burn in the roome where it is, and though it come never so loud and on a sudain, yet no dog will bark: it hath been often so loud that it hath been heard up into the fields and has wakned my neighbours in the towne. I have not been without strangers to heare it this many nights which have troubled me half as bad as the spirit; now it comes a little seeming a farre off at eight of the clock in the night, and layes still all night till about five in the morning, and then it will drum us up, but it often changes its course, and has not mist one night these seven weeks.

We come now to Mompesson's letter of 26 December 1662. It describes events which took place between 6 December and 26 December 1662.

Since I wrote my last unto you, we have constantly at night been troubled with this evil companion, but with much variation: we have but litle of the Drum noyse, but very much of Gingling, occasioned as we think by some discourse that fell from my Mother at Noonday, for certeinly it is here all day as well as at night, although it be in greater silence at some time than at other; It was thus. A neighbour coming and discoursing with my Mother, told my Mother that she had heard storyes of Fayries, that did use to leave money behind them in Maydens shooes, and the like; My Mother replied, I should like that well if it would leave us some money to make us satisfaction for the trouble and charge it putts us to. And that night there was such a chinking of Money all about the house, that we thought we should have found all the house strewed with halfe Crownes in the Morning: which kind of noyse it still most resembles, but it doth not now make such great sounds, but more applies it selfe to unlucky trickes.

On Christmas Eve about an houre before day, one of my little boyes arising to make water, all being quiet, a pin of the latch of the dore was pulld out, and the dore throwne open, and the latch hit the boy directly in a sore place of his heel, and made him cry out: one would wonder how such a little pin could be found out in the night. And on Christmasse day at night it took my Mothers clothes and threw all about the roome and took her Bible and hid it in the ashes of the chimney, and such odde trickes every night it does.

I shall acquaint you with some Mirth we have with it: I have a man[,] a Clowne of a great Courage but no great witt, but of good conversation and sober; this fellow offered his service to lay within where the greatest trouble was, so I lay him in the next Chamber to me and gave him a sword to stand by his bed side; there is scarse a night but there is a conflict between these two, sometimes John (for so is his name) hath the best of it, and sometimes the Goblin: sometimes Johns Breeches and Doublet are pulld about the room and his shooes thrown at him; then John takes his sword and recovers it, but now and then it takes John at the advantage when he is asleep and his Armes in the bed, and layes so hard upon him, that for his life he cannot get one hand loose for a quarter of an houre, and then he will be in a great sweat: but as soon as he can get out his hands, then he beats him away, and sometimes the fray is so loud that I rise or send to relieve John which he takes for some disparagement. And these things others also have tasted as well as strangers as others, some have had their hands catched as they have been feeling for a chamber pot, and held, their feet and stomachs layd on, but thus much we have discoverd of it, that it is afraid of weapon or to be handled, and very shy of much light.

My Jelousie of the Drummer still increases; the Drum I burnt in the field long agoe, but I question not but I shall meet with him at home at Broad Hinton neere Marlborough after Glocester Sessions. There was one Miller Vicar of Barwick by Broad Hinton that was convented before the Committees for practicing Magick, he confessed he had skill therein, he used to help people to lost goods. This Drummer was a reteyner to his house: Miller is dead, this fellow often repaired to his Widow, and has reported that Mr Miller had gallant Bookes which he had seen, and understood by them how to tell fortunes, which he practiced etc: . . . .

It never comes neere me nor my wife, unlesse we go to that, which I also wonder at, unlesse we take any children to us. I am the more unwilling to leave my house, because it seems to me to be the very designe of the Devill to drive me out of it.
The Presidents man of Ma. [Magdalen] Coll. saw and heard some of the prancks.

Mompesson's final letter is dated 4 January 1662/3 (readers will recall that until 1752 the legal year ended on 25 March), and refers to events of the previous nine days.

We doe often heare (especially of late) a tinging [Glanvill says 'singing'] in the chimney before it comes downe, and many other things we have experimentally found to be true as the letter mentions. Since I wrote my last, we have constantly every night been troubled, and one night more than ever, there being great lights, one whereof came into my chamber which my wife did see [Glanvill talks of 'those that saw it'], which she conceived to be very blue and glimmering, and caused as she thought some stiffnesse on her eylids: it continued whilst forty might be distinctly told, and before she perceived it, heard something come up the staires resembling one coming up without shooes: that light was foure or five severall times in my childrens chamber, and as the maids constantly affirme, the dores were at least ten or more times opened and shut in their sights, and when they were opened there came in a noise as if half a dozen had come in and pressed who should come first in, and walk about the roome, one whereof rusled so that they thought it had a silk garment on (the same I once heard) but all this while they saw nothing but the dores open and shut, and the lights, but when they first were troubled with the noise of the dores they set up a candle, by which they perceived the motions of the dores.

This light came to my man, who being asleep it awakened him, and he confessed that his haire stood on end, and that for some time he knew not where he was; which made him the next night desire a candle by him, which he set burning in the chimney, and got a neighbour to ly with him: Within a quarter of an houre the candle was taken away burning, the candlestick being left behind, and the candle so disposed of that none of it could be found though sought after.

One passage more I shall trouble you with, which was this; When the knocking was, many being present, a Gentleman said, Satan, If the Drummer set thee on worke, let us understand so much by giving three knockes and no more; it presently gave three knockes distinctly and audibly: then the Gentleman knockt to see where it would imitate him or no, as it had done severall times before, but it remained silent: He then further replied, For the further confirmation of this, If the Drummer set thee on work, let us have five knockes and no more; It gave five knocks, and then ceased from knocking that night any more. This was in the presence of Sir Thomas Chamberlaine of Oxfordshire (truly at present I doe not remember whether he were the person that spake himself or no) Mr Gyles Tooker [1625–1675, later Sir Giles, of Maddington, Wiltshire] and others. This I suppose is no evidence to a Jurie, for the Devil ought not to be believed, yet I suppose it may be an argument that this Spirit comes not to discover any murthers committed, Treasures hidden, or the like.

I observe you say that some that had the sight of my letter admired, others doubted: Indeed they are things of so strange a nature that at a distance they may well be doubted of: for although I have heard that many houses have been troubled with unusual noises and sounds and other disturbances, yet I never heard that for 14. weeks together a spirit should come, and in the sight of so many hundreds should doe such things, as if it were his chiefe businesse and designe to convince the World of their infidelity in that point.

I shall trouble you with one story more: the last night there came some Gentlemen afarre off to see this; I admitted them; so they inquired at what time it usually came, it was answered neer about this time; so they sat half an houre longer in expectation, and asked where it was yet come, the maid said No: whereupon I perceived them to smile: shortly after it was told them it was come, whereupon they rose up and ran into the roome, so they heard the knocking it usually made; they began to search and very curiously to look where or no they could discover any secret Angles or holes where any body might be put to make noises to deceive them, but found none: then they called out, Satan, Doe this, and that, and Whistle if thou canst, or let us see where thou canst tell money, or make chaires dance, as we have heard, let us see it: I protest I was afraid at their cariage, and begd of them to be more sober and to withdraw themselves, for there was most to be heard when there was most silence; they were impatient and would not heare me; the spirit kept knocking, but medled not with any chaires or stooles: So I perceived they imagined there was a trick, and one before askt me leave, if they thought fitt, to pull up my boards, I told him no indeed: So when the Spirit was silent they discoursed of it, and I perceived remained doubtfull. There were two Ministers present who both assured them they had seen the motions of the chaires and stooles as reported, but because they could not see it would not believe (the devill was a fool to let them see so much) and began to hold discourses with these two Ministers, in which they declared their diffidence of the being of Spirits, and so departed with some kind of suspicion that what they heard was onely a cheat or a fancy, all but one, who seemed to be well satisfied upon a particular observation that he made, and in their way have reported it to be as before I have said, and not worth regarding, and told it to a person of honor. They were the onely persons that ever I observed went away with so much dissatisfaction, and whole carriage was of that nature, that I shall be more carefull how I admitt strangers for the future. If any be so uncharitable as to believe that a whole family can be so monstrously impious as to fast and pray, and to desire the help of Ministers and other good people to remove that which themselves have contrived to deceive the World, I wish them better Christians . . .

I subjoin next William Maton's letter of 6 January 1662/3 to his nephew Francis Parry. 'Last Sunday night' would have been the night of 4 January.

I am glad to heare you are well, and for the intelligence concerning Mr Mumpessons you may be satisfied by the Letter you saw of Doctor Creeds: I have heard it many times, and severall tones, which are these, Drumming, Scratching, Threshing, all at once, and last Sunday night it spake, the words are these, A Witch, A Witch, many times. And what you desire it to doe, it is much at command: and it will heave up the beds two foot from the boards: I can affirme this to be true, and that it did Cover Mris Mompessons Bible in the ashes, and many strange things more which will be too tedious to relate, being enough to convert an Infidel . . .

The story is now taken up in a brief journal kept by Mompesson from 10 January to 22 January 1662/3:

On Saturday morning being the tenth of this instant January, and the day Mr Parry returned to Oxford, about an houre before the break of day, the Drum was beaten up severall times in the outside of my Chamber, and then went to the other end of the house, where my Cosen St John of Lediard [the St Johns of Liddiard Tregose were a well-known Wiltshire family] and Mr Pleydell [the Pleydells were also a well-known Wiltshire family] lay, and plaied at the dore and in the Aire foure or five severall tunes, and so went off in the aire.

Sonday next night [11 January] a young man being a Smith, lodging with my man as he useth to do, there came a snipping to his nose which continued most part of the night, as it had been a paire of Smiths Pincers, and my man rising and reaching after his hat, his hat flew from him to the other side of the Chamber.

Monday night [12 January] (as once before) the Candle going out in my Childrens Chamber, the maids attempted to strike fire with a steele and flint, but could not make any fire take, the Spirit sitting at the bedshead and mocking them every stroke they struck: they tryed when they were up, and made fire come presently.

Tuesday night [13 January] all was quiet, but I rising early to goe to Sarum, halfe my cloths being on, I heard a great noise below where my children lay, and so ran downe with a pistol in my hand into the roome, where there was a voice crying a witch a witch, as once before, and the chaires jumbling together, and presently vanished.

Wednesday [14 January] there was no noise but up in my cock loft.

Thursday night [15 January] as soon as my Wife and I were into bed, the chaire at my beds feet rocked very hard up and downe, and it knocked very hard upon the boards: I rose and lighted a candle and it went away.

Friday night [16 January] it came into my Chamber (I being at a neighbours) before I went to bed, and went into the bed teeke where my Daughter lyes, and ran from one side of the bed to the other, and heaved her up; it continued two houres, many being in the roome there were at one time three severall noises in the bed; one whereof seeming to blow and pant like a dog out of breath, and continued not with standing two lights were held to the bed, and naked swords, but it was so swift that we could not thrust it without indangering her, for it would be at the head and at the feet, and yet as soon as we were ready to thrust at it, it would run under her body.

Saturday night [17 January] the like panting was in her bed, and one lying with her, they going to bed before us, we bid them knock when they heard it; her bedfellow knockt with a bedstaffe, which the second time shee knockt was catcht out of her hand, and throwne to the other side of the chamber, we hearing it ran up, some neighbours being with us, we, as soon as we put our noses into the roome smelt a bloomy, hot, ill smell, and the roome though without fire was very hot, and the children in the bed in a great sweat that it run down their faces, and sweat so violently that we durst not remove them out of the bed, and the greatest heat was about their bed and in it: it continued thus panting in the bed and scratching an houre and half, heaving up the bedcloths, and at last went into the next chamber where it knockt a little and seemed to rattle a chaire.

The like the next night and the night following [18 and 19 January] except the smell.

And the next night [20 January] the like with something againe of the smell, and the panting continuing very long, sometimes it would resemble the palpitation of the heart, and although the noise were but small yet we could plainly feel the whole roome many times to shake.

The next night [21 January] there was litle to be heard, but the last night [22 January] Sir Thomas Bennetts son of Salthropp coming to see me, whose workman this Drummer had sometime been, living hard by him, he gave me some account of words spoken by the Drummer and some other passages; his man lay with my man, and another Gentleman with him; as soon as we were into our beds the Drum came with a rattle to the purpose, they rose and called their man to them, as soon as he departed from my man, there came one rusling like a Gentlewoman in silk to my mans bed side, he catcht at his sword which was held, and he gave many tugs before he got it, but when he got it, it left him; his shooes were taken away and every thing in the chamber and piled up in the chimney, and took a sylver spoon and hid it behind the hangings, so that we could not find it in three houres, and at last found it behind a wing that was pinned upon the hangings: it was very troublesome to Mr Bennet, it may be because he spake so ill of the Drummer.

That is as far as Mompesson's first-hand account goes. Glanvill gives us a few more particulars of events which took place about the end of January 1663:

> After this, the old Gentlewomans Bible was found in the Ashes, the Paper side being downwards. Mr. *Mompesson* took it up, and observed that it lay open at the third Chapter of St. *Mark*, where there is mention of the unclean spirits falling down before our Saviour, and of his giving power to the Twelve to cast out Devils, and of the Scribes opinion, that he cast them out through *Beelzebub*. The next night they strewed Ashes over the Chamber, to see what impressions it would leave. In the morning they found in one place, the resemblance of a great Claw, in another of a Lesser, some Letters in another, which

they could make nothing of, besides many Circles and Scratches in the Ashes.

Glanvill next goes on to describe his own visit to Tidworth, which would appear to have taken place about the end of January or beginning of February 1663.

About this time I went to the house, on purpose to inquire the truth of those passages, of which there was so loud a report. It had ceased from its Drumming and ruder noises before I came thither, but most of the more remarkable circumstances before related, were confirmed to me there, by several of the neig[h]bours together, who had been present at them. At this time it used to haunt the Children, and that as soon as they were laid. They went to Bed that night I was there, about Eight of the Clock, when a Maid-servant coming down from them, told us it was come. The neighbours that were there, and two Ministers who had seen and heard divers times, went away, but Mr. *Mompesson* and I, and a Gentleman that came with me went up. I heard a strange scratching as I went up the Stairs, and when we came into the Room, I perceived it was just behind the Bolster of the Childrens Bed, and seemed to be against the Tick. It was as loud a scratching, as one with long Nails could make upon a Bolster. There were two little modest Girls in the Bed, between Seven and Eleven years old as I guest. I saw their hands out of the Cloaths, and they could not contribute to the noise that was behind their heads. They had been used to it, and had still some body or other in the Chamber with them, and therefore seemed not to be much affrighted. I standing at the Beds-head, thrust my hand behind the Bolster, directing it to the place whence the noise seemed to come. Whereupon the noise ceased there, and was heard in another part of the Bed. But when I had taken out my hand it returned, and was heard in the same place as before. I had been told that it would imitate noises, and made trial by scratching several times upon the Sheet, as 5, and 7, and 10, which it followed and still stopt at my number. I searcht under and behind the Bed, turned up the Cloaths to the Bed-cords, graspt the Bolster, sounded the Wall behind, and made all the search that possibly I could to find if there were any trick, contrivance, or common cause of it; the like did my friend, but we could discover nothing. So that I was then verily perswaded, and am so still, that the noise was made by some *Daemon* or *Spirit*. After it had scratcht about half an hour or more, it went into the midst of the Bed under the Children, and there seemed to pant like a Dog out of breath very loudly. I put my hand upon the place, and felt the Bed bearing up against it, as if something within had thrust it up. I graspt the Feathers to feel if any living thing were in it. I looked under and every where about, to see if there were any Dog or Cat, or any such Creature in the Room, and so we all did, but found nothing. The motion it caused by this panting was so strong, that it shook the Room and Windows very sensibly. It continued thus more than half an hour, while my friend and I stay'd in the Room, and as long after, as we were told. During the panting, I chanced to see as it had been something (which I thought was a Rat or Mouse) moving in a Linnen Bag, that hung up against another Bed that was in the Room. I stept and caught it by the upper end with one Hand, with which I held it, and drew it through the other, but found nothing at all in it. There was no body near to shake the Bag, or if there had no one could have made such a motion, which seemed to be from within, as if a Living Creature had moved in it . . . . It will I know be said by some, that my friend and I were under some affright, and so fancied noises and sights that were not. This is the Eternal Evasion. But if it be possible to know how a Man is affected, when in fear, and when unconcerned, I certainly know for mine own part, that during the whole time of my being in the Room, and in the House, I was under no more affrightment than I am, while I write this Relation.

I omit here passages concerning nocturnal bangings and a voice outside Glanvill's chamber door, and about the laming of his horse; and proceed with 'Mr. Mompesson's own particulars', as somewhat briefly retailed by Glanvill, of the events which took place around February and March 1663.

There came one Morning a light into the Childrens Chamber, and a voice crying, *a Witch, a Witch*, for at least an hundred times together.

Mr. *Mompesson* at another time (being in the day) seeing some Wood move that was in the Chimney of a Room, where he was, as of it self, discharged a Pistol into it, after which they found several drops of Blood on the Hearth, and in divers places of the Stairs.

For two or three nights after the discharge of the Pistol, there was a calm in the House, but then it came again, applying it self to a little Child newly taken from Nurse. Which it so persecuted, that it would not let the poor Infant rest for two nights together, nor suffer a Candle in the Room, but carry them away lighted up the Chimney, or throw them under the Bed. It so scared this Child by leaping upon it, that for some hours it could not be recovered out of the fright. So that they were forced again to remove the Children out of the House. The next night after which, something about Mid-night came up the Stairs, and knockt at Mr. *Mompesson's* door, but he lying still, it went up another pair of Stairs, to his Mans Chamber, to whom it appeared standing at his Beds foot. The exact shape and proportion he could not discover, but he saith he saw a great Body with two red and glaring Eyes, which for some time were fixed steadily upon him, and at length disappeared.

Another night strangers being present, it purr'd in the Childrens Bed like a Cat, at which time also the Cloaths and Children were lift up from the Bed, and six Men could not keep them down: hereupon they removed the Children, intending to have ript up the Bed. But they were no sooner laid in another, but the second Bed was more troubled than the first. It continued thus four hours, and so beat the Childrens Leggs against the Bed-posts, that they were forced to arise, and sit up all night. After this it would empty Chamber-pots into their Beds, and strew them with Ashes, though they were never so carefully watcht. It put a long piked iron into Mr. *Mompesson's* Bed, and into his Mothers a naked Knife upright. It would fill Porrengers with Ashes, throw every thing about, and keep a noise all day.

About the beginning of *April* 1663. a Gentleman that lay in the house, had all his money turned black in his Pockets; and Mr. *Mompesson* coming one Morning into his Stable, found the Horse he was wont to Ride, on the Ground, having one of his hinder Leggs in his Mouth, and so fastened there, that it was difficult for several Men to get it out with a Leaver. After this, there were some other remarkable things, but my Account goes no further. Only Mr. *Mompesson* writ me word, that afterwards the House was several nights beset with seven or eight in the shape of Men, who, as soon as a Gun was discharged, would shuffle away together into an Arbour.

No doubt the seven shufflers were local persons in search of excitement. More or less coincident with the dying away of the phenomena came a crisis in the affairs of the feckless drummer, William Drury. About the beginning of April 1663 he was sentenced at the Gloucester assizes to transportation for stealing hogs. On 10 April he was put on a barge with some other prisoners, presumably to be taken to a larger ship at Bristol. He managed to escape by swimming to the shore. He was foolish enough to buy another drum and return to his home at Uffcot,

Wiltshire. Unfortunately Mompesson, who had gone to Gloucester to see what had become of him, chanced to be in the neighbourhood. He had him arrested on a charge of witchcraft. An account of the hearing before the magistrates was published in the *Mercurius Publicus* for 16–23 April 1663, and in *The Kingdom's Weekly Intelligencer* for 20–27 April 1663. There is also a manuscript copy among the Harleian Mss in the British Library. Drury was remanded in Salisbury gaol for the next assizes.

We learn from a letter of Mompesson's to James Collins, dated 8 August 1674, and published in *Saducismus*, that Drury was indicted at the assizes under the Witchcraft Statute of 1604. He had been unwise enough whilst in prison to claim before a witness that 'if he had not taken away my Drum, that trouble had never befallen him, and he shall never have his quiet again, till I have my Drum, or satisfaction from him'. Mompesson himself, together with William Maton, Walter Dowse, and Mr Cragg the minister, all testified upon oath to phenomena which they had witnessed. However, '... the Grand Jury found the Bill upon the Evidence, but the Petty Jury acquitted him, but not without some difficulty'. What became of Drury thereafter does not appear. There seems to have been a recrudescence of phenomena at Tidworth toward the end of 1663, with 'tricks farr different from the former' (*Conway Letters*, pp. 218–19; J. I. Cope, *Joseph Glanvill*, St Louis, 1956, pp. 15, 16); but we do not have the details – unless, indeed, the reference is to the activities of the seven shufflers mentioned above.

It is curious that many writers who mention this case (including even so notable an authority as C. L'Estrange Ewen) assume without question that Drury himself caused the phenomena in Mompesson's house, directly and by natural means. Clearly he could not have so caused them; during four or five months of plentiful phenomena, he was shut up in prison. At the time (for the affair quickly became famous, was the subject of a broadside ballad, and is mentioned in Pepys's *Diary* for 15 June 1663) Mompesson was widely suspected of knowingly and for his own reasons conniving at an imposture. Many persons had visited Tidworth in the hope of witnessing the phenomena. Some had gone away satisfied; others had not. The King sent down Lord Falmouth, and the Queen Lord Chesterfield, to look into the matter; but they could 'neither see nor heare anything that was extraordinary'. ('By the same turn of reason,' Glanvill remarked, 'the Spaniard inferred well that said, "There was no Sun in England," because he had been six weeks here, and never saw it.') According to Aubrey's *Natural History of Wiltshire* (1847), Sir Christopher Wren went down, and suspected a servant-maid of drumming on the wall. It was soon put about that Mompesson, summoned to the King's presence, had confessed he had discovered it was all a cheat. However, Mompesson sent Glanvill a letter for publication (it is dated 8 November 1672) in which he denies in the strongest terms that he ever made such a confession, and remarks: 'I must bely my selfe, and perjure my self also to acknowledge a Cheat in a thing where I am sure there was nor could be any, as I, the Minister of the Place, and two other Honest Gentlemen deposed at the Assizes . . . .' Mompesson was not a man to whom his oath meant nothing. Furthermore Mompesson's son Thomas assured Samuel Wesley (the Wesley who collected the evidence in the Epworth case of 1716) when both were at Oxford that no cheat had ever been discovered in the affair.

Of course an important question is whether Mompesson, our central though not our only witness, was so hopelessly gullible that some member or members of his household could have imposed on him more or less continuously for upwards of a year. I can only say that to me he appears from his letters to have been neither a fool nor a fanatic, but a manly and sincere Christian, who faced with some courage, and with no sign of loss of balance, manifestations which he certainly regarded as satanic. The reader is in as good a position as I am to make up his mind on the issue.

It is worth pointing out perhaps that many of the happenings which Mompesson records – responsive rappings, imitative noises, objects falling 'softly', nocturnal luminosities, the tendency of the phenomena to follow the 'little modest girls', especially in bed – have parallels in cases of which he could never have heard. He fails, of course, to give us information upon many questions to which modern parapsychologists would wish answers. He can hardly be blamed for this. However, some at least of these questions were put to him by the Cambridge philosopher, Henry More, with Glanvill as intermediary, and the answers are given in Glanvill's *A Whip for the Droll* (1668).

POLTERGEISTS AND WITCHES 61

The relevant passage, though important, is little known, so I will conclude my account of the Tidworth case by giving it in full. It is in the form of a letter from Glanvill to More.

The scrupulous care you take in examining the Story of the Disturbance at *Tedworth*, is no more than becomes a Philosopher, and one that is not willing to be deceived. And without such a cautious and particular inquiry you could not answer the murmurs and petty evasions of wilful Unbelievers. Those *Objections* you pickt up at *Cambridge* have the ill fortune to miscarry in almost every circumstance, and are in no likelihood of being believed but at a great distance. Some of them I could have answered upon mine own knowledge; and concerning the rest I have made a strict enquiry of Mr. *Mompesson* himself and others, when I was last in those parts, and upon certain [i.e. reliable] information I give you this account.

To the (1.) that saith, *The House is rented and that this is a device to beat down the value of it.* I answer from his own Mouth, That the House is his own, and so the foundation of this shift is over-turned. The second, of those that say, *It is a trick to get Money from those that come to see the Prodigy*, hath as little truth, but much more malice in the first Contrivers than the former. For this Gentleman being a Person of Estate, I am confident scorns so base and so beggarly a Policy, and is so far from making any advantage, that it hath done him very material prejudice in his Fortunes and Affairs. And those Strangers that come to see the Prodigy use to leave nothing behind them except thanks for the civility of their Entertainments. 'Tis true (3.) as others say, That *the House is boarded without*, at least a great part of it. But there are no *Cellars* as the *Objection* adds, save only under the Parlour, and the disturbance was most in other Rooms. And whereas (4.) 'tis objected, That *a Knight that offered to go down could not be permitted*. 'Tis answered me, That the Gentleman might have gone down had he pleased, and his Servant did, who made a careful search, but could find nothing that might be a cause of the noise, which he affirmed to be above, and that it proceeded not from the Cellar. And to disable what other Objectors say, viz. (5.) *That there was no Drumming in the midst of any Room, but only a striking on the Boards as it were with a Hammer in a corner of the outsides of the House.* I say, to null this pretence, Mr. *Mompesson* and others assured me, that the noise was oft in the *midst* of the Room, and oft *over head*; and, he saith, that there is scarce a Man or Child in the Village but hath heard and can witness it. And after the first month it was almost *always* within. Thus, Sir, to the *Objections* of others, which you have gathered. And to your own *Queries* I make this return.

Whereas you inquire (1.) What part of the Childrens Bed did the Daemon beat, and what noise did it make? 'Tis answered, That it beat against the Head and Posts of the Bed, and that when hands were laid on each side of them, at those times they would shake as if they would fall in pieces, but nothing else could be perceived or felt. The noise was like to that of striking with a Hammer. And then (2.) To that whither the *Drummer's Drum was ever looked on while it beat, or was it only in the dark*, I am assured that it was seen while the noise was made upon it both by the light of Fire and Candle. (3.) To the Query, *What were the Boards that moved, by what* Light was their motion seen, and by whom? Mr. *Mompesson* answers, They were seen move forwards and backwards in the light of clear day, before the Sun was set, and by a whole House full of people. And whereas (4.) you ask, *In what clearness of Light were the Chairs seen walk about, and by what Witnesses?* 'Tis answered, That they were seen to do so by Candle light, and by divers persons.

As to what I was a witness of my self, I add these circumstances for the satisfaction of your *Queries*; The Children were in Bed when the *Scratching* and *Panting* was, but I am sure did not contribute to those noises. I saw their hands above the Clothes during the *Scraping*, and searched the place where the noise came. To which I might add, That they were little harmless modest Girls that could not well have been suspected guilty of the confidence of such a Juggle, had it been possible they could have acted in it. For the *Panting* I am certain there was no Dog in the Bed, for I graspt it with my hand, and felt it in all parts, especially there where the original motion was. The Bed also was searcht *under*, but no Dog, nor any Creature else could be found there. The *Floor* I said shook with the *Panting* sensibly, and yet it was as strong and substantial an one, as ordinarily is seen. But the Children indeed did not seem to be much concerned, having been used to those and ruder noises, and there was company in the Room to assure them.

It will not have escaped notice that in the seventeenth century poltergeist phenomena were very commonly attributed to witchcraft. And things might go ill with the suspected witch – William Drury, for example, could easily have been hanged. This point is well illustrated by two further seventeenth-century cases of which we have diary or court records. These two cases, both American, are the case at Newbury (Newburyport) Mass., in 1679–80, and the case at Portsmouth, New Hampshire, in 1682 and 1683. In the afflicted house at Newbury lived an elderly shoemaker, William Morse, esteemed 'a sincere and understanding Christian', his wife, Elizabeth, and their grandson, John Stiles, who was clearly a lively lad. Elizabeth Morse was, or had been, a midwife. Midwives, owing to the ready access which they had to certain items of magical import, were frequently suspected of witchcraft; and it is clear that such suspicions had been directed at Goodwife Morse long before the events of which I shall speak.

On 27 November 1679 poltergeist phenomena began in Morse's household. They were of a fairly characteristic sort – stones and other objects were flung around; a long staff danced up and down in the chimney; a chair flew about and lighted on the table; and so on. The phenomena continued, and became quite violent. Within a day or two local gossip began to lay them at the door of Goodwife Morse. At this point a seaman, named Caleb Powell, the mate of a ship, appeared on the scene. Powell's later story (told, however, when he was himself on trial) was that looking into the house one day he saw young Stiles throw a shoe at his grandfather, who was at prayer. Believing that the lad was behind the whole thing, and wishing to have an opportunity of proving it, he represented himself as an expert in astrology, and said that he could alleviate the troubles if the lad were given over to him for a day. Accordingly on 2 December 1679, Powell was put in charge of John Stiles.

Phenomena did indeed temporarily quieten down thereafter (Andrew Lang cynically proposes that the seaman presented young Stiles with arguments not unconnected with a rope's end). But on the very next day Morse complained to the magistrates that Powell was working with the devil against him and his family. Powell was arrested. Perhaps Morse hoped that suspicion would thereby be turned from his wife; if so, he was to be disappointed. Powell did not come to trial until March. In the meanwhile the phenomena became still more violent, and began to show a new streak of vindictiveness. The boy was flung violently around, pinched and struck, pins and knives were stuck into him, and Morse and his wife were scratched, pinched and beaten. Eventually the lad began to rave and have fits, and to bark like a dog, cluck like a hen, and to have visions of Powell. In short he showed all the traditional symptoms of a person afflicted by witchcraft (cf. chapter 7).

Powell succeeded in gaining an acquittal; and at once the flood of public suspicion was directed back to Goodwife Morse. All kinds of old incidents and old grudges were resurrected from dark corners of spiteful minds, where they had festered for years; and the unfortunate woman was arraigned upon witchcraft charges, most of which had nothing to do with the recent events in her home. In May she was sentenced to death, but, much to the disgust of the locals, the Governor, who had doubts about the whole business, reprieved her, and after urgent representations by her husband, she was allowed to return home in June 1681. Till her dying day she denied that she had ever been guilty of the sin of witchcraft.

In the Portsmouth case, however, the suspected woman may well have been guilty in intent. The case was predominantly one of stone-throwing, and it is described in considerable detail and in diary form by Richard Chamberlain, Secretary in 1682 of the Province of New Hampshire, who lodged in the afflicted house. The house and lands (for these too were troubled) were those of a Quaker named George Walton. An elderly lady named Hannah Jones had claims, too complex to be gone into here, upon land purchased by Walton. There was continual bickering between the two, taking the form of complaints to the President and Council. Goodwife Jones was reputedly a witch and the daughter of a witch, and when the stone-throwing began, Walton's suspicions naturally lit upon her – not, it must be said, without cause; for she had uttered some incautious words on the subject, and on one occasion, following a threat from her that stones would be thrown at his head, he was struck several times by stones, though witnesses testified before the Council that they 'saw no hand or person to throw them'. However, Goody Jones was no sluggard herself at accusation and litigation, and she does not seem to have been prosecuted as a witch.

It thus appears to have been widely believed in the seventeenth century that poltergeist phenomena could be instigated and sustained by witches, presumably through the instrumentality of their familiar spirits. Not only witches, but 'cunning men', those curious compounds of herbal doctor, clairvoyant and white witch who survived in our countryside almost to within living memory, were credited with the power to stir things up. Indeed in the case at Kabsdorff in 1666, the Lutheran pastor whose house was involved suspected a Franciscan friar who had visited him, and whom he had worsted in a theological dispute. Such ideas are by no means confined to the seventeenth century. In the twentieth century, for instance, accusations or suggestions of witchcraft have been made in connection with poltergeist phenomena in cases at Monneville (early twentieth century), Gerolstein (1901), Molignon (1914), Cieurac (1926), Cork (1928), Seyssuel (1930), and Pursruck (1970). This list does not profess to be exhaustive. Indeed within the last two years I have heard a fairly educated man, in whose place of work poltergeist phenomena were ostensibly happening, ascribe them to 'black magic'.

I do not suppose that many modern parapsychologists would subscribe to the view that a witch or other such person may by occult means initiate poltergeist phenomena at a distance. They would, perhaps, be more apt to explore another line of thought, one which is suggested by a modest number of cases. An idealized case of this kind would run as follows: old hag of sinister aspect comes to kitchen of substantial house and asks maid to hand over food or goods not belonging to her. Indignant young maid refuses. Old hag departs, muttering curses of ill-omen. Next day poltergeist phenomena break out around the maid, possibly accompanied by psychosomatic disturbances. Cases somewhat of this type occurred at Glenluce (1654), Brightling (1659), Youghal (1661), Ewell (1681), Boston (1692–3), Bargarran (1696), Annandale (1707), Canton de Auberire (1816), Dijon (near) (1838–40), Devonshire (1840s), Clairefontaine (1846), Pleaston (1852), and Cumminsville (1870). In some of these cases the fright which apparently precipitated the phenomena had nothing directly to do with witches; and the conclusion to be drawn is that it was the *fright* which, by disturbing the victim's nervous system in some way as yet obscure, triggered the happenings. Having established this point, we might perhaps try to fit other cases into the same mould, e.g. by proposing that at Lolworth Richard Curtis was frightened by Robert Norton's threats; that someone in Mompesson's household was somehow frightened by the drummer or the drum; and so on.

This sort of procedure strikes me as risky and quite illegitimate. Poltergeist phenomena are so many-faceted, and we know so little about them, that nothing but confusion and muddying of the waters is likely to result if we invent imaginary facts in order to reconcile particular cases with our own over-simple hypotheses. However, the cases we have so far touched on do fairly strongly suggest two things: that in some poltergeist cases the phenomena centre around, and depend upon the presence of, particular individuals (the 'poltergeist agents'); and that in some of these cases the phenomena have been triggered off by the agent's receiving an emotional shock. In other words, there is some evidence that the occurrence of poltergeist phenomena may be related to the psychological state of the poltergeist agent. This is a view at which I will begin to look in the next chapter.

4 Poltergeist people

The idea that poltergeist phenomena may sometimes or even always be related to the emotional state of a particular person round whom they centre has become almost a commonplace of the popular press. It accords very well with another such commonplace, namely that 'poltergeist agents' are very often adolescent children, adolescence being widely supposed by non-adolescents to be a period of particular susceptibility to emotional stress. Proponents of the idea have, however, not all been agreed upon which emotional states are especially liable to provoke poltergeist phenomena. Repressed sexual feelings, repressed aggression, 'family tensions', and hysteria, have all been proposed, and, as we have seen, there is quite a lot of evidence to implicate plain fright. So far as I can see, the only common denominator amongst these various conditions is that they are such as one might well wish to avoid. I have not heard it claimed that a surfeit of happiness may cause a poltergeist outbreak. Of course if levitation of the human body be reckoned a poltergeist phenomenon – as no doubt it must, since it has allegedly occurred in various poltergeist cases – it might be pointed out that according to the biographies of certain saints a state of rapt ecstasy and holy joy appears especially conducive to it. St Joseph of Copertino (1603–63), concerning whose feats in this direction there is a surprising amount of first-hand testimony, was wont to pass into a state of rapture at the sight of some holy object, and to fly with a shriek into the air. On one occasion he was thus enraptured at the sight of Pope Urban VIII and remained for some time floating before that astounded Pontiff. It is apparent, however, that quite apart from his propensity to fly or float over the heads of bystanders, Joseph was not a healthy person. He practised the most fearful austerities and was liable to all kinds of hysterical or perhaps psychotic hallucinations. So perhaps his case does not really provide a counter-example.

In this chapter I shall briefly describe and compare four cases of poltergeists in which the phenomena have clearly centred around particular persons. In each of these cases a plausible attempt might be made to link the poltergeist outbreak to the emotional state or psychological situation of the person concerned. The cases are those at Boston, Massachusetts (1867), Ylöjärvi, Finland (1885), Hopfgarten near Weimar (1921) and Sauchie, Scotland (1960–1).

The case at Boston, Massachusetts (1867), is commonly referred to as the 'Atlantic Monthly' case, because it was described in the *Atlantic Monthly*, vol. 22, 1868, by one of the principal witnesses, Mr H. A. Willis. Mr Willis represents himself as a sceptic concerning, and a firm opponent of, Spiritualism in all its aspects. None the less he was interested and impressed by the phenomena which he witnessed, and he made attempts to persuade 'two of the learned professors of one of our educational institutions' (presumably Harvard) to investigate them. Failing in this, he attempted various experiments himself, and kept a daily journal of events, in which such possibly relevant matters as the state of the weather were also recorded. His account (which includes extracts from the journal), though short, is clear and to the point, and inspires some confidence in the writer's honesty and abilities.

The poltergeist agent in this case was a servant girl named Mary Carrick, a recent arrival from Ireland who had come to live in Willis's household about the middle of May 1867. (I call it Willis's household because, though he adopts a curiously detached style of writing, and does not specifically tell us so, it is clear that it must either have been his household, or one in which he freely came and went.) It appears that in Ireland Mary had shown some tendency towards sleepwalking, but in Massachusetts 'she performed the duties required of her in a most acceptable manner. . . . She seldom left the house, and . . . she did not have the acquaintance of six persons outside the family'. The poltergeist began its activities on 3 July 1867. The bells hanging in the kitchen, which were, of course, connected by wires to bell-pulls in the various rooms and beside the various outer doors, began ringing violently and in unison at intervals of half-an-hour or so during daylight hours. The bells were detached from the wires, but the ringing went on as before. The bells hung near the ceiling of a room eleven feet high.

They never rang unless the girl was in that room or the adjoining one, but were often seen and heard to ring when different members of the family were present in the room with the girl. A careful examination by the writer and others showed that there was no mechanism or other appliance by which the ringing could be produced.

After a few days another kind of phenomenon made its appearance. Loud and startling raps were heard, which seemed to be on the walls, doors or windows of the room where the girl might be at work. These noises 'were quite as loud as would ordinarily follow a smart application of the knuckles to any article of wood'. They followed her from room to room, and 'could be heard in her chamber at night, when she was found to be in a profound sleep'. If during her sleep they became very loud, she would start and scream as if in the utmost terror. They were heard by all the members of the family, and by many outsiders 'whom curiosity prompted to come in'. Later on attempts were made to communicate with the rappings in a Spiritualistic fashion, but without the slightest success.

Meanwhile the unfortunate Mary was fearfully upset. It was with the greatest difficulty that she could be kept in a state of comparative calmness during the day, and in her sleep at night she raved continuously.

> She wept very much, protested that she had no action in the occurrences, and begged of the family not to send her away, for she had not a single friend in the country to whom she could go, and none of her countrymen would take her in, for the matter had already become notorious, and they shunned her as they would the Evil One himself.

It seems to me that we have here a very strong argument against the view that Mary was deliberately faking the phenomena. Had the family with whom she was living cast her out (the general fate at that time of servants who turned out to be poltergeist agents) her plight would have been dreadful indeed. Fortunately for her, the family was convinced by their own observations that she was not faking the phenomena, and it showed a somewhat unusual sense of responsibility for her welfare.

Towards the end of July occurrences of a still more extraordinary character began to take place. Chairs were upset, crockery was thrown down, tables were lifted and moved, and various kitchen utensils were hurled about the room. 'No particular record of these occurrences was made until August 1st; after which time, and until the phenomena had entirely ceased, accurate daily memoranda were noted.' I shall now give a few extracts from these memoranda, with Willis's additional comments.

'On the 5th of August, Mary was washing clothes, when a bench, having upon it two large tubs filled with water, was suddenly moved several inches. The lid of a copper wash-boiler was repeatedly thrown up, when the girl was not near enough to touch it. These occurrences were observed by different members of the family.'

'August 6th, Mary was ironing. The table at which she worked continually lifted itself, and troubled her so much that she took her work to another table, where the same operation was repeated, and her flat-iron, which she left for a moment, was thrown to the floor.' This annoyance was always repeated whenever she worked at ironing, and more or less at other times. It was seen by all the members of the family and other persons. The writer saw the table thus lifted when neither the girl nor any other person was near enough to touch it. It has happened when a child nine years of age was sitting upon it, and also when persons have tried to hold it down. This *lifting* propensity seemed to communicate itself to everything movable. The covers to the woodbox and wash-boiler were constantly slamming. A heavy soapstone slab, one and a half inches thick, weighing forty-eight pounds, which formed the top of a case of drawers, was often affected in a similar manner.

'On the 6th of August, as Mary was putting away the "tea things", and about to place a metallic tray filled with dishes upon this slab, it suddenly flew up, and struck the bottom of the tray with such force as to upset the dishes upon it.' This was seen by one of the family, and frequently occurred afterwards. The stone would also often be thrown up violently when Mary was at work at the sink near it. On the last occasion that this happened, August 25th, the writer was seated near to it, and watching for the movement, which had been repeated several times within an hour. Suddenly it raised itself, and fell with great force, breaking in two through the centre, Mary at the moment being in the act of wringing our her 'dish-cloth'. Soon after, one half of the same was thrown to the floor; and the fragments were then thrown out of the house on the ground, where they remained quiet.

Willis seems to have favoured the idea that the phenomena were electrical in origin. He tried the experiment of insulating the girl's bedstead by placing the bedposts on glass. From that time onwards the nocturnal rappings in her chamber ceased. He found likewise that when the kitchen table upon which Mary took her meals, and the chair at which she sat, were similarly put on glass, the rappings and table-movements which had previously disturbed her meal-times no longer took place. He noted also that phenomena were most prolific in rooms with bare floors or oil carpets and matting; woollen carpets seemed to have an inhibiting effect. However, despite careful recording of daily weather conditions, no clear correlation emerged between the occurrence of the phenomena and dry, clear skies.

The phenomena continued with only one day's respite from 3 August to 27 August 1867. At this point Mary was sent away for two days. During her absence neither she nor the family witnessed anything untoward. However within two hours of her return the happenings recommenced. Two weeks later, on 12 September, 'her nervous system succumbed, and she was suddenly seized with a violent attack of hysteria. During the paroxysm, which continued two or three hours, she was in an unconscious state, and could be restrained upon her bed only by the combined strength of her attendants'. For the next few days, similar paroxysms (which may be compared with the symptoms of 'possessed' or 'obsessed' persons, cf. chapters 7 and 9), and which were accompanied by 'a very distressing sensation referred to the base of the brain', alternated with periods of great excitement. On 18 September she was removed to an asylum. She returned after three weeks in a much happier frame of mind, but at the end of November she began once again to sleepwalk. After five nights of this 'nature gave out, and she again passed into the condition of hysteria. She was again conveyed to the asylum, where she now remains, though she seems to have entirely recovered, and is there employed as a housemaid'. It is to be noted that the poltergeist phenomena ceased for ever at the time of Mary's first 'hysterical paroxysm'.

Our next case occurred in 1885, and is thus fairly close in time to the previous one. It could, however, hardly be more different in other respects. It took place some 3000 miles away, in the village of Ylöjärvi, Finland, some 15 kilometres from Tampere (then Tammerfors). The setting was not a substantial middle-class dwelling, but the poor three-roomed cottage of Efraim Martin, a seventy-one-year-old former elementary school teacher, and his wife Eva, aged 77. We hear not talk of electricity and attacks on Spiritualism, but accusations of magic and of traffic with infernal powers. The Martins kept as servant a thirteen-year-old girl named Emma Lindroos, and it was round her that poltergeist phenomena centred from 12–27 January 1885. At the end of that period she was taken away ill (she had tuberculosis), and died a few months afterwards. With her departure the phenomena ceased completely. However, in March 1885 an official prosecution was launched against the Martins and Emma Lindroos on the grounds that they had perpetrated the phenomena with the help of the powers of darkness in order to sell brandy to curious visitors. On 24 March 1885 the statements of fifteen eyewitnesses to the phenomena were taken down, together with statements by the Martins themselves (Emma Lindroos being too ill to attend). Many years later, in 1921, these statements were unearthed by Yrvö Kulovesi, a medical practitioner of Tammerfors who was interested in parapsychology. He visited Efraim Martin's son, who had not been present at the time, and obtained some useful background information; he also interviewed a surviving witness. Then he translated the court records into German and sent them with a commentary to Freiherr Albert von Schrenck-Notzing, a noted German parapsychologist of the time. Schrenck-Notzing edited Kulovesi's communication and published it as 'Der Spuk in Ylöjärvi (Finnland)' in *Psychische Studien*, vol. 49, 1922; this piece appeared again in Schrenck-Notzing's *Gesammelte Aufsätze zur Parapsychologie* (Stuttgart, 1929).

Phenomena began on the night of 12 January 1885. The front door, though fast closed, was three times beaten open. Plaster burst from the walls in large quantities. The contents of locked drawers were scattered all over the place. Objects were thrown and broken. A hymnbook flew from the table against the door. Keys disappeared. A sheep was found in the cowstall with all its four legs tied together. The harness of a cow was turned inside out. These and other manifestations 'occurred daily, without anyone being able to see how they were produced'. The 'other manifestations' included such oddities as objects being moved in curved paths as though carried, and a voice of unknown origins saying 'the Devil has poured the beer out of the barrel', a statement which, upon investigation, proved to correspond with fact. 'Many of the phenomena,' we are told, 'happened by lamp- and candle-light; but they could not uncommonly be observed in clear daylight.'

Small wonder, then, that numerous sightseers were drawn to the place. It is the statements which some of these sightseers later gave to the court that I shall now proceed to quote. Out of the fifteen statements I shall give, in whole or part, numbers 1, 7, 10, 11 and 12.

1. *Statement of the Smith, Gerhard Grönfors.* On the evening of January 17th, 1885, the witness, together with Efraim Eerole and the tailor Gustaf Hellèn, visited the Martin's house, and observed how an awl was suddenly thrown out of a corner onto the floor, whilst Eva Martin lay in bed. The bed stood in the direction from which the awl was thrown. Whether Eva Martin or another person had thrown it, he could not tell. At that time were present in the room only the two visitors, the old couple and the servant girl, Emma Lindroos. They were all sitting at the table when the awl was thrown out of the corner. This happened about ten in the evening. Then a pair of shoes moved on the floor, each shoe after the other. An old psalter was thrown against the door, so that it resounded through the whole room. The witness could not see that anyone present had produced these phenomena, and believed that . . . they were brought about through some unknown, unexplained and invisible force.

On Sunday, January 18th, the witness again visited the Martins, and when neither one of the old couple nor Emma Lindroos were in the room, thin pine boards, which stood in the corner, began to hop and to dance round each other. Two bread sticks in the corner began to dance up and down on the floor and to strike against each other. Martin's wife came directly in, took one of the bread sticks in her hands, and said 'Be still indeed!' After she had said this, she put it in the corner and turned aside. Nevertheless the bread stick hopped three more times and was then thrown on to the floor. All this happened by clear morning daylight, and the witness searched the corner thoroughly and found nothing suspicious . . . . He had not seen the Martins sell brandy.

Asked particularly, the witness stated that the Martin's house is built on the hill, and is provided with such a low foundation wall, that no cellar has been installed, where anyone could have hidden himself and executed the things.

After this testimony, the Martins stated that the awl flew out of the drawer of the table, where it was ordinarily stored.

[Grönfor's testimony about the pine boards and the bread sticks was confirmed by Gustaf Hellèn.]

7. *Statement of the Sexton Lindell.* The witness visited the Martins for the first time on January 27th with his wife. After they had talked for a little, a stool was thrown upside down before the witnesses. Those present were Efraim Martin, and Emma Lindroos who lay on a bed made up on the floor. Neither could have thrown the stool, for neither had a string. The witness was convinced that this happened in a supernatural manner . . . . Then both he and Martin went into the building at the end of the yard, and as they set out, a basket made of pine wood was suddenly thrown after him, to be sure quite gently as if it were carried by an invisible force, and it touched the witness's side . . . . Even as he returned to the living room, he could hear in the yard a noise coming from the room. However in the room were only Eva Martin and Emma Lindroos, of whom the former lay awake in her bed, and the latter, in her bed on the floor, was probably already asleep. He saw the big dining table, with two plates on, dash the plates against each other. He could, however, see nothing suspicious. When the witness's wife and Efraim Martin likewise came in, the plates began to move faster, and with a louder noise, that resounded through the whole room. When the witness pressed the one plate against the table with his knee, the other clattered still harder. Then they decided to tie the two plates down with a piece of string, and for security they furnished the string with wedges. The plates now remained immoveable, but a groaning noise was heard between them. The whole table then sprang three inches into the air. When they placed it in the middle of the floor, the two plates stayed motionless, although the string had become unwound. Neither flap nor loose cross-piece communicated with the floor, nor was there any hidden cord with which the movement might have been executed. The witness swore that the phenomenon happened through the influence of an unseen force. When they had put the table back in its place, Emma Lindroos, who had lain the whole time in her bed, stood up and called: 'Now he has tied up me too', and began to disentangle herself from the string which was would round her body. She had remained motionless the whole time, seemed to be asleep, and appeared ill. The witness also knew nothing of the sale of brandy . . . .

[Compare the basket carried gently to touch sexton Lindell's

side, with the staff which, in the Tidworth case, struck Mr
Cragg, the minister, as softly as if it had been a lock of wool.]

10. *Statement of Amanda Lindell.* The witness visited the Martins'
house together with her husband, sexton Lindell, and saw a
stool thrown towards her husband. Furthermore, everything
happened which her husband had already related. She added
that, whilst her husband and Efraim Martin were in the other
room, three old shoes were thrown from a corner of the room
into the middle of the floor. Emma Lindroos, who was in the
room, had not thrown them. Plaster fell from the wall, and the
table began to dash the plates together in such a way that it
resounded through the room. While that continued, the witness
went out to fetch her husband and Efraim Martin. When they
came into the room, everything happened as her husband had
already told. The witness knew nothing of the sale of brandy.

11. *Statement of Karl Lindholm* [a cobbler]. On January 22nd the
witness visited the Martins' house, and at that time saw a
candle-holder flung twice against the door, and a third time
against the outer end of the room. He could not establish
whence it came, but he believed that no human being could
have thrown it because it moved in the air as if under the
influence of an invisible force, and rotated itself. It moved
soundlessly, whirling around in circles, always remaining
upright. Then came a rattling under the table. The witness
swore that no human being could have thrown the candle-
holder, or kept it upright in the air with a string . . . .

[Compare this moving of the candle-holder in circles with
Heinisch's account of his observations in 1718, which I quoted
at the beginning of the last chapter.]

12. *Statement of Helene Punala.* The witness visited the Martins'
house at the same time as Karl Lindholm, and confirms the
events equally with the latter. She sat beside the table from
which the candle-holder was thrown, and therefore saw quite
clearly that no human hand could have thrown it.

Efraim Martin, who had, according to his son's later testimony, always been sceptical about such matters, stated firmly
that there had been no profitable sales of brandy; rather he had
lost money through the influx of visitors to his house. He
believed the phenomena to be due to an unknown natural force.
It was true, he added, that Emma Lindroos had occasionally
thrown things out of the corner, and urged on the devil to
renewed activity; but that had nothing to do with the issue, for

many others had done the same. The accused persons were acquitted.

I have very much the impression that this trial was to some extent at least a put-up job, instigated so that the Martins, who seem to have been much respected locally, could clear themselves from malicious gossip.

In the next case that I shall briefly describe, that at Hopfgarten, near Weimar, in 1921, our principal source material again comes from court records. Once again we owe publication of the records to Schrenck-Notzing. They are to be found in *Psychische Studien*, vol. 48, 1921; in the report of the Copenhagen International Congress for Psychical Research (1921); and in Schrenck-Notzing's *Gesammelte Aufsätze zur Parapsychologie* (Stuttgart, 1929). A useful summary of them is in the *Journal of the SPR*, vol. 20, 1922. The background to these records is as follows. At the beginning of 1921 there lived in the village of Hopfgarten a clock-maker named Ernst Sauerbrey, together with his second wife, Minna, and her daughter, Frieda Pappe. Minna Sauerbrey was dying of cancer, and was in a condition of utter weakness and total prostration. She lay all the time on a sofa in the kitchen, so enfeebled that she could hardly raise a hand.

Ernst Sauerbrey had by his first wife a son named Otto, who since the summer of 1919 had been giving public exhibitions of hypnosis. Otto came to visit his father on 10 February 1921, and stayed until 12 February. During this time he hypnotized his stepmother, apparently in an endeavour to alleviate her suffering in some respect. However, the lady reacted adversely to his attempts, and the very next day complained of headache and weariness. She seems to have passed much of the time between then and 28 February, when she was hypnotized by a nerve-specialist and given counter-suggestions, in a sort of rambling dream or twilight state in which she exhibited a pathological fear of her stepson and saw his eyes before her during the night.

There were, however, other symptoms more curious than these. On the evening of 14 February, Ernst Sauerbrey and his stepdaughter were puzzled by loud raps which resounded through the kitchen, and continued intermittently throughout the night. They were heard again in each succeeding night until 28 February. The noises resembled blows with the fist or knuckles upon furniture, walls and doors. They moved around the room, never remaining in the same place long. Sometimes the rapping was heard simultaneously in two separate places. Occasionally, too, small objects in the room would be displaced, usually in a direction away from Frau Sauerbrey. These objects are stated to have been beyond her reach, she being in any case too weak to leave the sofa on which she lay. The phenomena never took place by daylight. They were, however, not inhibited by the light of an electric table-lamp, and were thus observed under relatively good conditions.

On 27 February the police were called in. They too witnessed certain phenomena, and called in the nerve-specialist, mentioned above, who succeeded in putting a stop to them. As a result of police investigations, a case was brought against Otto Sauerbrey in the Schöffengericht (roughly speaking, the magistrates' court) at Vieselbach near Weimar in April 1921. It was alleged that his attempts at hypnosis had shortened his stepmother's life (she had died on 27 March). He was acquitted after medical evidence had been heard.

The records of the hearing were procured by Schrenck-Notzing, and he publishes them together with some answers to queries sent him by the presiding magistrate. I will now, following my policy of quoting first-hand testimony whenever possible, give such extracts as are especially relevant to the alleged poltergeist phenomena.

> Witness Sauerbrey: Ernst Sauerbrey, 53 years old, clockmaker in Hopfgarten, father of the accused . . . .
> My wife lay in the kitchen. She had remained in her bed since October 1919, and had left it only once, about New Year 1920, for half an hour. Because of her bodily weakness she had to lie down again.
> On the second day after my son's departure, I heard at night the sound of rapping in the table and on the door. I slept in a room near the kitchen. My wife drew my attention to the rapping, and said I should at once see who was knocking. I went into the kitchen, and when I perceived that the knocking came thence, I searched everywhere, but found nothing. As soon as the lamp was lit, the rapping ceased. Thereupon I went back to bed. Soon afterwards the rappings were again heard. They became very loud. These rapping sounds were heard at an interval of about five minutes. My wife lay on a sofa in the kitchen and kept quite still. Sometimes she even slept. Since the rapping did not cease all night, I woke my step-daughter, Frieda

Pappe, who stayed awake for the rest of the night. These ghostly phenomena began again on the second night. The rapping was heard from six in the evening until towards seven in the morning. On one of the next nights several objects moved. A coffee-cup, which stood on a chair in the kitchen, fell down from the chair, which was itself moving, and broke in pieces. Likewise the table moved, and also a bucket and a wash-basin. It is inconceivable that my wife did these things herself.

Since we could no longer get any rest at night, my step-daughter went to Weimar and told the police about it. The next night eight policemen came from Weimar and surrounded the house. Several of them came into the house, and there witnessed the psychic phenomena, which were in evidence that night also. In the presence of police-commissioner Pfeil from Weimar, several objects were placed in the middle of the room about two metres from where my wife lay. It could be seen that these too moved from the place where they stood without anyone touching them. The rapping sounds were likewise heard . . . .

Witness Pappe: Frieda Pappe, 22 years old, Protestant, from Eisenach, step-sister of the accused . . . .

On the second day after the last departure of the accused, about February 13th, we heard a sound of rapping on the kitchen door. On the second night we also heard it on the table and the chair in the kitchen, where my mother was lying. My mother did not produce these noises. As soon as the light was put on the knocking was not so powerful. My mother did not move her hands at all.

In reply to a question: It is impossible that my mother moved the objects or caused the rappings herself, for in the presence of the police we undertook tests, and moved the objects so far from my mother's sofa that she could not reach them; none the less they moved from their places. I observed that the objects, chair, pail, wash-basin, and so on, moved away from my mother. When there was rapping and my mother answered, the noise ceased. The rapping could be heard the whole night. A chair and a bucket, which stood next to each other, knocked loudly together.

Witness Degenkolbe: Walter Degenkolbe, tailor, dwelling in Eisenach, no relation of the accused . . . .

During the time in question I went to Hopfgarten nearly every Sunday . . . . On the second night I was there, I heard a sound of rapping on the furniture and the walls. It is inconceivable that Frau Sauerbrey made these sounds. She lay still, and I must have seen if she had moved. Also the rapping sounds were heard on a door which Frau Sauerbrey could not reach. I also saw a chair, a table, etc., move from their places, and a cup fall off the chair and break.

In reply to a question: .... The phenomena, which began about six in the evening, lasted until about seven in the morning. In the daytime it was quiet. Only once did I hear rappings during the day, about nine in the morning. Usually the phenomena in question began towards nine in the evening.

Unfortunately the police officers who witnessed the phenomena did not give evidence in court; but the presiding magistrate forwarded the following to Schrenck-Notzing:

Detailed statement of Police Commissioner Pfeil: A police-officer set a bucket of water two metres away from Frau Sauerbrey. At the very moment that he turned away, the bucket moved. The same thing happened with a wash-basin. A dog, which at other times was unusually bold, was unusually oppressed by the onset of the phenomena. The clock would not go, although according to Sauerbrey's statement, he being a clock-maker, there was nothing wrong with it. Sometimes a sound was heard as though someone were stroking the furniture with the flat of his hand.

These observations were made by 10 or 12 police officers whom Pfeil had sent out. They saw everything either through the open kitchen door, or through the key-hole.

Schrenck-Notzing sees in Frau Sauerbrey's hypnoidal state certain analogies with the trance states of certain physical mediums.

The last case of which I shall give some account in this chapter is that of the well-known Sauchie poltergeist, which took place at the end of November 1960, in the town of Sauchie, Clackmannanshire, Scotland. In choosing this case I am departing slightly from my policy of selecting cases in which contemporary diaries or court records are available. However, Dr A. R. G. Owen, then of Trinity College, Cambridge, who visited Sauchie in the middle of January 1961, obtained detailed statements from four of the principal witnesses – the Rev. T. W. Lund, Dr W. H. Nisbet, Dr William Logan, and Miss Margaret Stewart – and the first two of these based their accounts on contemporary diary notes. Dr Owen prints this material in his *Can we explain the Poltergeist?* (New York, 1964). In his *Beyond*

Belief (London, 1974) Mr Brian Branston supplies some pieces of additional information, and prints the transcript of an account of the case which Dr William Logan gave for a BBC film on spooks.

The phenomena in the Sauchie case centred around an eleven-year-old schoolgirl, Virginia Campbell. Virginia had been brought up by her parents on a small farm in County Donegal, Eire. There she had had a rather lonely life, her chief companions being her pet dog, Toby, and a little girl named Anna. In 1960 her father decided to dispose of his interest in the farm and, in the autumn, whilst he was engaged in so doing, Virginia and her mother went to Scotland, her mother to take a job in Dollar, near Sauchie, and Virginia to live in the family of her elder brother Thomas, a miner, in Sauchie. The Thomas Campbells had two children, and Virginia shared a room with her niece Margaret, aged nine, a state of affairs which she does not altogether seem to have liked. In mid-October 1960, Virginia was sent to Sauchie Primary School. According to her teacher, Miss Margaret Stewart, Virginia, though shy, was outwardly quite placid and normal. She was big for her age, fond of games, and above average in intelligence. She was, Miss Stewart said, of a very honest disposition.

The first curious phenomenon occurred on the evening of Tuesday 22 November 1960, when a sound like a ball being bounced was heard, without obvious cause, in Virginia's bedroom, on the stairs and in the living room. The following day, Wednesday 23rd, at tea-time, Virginia was sitting in the living room near a heavy sideboard. Mr and Mrs Campbell both saw this move *bodily* outwards a distance of about five inches and return to its original position. Virginia did not touch it.

That evening, while Virginia was in bed, though not asleep, loud knocks were heard in her bedroom. A neighbour summoned the Rev. T. W. Lund, the Church of Scotland minister of Sauchie, who prudently consulted the *Encyclopaedia Britannica* article on poltergeists before setting forth. He investigated the knockings, and concluded that they came from the bedhead. He moved Virginia down the bed, so that no part of her body was touching the bedhead, and also verified that her feet were tucked in under the bedclothes. The knockings, however, continued.

Mr Lund then saw a large, and full, linen chest, 27" × 17" × 14", which was standing a foot and a half from the bed, rock sideways, raise itself, and travel jerkily along parallel to the bed for a distance of about eighteen inches and back again. Mr Lund and the neighbour mentioned before lifted the linen chest, which weighed about fifty pounds, out on to the landing. Eventually it was proposed that Virginia's niece Margaret should rejoin her in the double bed; at this suggestion there was a burst of 'violent and peremptory knocking'.

On Thursday 25 November, Mr Lund came again in the evening. He heard more raps, and witnessed further rockings of the linen chest. He was told by members of the family that some curious movements of Virginia's pillow had been observed. He saw one such movement himself – Virginia's pillow was rotated beneath her head to the extent of about 60 degrees. Dr W. H. Nisbet, a physician, of Tillicoultry, who had been called in by Mr Lund, also came to the house, along with another minister and another medical man. Dr Nisbet heard the knockings and a mysterious sawing noise. He saw a curious rippling movement pass across the surface of the pillow on which Virginia's head lay, but could find no explanation.

Virginia had stayed away from school on 23 and 24 November, but returned again on the afternoon of Friday 25 November. During a period of silent reading that afternoon, Miss Stewart, Virginia's teacher, saw her trying to hold down her desk lid, which several times raised itself to an angle of 45 or 50 degrees. Miss Stewart could see Virginia's hands flat on the lid of the desk, and her legs underneath the desk.

Shortly afterwards, Miss Stewart, happening to look up, saw an empty desk behind Virginia, slowly rise bodily upwards about an inch, and settle down again gently a little way from its original position. Miss Stewart went to it immediately, and made sure that no strings, etc., had been attached to it.

That evening, before Virginia went to sleep, Dr Nisbet sat in her bedroom. He heard knocks even when Virginia was lying motionless on the bed without bedclothes over her. On a number of occasions he saw the linen chest move about a foot. He carried it to the other side of the bed, and there its lid opened and shut several times in succession. He saw horizontal rotations (up to 90 degrees) of the pillow under Virginia's head, and also saw inexplicable ripplings pass across the bedclothes.

On Saturday 26 November, Dr William Logan, Dr Nisbet's partner, sat up in the bedroom. He witnessed a puckering of the bed-cover, and pillow rotations similar to those reported by Dr Nisbet. On Sunday 27 November, Dr Logan visited Virginia again. He brought his dog, with whom Virginia was much taken, saying that he reminded her of her own dog in Ireland. Later she passed into a 'trance' in which she seemed not fully aware of what was going on, and called out for her dog, Toby. About 11.30 p.m. Mr Lund arrived. Virginia cried out loudly and struck about with her fists; but when Dr Nisbet and Mr Lund left the room she became quiet and passed into a normal sleep.

On Monday 28 November, Virginia went to school in the morning. She had occasion to come to Miss Stewart's table, and stood to Miss Stewart's left, somewhat away from her, with her hands clasped behind her back. A blackboard pointer lying on the table began to vibrate, and travelled across the table until it fell off. While the pointer was moving, Miss Stewart put her hand on the table, and found that it too was vibrating. The right-hand end of the table began to move away from her, so that the whole table swung round anticlockwise. Virginia started to cry, and said that it was not her. To conceal the affair from the class, Miss Stewart hastily told her to help straighten the table.

That afternoon Virginia was taken to stay with a relative at Dollar, a few miles away. Dr Nisbet visited her and again heard knockings, this time very loud ones.

On Tuesday 29 November, Dr and Mrs Logan (also a qualified physician) went to Dollar. They heard several bursts of rappings, which originated from the neighbourhood of Virginia. Mrs Logan, who had previously been sceptical, satisfied herself that Virginia was not responsible.

Later in the evening Virginia went into another 'trance'. She talked loudly and unnaturally, called for Toby and Anna, and tossed around in her bed. She answered questions in an unusually free and uninhibited way. She woke up after about ten minutes.

On Wednesday 30 November, Virginia returned to Sauchie. There were no phenomena.

On Thursday 1 December, Drs Nisbet and Logan went round in the evening, armed with a tape recorder and a cine-camera. Virginia went up to bed at 9.00 p.m. Between 9.00 p.m. and 10.30 p.m. there were continuous rappings, occasional loud sawing noises, and some ripplings of the bedclothes. Tape recordings of the noises were obtained, but attempts to catch the ripplings of the bedclothes on cine-film were unsuccessful. Between 10.00 p.m. and 11.00 p.m. Virginia talked a good deal in a rather uninhibited and hysterical way. At 11.00 p.m. Mr Lund and two ministers arrived to conduct a service of intercession. During the service there were several knocks.

After 1 December the phenomena considerably diminished. Minor occurrences persisted until about March, but are not so well authenticated as the early ones. The most interesting were perhaps occasional pinches which both Virginia and her niece Margaret claimed to have felt – foreshadowing perhaps the 'assault' cases which I shall discuss in chapter 7. The best attested later occurrence happened on Monday 23 January, 1961. Virginia placed a bowl of bulbs on Miss Stewart's table in the classroom. It moved across the table-top.

A curious feature of the case was that the rappings and other physical phenomena did not occur during Virginia's 'trances'. It seemed as though the rappings and the trances might be alternative outlets for the suppressed emotions of a girl transplanted from her accustomed environment, and subjected to the stresses of an early adolescence. However, Virginia seems quickly to have settled into a more cheerful frame of mind. Perhaps the fuss and attention which the case brought her did her good; and I understand that she was before long reunited with her favourite dog.

A case similar in many respects to this one came to my own notice in 1967 (see chapter 14).

I have now given some account of four poltergeist cases in which the phenomena clearly centred around a particular person. In all four cases the person concerned was female, in three cases a young one. In all four cases, it might plausibly be claimed that the presumed poltergeist 'agent' had psychological problems. Mary Carrick was a somnambulist, and developed the once classical bodily symptoms of 'hysteria'; Emma Lindroos had contracted a fatal illness, and very possibly knew that she was destined for an early grave; Frau Sauerbrey was in an hypnoidal condition in which she suffered obsessive fears of the hypnotist; Virginia Campbell was, temporarily at least, in a situation that must have been somewhat trying for her. But that the psychological problems of these four persons had any fundamental similarity remains undemonstrated. *Prima facie* it seems most unlikely. Indeed, it would seem more reasonable to propose that a few persons, peculiarly constituted in some way that we do not understand, have available to them this means of 'letting off steam' when under *any kind* of stress.

Nor is it possible to make any generalizations about the state of mind of the various agents at the time of occurrence of the phenomena, beyond, that is, the simple remark that none is reported to have claimed any conscious control of the events which surrounded her. In the cases of Mary Carrick and Virginia Campbell, the phenomena ceased when the agent passed into a peculiar psychological state, loosely referred to as 'trance'. On the other hand it was not until Frau Sauerbrey entered a 'trance' state that the phenomena which centred on her began.

The phenomena observed in all four cases were, however, very similar. The staple ones were raps, and the movement of small objects – sometimes also of objects that were not so small. It is debatable whether in any of the four cases the phenomena could be described as intelligent. Perhaps the way in which objects were manipulated in the Ylöjärvi case could be said to have required 'intelligence'. There was, however, little sign of an 'intelligence' behind the phenomena in the other three cases, whether the intelligence of the presumed poltergeist agent, or of some other sort of entity altogether. In none of the cases was there any 'communication' with the phenomena such as had been reported in some other cases, though in the Ylöjärvi case an intelligible voice of no obvious origin once spoke a meaningful sentence.

From the point of view of providing evidence for paranormal physical happenings, these cases are in some respects strong ones. They all have this in common. There was in each instance no serious question as to which person must have been faking the phenomena, if faking indeed there were. Thus there was only one person who needed to be strictly watched. And strictly watched that person was, if we are to take the contemporary records at face value, by more than one person, and over a period of days or weeks. In each case phenomena took place, at least some of the time, by good light; and in each case, occasionally, while the prime suspect was ostensibly asleep, or else lying perfectly still. It seems perfectly incredible that attempts at fraud would not under these conditions have been quickly discovered.

5 Destructive poltergeists

I suspect that a considerable percentage of people, if asked what poltergeists do, would reply 'they break things'. It is breakage that dominates the popular picture of a poltergeist – smashing of windows, flinging of crockery and ornaments, fusillades of destructive stones. And there is no doubt that breakage in one form or another does figure in many poltergeist cases. A few instances have already been given. In some cases, the damage seems to be merely incidental – if solid objects are thrown about, damage must occasionally result. In other cases, however, damage seems to be deliberately aimed at, and the poltergeist explodes into a frenzy of breakage and destruction. Naturally it is this sort of case which sticks in the public mind and somewhat slants its idea of what poltergeists do.

The archetypal case of a destructive poltergeist is the famous 'Stockwell Ghost' of 1772. This is described in an anonymous pamphlet of that year entitled *An Authentic, Candid, and Circumstantial Narrative, of the Astonishing Transactions at Stockwell, in the County of Surry* .... The narrative is an extremely lucid one, and to it is appended a statement that it is 'absolutely and strictly true', dated 11 January 1772 (four days after the phenomena had ended) and signed by six of the principal witnesses. This rare pamphlet has been frequently reprinted or paraphrased, for instance by Catherine Crowe in *The Night Side of Nature* (London, 1849), by William Hone in *The Every Day Book* (London, 1826) and by Harry Price in *Poltergeist over England* (London, 1945). Some further details of the case, drawn from contemporary newspapers, will be found in J. P. Malcolm's *Manners and Customs of London during the Eighteenth Century* (London, 1810), vol. I.

The 'astonishing transactions' of the title began on Monday 6 January 1772 in the house of Mrs Golding, an elderly lady 'of an independent fortune'. Mrs Golding, we may note at this point, had one week and three days before taken as her maid Ann Robinson, a young woman of about twenty, daughter of the clerk of Lewisham Parish. About ten o'clock in the morning, when Mrs Golding was in her parlour,

> she heard the china and glasses in the back kitchen tumble down and break; her maid came to her and told her the stone plates were falling from the shelf; Mrs Golding went into the kitchen and saw them broke. Presently after, a row of plates from the next shelf fell down likewise, while she was there, and nobody near them; this astonished her much, and while she was thinking about it, other things in different places began to tumble about, some of them breaking, attended with violent noises all over the house; a clock tumbled down and the case broke; a lanthorn that hung on the staircase was thrown down and the glass broke to pieces; an earthen pan of salted beef broke to pieces and the beef fell about; all this increased her surprise, and brought several persons about her.

Understandably alarmed by these events Mrs Golding ran to the house of her neighbour, Mr Gresham, and fainted. While attempts were being made to revive her, many of the more fragile objects were removed from her house and brought into that of Mr Gresham. This, unfortunately, did not save them, for before long further wholesale destruction began.

Mrs Golding and Ann Robinson then went on to the house of Mrs Golding's niece, Mrs Mary Pain, whose husband, John, was a farmer 'at Rush Common, near Brixton-Causeway'. For a few hours all was quiet, but about eight o'clock in the evening, a fresh scene began:

> the first thing that happened, was, a whole row of pewter dishes, except one, fell off from a shelf to the middle of the floor, rolled about a little while, and then settled, and what is almost beyond belief, as soon as they were quiet, turned upside down; they were then put on the dresser, and went through the same a second time: next fell a whole row of pewter plates from off the second shelf over the dresser to the ground, and being taken up and put on the dresser one in another, they were thrown down again.
>
> The next thing was two eggs that were upon one of the pewter shelves, one of them flew off, crossed the kitchen, struck a cat on the head, and then broke to pieces.
>
> Next, Mary Martin, Mrs. Pain's servant, went to stir the kitchen fire, she got to the right hand side of it, being a large chimney as is usual in farm houses, a pestle and mortar that stood nearer the left hand end of the chimney shelf, jumped about six feet on the floor. Then went candlesticks and other

brasses: scarce any thing remaining in its place. After this the glasses and china were put down on the floor for fear of undergoing the same fate, they presently began to dance and tumble about, and then broke to pieces. A tea pot that was among them, flew to Mrs. Golding's maid's foot and struck it.

A glass tumbler that was put on the floor jumped about two feet and then broke. Another that stood by it jumped about at the same time, but did not break till some hours after, when it jumped again and then broke. A china bowl that stood in the parlour jumped from the floor to behind a table that stood there. This was most astonishing, as the distance from where it stood was between seven and eight feet but was not broke. It was put back by Richard Fowler, to its place, where it remained some time and flew to pieces.

One could extend this catalogue considerably, but it would grow repetitious. Two curious, but by no means unparalleled, kinds of phenomenon that were observed in this case were the spontaneous breakage of crockery and china, i.e. its fracturing *without* being thrown or struck by a missile, and the 'boiling over' of liquids from their containers – in one instance the liquid concerned was blood, recently drawn by a surgeon from Mrs Golding to relieve her faintness!

Next morning the miserable Mrs Golding, together with her maid, removed to the house of one of Mrs Pain's neighbours, but phenomena at once broke out there. So she returned home, and shortly afterwards, having noticed that Ann Robinson seemed surprisingly used to such occurrences, discharged her. The phenomena ceased at once.

Many years later William Hone published in his *The Every Day Book* (London, 1826), an account of some particulars relating to the case given to him in 1817 by 'the late Mr. J.B.——' (said by Sir Walter Scott, a friend of Hone's, to have been a Mr Brayley). Brayley stated that some years after 1772 he became acquainted with Ann Robinson, who told him that she had produced the phenomena by sleight of hand, by affixing wires, horsehairs, etc., to the objects that moved, and by the use of 'some simple chemical secrets'. I quite agree with Harry Price, who observes that this story is sheer invention – whether it was Mr Brayley who invented it, or his lady informant, we shall never know. As Price, an authority on conjuring, remarks: 'The greatest conjurer living could not produce the Stockwell effects by means of wires, etc., surrounded by people on the look-out for tricks, and in a well-lighted room, without instant detection'.

One must, I think, make it a rule in this field not to accept at face value unsubstantiated claims to have discovered trickery. Otherwise any case whatsoever would be vulnerable to the allegations of any joker or crank.

Poltergeist destructiveness does not always take the form of breakage of windows or crockery. Also reported from time to time in association with poltergeist phenomena are spontaneous outbreaks of fire. These may also occur in the absence of poltergeist phenomena of other kinds. This is also true of another variety of destructive poltergeist phenomenon, the inundation of an unfortunate household with large quantities of water of unknown origins. In fact such inundations so frequently occur unaccompanied by other kinds of poltergeist phenomena, that 'water poltergeists' might arguably be set aside as not poltergeists at all.

I shall not in this survey devote chapters to incendiary and to water poltergeists. I have omitted such chapters chiefly because I cannot find in sufficient quantity detailed contemporary records of the kind I am particularly looking for. However, occasional incendiary phenomena took place in some of the cases which I shall describe; and two 'water poltergeists' investigated by my co-author will figure in the second part of this book. In the remainder of this chapter, I shall give accounts of two recent examples of destructive poltergeists. The first case, that of the Miami poltergeist of 1966-7, is so like the Stockwell case (though separated from it by 200 years and 3000 miles) that I shall not even bother to point out the similarities. The second, the Rosenheim case of 1967-8, is superficially very unlike it; but I shall argue that the unlikeness is only superficial. Both these cases are very well-known, and describing them goes against the policy of this book, which is to include as few well-known cases as possible; but both are evidentially so strong and theoretically so interesting that some mention of them is inevitable.

The setting of the main events in the Miami case was the largish rectangular warehouse room of a novelty and souvenir firm, Tropication Arts. Much of this room was used as storage space. It had shelves on some of the walls, and longwise down the middle ran three tiers of shelving, separated by aisles. On the shelves were stored, individually or in boxes, glasses, mugs, jars, bottles, and all kinds of pre-eminently breakable objects. It is impossible to imagine a more congenial stamping ground for a destructive poltergeist.

The end portions of the warehouse, clear of the tiers, constituted working space for two shipping clerks, one of whom, Julio Vasquez, a nineteen-year-old Cuban, was the poltergeist agent of our story, and also for a girl whose function it was to paint certain of the souvenirs.

The case began about the middle of December 1966, but did not come to the notice of parapsychologists until 12 January 1967, when it was learned of by Susy Smith, a writer of popular but excellent books on parapsychology, who was then in Miami. Her account can be found in her *Prominent American Ghosts* (Cleveland, 1967). Through Miss Smith two well-known American parapsychologists, Mr W. G. Roll, Director of the Psychical Research Foundation in Durham, North Carolina, and Professor J. G. Pratt, of the University of Virginia, were brought into the case. Roll visited Miami from 19 January to 21 January and again from 25 January to 1 February, whilst Pratt was there from 27 January to 30 January. These three persons made strenuous efforts both to collect accounts from previous witnesses, and to observe the phenomena for themselves. The results are to be found in Roll and Pratt's article 'The Miami Disturbances' in the *Journal of the American SPR*, vol. 65, 1971, and in Roll's book *The Poltergeist* (New York, 1972).

Roll and Pratt observed or received accounts of 224 separate incidents. The incidents consisted in the projection, falling, displacement, etc., of the small objects which were stored on the shelving in the warehouse room. The greatest displacement involved was one of twenty-two feet. Many of the objects were fragile, and breakages were frequent.

One hundred and two of the incidents on Roll and Pratt's list happened before either of them reached the scene. There must, however, have been many more incidents than these during the period concerned. Indeed at times objects were falling from the shelves as fast as they could be picked up or swept up. It pretty soon became evident that the phenomena centred around Julio – only one reliably reported incident took place when he was not present. It does not appear, however, that the phenomena followed him home. The owners of the firm seem to have been remarkably tolerant of the destruction that followed in Julio's wake.

On 14 January the police were called in, not, apparently, because of any suspicions of Julio, but rather because of gossip, the amount of damage, and the distress occasioned to other employees. Police witnesses later told the investigators that at one point four police officers were present, and had everyone in the warehouse room in sight. Phenomena still took place.

On thirteen occasions witnesses actually saw the start of object movements. Thus on 19 January, Mr Howard Brooks, a professional conjurer, who was a friend of the co-owner, Mr Alvin Laubheim, was in the area in front of the tiers talking to a television cameraman when Julio came past, carrying a stack of boxes. There was a crash from the tiers (event 101). Brooks grabbed Julio, so that the cameraman could collect the object. It turned out to be a beer mug which Brooks himself had put there as a decoy. Also in the warehouse room was Mr Laubheim's sister, and she was looking directly at the mug when it moved. She stated that it 'sort of scooted off' the shelf, moving straight out into the air, then dropping straight down. I have already pointed out several times how often witnesses have stated that poltergeist projectiles have moved through the air in an erratic path.

Of the one hundred and twenty-two incidents which occurred after Roll's first arrival on the scene, forty-four took place in the presence of either Roll or Pratt or both. Thanks to the co-operation of the owners, Roll and Pratt were able to maintain a fair measure of observational control of the persons and activities in the warehouse room. They arranged certain specially selected 'target objects' in specific areas which they kept under surveillance. Persons in the room were requested to 'freeze' should anything take place. Although Roll's presence appeared somewhat to inhibit the occurrence of phenomena (his known status as an investigator may have contributed to this), Pratt's did not (he had been introduced simply as 'a friend' of Roll's) and he was able to establish himself at an 'observation point' in the south-west corner of the room (Roll had one in the opposite corner) and dictate into an inconspicuous battery-driven tape recorder a continuous commentary on the positions and the comings and goings of people in the room. Thus when an incident took place, the positions and activities of all possibly relevant persons could be determined from the tape; and after the incident had been investigated, the particulars could similarly be recorded or noted down. The protocols thus derived marked a new high point in the recording of poltergeist phenomena; the quantity of relevant detail obtained was maximal, and the possibility of errors of memory minimal. I shall now give sample extracts from three of Pratt's protocols. The first and third of these involve the displacement of 'target' objects (altogether target objects were moved eighteen times, thirteen times in the presence of one or both of the investigators).

Event 181 (January 27th, 1967)
W.G.R., who was still considering the possibility that his presence was an inhibiting factor, told Julio and me that he was going outside for a stroll. Five minutes after he had left, at 3:00 p.m., the spoondrip tray that had been on the target area of the second shelf of Tier 2 near the north end fell into Aisle 2 and broke. This was the tray that Julio had placed on the shelf at the suggestion of W.G.R. to replace the one that had fallen from the same spot and broken late in the forenoon. Both investigators had examined the replacement object at the time and both of us had periodically inspected it afterwards in the course of our individual 'touring' of the premises to inspect objects in different parts of the room and to insure that everything was in normal order.

During the period preceding this event I was observing the activity in the room and recording a running description of the situation on tape from my position in the southwest corner of the room. This record continued right up to the instant when the tray fell and broke. The point on the shelf where it was standing was not visible from my observation point. I could, however, see Julio. He was working in the south part of Aisle 3 and was separated from the disturbance by the tier of double shelves. I could see both his hands. In one he held a clipboard, and the other was by his side. At the time of the incident he was walking toward my position. No one was in Aisle 2 where the tray fell and broke, and Julio was the nearest person. I was not able to conceive of any way in which the falling of the tray could have been caused to happen in a normal manner.

Event 184 (January 28th, 1967)
This event occurred at 10:55 a.m., while W.G.R. had left for fifteen minutes to encourage the phenomena. I was talking with Julio south of Tier 2. At that moment there was a crash of

breaking glass in the west side of the room. I went immediately in the direction of the noise, entering Aisle 4 from its south end. About two-thirds of the way up the Aisle I found on the floor shattered glass that appeared to be the remains of a large-sized jar. The metal cap was still screwed onto the threaded opening, and the round base of thick glass was still in one piece . . . .

I asked Julio if he knew where the jar had been before it crashed on the floor. He appeared to think a moment, then he led the way to the north end of the room and pointed to a spot on the table near the back door. There we found a circle on the table that was relatively free of dust. W.G.R. and I found later that the base of the jar fitted the circle on the table, so the jar could have been standing there previously.

This incident differs in several important respects from others that happened while I was present. It occurred when Julio and I were the only two people in the room and when we were together and engaged in conversation. I had been watching Julio during the period of approximately an hour since he had first arrived in the morning. During that time I had observed nothing unusual in his actions. The jar was a relatively large one (approximately two quarts). It would have been to invite detection if such a large and 'unusual' object had been placed on the shelf among the souvenirs, where it obviously did not belong, and rigged in any way to make it fall.

Assuming that the jar moved from the back table, this was the greatest distance that any of the disturbed objects traveled while an investigator was present. The distance was approximately twenty-two feet. The circumstances before the event and our close inspection of the situation immediately afterward did not reveal any normal explanation of how the jar came to fall on the floor and break when it did.

Event 185 (January 28th, 1967)
At 11.03 a.m., approximately seven minutes after the disturbance involving the breaking of the glass jar, W.G.R. (who had returned at 11.00 a.m.) and I were standing just beyond the north end of Aisle 4 facing east. Julio was standing at the end of Tier 3 close to Aisle 3. He was facing us, four feet away, and the three of us were talking in general terms about developments connected with the case. We heard the sound of glass breaking in Aisle 2, and we went immediately to that location. There we found fragments of a drinking glass scattered on the floor near the north end of the aisle. This was a Zombie glass like the one that had been broken the previous day . . . . We had taken it

from the general stock and placed it on the shelf in the place
where the two spoondrip trays had been before they were broken
. . . . We used the glass because there were no more spoondrip
trays and because this kind of glass had been involved in several
earlier incidents.

Both investigators had inspected that area frequently between
the time when the glass was placed on the shelf and when it was
broken. We never found any indications of anything unusual
about the situation, and we discovered nothing immediately after
the disturbance that could suggest any ordinary basis for the
event. Mr. Hagemeyer [the other shipping clerk] was working at
the shipping desk. He was participating in the discussion and
was facing Julio at the time the glass fell and broke. No one else
was in the room.

It should be emphasized that despite being, for a period of several weeks, the object of close scrutiny and attention by a diversity of people, Julio was never caught faking the phenomena. After Pratt's departure, Roll and Miss Smith investigated the possibility that some chemical or device that would disappear from sight might be responsible. They tried balancing an ashtray half over the edge of a shelf, using a piece of dry ice (frozen carbon dioxide) as a counterweight. When the dry ice had dissolved sufficiently, the ashtray tipped off and fell. However, the dry ice left obvious traces, to which nothing comparable was ever observed in the warehouse.

Cases of destructive poltergeists give plenty of scope to those whose forte it is to speculate about the possible relationships between poltergeist outbreaks and the mental states of the presumed poltergeist agents. Surely behind so much destructiveness must lie deep-seated aggressive urges, finding, we know not how, an outlet in these bizarre phenomena? Julio seemed to Roll to have self-punitive and even suicidal tendencies. Shortly after the period of which I have been writing he was arrested after walking out of a jeweller's shop with a ring. He received a six-month jail sentence. One psychologist who tested him found '(a) early family tenderness, love, and training in high moral standards; (b) feelings of unworthiness, guilt and rejection; (c) development of the personality traits of passivity and inaction; (d) development of inner feelings of detachment and unhappiness; (e) dissociated tendencies, especially in relation to expressing aggression'.

Such speculations will be touched upon later (chapter 18) in the context of a wider range of cases. Also touched on (chapter 17) will be Mr Roll's interesting analyses of the kinds and locations of the objects moved in such cases and of the direction of the movements with regard to the position of the presumed agent.

The last case which I shall discuss in this chapter seems to have begun as a destructive poltergeist, but thereafter to have branched out into a variety of other forms of nuisance which might more accurately be called 'disruptive'. Despite this, the case has various points of similarity with the preceding one. It centred around a young person of nineteen (this time a girl), who possessed, if a battery of psychological tests is to be believed, a somewhat similar personality profile to Julio's – she is said to have had a tendency to dissimulate conflicts and mental tensions of a kind which might lead to aggression, and to be liable to displace short impulses of aggression away from their real objects on to substitute ones. As in the Miami case, phenomena were confined, or largely confined, to the agent's place of work; and in both cases it appeared possible that some of the agent's frustrations and tensions had become so to speak focused on the work situation (though both agents seem to have had considerate employers). Despite the fact that in the present case many of the happenings centred upon pieces of electrical equipment, it seems likely that, as in the Miami case, the forces at work were of a kind that might loosely be called mechanical. A possible difference is that in the present case certain of the phenomena gave the impression of being performed by intelligently-controlled forces. There was little about the Miami poltergeist to create such an impression, unless, indeed, the mere occurrence of a few apparently 'controlled' object-movements be sufficient to create it.

The case in question is of course the well-known Rosenheim case of 1967–8. It was investigated by Professor Hans Bender, Professor of Parapsychology at the University of Freiburg, West Germany, and a leading investigator of poltergeist cases, together with various associates. The printed reports, or such of them as I have seen, are rather short. The principal ones are by Bender in the *Zeitschrift für Parapsychologie und Grenzgebiete der Psychologie*, vol. 11, 1968, the *Proceedings of the Para-*

Psychological Association, no. 5, 1968, and no. 6, 1969, and by F. Karger and G. Zicha in the same, no. 5, 1968; further versions will be found in Bender's article 'Modern poltergeist research – a plea for an unprejudiced approach', in a volume edited by John Beloff, *New Directions in Parapsychology* (London, 1974), and in Bender's *Telepathie, Hellsehen und Psychokinese* (Munich, 1972). The case qualifies for inclusion in a survey whose professed aim is to concentrate upon cases in which there is contemporary eye-witness testimony because of instrumental recordings of the phenomena, and because of material gathered for television broadcasts by the Bavarian and the General Western German television companies. A television documentary about the case has been broadcast in Britain.

The case began at the end of November 1967, when inexplicable events started to occur in a lawyer's office in the Bavarian town of Rosenheim. Neon lights on a two and a half metre high ceiling repeatedly went out, and were afterwards found to have been unscrewed from their sockets. Electric light bulbs exploded, sharp bangs were heard, electric fuses blew without apparent cause. Developing fluid in photocopying machines was again and again spilled. The telephones became subject to curious disturbances – calls were cut off, all four telephones often rang simultaneously, the telephone bills swelled unprecedentedly. It can be imagined that under these conditions the lawyer's office did not run smoothly.

Suspicion in the office at first centred on the power supply. The maintenance department of the power station and the post office authorities were called in. The power station's monitoring equipment registered large deflections in the power supply. These deflections sometimes coincided with the peculiar phenomena, and continued even when a special power supply was installed to ensure 'undisturbed' electric current.

The post office fitted to the telephone a device which recorded for each outward call the number dialled, the time of dialling, and the length of the call. Over a period of weeks this device recorded innumerable calls to the speaking clock (0119), often dialled six times a minute, and at times when it seemed absolutely certain that no one in the office could have been responsible.

Bender and his colleagues came on the scene on 1 December 1967. They speedily noticed that the phenomena seemed to depend on the presence of a new employee, a nineteen-year-old girl referred to as Annemarie Sch. A first deflection of the instruments monitoring the power supply was often registered the moment Annemarie arrived for work in the morning. When she walked along the corridors, electric lights hanging from the ceiling began to swing behind her (this phenomenon was photographed). When bulbs exploded, the pieces flew towards her. Phenomena decreased in frequency with distance from her.

In an attempt to demonstrate conclusively that the phenomena were not due to variations in the mains power supply, the co-operation of two physicists from the Max Planck Institute for Plasmaphysics in Munich, F. Karger and G. Zicha, was obtained. On 8 December 1967, they fitted the power station's recorder, which monitored the mains supply, with a voltage magnifier, and set it up in the corridor to record the mains voltage. Between 4.30 p.m. and 5.48 p.m. the recorder registered an irregular sequence of strong deflections. Some of these were accompanied by sharp cracks, similar to those produced by electric sparks (these sounds were tape recorded). Then, and on subsequent days, they set up equipment to record the electric potential and the magnetic field in the vicinity of the recorder, and also equipment to record the sound amplitude in the office. They were able (at least if one assumes that *their own* equipment was not also being interfered with) to rule out as explanations of the recorder deflections the following: mains voltage variation; HF voltage, demodulated at component with non-linear characteristic; electrostatic charging; external static magnetic fields; loose contacts in the electronic amplifier system; extraneous mechanisms in the recorder; ultrasonic or infrasonic effects, including strong vibrations; and manual intervention. They were forced to the conclusion that some unknown mechanical influence had acted on the pointer of the measuring instruments.

Bender describes the end of the case as follows:

> The discovery of the PK nature of the occurrences led to an intensification of the events: paintings began to swing and to turn, drawers came out by themselves, documents were displaced, a 175 kilogram cabinet moved twice about 30 cm from the wall, etc. Annemarie Sch., getting more and more nervous, finally displayed hysterical contractions in her arms and legs. When she was sent on leave, nothing happened, and when she definitely left the office for a new position, no more disturbances

occurred. But similar events, less obvious and kept secret, happened for some time in the new office where she was working.

A video-recording of one of the picture rotations was obtained.

6 Fantastical poltergeists

In chapters 4 and 5 I have been describing poltergeist cases that are, in a sense, simple – simpler, certainly, than the Stans case or the Tidworth case. By this I mean that the poltergeists concerned had only one string to their bows, or at best a small number. They could rap or throw things or break things, etc., and little else beyond. Even within their own special spheres they tended to be repetitious. They lacked the versatility and gift for improvisation of the true artist. In this chapter I want to consider certain more complex cases. 'Fantastical' may seem an archaic and not very precise word with which to characterize them; but no other seemed adequately to convey their curious mixture of the capricious, the extravagant and the grotesque. In these cases a certain 'intelligence' is commonly manifested, but it is intelligence of a lunatic and disruptive kind. The interactions of this 'intelligence' with the intelligences of the persons plagued or victimized may lead to the victims building up a whole framework of beliefs about the phenomena. The phenomena in turn accommodate themselves to the beliefs, and the beliefs may be supported by shared visions and hallucinations. The upshot can be a series of happenings which strain the credulity even of persons who are prepared to accept 'simple' cases of stone-throwing, raps, etc. And yet it must be emphasized that the evidence in complex and fantastical cases is sometimes nearly, if not quite, as good as the best which we have in simple cases.

One or two of the cases that we have already looked at, e.g. the Tidworth case of 1662–3, fall almost within the 'fantastical' category. An archetypal instance is perhaps the Clarendon case of 1889. In this case the spook stole money, spread excrement around, stole food, broke windows, caused fires, cut off hair, threw things, appeared in grotesque forms, developed a voice, swore, blasphemed, repented, became pious, blamed a witch, sang hymns, assumed the figure of an angel and said farewell to three children who collectively saw it. It must not be thought that 'fantastical' cases do not occur in the present century, which

FANTASTICAL POLTERGEISTS 99

is, after all, not just the century in which men have reached the moon, but the century in which men have fancied that they saw on earth flying saucers and their Venusian occupants. At the parapsychological association conference in 1972, Dr James F. McHarg reported on a case of poltergeist in the English Midlands. It centred around a thirteen-year-old girl, formerly liable to epileptic seizures, and came to involve various of her friends and relatives. There were object-movements, and apparitions (sometimes collectively perceived). The apparitions assumed a grotesque character – there were overtones of supposed 'black magic' – and several of the persons involved underwent transient episodes of 'possession'.

However, my aim in this survey is to concentrate upon cases in which we have diary accounts or other comparable contemporary records. In pursuit of that policy I have selected two examples of 'fantastical' poltergeists which, though well separated in space and time, possess many features in common. The first of these took place in 1722, in the village of Sandfeldt, near Gadebusch in East Germany (then in the Duchy of Mecklenburg-Schwerin). The phenomena lasted from 22 January 1722 to 30 March 1722. They took place in the house of a farmer, Hans Joachim Dunckelman, which must have been of moderate size, since he had a wife, five children and several lodgers. The case was recorded by a certain Heinrich George Haenell, who seems to have been a sort of factor or estate manager to the local landowner. Dunckelman complained to Haenell on 30 January that it had spooked now in his house for several days, with such mighty noises and apish tricks that he and his family could no longer remain there. Haenell reported the affair to his master, who instructed him to investigate and keep a careful record. This Haenell, with two helpers – a gardener and a watchman – faithfully did, and his journal, published later in the year at Hamburg as *Curieuse und Wahrhaffte Nachricht oder Diarium, von einem Gespenst und Polter-Geist* . . . (Curious and Truthful Report or Diary, of a Ghost and Poltergeist) is, for its time, rather an impressive document. It begins on 5 February, with the statements of witnesses to the earlier phenomena. Thereafter Haenell visited the house very frequently, sometimes more than once a day, and heard the stories of the occupants and other witnesses, and of his watchers. These he transferred to his journal, together with accounts of what he had observed himself. The phenomena became more and more grotesque throughout February and most of March, but eventually died out of their own accord. The children were undoubtedly much involved in them, but it is not clear whether or not any one person was the poltergeist 'agent'. On at least one occasion phenomena took place in a room in which no member of the household was present.

At the end of his pamphlet, Haenell presents the names of twenty-seven eyewitnesses who have stated upon oath before the public notary of Gadebusch that the record is, so far as it concerns each of them, a true one.

My second 'fantastical' case is a relatively well-known one, that of the Poona poltergeist of 1927–30. The background to this case is somewhat complex. The young boy, Damodar Bapat, round whom most of the phenomena centred, was born in May 1919, the youngest of three sons of his father's second marriage. The eldest of these sons, Lakshman, had died at the age of about nine; the second son, Ramkrishna, was eight years older than Damodar. Their mother, who had taken to seeing apparitions, became insane and committed suicide about 1920. Their father, a Brahmin aged 60, died about June 1922. Ramkrishna was found employment, and Damodar was sent to an orphanage.

In May 1923, Damodar was adopted by a married couple from Poona, Dr and Mrs Ketkar, who had seen him in the orphanage and taken a fancy to him – he seems to have been a perfectly ordinary and amiable little child. He assumed the surname of Ketkar. The following year Dr Ketkar looked up Ramkrishna, the elder brother, now about thirteen, in Bombay, where he worked in a teashop. Finding him half-starved and miserably exploited, he arranged for him to be educated, and placed him in his Bombay office (Dr Ketkar had a printing and publishing business).

It appears that when Ramkrishna had been about nine years old, he had become the focus for assorted poltergeist phenomena. These were temporarily cured through a visit to some holy place, but broke out again during the period of his servitude in teashops. He was 'dismissed by one employer after another, because, while he was in the act of serving soda-water or lemonade, the liquid would suddenly leap up into the air, and cups and glasses would fall and break'. After he was rescued by Dr Ketkar, the happenings seem to have continued sporadically, and in 1927, when he was working for Dr Ketkar in Bombay, they became so frequent that the Bombay clerk 'asked for the boy to be removed, as daily supernormal things were happening'. In August 1927 he was transferred to Poona to train as a compositor at Dr Ketkar's printing works, and thereafter stayed for extended periods in the Ketkars' house. From that time onwards poltergeist phenomena began to happen there, at first centring upon Ramkrishna, but from April 1928 centring also, and even more markedly, upon the younger brother, Damodar. They continued to afflict Damodar, with intervals, until around October 1930, when they died out. It is not clear whether we have here one poltergeist case with two agents, or two poltergeist cases which happened to occur in the same family. I shall treat it as one case.

We have, in fact, no less than two diary records of it. One is by a Mr J. D. Jenkins, who seems to have been a medical man in attendance on the Ketkar family. His diary runs from June 1928 to January 1930, and parts of it were published in *The Times of India*, and in *The Statesman*. I have, however, seen only a few extracts. A second diary, the one on which I shall here draw, is by a Miss H. Kohn, and is printed in full, with introductory remarks by Harry Price, in the *Journal of the American SPR* vol. 24, 1930. Miss Kohn, it should be explained, was Dr Ketkar's sister-in-law. She was of German origin, and taught languages in the Deccan College, Poona. She lived with the Ketkars during substantial periods of the phenomena, and seems to have taken charge of Damodar, who slept in her room. Her account starts with a résumé of events up to 23 June 1928. Part of this résumé is based on personal recollections, part on Mr Jenkins's articles (mentioned above) and part on her sister's letters. The diary proper begins on 24 June 1928 and continues until 17 January 1929, with a few notes thereafter. In October 1929 Miss Kohn came to London and called upon Harry Price and upon Father Herbert Thurston, two leading authorities on the subject. They were both very struck by her. Father Thurston says 'she impressed me, as she did others to whom she was introduced, as an exceptionally intelligent and level-headed observer'.

I should perhaps add that neither Damodar Ketkar, nor his brother Ramkrishna, was ever detected in fraud, and this despite constant scrutiny. Nor was fraud at any time observed in the Sandfeldt case.

I shall now proceed to spell out some of the similarities, and also the differences, between the two cases, with regard to the kinds of phenomena prominent in both of them.

1 Object-movements

The very first odd things reported in the Dunckelmans' house at Sandfeldt, belonged in this class. Lighted lamps were snatched away or thrown down before their eyes and turned up later in various odd places. This went on for several evenings. Then, on 26 January, as it was growing dark, the children, who had been alone in the living room, rushed out and said that there was such a roaring in there. At this the Dunckelmans lit a candle and went into the room together. They sat down in a corner and began to pray. The spinning wheel, the distaff, and all kinds of household objects lying in the room were thrown about around them. Haenell, a truly methodical man (he must have been very good at his administrative job), itemizes these one by one – wooden trenchers and bowls, two mugs, glasses, gloves, hats, stockings, etc. They were all flung into a heap. Then the Dunckelmans were bombarded with lumps of lime and other missiles. A glass standing before the window was hurled into the middle of the room, and a window pane was smashed. At bed-time, however, all became quiet.

During the next few days the poltergeist raged with increasing violence. All kinds of objects, sometimes quite large ones, were thrown around inside the house, and were also precipitated out of it into the garden. Windows were smashed. Haenell gives a graphic account of the mess which he saw when he visited the house on the morning of 31 January.

> In the dining room, table, shelves, cupboard, and all other kinds of objects and utensils therein, and likewise two large pickle-barrels, lay one on top of the other. It was a wretched enough sight, made worse by the fact that the door was in two pieces and the window-wall smashed in. In the garden groats, meal, beans, etc., lay strewn all about, together with assorted household objects which had been thrown out through the window-wall.

It was some while before Haenell was able to observe any of the happenings himself. However, on the evening of 14 February his curiosity was at last gratified. He went to the Dunckelmans' house with his ally the gardener:

> We could hear the noise from in front of the house. However, only when we entered the house and said good evening did we hear that it racketed loudly in the living room.... We betook ourselves to the living room, and found everything flung into a heap. There was a pitiable wailing and lamentation from young and old. At this moment it tore free a work-table which was firmly nailed down, and threw it the length of the room. I gathered to me all the people young and old, except a small child of three, who lay in bed, and at once went out of the room to stand in front of the [kitchen] hearth. I left the living room door open to see what would happen. It shortly threw an old herring tub (which lay under the bed in the living room, and, fully packed with assorted objects, was so heavy that I could scarcely lift it from the ground) with a mighty clatter out in front of the living room door.... Then came a fall on the floor like something made of iron. We found an iron ring which was quite hot.... Since at this moment it again began to racket in the living room, I and the gardener went in alone with a candle to see what it might be. It bombarded us about the head and nape of the neck with pieces of lime and earth.

Sometimes very weighty objects were moved. In the early morning of 20 February two watchers, Frantz Timcke and Frantz Stüve, were in the house with their wives. Dunckelman and his wife were also present. After divers strong phenomena, so they assured Haenell the same morning, the bed in the living room, in which Dunckelman's thirteen-year old daughter lay ill, was repeatedly lifted up and down as though swine were rummaging under it. The other children were made to sit on it, but the movements continued. In the end the two wives had to restrain it.

If the Poona case is reckoned to have begun with the disturbances which are said to have afflicted the elder brother, Ramkrishna, at the age of nine, then we have no record of precisely what the first phenomenon may have been. However, curiously enough, the first phenomena reported when, in August 1927, the case came under serious investigation, involved lamps, as had been the case at Sandfeldt. The wicks of the lamps were tampered with. Shortly after this, inexplicable object-movements began. These reached a peak of intensity in April and May 1928, by which time the younger brother,

Damodar, had become the principal focus. Miss Kohn was away at this period, and heard about the happenings through letters from her sister. At their worst the phenomena were violent and almost continuous.

> On *April 28th*, things reached a climax. The little boy's food and toys were repeatedly snatched from his hand, and his drink from his mouth, though he made frantic attempts to retain his hold of these things. His toys came literally in showers from his cupboard when no one was in the room who could have done this. As the child moved through the rooms, he was surrounded . . . by broken glass, scattered liquids (including bottles of citronella oil, liniment, brilliantine, eye-drops, and saccharin, all of which were hurled from their accustomed places), and the noise of the crashing objects. The child was exceedingly brave, but hysterical. For a great part of the time, the smashes were occurring at intervals of not even one whole minute.

Things were never quite as violent as this when Miss Kohn was actually present. None the less she witnessed many very curious object-movements. Thus on Thursday 26 July 1928.

> At 9:30 p.m. D. fell asleep, in the presence of my sister and myself. We sat for some minutes, both looking in his direction. When he was quite asleep, he turned over to the wall. A minute or two later, my pillow was gently lifted from its place at the head of my bed (which adjoins D.'s bed), and was placed by an invisible hand at the foot of my bed, making a slight sound. This was so gently done that, had one of us chanced to be looking in another direction, the other who saw the phenomenon could have been inclined to think that it had been a mere optical illusion – but we both distinctly saw the pillow moved. D. did not wake, but during the transit of the pillow, he stirred uneasily, and murmured in his sleep.

On the evening of Sunday 29 July, a group of people, including Miss Kohn, had gathered in the dining room, apparently to hear the deliverances upon the case of a clairvoyant gentleman. Between 6.30 p.m. and 8.00 p.m., during the whole of which time Damodar was sitting on the clairvoyant's knee, small objects – a nail-brush, a mug, a pillow, a comb, etc. – were thrown across or into the room on sixteen occasions, which Miss Kohn itemizes in her diary. Objects were even moved, or precipitated, in the bathroom, while Damodar was under observation in his bath.

The objects moved in the Poona case seem, in general, to have been rather smaller than those moved at Sandfeldt, though on 4 August 1928 a chair and two largish tables were violently thrust at Ramkrishna, who was trying to sleep on the dining room floor. In both the Sandfeldt and the Poona cases, the object-movements had certain further curious features which have been commonly reported. Sometimes objects moved through the air not as if they had been thrown, but as though they were being carried – they floated, turned corners, etc. (compare the 'slow transit' of the pillow described by Miss Kohn). In the Sandfeldt case, stones and iron objects which had been thrown were found to be hot (I have notes of seventeen other cases in which this is said to have happened). On 14 February 1722, an iron ring from a plough wheel was flung at the feet of Haenell's two assistants, the gardener, Hieronymus Heinrich Schultz, and the watchman, Cordt Fieck. When Schultz tried to pick it up, it burnt his glove. They carried it to Haenell at the manor house 1500 yards away, and it was still quite warm when he felt it.

2 Apport phenomena

It is very dificult to draw any proper distinction between those poltergeist object-movements in which the objects concerned are thrown or as it were carried from place to place, and so-called 'apport' phenomena. I have chosen, more or less arbitrarily, to talk of 'apports' when the objects concerned are transported from one place to another without the object being observed in passage by persons in a position to have done so; or when objects are transported into or transported out of closed containers (including rooms), the inference being here that there could have been no ordinary transit for anyone to have observed. But it may of course be that there is at bottom no difference between such 'apports' and the more commonplace kinds of poltergeist object-movements. In fact in both the cases under discussion there were observed examples of happenings which might plausibly be presented as midway between object-movements and apports. Miss Kohn's diary entry for 27 June 1928 runs in part as follows:

> At midday . . . . Two packets of butter, placed on a shelf temporarily, changed their positions twice during an interval of about five minutes, *i.e.* one of the packets hopped, as it were,

from the shelf down on to a trunk a few inches away from the shelf; then suddenly both packets were on the trunk; then again one of the packets was once more on the original shelf. My sister, D[amodar], and myself witnessed this little performance without rising from our seats.

Dunckelman and his wife described to Haenell rather similar happenings which took place in their home on 18 February 1722.

> Earthenware pots and many other things that stood in the living room on a shelf came thence in a moment, before the eyes of all, to stand in the middle of the living room floor, without anyone being able to see in what way they did so.

Apport phenomena figured prominently in both cases, and there were some marked similarities in the kinds of object apported. Foodstuffs were particularly affected, even to the extent of being snatched away from persons about to eat them. Eggs were an especial target in both cases. At Poona, cooked and uncooked eggs would be removed one by one from bowls or containers despite all attempts to prevent it by watching them or locking them away. A most extraordinary incident occurred there in Miss Kohn's absence on the night of 15 June 1928. Someone, hoping to placate the 'spirits', had put out some fruit, inviting them to eat it and depart. The fruit was removed and ostensibly eaten, to the accompaniment of sounds of lip-smacking, heard by Dr and Mrs Ketkar. The rinds were flung back with teethmarks on them. At Sandfeldt, on 19 March 1722, a newly baked pancake vanished in an instant from the oven, and could not be found. A piece was later thrown at the biggest boy, a lad of 10, and a voice said 'I haven't eaten it all on my own; you've got a piece again'.

The other favourite targets for apport phenomena in the Poona case were toiletries and money. Money disappeared from purses, pockets, money boxes and locked trunks in a fashion that was sometimes highly embarrassing, especially to Miss Kohn, the most frequent victim. The money was not infrequently returned in whole or part, sometimes in the form of small change. At Sandfeldt money and toilet articles were on occasion affected, but did not figure so prominently in the phenomena. It is quite likely that neither was abundant in the Dunckelman household.

In the Poona case objects were, ostensibly, apported over appreciable distances, and therefore, of necessity, out of closed containers, through locked doors, etc. On Sunday 8 July 1928,

FANTASTICAL POLTERGEISTS 107

for example, a jar was flung into Miss Kohn's bedroom, where Damodar, in Miss Kohn's presence, was about to open his cupboard. It later transpired that the jar was one which Damodar had taken to school on the previous Friday, and had left there.

In both the Sandfeldt and the Poona cases, apports were observed which, on the face of it, must have involved the transportation of objects out of closed containers. Here is Haenell's diary note of his experience of 20 February 1722:

> In the evening I went again to Dunckelman's house .... The glass from a mirror fell on the floor before my very eyes, without my being in the slightest able to see from where it came. I stood so that I had the people with whom I was talking in front of me and in sight all the time, and there was no one behind me. Dunckelman's wife told me that she kept this mirror-glass in a frame which was in a box. She picked up the glass and put it back in the box. I saw the frame really in the box – the frame was rather more than a foot square. Shortly afterwards this mirror frame fell likewise at my feet, having first lightly hit my head. I could not see when it came out, though I stood right in front of the box. This made me shudder a little. It was not yet dark; not yet sunset.

The following day, 21 February 1722, two watchers, Frantz Timbke [sic] and Frantz Stüve, were in the house at daybreak, at which time various phenomena took place.

> a blue apron and a table cloth came flying in front of them. The householder and his wife stated that they were kept in the box. The householder took them and placed them back in the box. Frantz Timbke and Lorenz Möller sat on top of the box. None the less the apron came flying out of the box again and into the room. Frantz Stüve testified that Franck Timbcke [sic] had not left the box, and they could not observe the least sign that the box lid lifted.

Compare with these incidents Miss Kohn's experience (one of many comparable ones) recorded in her diary for 19 July 1928:

> At 9.30 p.m., while D. was going to bed, some of his toys became active. My sister took care that the lid of his wooden toy-case was properly shut. D. and I got into bed, when a wooden wheel came pelting on to his bed, and he dodged it, as it went very near his head. (He is compelled to dispense with a mosquito net, owing to the furious nature of the occurrences last April, when stones and toys would appear inside his net just after he had been tucked safely in – the memory of these horrors

has made him nervous of mosquito-nets for the present.) The wheel was followed by a spinning-top.

I got 'fed-up' and fetched an enormous German dictionary weighing about five pounds. I placed this upon the toy-box, and got into bed again. Two minutes had not elapsed when another top (not the same one as before) came towards us, again out of the toy-box. I called my sister's attention to the heavy dictionary. She looked into the box to see what toys were there. After a moment, when she had just left the room, the same top as at first, came out as if to mock our vain imagining that a mere dictionary would prove an obstacle.

A curious feature of the Poona case was that when objects which had been apported away were returned they were sometimes seen to appear in mid-air and drop down – an observation for which a good many parallels could be cited from other poltergeist cases. A most curious example is related by Miss Kohn in her diary entry for 26 July 1928:

At eight p.m., D. and I sat in my room, burning a wick rolled round a small scroll containing verses which a friend had given us. (I had burned a similar wick once previously without anything happening.) We sat with our heads close together watching the wick burn out. All of a sudden, quite quietly a round glass button (which belongs to an old set in our possession) was dropped deliberately into the small bowl (*wati*) in which the wick was burning. It did not fall from a height, but appeared only one inch above the edge of the *wati*, *i.e.*, the 'spirit' must have been hovering quite near to our very faces, to produce this act.

At least one such sudden re-emergence of an object into view was reported in the Sandfeldt case. On the evening of 27 January 1722, an old piece of cannonball, which had been taken outside that same morning because it had damaged a door the previous day, was thrown at the Dunckelmans' feet. They did not see it until it dropped down in front of them.

3 Intelligence and responsiveness

I have already described several poltergeist cases in which the phenomena have assumed a form as if an invisible 'entity' were aware of the words and actions of persons present and were adjusting its own doings accordingly. The most obvious examples are cases in which intelligent communications have been received through rappings. But intelligence, often mischievous or spiteful, has in many cases been exhibited through other kinds of responsiveness. A much-quoted example is the Durweston poltergeist of 1894–5. One of the principal witnesses here (we have his first-hand statement) was a gamekeeper named Newman (and gamekeepers are, and have to be, good observers). A boot, which had flown into a cottage, was cast out again by the occupant. Newman went and put his foot on it and said 'I defy anything to move this boot'. The moment he stepped off it, it rose up behind him and knocked his hat off.

Responsive intelligence was a marked feature of the Poona poltergeist. On at least one occasion, indeed, a table-rapping seance was held, though Miss Kohn is exceedingly reticent as to what was spelled out and who the purported communicators were. Sometimes money, or other objects, which had been 'apported' away would be returned on request. Once, when the boot-polish had been removed in this way, Miss Kohn, who wished to polish her shoes, asked for it back again, and it was at once dropped, or rather carried down, to land conveniently at her feet.

The intelligence concerned could sometimes be, as it were, creative rather than merely responsive. The creativeness tended to be directed to spiteful or mischievous ends. Sometimes it seemed as though its aim were to get the boys into trouble for fraudulently producing phenomena in which, as a matter of fact, they had had no hand. Thus when the poltergeist was in a stone-throwing humour, Damodar's pockets might be found full of stones as though he were responsible for the manifestations. On his ninth birthday, 23 May 1928, says Miss Kohn, stones fell, apparently from the roof. Damodar became excited and hysterical.

> We repeatedly searched his pockets and found nothing there: I then followed him about, watching him closely and seeing that he picked nothing whatsoever up. Then a stone would be thrown: I again put my hand in his pockets, which were full of stones. I emptied out the stones, and again watched closely: the procedure would be repeated. To the ordinary [person nothing could be] simpler: in this instance, he would naturally accuse the child of mischief. But to myself, who knew very well he had not picked up the stones, no explanation offered itself.

In the Sandfeldt case too, there were signs of what might be called a creative intelligence, sometimes one with a bizarre or even sick sense of humour. For example, on 4 March 1722 Frau Dunckelman was in the garden behind the living room window, when she heard an unknown voice (a voice of unknown origin was sometimes heard in this case) call out 'Your health!' and a tankard full of human excrement was thrown into the house. On 19 February 1722, a servant of Haenell's, Lorentz Buckman, was in the house, and witnessed mighty racketings and throwings of objects in the living room. Thereafter there arose in that room a powerful and appalling stench, which caused Buckman to leave precipitately, taking the children with him (the Dunckelmans were absent). They all stood by the kitchen fire. Noises continued to come from the empty room, and at intervals Buckman looked in. To his astonishment he found that objects in the room were gradually being arranged into a little scenario. Each time he looked, more objects had been added. The scenario resembled a sort of picnic. A cloth was spread on the floor, and on it were laid numerous dishes and various kinds of foodstuffs. The figures of two picnickers were made up out of clothes ingeniously put together. Various other persons came to observe this, including the pastor and the sexton from nearby Roggendorf (summoned to read prayers), and Haenell himself. Haenell, in his usual methodical manner, lists the items which they found laid out. This curious phenomenon (the arrangement of a *tableau* inside an empty room) has parallels from quite a few other cases (twenty-one other examples are mentioned in the appendix).

A further development of such *tableaux* would, I suppose, be that they should become animated, creating what might well be called *tableaux vivants*. I know of only one case (see chapter 9) in which so horrific a development has reportedly taken place. There have, however, been several cases in which inanimate objects have allegedly been 'animated' so as to act like living things. I shall describe one such case later on (chapter 8). My favourite of them all is the distant, and alas not especially strong, Spreyton case of 1682–3, in which, we are told, one of a victimized lad's shoestrings came out of its shoe and was flung across the room, and the other shoestring began to crawl out after it. A maid pulled it out, and it clasped and curled about her hand like a living eel or serpent.

There are some indications of this animation of the inanimate in both the Sandfeldt and the Poona cases. In the former, on one occasion, two of Dunckelman's children (aged thirteen and nine) were in the garden, when they saw a bag of beans flung out of the house. The bag began to move through the garden, and had already covered a fair distance when the shepherd's little daughter, aged nine, ran up and said 'O ha, where do you want to go with that?' and put her foot on it. After that it lay still. Haenell, that admirable investigator, interviewed the two Dunckelman children and also the shepherd's daughter. In the Poona case, a wastepaper basket once 'walked' up to Miss Kohn as she was about to leave the house and nudged her as if to say 'be off!'

4 Apparitions

In his perceptive and scholarly collection of papers, *Ghosts and Poltergeists* (London, 1953), Father Herbert Thurston writes (p. 168):

> it is unquestionable that in a considerable number of accounts of poltergeist phenomena, the spook, while remaining invisible to all grown-up people, is said at times to have revealed himself, often in a highly fantastical guise (*e.g.*, under the appearance of a man they have never seen, an old witch, a black dog, etc.), to some child medium involved in the disturbances.

I can fully confirm Thurston's remarks. Such apparitions, sometimes collectively perceived, were reported in, for instance, the following cases over and above those mentioned earlier: Youghal (1661), Newbury (1679), Döttingen (1689), Boston (1692), Boston (1693), Naples (1696), Epworth (1716), Bristol (1761–2), Cideville (1850–1), Oderwitz (1862), Ooty (1897), Grosserlach (1916) Suri (1919) and Nidamangalam (1920). Occasionally, but less frequently, the apparitions have been seen by adults. Thurston does not think that these child percipients have in all cases been lying or capitalizing on the credulity of marvel-hungry adults. A more probable theory, he believes

> would suggest that some telepathic influence affected simultaneously the susceptible mental faculties of the children, enabling them to visualize a scene which existed only in their own imagination. Fancy and reality lie nearer together in the mind of the child than in that of the adult, and, even in the case of adults, they commingle strangely in our dreams. But what could be the source of the telepathic influence? One speaks very much

in the dark, but, accepting as I do the existence of a spirit world, angelic, demonic and possibly nondescript, I should be more inclined to look for the influence there than to identify it with any terrestrial agent. Children may very probably be more susceptible to such telepathic influences from outside than the normal adult is!

Thurston's views about the origin of this phenomenon are not our concern just now. The phenomenon itself, however, and much of what Thurston says about it, is perfectly illustrated by the two cases under discussion. In fact in the Poona case (I am tempted to say) it would have been surprising if little Damodar had *not* begun to see apparitions. The distraught family had brought several reputed clairvoyants to the house in the hope of procuring an end to the disturbances. The clairvoyants, sometimes at least in Damodar's presence, had seen visions which seemed to implicate, separately or together, his deceased brother Lakshman, his former *ayah* (nurse), and his late father's first wife. In August Damodar too began to see the apparitions of these persons, and when items of furniture were moved, he would say which of them had been responsible. After a while he began to see other apparitions, sometimes crowds of them; but, fortunately for him, their frequency tailed off and these visions became sporadic. On one occasion he seemed to exhibit a knowledge of the appearance of a recently deceased person whom he did not know and who had not been described to him.

In the Sandfeldt case the apparitions seen by the children, which were often collectively perceived, became, if their stories are to be taken seriously, more and more grotesque. The apparitions began on 12 February 1722 with a plague of mysterious cats in and about the house. These cats were visible only to the children, who also saw a ghost dog with short ears. On 20 February 1722 the children, who were playing in the attic, were terrified by the apparition of a great yellow dog. It had a huge ugly head, with eyes as big as a child's head, a cow's snout, and only three legs. This creature took several large barrels and placed them in front of the living room door (a feat which must have occasioned it some difficulty in view of its anatomical peculiarities) thus preventing the adults below from emerging to rescue the shrieking children. Haenell several times cross-examined the four children involved (as well he might) but their stories remained constant.

The next day, 21 February 1722, the children saw the apparition of a child in the garden and, on their mother's instructions, began to say over various names. The phantom indicated that its name was 'Nörcken' (i.e. Eleonora). It asked for a certain apron, which it was given. It tore the apron into four pieces and returned them with instructions that the mother should make neckcloths and a cap out of them. Apparently it also claimed to be an angel and gave the children good advice. (One assumes therefore that it can hardly have been the same apparition as that of a little woman who stole the youngest child's pancake on 18 March.) The adults who were watching could see and hear only the children; Frau Dunckelman, watching from the garden door, saw the apron come over the hedge, but could see no one pulling it. Later on the same spectre gave the children instructions as to how the wicked spirits could be expelled from the house. Following these instructions, the parents hunted these invisible beings through the house, prodding at them with a pitchfork. On 26 February 1722 the children saw a cavalcade of strange rough things almost like calves, but smaller, fly up out of the shed in front of the house, flogged onwards by a big man with a great whip.

I imagine that by this time the children were thoroughly enjoying the fun. But does it follow that they were making up all of these grotesque stories of apparitions? I can only refer again to Thurston's remarks, quoted above; the psychological aspects of these cases can be very complex, and bizarre apparitions, especially of animals, have been too often reported by poltergeist children, and in too many different milieus, for us to set them all aside as confabulations. In the Sandfeldt case there are yet taller stories to be narrated; but these will have to be held over for a moment.

5 Levitation and transportation of people

If poltergeists have the power to move, or to apport, inanimate physical objects, sometimes even quite sizeable ones, there does not seem any reason why they should not also move or apport the bodies of human beings. And indeed such phenomena are alleged to have occurred in a number of cases. The two 'fantastical' cases which I am discussing in this chapter are amongst them.

In the Poona case, Damodar on several occasions found himself lifted up and transported into the car, which stood in a shed. At least once the shed seems to have been closed, so that he had to open it from the inside. Damodar was the only witness of these occurrences, which must be treated with a corresponding reserve. He seems, however, to have been thoroughly frightened by them, and after the first one he became very ill.

Damodar's elder brother, Ramkrishna, also claimed to have undergone rather similar experiences during the period before the Ketkar family got to know him well. No-one treated these tales seriously. However, on 23 April 1928, Miss Kohn's sister (in Miss Kohn's absence) had an extraordinary experience which she described in a letter partly transcribed into Miss Kohn's narrative:

> At 9.45 a.m. on *April 23rd*, my sister says in a letter, the elder boy 'suddenly materialized in front of me in your doorway like a rubber ball. He looked bright but amazed, and said "I have just come from Karjat". He didn't come through any door'. My sister describes the posture of the boy as having been most remarkable. When she looked up from her letter-writing, she saw him bending forward: both his arms were hanging away from his sides, and the hands hanging limp – his feet were not touching the floor, as she saw a distinct space between his feet and the threshold. It was precisely the posture of a person who has been gripped round the waist and carried, and therefore makes no effort but is gently dropped at his destination.

Perhaps I should point out that Miss Kohn's sister, Mrs Ketkar, was no simple dupe, but a scholar of considerable attainments. Later on Miss Kohn herself observed the end of a similar, but less dramatic, occurrence.

The levitations and transportations which allegedly took place at Sandfeldt bring that case to what many will regard as the very apex of incredibility. These happenings began on 5 March 1722, when Dunckelman's youngest child, aged three, was found upside-down on the living room table, and nearly suffocated. The child claimed that a little white girl had put him there. This same child was later (10 March) several times carried up into the air before his parents' eyes. On 6 March 1722, towards evening, the children were playing on the floor. In the twinkling of an eye, so the others anxiously told their parents, the eldest and the youngest girls vanished. They were sought and called for everywhere, but in vain. Half an hour later both girls reappeared, standing once again on the floor. The following day, 7 March 1722, the girls were likewise carried off and replaced, and so was a lad of ten. This boy was standing with his mother when he vanished. His mother took this very ill, and he was shortly returned, crying, to his former position. All the children who were carried off like this returned with great tales of having been transported under the earth, where they had met a race of little crooked people. These people had offered them money to remain with them, but when they refused it, had returned them. Whether these little people are to be identified with the fairies of British tradition I leave to students of folklore to determine; for clearly these childrens' experiences, or else their story telling, had been shaped by the folk-tales then current in Mecklenburg.

6 Transition to assault

The phenomena which I have so far described in this chapter, sometimes whimsical, sometimes malicious, have stopped short of directly causing personal injury. Not all poltergeists have been so forbearing, and in fact in both the Sandfeldt and the Poona cases, personal injuries were sometimes meted out. In the Poona case, towards the end of the period covered by Miss Kohn's diary, the phenomena went through a phase of being positively vicious. Damodar was bitten and slapped, and his clothes and bedclothes were cut and torn. A little girl, described as his sister, was cut and pricked and an attempt was made to strangle her by tightly knotting up her bib. Dr and Mrs Ketkar were pinched and scratched, and had a most unpleasant thick saliva smeared over them; and the former was smacked hard and audibly. It seems that a prayer meeting, held in the house on 29 April 1929, calmed things down, at least temporarily. However, with these phenomena of poltergeist 'assault' we reach the topic of the next chapter.

7 Poltergeist assaults

The question that one most frequently hears asked about poltergeists is this. Poltergeists frequently break windows, smash ornaments, cause fires, and otherwise damage houses and household objects. Do they ever damage *people*? In some cases, at least, the forces at work, whatever their origin, have been violent enough to appear very dangerous. However, as a general rule they have been muted or turned aside whenever harm seemed imminent. Of course all poltergeists are to a greater or lesser extent frightening and annoying, and are therefore in some sense injurious. Moreover the activities of a poltergeist may create or unleash personal animosities of a highly distressing kind. In at least one case (Kosten-Steinhügel, 1927) a murder has resulted. But direct injury of a person by a poltergeist is fairly uncommon.

Uncommon, perhaps, but not unknown. Indeed, if we simply think back to some of the cases already discussed, we can see grounds for supposing that personal injury by poltergeists is quite on the cards – grounds, I should add, independent of whether one considers the phenomena genuine or fraudulent. Sometimes poltergeists have been wildly, one might say insanely, violent and destructive. Sometimes the phenomena have seemed undeniably, if obscurely, linked to the fears, frustrations and hostilities of a particular person round whom they have centred. Sometimes the phenomena have given rise in the minds of the persons most involved to a whole set of delusory beliefs, generally shaped by folk-lore, and occasionally reinforced by confirmatory hallucinations; and the phenomena have in turn accommodated themselves to this set of beliefs. Given these tendencies in the phenomena, one can readily imagine that the following state of affairs might arise: a poltergeist 'agent' (often, though not always, a teenage girl), one whose phenomena have a violent or destructive tendency, has, consciously or otherwise, attitudes of dislike and aggression towards a certain person – perhaps even, for complex psychological reasons, towards herself. Then the phenomena, reflecting these attitudes in ways which we do not understand, turn their violence more and more upon the disliked person. Finally a delusory set of beliefs arises with regard to them and receives support when the phenomena begin to conform to the beliefs. A kind of paranoid state ensues in which the phenomena, really self-generated, are ascribed to some external persecutor, and then assume a form which supports that belief. This state of affairs, unless interrupted in some way, becomes more or less self-perpetuating.

There are in the literature a number of cases which it would, *prima facie*, be very easy to interpret like this. For instance certain cases of supposed diabolical assault on holy persons are obvious candidates. The best-known instance is probably that of St J.-B. Vianney (1786–1859), the celebrated *curé* of Ars; but perhaps even better documented are the poltergeist assaults which centred upon the Blessed Christina of Stommeln (1242–1312) in the period from about 1260 to about 1288, of which we have moderately detailed accounts in contemporary letters. I have not studied the original materials, but there is a careful account of the case in Father Herbert Thurston's *Surprising Mystics* (London, 1955). Christina was, apparently, subjected not just to the ordinary poltergeist annoyances – such as objects being moved and stones being thrown in her vicinity – but to many other even more unpleasant manifestations. Her bedclothes were pulled off and she herself was dragged about. She was struck and scratched, leaving visible wounds. Nails were thrust into her – sometimes they were found to be hot. She was bitten as if by invisible beings, toothmarks being left in her flesh. Visitors were sometimes likewise bitten. Hot stones were pressed into her body. Her clothes and shoes were cut to pieces. Her room, her clothes, sometimes her visitors were spattered with excrement. When an exorcism was attempted, a loud explosion was heard, and a deluge of filth descended on the exorcist. Christina suffered from numerous, and sometimes grotesque, hallucinations of a divine or diabolic character; and sometimes she was roughly dragged away to a distance as if by diabolic agency. All these phenomena ceased around the time at which she reached the menopause.

Such phenomena have generally been regarded by the victims, and by the devout in general, as signs of the malice with which Satan regards persons of particular sanctity. The phenomena themselves, or aspects of them, may accommodate themselves to this way of thought. Of course neither the phenomena, nor this view of them, are peculiar to any one religious denomination. We have, for instance, an account by an eminent Lutheran theologian, Professor Schuppart of Giessen, of poltergeist assaults directed upon himself and his wife over a period of six years (about 1703–8), during which he was pastor of Pfedelbach in Swabia. The happenings which he describes are very similar to those which had taken place at Stommeln over four hundred years previously. The victims were pinched, struck, slapped, bitten (leaving toothmarks), pelted with stones and pierced with needles. A knife was thrown at Schuppart and a sword at his wife. His pupils found stones and excrement in their satchels. Clothes and wigs were damaged or hidden. And there were numerous minor annoyances.

The victims of poltergeist assaults have, however, not always been persons whose piety was such as might seem likely to excite the malice of the Evil One. Sometimes they have been ordinary poltergeist 'agents', teenage girls, winning but wayward, like the general run of their kind. In such cases the folk-lore of many lands provides another ready explanation of why these girls should be singled out for persecution – they, or their families, have fallen foul of a witch, and the vengeful witch has set her familiar spirits to work; or perhaps the witch has been hired by a third party with a grudge to settle. I have already remarked (chapter 3) upon the links between witches or 'cunning folk' and poltergeist outbreaks in the seventeenth century, and indeed far later. How much more obvious must the link have appeared to contemporaries when the poltergeist phenomena seemed to persecute and even endanger a particular person or persons, and when, indeed, as in a case I am about to discuss, they had features which seemed directly to support this kind of interpretation.

The case in question lasted, with some interruptions, from November 1761 to December 1762, and was thus partly contemporaneous with the more celebrated Cock Lane ghost. It is described by an eyewitness, Henry Durbin, in a rare little pamphlet, published at Bristol in 1800 under the title *A Narrative of some Extraordinary Things . . .* , and recently reprinted as *Witchcraft at the Lamb Inn, Bristol* (Leicester, 1971). Durbin's narrative, though not published until after his death, seems to have circulated in manuscript (the editor speaks of minor errors made by 'the transcriber'). It is in diary form, and is without doubt based on contemporary notes. Durbin (or his editor) has a rather irritating way of substituting blanks for the names of the other witnesses. However the affair made some stir at the time in Bristol newspapers, and quite a few of the missing names can be obtained from them (see John Latimer's *Annals of Bristol*, Bristol, 1893, Vol 2, pp. 348–50, and *Felix Farley's Bristol Journal* for the relevant period).

The 'agents' and victims in this case were two girls, Dobby (eight) and Molly (thirteen), especially the former, both daughters of Mr Giles, a carrier, who kept the Lamb Inn, without Lawford's-Gate, Bristol. Durbin first visited them on 18 December 1761, by which time the phenomena had been under way for several weeks. So intrigued was Durbin by what he was told, and by what he witnessed himself, that he returned day after day to observe and record. His pamphlet is still among the fullest accounts of a British poltergeist.

The first phenomena to startle the Giles family were inexplicable scratchings and rappings, especially from the girls' bedroom. They were most marked at night. They soon became stronger and more persistent, and in fact continued alongside the other phenomena during the whole period of the disturbances. In January the rappings began to show signs of intelligence – they several times beat the tattoo – and on 23 January the first attempts were made to communicate with the raps and scratchings by means of a code. During the next few weeks a very circumstantial tale as to the origins of the phenomena was spelled out by the scratchings in reply to leading questions put by Durbin and others. The mischief, it appeared, was being worked by the familiar spirit of a witch, from Mangotsfield in Gloucestershire, who in her turn had been hired for ten guineas by one of Mr Giles's rival carriers. The spirit would have power over the children for a further forty weeks. In keeping with this story, several of Mr Giles's wagons broke down for no good reason. Dobby began to have visions of a hag, who transported her mysteriously from one part of the house to another. On 12 May Mr Giles himself caught sight of a similar woman standing by his trap, and shortly afterwards he sickened and died.

Durbin was particularly impressed by the fact that the scratchings would correctly or appropriately answer questions posed in Latin and Greek (of which the girls were ignorant) and by the fact that they would correctly answer *mental* questions, and in other ways exhibit what we should now call ESP (a circumstance that has been reported in a number of other cases). The communications were occasionally supplemented by a mysterious voice, usually heard by the girls only, as if whispering in their ears, but occasionally heard by all present. When it was heard by all, its remarks tended to be of a scurrilous and abusive character. Durbin himself does not seem to have heard it; but he heard curious squeakings when the spirit's supposed location was beaten and cut, and once he heard 'a laugh, ha! ha! ha! like a hollow shrill voice in a place where it echoes'.

Not long after the rappings and scratchings began, objects in the house started to be moved or thrown by no detectable agency. Phenomena of this class included the complete inversion of a heavy table, the displacement or throwing of chairs, chamber pots, teacups, and other domestic utensils, and the carrying (as distinct from projection) of a brush across the room. A particularly striking incident is described by Durbin as occurring on the morning of 5 January 1762.

> I went up, and the nurse went up to show me where the great knockings were last night, by the childrens' bed; on my left hand was a sash window; about three feet from the window, was a case of drawers, on the drawers stood a wine-glass, which I saw glitter in the sun, and was astonished to see it rise from the drawers without hands. It rose gradually about a foot, perpendicularly from the drawers; then the glass seemed to stand, and thereupon inclined backwards, as if a hand had held it; it was then flung with violence about five feet, and struck the nurse on the hip a hard blow, so that I heard it give a loud report . . . .
> There was no person near the drawers when it rose; the children were standing by me who saw it, and ran to the other end of the room, fearing it would be flung at them, as things generally were. I was so amazed at it, that I said, 'Do I see, what I see?' I then thought I would examine the glass, whether there were any wires or hairs tied to it. I then took up the glass from the floor, and found no wires nor any thing else; but the glass was quite whole, except that the foot of it was broken, as if pincers had pinched it all round. – This was about nine in the morning, clear day-light, close by a sash-window.

On 26 April, in the evening, Durbin saw a chamber pot, which stood in the middle of the floor of Dobby's room, move backwards and forwards several times. No one was within six feet of it. Durbin and a maid

> then looked under the bed and about, but could see nothing that could possibly do it. Indeed I stood still while it was moving, so I am certain nothing visible did it; but for greater proof, after it stood still, I kneeled down, and put my hand round the outside of the pot, to feel if any wires or hairs were tied to it, but found none.

The most singular feature of this case, however, was not the object-movements, remarkable though these were, but the assaults upon and bodily afflictions of the two girls. Throughout the period of the phenomena the girls were physically tormented in a variety of ways. At first they were simply pinched. After that they began to be frequently bitten, especially on the hands and arms, but occasionally on the neck or shoulder-blades. The bites left behind toothmarks (presumably human in pattern) and also copious quantities of spittle. Next pins, sometimes twisted into fantastic shapes, were thrust into the girls by some undetected agency. Both girls were many times cut as with a sharp knife, and neither searching nor the interposition of clothing could prevent the injuries. The children were pulled about, both sideways and upwards, with such force that several strong men could hardly hold them.

This catalogue of sufferings prompts two obvious reflections. The first is that phenomena of the kinds in question could very readily be counterfeited by sleight of hand or other trickery. The second is that certain of the phenomena – the ones involving the appearance of marks on or injuries to the skin – are of a sort which, it has often been claimed, may be produced on persons with very sensitive skins simply by strong suggestions with or without the use of hypnotic techniques. (It will be recollected that Christina of Stommeln, whose skin was similarly wounded and marked by bites, suffered from stigmata corresponding to Christ's wounds on the cross, and was therefore, presumably, just such a hypersensitive person.)

The first of these points was quite as obvious to Durbin and others who investigated the case as it is to us, and they made repeated efforts to obtain the phenomena under conditions which excluded fraud. I can only give a couple of examples here.

For instance, Durbin's record for the afternoon of 15 February 1762 runs as follows:

> I made Molly sit down in a chair in the middle of the parlour: I took a large pin, and marked it at the top with a pair of scissars, I put her hands across, and bid her not move. I desired the above Gentlemen to watch her narrowly; none were in the room besides ourselves; I then put the marked pin in her pincushion in which the other pin was; I put the pincushion that hung at her side into her pocket hole, and pulled her clothes over it. As I moved one hand (my watch being in the other to see the time), she cried out she felt somewhat at her pincushion, and directly was pricked in the neck (her hands being still across). The identical pin that I marked, was run through the neck of her shift, and stuck in her skin, crooked very curiously. It was not a minute from the time I put the pin in, to her being pricked in the neck: those two Gentlemen were witnesses of the Fact. We then marked four other pins, and I put them in her pincushion singly, as before; and all of them were crooked, and stuck in her neck.

Again, this is how he describes events of the afternoon and evening of 30 January 1762:

> I saw Dobby wiping her hands in a towel, while I was talking to her, she cried out she was bitten in the neck. I looked and saw the mark of teeth, about eighteen, and wet with spittle. It was in the top part of the shoulder, close by the neck; therefore it was impossible for her to do it herself, as I was looking on all the time, and nobody was near her but myself. – At night I went with Mr. ——, and met there Mr. —— . . . . Dobby was bitten twice following in the back, and it was wet with spittle. We saw their faces all the time. Molly was bitten on the arm and shoulder. While we were examining the bite on the arm, the other arm was bitten close by us in sight.

The second point, that the marks on the girls' skins might have been psychosomatic in origin, does not seem to have occurred to Durbin, and how indeed could it have done in that day and age? There are, however, a few indications that the marks were of mechanical rather than psychological origin. For instance, on his very first visit, 18 December 1761, Durbin, watching Molly, 'saw the flesh pressed down whitish, and rise again, leaving the print of a finger-nail, the edges of which grew red afterwards'. Again, he says

> Jan. 2, 1762, I went and met there Mr. ——, and several other gentlemen. We went into a room called the *George*, and saw the

children pinched with the impressions of nails, and the children said they saw the hand that did it .... Dobby cried, the hand was about her sister's throat, and I saw the flesh at the side of her throat pushed in, whitish, as if done with fingers, though I saw none. Her face grew red and blackish presently, as if she was strangled; but without any convulsion or contraction of the muscles.

Furthermore bystanders, particularly ones who treated the spirit with disrespect, were on several occasions pinched and bruised.

The strange happenings which surrounded these two girls were at the time popularly supposed to be fraudulent, and historians of Bristol have for the most part endorsed this verdict. John Evans, for instance, asserts that the whole imposture was planned by 'Mrs Nelmes [Elmes], and her daughter Mrs Giles, the grandmother and mother of Molly and Dobby, for the purpose of depreciating the value of the house, of which Mrs Nelmes became the purchaser'. Evans, however, was writing fifty years after the events concerned, and fifty-year-old gossip, or for that matter contemporary gossip, can have no standing against a first-hand narrative of personal experiences. In any case, Molly and Dobby were removed to other houses, and the phenomena followed them thither, so that it must have been clear even at the time that it was the two children that were haunted and not the house.

A recent commentator thinks it 'likely that Molly and Dobby were aided and abetted by their six brothers and sisters'. However only one other child is mentioned in Durbin's narrative, and it seems likely that the rest lived away from home. And before supposing Molly and Dobby parties to a deliberate imposture we must reflect how much they *suffered*. Here, for instance, is Durbin's description of the sort of cuts which were inflicted on them:

She [Molly] had above *forty* cuts on her arms, face and neck, with the blood dried on them, and very sore. They looked very black, and were all about two inches and a half long, and about the thickness of a shilling deep; the skin not jagged, but smooth, as if cut with a penknife.

Of course if Durbin's account of the phenomena, and of his attempts to investigate them strictly, are correct, those phenomena could not have been fraudulent, or rather could not all have been fraudulent. One's assessment of the case is bound to depend very much on one's opinion of his honesty and intelligence. Unfortunately not a great deal is known about him. He appears to have been a prosperous Bristol druggist, of great piety and ample charity. It is obvious from his narrative that he was neither a fool nor a fanatic. He omits, of course, details that we should like to have; but he never lost sight of the need to search for trickery. When one calls to mind that his investigations were carried out, and his narrative written, more than two hundred years ago, both appear decidedly impressive. If one is to impugn them, it must be upon the general ground of the fallibility of human testimony in all matters of this kind.

It remains for me to relate the ending of this singular affair. The phenomena continued beyond the period predicted by the scratchings, which then answered that the services of the witch had been retained for a further period. At this Mrs Giles (against Durbin's advice) visited the 'cunning woman' at Bedminster, who told her much that was already common knowledge about the phenomena and their supposed causation, but also had some practical advice.

> She bid them . . . take the two children's first water in the morning, and put it in a pipkin on the fire; and if, when it boiled, all colours of the rainbow came out of it visibly, she could cure it; and she would do the rest at home. They accordingly put the water on the fire, and . . . beautiful colours came out of it, like the rainbow.

From that day the phenomena ceased. 'How far the *cunning woman* may have contributed to this,' Durbin prudently adds, 'I will not pretend to say.'

Not the least interesting feature of this case is that the phenomena accommodated themselves not, as would probably happen today, to Spiritualistic beliefs and practices, but to the witch-lore of the preceding century. It is worth turning aside for a moment to note how completely the witch-superstitions had survived. Some curious parallels present themselves between the Bristol poltergeist case of 1761–2, and a case of supposed witchcraft which took place in the remote Yorkshire hamlet of Fewston in 1621–2. The witchcraft case, which is described by Edward Fairfax, the father of the victims, in his *Daemonologia: a Discourse on Witchcraft* (reprinted London, 1971), perfectly exemplifies the leading features of seventeenth-century English witch beliefs. Two of Fairfax's daughters, Helen (twenty-one) and Elizabeth (seven), began to suffer from mysterious ailments, sensations as of being strangled, etc., and to pass into trances in which they saw and conversed with the phantasms of the witches who afflicted them, and also those of the witches' familiar spirits. Fairfax took detailed notes (which he presents in diary form) of his daughters' troubles and trance utterances, and unsuccessfully attempted to secure the conviction of the alleged witches. Although in the Fewston case, with a few doubtful exceptions (apports), no poltergeist phenomena took place, some obvious parallels with the Bristol case may be drawn:

Fewston case (1621–2)	*Bristol case (1761–2)*
Centred round two girls	Centred round two girls
Visions of witches and familiars who claimed responsibility for phenomena	Intelligent scratchings implicated a witch who was said to work through a 'spirit'
Witches said they were hired by Henry Graver, a neighbour	Scratchings stated witch hired by business rival of Mr Giles
Girls subjected to divers bodily afflictions	Girls subjected to divers bodily afflictions
Witches and familiars correctly predicted course of girls' afflictions	Scratchings correctly predicted length of girls' afflictions
Helen supposedly carried away by phantasmal witches	Dobby supposedly transported to other parts of the house by figure of old woman
Victim threatened with knife by apparition of witch	Both children cut as by knife
Phantasms discomfited when their reported location beaten with stick	'Spirit' cries out audibly when cut at with knife or beaten
Fairfax's youngest daughter died – death claimed by witches	Giles's youngest daughter, and also Giles himself, died. 'Witch' claimed responsibility
Witches claimed responsibility for afflictions in other families	'Witch' claimed responsibility for afflictions in another family
Visions conveyed apparently correct information about distant scenes	Scratchings conveyed information apparently unknown to persons present and answered 'mental' questions

| Resort to 'cunning men' suggested and rejected | Giles family resorted to 'cunning woman' |

At this point some writers on poltergeists would be very likely to develop the following line of argument. The Fairfax girls show many of the classical symptoms of 'hysteria', a supposed state of mental disturbance in which underlying states of emotional conflict may manifest themselves (be 'converted' into) in bodily disorders, disturbances of the senses, and limb movements, all of which are outside the conscious control of the sufferers. Such symptoms are often markedly influenced by suggestion and by social and cultural factors which may together lead to so-called hysterical 'epidemics', like the outbreaks of epidemic 'possession' that in earlier centuries afflicted whole convents of suggestible and probably frustrated nuns. We do not have to suppose that the Fairfax girls were conscious imposters; in fact there is a good deal that tells against this idea. They were hysterics in whose symptoms the influences of suggestion and of superstition can be readily traced. Now what about the Giles children? The phenomena which surrounded them were equally and very similarly influenced by suggestion and by superstition, yet there is likewise every reason for supposing that these phenomena were not within their conscious control. Is it not plausible to say that the Giles children too were hysterics, though in their case the emotional conflicts which were no doubt at the root of their troubles found expression not in bodily movements and afflictions but, for reasons which we do not as yet understand, in 'poltergeist' phenomena external to their bodily organisms? This interpretation of certain sorts of poltergeist cases will have to be discussed in more detail later on. But for the time being we may perhaps note that it can be supported by one further sort of consideration, namely that there are some cases which seem to fall, as it were, mid-way between the two which we have just been considering. There are cases, in other words, in which it seems as though a certain underlying psychological condition in an hysterical person has given rise more or less indifferently *both* to hysterical symptoms of the classical kind, *and* to poltergeist phenomena with overtones of assault. A central example here is that of Christian Shaw in 1696–7 (she is usually known as the 'Bargarran imposter', though it seems to me fairly unlikely that she was a complete and conscious charlatan). In addition to the usual hysterical symptoms – convulsions, visions of the tormenting witches, etc. – Christian was a victim of poltergeist assaults. She was cut, hit, pinched and bitten. The pinches and bites left appropriate marks and, in the latter case, spittle, on her skin. Some minor object-movements and incendiary effects allegedly took place in her presence. She was transported around the house as if by invisible agencies. She vomited pins, excrement, and other foreign substances (a kind of happening which, though once common, I have chosen, perhaps wrongly, not to include amongst poltergeist 'apport' phenomena). I need hardly spell out the analogies between these alleged occurrences and the phenomena which took place in the other cases which we have been considering.

To return now to the main theme of this chapter, cases of poltergeist assault. It remains for me to describe, though of necessity too briefly, the best-known of all such cases, namely that of Eleonora Zugun in 1925–7. The agent in this case, and victim of the poltergeist assaults, was a Rumanian peasant girl named Eleonora Zugun. Eleonora was born on 24 May 1913, and lived in the village of Talpa, a few miles west of Dorohoi, in the northern part of Rumania. It appears that sometime in February 1925, Eleonora set out to visit her grandmother, at the village of Buhai, a little to the north-east of Talpa. This old lady was 105 years old and reputedly a witch. During the journey Eleonora found some money by the roadside. When she arrived she spent it on sweets, all of which she proceeded to eat. This led to a sharp quarrel with a girl-cousin. The witch-grandmother overheard the quarrel and informed Eleonora that since the sweets had been bought with money left by the Devil, she, Eleonora, had swallowed the Devil with the sweets, and would never more be free of him. The very next day poltergeist phenomena began! Stones hurtled against the house from the outside, breaking windows; and small objects in Eleonora's vicinity jumped and flew. Her grandmother's diagnosis of possession gained wide currency among the peasants. She was quickly sent home to Talpa, where, three days later, phenomena broke out again.

Our information about the phenomena of this period comes almost entirely from statements obtained from the local peasants several weeks later by Kubi Klein and Fritz Grunewald, the first serious investigators to visit the scene. These statements are not without interest, but my policy in this book is where possible to present diary accounts and other detailed contemporary records, and I shall pass over nearly all of them. It is, however, perhaps worth quoting one or two brief passages. Joan (i.e. Johan) Teodorescu, a schoolmaster, was present when Eleonora was brought by her father and other peasants to visit a venerable priest named Macarescu at Zamostea. On Eleonora's first evening with Macarescu, Teodorescu was in the room with several other persons. A number of object-movements took place, for which he did not think Eleonora could have been responsible.

> I decided to turn my gaze on a selected object . . . . I fixated a water-jug which stood below the window on a big stool, and leant obliquely against the wall. The jug was full of water. After about five minutes I saw the jug rise slowly upwards about half a metre, after it had raised itself from its leaning position. Then it went in a slanting line on to the other end of the stool, where it remained standing upright. Not a drop of water was spilled . . . . All the people in the room saw this with their own eyes, so that it was impossible that one of us could have moved the jug with his hands. (Z. Wassilko-Serecki, *Der Spuk von Talpa*, Munich, 1926, pp. 20–1)

On Eleonora's second evening with Macarescu, after various exciting events, only the old priest himself, Eleonora, and a young man named Nicolai Ostafi, were in the room; several others, including Teodorescu, were looking in through the windows. The young man, Nicolai Ostafi, deposed as follows:

> Eleonora sat down on the trunk and I stood in front of her. Suddenly I heard a noise in the trunk. Eleonora instantly stood up. Then I observed that the trunk made rocking movements. Next I told Eleonora to sit on the seat by the oven. I took a stick, rapped with it on the trunk and said to the Devil: 'Get out, you unclean thing'. Then I seized the trunk by the lid, to turn it round and see whether there was anything under it. I stood beside it with my back towards the girl. In order to be able to watch her none the less, I turned my head leftwards towards the rear.
>
> Suddenly I saw an object rise up from behind the oven and fly at me. I afterwards learned that it was the *polentabrett* [a board for mixing a kind of porridge] which stood behind the oven in the back corner. When I saw the board coming, I turned my head quickly to the right, in order to avoid being struck in the face. However, it hit me on the left side of the back of the head with its handle [making a nasty wound] . . . . I am quite sure that

Eleonora did not throw the *polentabrett* at me, for I had my eyes fixed on her. (*Ibid.*, pp. 26–7)

The visit to Macarescu failed to damp down the phenomena, and thereafter Eleonora seems to have had a fairly miserable time among the superstitious villagers. For three weeks she found sanctuary in the monastery of Gorovei, but the (extremely destructive) phenomena continued unabated, and by April she was shut in a lunatic asylum, apparently as a result of newspaper controversy about the case. From this dreadful situation she was rescued in a somewhat roundabout way. Newspaper accounts reached a well-known parapsychologist, Fritz Grunewald, of Charlottenburg in Germany. Grunewald was an engineer, and was particularly interested in the physical phenomena of mediumship and the problems of instrumentally recording them. Upon reading about Eleonora he set out for Rumania. He enlisted the help of Kubi Klein, a journalist of Czernowitz, who had written sympathetically about her, and of Victor Setnik, proprietor of a motorbus line near Talpa, who had first told Klein of the case. Between them, and no doubt by the judicious use of that oil which best frees obstinate locks, they contrived to have Eleonora removed from the asylum and returned to the monastery of Gorovei, where they could observe the phenomena at leisure. They arrived at Gorovei on 9 May 1925. Grunewald's shorthand notes of the phenomena which took place between then and 18 May were edited and published after his death by Professor Christoph Schröder in the *Zeitschrift für psychische Forschung*, vol. 1, 1927. These notes constitute what is perhaps the fullest minute by minute record of poltergeist phenomena prior to the invention of the tape recorder. It is unfortunate that I can only give some brief representative extracts.

The principal scenes of poltergeist activity were the monastery kitchen, and the guest house in which Grunewald and Eleonora were accommodated, a wooden bungalow with two rooms opening off a corridor, and a covered veranda at one end. By far the commonest kind of phenomenon was object-movements. These ranged from the slow tilting of a large pot on the oven, to quite violent hurlings of moderate-sized objects at or near people. There were also apports, occasional raps, and, on one or two occasions, the mysterious conflagration of matches. Sometimes – a development foreshadowing things to come – Eleonora was struck as if by an invisible hand.

The phenomena which took place when Eleonora was in the monastery kitchen were often not observed by Grunewald and his colleagues. In that case Grunewald had to rely on translations by Klein of what the witnesses, usually servants, had to say. An entertaining little war developed between Mihai, herdsman at the monastery, and 'Dracu', the devil whom Eleonora firmly believed was plaguing her. Mihai would insult 'Dracu' with the greatest impudence, and 'Dracu' would, in apparent exasperation, respond by hurling any available object at Mihai or at Eleonora. Here are some extracts from Grunewald's records of the events of 11 May 1925:

> 1. Phenomenon.... Towards 10.00 a.m., Eleonora (E.) stood in the kitchen at the cupboard, where she was later struck by the salt-cellar. The herdsman Mihai sat right beside her on the bench and insulted the devil as if he had been schooled to it. Then the *polenta* mixing stick, which was on the wall which contained the door, flew at Eleonora and hit her, striking obliquely, on the right upper arm .... There was no-one in the corner by the oven from which the grater came. The cook saw the stick fly, as did brother Joseph.
> ... The following was now the situation: Brother Joseph sat on the bench, at the oven young Ivan; E. stood by the cupboard, Klein in front of the oven fire; Gru. in the middle before the door; the cook stood on Grunewald's right at the table.
> 2. Phenomenon. Suddenly Gru. saw ... an object drop from E.'s head to her left (as Gru. saw it) and down in a curve to the floor. It was a small glass salt-cellar in two parts, which was broken through the middle. The cook, who remained quite still during the occurrence, said that it had stood on the table.
> E. stood during this at the corner of the cupboard, shrinking a little, with her face towards the middle window. Klein saw the salt-cellar fall on her head. E. called out 'Waihau', and shrank a little.
> The young man from his seat saw the salt-cellar fall down from E.'s head. The cook, who stood in front of the middle of the table, saw it fly up from the table, at her right, to Eleonora's head, and then drop downwards on the floor.
> Gru. made his note immediately after the phenomenon. It finished at 2.24 p.m.

The following extracts from Grunewald's protocols for 15 May 1925 (a day on which he recorded nineteen phenomena altogether) refer to events which took place in the bungalow:

> 6. Phenomenon, 10.08 a.m. E. had fetched herself a chair out of

the guest room and seated herself opposite Gru. on the other side of the table [on the veranda]. A small coin fell on the table to Gru's right, about 70 cm. away from him. E. sat opposite at the 88 cm. wide and 1.78 m. long table; she had, and had had, both her hands on it, and Gru.'s tape measure in the right one. Gru. saw the coin fall down from a height of about 20 cm.; he sat upright, as he stressed, with his gaze deliberately fixed on E., so that he observed closely.

E. shrank a little when the coin fell. It is quite impossible that she should have thrown it; for she had both hands on the table. Although the veranda gave shade, it was nevertheless very well lit on account of the beaming sunshine outside . . . .

8. Phenomenon, 10.55 a.m. E. sat quite still in front of Gru. as previously, and he watched her. Something came from behind E.'s back, about 80 cm. above the table, and 20 cm. above her head. It went away towards her left (Gru.'s right), and dropped outside the table-edge to the floor, about 1 m. from E.'s left side (Gru.'s right). It was a little silver chain with a blue stone, a present from Klein, which E. had in turn given to the cook. It must accordingly have come from the kitchen or the Prior's house . . . .

Gru. stresses that this phenomenon had been of especial value to him, because he saw the chain fly away over E. in not exactly fast motion. She was sitting quite still.

Grunewald was intensely interested by these and the numerous other phenomena which he observed. As soon as he left Gorovei he began to make arrangements for Eleonora to live, under his supervision, with a family in Berlin, where he had his laboratory. Had his plans gone forward it is possible that we should now know more than we do about the mechanics of poltergeist phenomena. But in July 1925 he died of a heart attack in his forty-first year, and the unlucky Eleonora was once again left to the not notably tender mercies of her family. Fortunately, perhaps, for her, she later in the year found another protector. This was the Countess Zoë Wassilko-Serecki, a handsome young Viennese woman, with Rumanian blood, much interested in psychical research and in psychoanalysis. The Countess visited Eleonora at Gorovei in September 1925. She found Eleonora dirty, wretchedly clothed, and thoroughly frightened. The phenomena, however, persisted, and the Countess witnessed them. She prepared a little book on the case, later published as *Der Spuk von Talpa* (Munich, 1926), and in January 1926, managed, after difficult and doubtless expensive negotiations, to bring Eleonora to live with her in her Viennese flat.

There is no doubt that Eleonora quickly adjusted to her new surroundings, and became very happy there. Indeed it is hard to recognize in the cheerful, clean and well-dressed girl who looks out from pictures of this period, the little urchin of Grunewald's photographs taken only a year or so before. Eleonora proved to be a bright and intelligent child, but in some ways emotionally backward. She delighted in toys designed for children much younger than she was, perhaps because such things had not often come her way in her own impoverished childhood. An examination by a nerve specialist showed her to be healthy and in no way abnormal, save for an unusual sensitivity of the skin. When she matured a little the Countess had her trained as a hairdresser, and after her return to Rumania in 1928 she was shortly able to set up in business for herself.

Sometimes the Countess induced Eleonora to take part in what were to all intents and purposes mediumistic sittings; but for the most part Eleonora was left to live a more or less ordinary existence, and the Countess kept a diary of the poltergeist phenomena. So far as I know this chronicle has not been published, but there are various extracts in articles by the Countess.

Object-movements and apports continued to be common, and took place in good light, even outdoors in the noontide sunshine. It was rather unusual for the objects to be seen in flight. Generally they just fell out of the air, landing with a loud noise, sometimes after having ostensibly come through closed doors, out of locked cupboards, etc. The Countess made some curious observations:

> Most interesting were the very rare cases when the last part of the hypothetical line of flight of a moving object was to be observed. Once I entered my room and looked at the window. Eleonore was standing behind me. Suddenly I saw a shadow which glided down slowly in front of the window and not straight, but in a zigzag line .... Then I heard a low sound of something falling. I looked and saw a little iron box filled with dominoes. The box was closed but some of the dominoes lay next to it on the floor .... Another time I was sitting with Mr. Klein at the round table, while Eleonore stood with a cat in her arms at the book-stand. Mr. Klein unintentionally looked at the girl, and on this occasion noticed a dark grey shadow come from

behind her, pass along her right side and fall under our table upon the cushion at our feet. It was a tin box which had before stood on the washstand on the other side of the room. I had always the impression that a returning object of the kind was only again submitted to the normal laws of the physical world when it was perfectly itself again . . . . The foregoing shadow has nothing at all to do with the appearance of the object itself. I think that the impression which this moving riddle makes, is described best by the words: 'Hole in the world', which I used for it. (*British Journal of Psychical Research*, vol. 1, 1927, p. 148)

Now and again raps were heard in Eleonora's presence, but attempts to communicate with them failed. She developed, however, the faculty of automatic writing, by which means 'Dracu' was able to air his views and make comments upon current events. Unfortunately his intellectual equipment seemed to correspond precisely with that of the child herself. On three occasions a breathy and toneless voice, apparently independent of Eleonora, was heard to speak a few words. These generally reflected the child's interests of the moment.

The most important development, however, of this period was as follows. The poltergeist, whether or not it was 'Dracu', had always been fairly spiteful towards Eleonora. Things were thrown at her with painful violence; she was slapped, pushed to the ground, thrown out of bed; her hair was pulled out and her shoes filled with water; her favourite possessions were 'apported' away, and sometimes not returned; or if returned, returned in a damaged state. Now – from late March 1926 – she became the victim of a full-scale poltergeist assault. Her hands and fingers were repeatedly pricked as if with needles; sometimes real needles were stuck into her; she was roughly scratched on face, neck, arms and chest, leaving painful weals on her hypersensitive skin; she was sharply bitten on her hands and arm (sometimes the bite-marks were damp). It was true that the injured places were always ones she could easily reach herself. None the less the Countess felt sure that she had witnessed these phenomena under conditions in which fraud was impossible. For instance, on the afternoon of 25 March 1926, Professor Hans Hahn, Professor of Mathematics at the University of Vienna, came to the Countess's apartment to observe Eleonora. Eleonora was badly scratched.

As this phenomenon became more frequent we took Eleonore

between us and each of us held one of her hands, naturally in full light, as always. Then there appeared suddenly on her hands and forearms marks, which one could recognize only as bites . . . exactly as though she had been bitten by somebody . . . . These teethmarks were first visible as heavy red depressions in Eleonore's skin; later they would get quite as thick and as white as the scratches which had preceded them. There even came, on the left forearm which I held, six bites at once, alongside one another. In the course of the hour during which Professor Hahn and I sat with Eleonore at the round table she was bitten about twenty-five times, under the most rigorous conditions, as Professor Hahn declared himself ready to confirm to anybody.
(*Journal of the American SPR*, vol. 20, 1926, p. 595)

On 30 April 1926 there arrived in Vienna a prominent British psychical researcher, Harry Price. Price, an authority on conjuring, was extremely interested in the physical phenomena of mediumship, genuine or fraudulent, and like his friend Fritz Grunewald, had assembled a laboratory of physical instruments with which to study it. He is now best remembered among the general public for his books on the alleged haunting of Borley Rectory in Essex. He is a controversial figure, and accusations of dishonesty have been levelled against him in connection with Borley Rectory and one or two other cases. I can only say here that these allegations appear to me to be based upon very debatable evidence. It is clear, however, that Price, though an exceptionally able man, was too fond for the fastidious of sunning his by no means diminutive ego in the light of newspaper publicity. None the less he had every claim to be reckoned an expert in all matters to do with the unmasking of trickery, and his opinions about Eleonora deserve attention.

Price was introduced to Countess Wassilko-Serecki by mutual friends, and paid three visits to her flat. He observed both object-movements and the appearance of scratch and bite marks. He became 'convinced that some of the telekinetic phenomena [i.e. object-movements] witnessed by me were not the work of normal forces' – he had, for instance, seen a cushion move off a chair when both it and Eleonora were in his line of vision. About the bite and scratch marks he was much less certain, but he remained extremely interested. He invited Eleonora and the Countess to visit the National Laboratory of Psychical Research in London. This was an institution which, though supported by various distinguished persons, was largely created and run by

Price. The Countess and Eleonora arrived in London on 30 September 1926, and remained until 14 October.

On most of these days Eleonora attended at the laboratory for a substantial number of hours, sometimes with and sometimes without the Countess. A number of formal sittings were held, but for the rest of the time Eleonora was allowed to play with toys and otherwise amuse herself while Price and other members of the National Laboratory, and also certain pressmen, observed her. The object-movements and apport phenomena were weaker than they had been in Vienna, and one or two possible attempts at cheating were noticed. None the less Price and the Laboratory Council believed themselves to have demonstrated with Eleonora 'that under scientific test conditions movements of small objects without physical contact undoubtedly took place'. To describe and assess these alleged object-movements would take a fair amount of space, and I can only refer any reader who may be interested to Price's long report in the *Proceedings of the National Laboratory of Psychical Research*, vol. 1, 1927, or to the summary accounts in several of his popular works. In some cases objects were ostensibly apported from fairly distant rooms in which Eleonora had never set foot.

Bite and scratch marks were of frequent occurrence, and Price's photographs of them have been frequently reproduced. Some particularly striking ones came on the afternoon of 5 October in the absence of both Price and the Countess. Eleonora was being watched by two members of the National Laboratory, Col. W. W. Hardwick and Mr Robert Blair, by the representative of the *Daily News*, Mr E. Clephan Palmer, and by Price's secretary, Miss Lucie Kaye. Price quotes (p. 15) Col. Hardwick as follows:

> At 5.40, after tea Eleonore was tying up a box, when she gave a gasp and moved her right hand towards her left wrist – distinct teeth-marks appeared on her wrist, then scores like scratches appeared on her right forearm, cheeks and forehead. Shortly after, a series of marks like some form of letters appeared on her left forearm, all rising to distinct white inflammatory swellings within three or four minutes, fading slowly. The girl was under close observation, and could not have produced these herself by any normal means.

After Eleonora's return to the continent, the telekinetic and apport phenomena largely died away. The bite and scratch marks, etc., continued, with the addition of a further unpleasant manifestation – for which the Bristol case of 1761–2 provides a parallel – namely the appearance on Eleonora's skin of copious quantities of highly offensive spittle. This phenomenon, with others, was investigated from November 1926 to January 1927 by a Berlin committee, consisting of a zoologist, Professor Zimmer, and four medical men, one of whom, Dr Walther Kröner, published the committee's report and conclusions, together with a sample seance protocol, in the *Zeitschrift für Parapsychologie* for May 1927. The report is probably the most interesting Zugun document of this period. Sessions were held in the Charlottenburg *pension* where the Countess and Eleonora were staying; none the less the committee members were satisfied with the conditions of control. Eleonora was surrounded, in bright light, by watchful persons, and when phenomena began to happen her hands would be held by a controller on either side of her. Attempts at helping out the phenomena were not uncommon; the committee had the impression that these arose not from systematic and malign deceitfulness but from childish bad manners and prima-donna-ish vanity.

Samples of the spittle which now very frequently appeared on Eleonora's arm and face were subjected to chemical and to microscopic analyses. The substance was not a secretion of her skin; nor was it saliva fresh from her mouth, for the latter was relatively free of micro-organisms, while the substance found on her skin swarmed with staphylococci.

Kröner and his colleagues adduced various findings to show that the skin markings were of external and mechanical origin. In some instances of scratching the skin was actually torn. The bites would sometimes ooze blood. Eleonora's arms and face were smeared with greasepaint, and it was found that the greasepaint was ploughed aside when scratches were made. Sometimes the greasepaint alone would be furrowed, as though by scratches not strong enough to damage the skin. (Rather similar measures were taken by an investigating group in Vienna under Professor Richard Hoffman. Greasepaint was applied to Eleonora's lips and fingernails, and her arms were examined for it after markings appeared. See the *Journal of the American SPR*, vol. 21, 1927, p. 286.)

Here is the first part of Kröner's protocol, dictated at the time, of the committee's investigation on 12 December 1926:

9.45. Control was reinstituted and maintained until 10.15. Eleonora sat in a high backed club chair. Dr Kröner held the right hand uninterruptedly, Professor Zimmer the left. Both watched Eleonora carefully. Drs Bruck and Körber sat in front of Eleonora and observed her movements. The Countess, about 1 m. away from her, wrote at Dr Kröner's dictation, sitting at the table. She did not come into contact with the medium.

Bright illumination

9.46. Impress as of a press stud in crook of right elbow with urticaria (*urticariabildung*).

9.50. Wetting of right cheek in front of the ear and wetting of hair.

9.51. Eleonora winced and announced a wetting in the same place, but this could not be verified because of the previous wetting. Her face was wiped and then again examined for dampness. It was quite dry, no perspiration.

9.52. Inner side of right upper arm, 3 scratches as with finger nails. No excoriation.

10.00. Wetting of right cheek on the spot wiped dry before.

10.10 Bite on knuckles of right hand. Scratch as with fingernail on left collar-bone without excoriation. 3 scratches underneath the left jaw with urticaria (one after the other).

10.11. Scratch on front side of right lower arm without excoriation.

10.14. 4 long scratches, inner side of right upper arm, with roughening of the skin.

10.15. 3 short oblique scratches, narrower than formerly, as if done by pointed, sharp fingernails, with severe ragged removal of the skin, the right upper arm, outer side, under the sleeve. Zimmer had let go of the [left] hand, however the right arm was still held by Dr Kröner, and visual control by the three observers was maintained unaltered. A trick would undoubtedly have been detected.

After their visit to Berlin, Eleonora and the Countess went in January 1927 to Munich for a fortnight as the guest of Baron von Schrenck-Notzing. Various sittings were held, and a cine-film of the phenomena was made by the Emelka-Kultur-Gesellschaft ('Eku' company). A copy of this film is in the possession of the British Society for Psychical Research. Amongst other things it shows Eleonora's bare arms being held by investigators whilst she winces as if in pain; close-up shots are then given of the marks which had (presumably) just appeared.

Present at two of the Munich sittings had been Dr Hans Rosenbusch, a medical man of that city, interested in parapsychology and co-author with W. Gulat-Wellenburg and Count C. von Klinckowstroem of a recently published and highly critical volume on the alleged evidence for the physical phenomena of mediumship. He invited the Countess and Eleonora who had gone off to Nuremberg *en route* for Vienna, back to Munich for a sitting in his own home. This was held on 10 February 1927. On 20 February, Rosenbusch published in the *Berliner Tageblatt* an article in which he stated not only that he had detected Eleonora in fraud, but that he had detected the Countess in helping her. He invited the latter to disappear from the scene in silence.

It can be imagined that these accusations caused a mighty fluttering in the dovecots. The March issue of the *Zeitschrift für Parapsychologie* painted a touching picture of the Countess as a maligned and helpless woman. The Countess, however, was very far from helpless. She replied to Rosenbusch in great detail, citing her own notes of the sitting concerned, and she instituted legal proceedings against him. (These were eventually dismissed for technical reasons.) Her Viennese colleagues Professors Hans Hahn, Richard Hoffman, Hans Thirring and Karl Wolf, Dr Alfred Winterstein, and Michael Dumba, signed a statement that they had observed the phenomena in bright light under stringent conditions for many months without observing anything to incriminate the Countess. An apparently successful test sitting from part of which the Countess absented herself was held in Vienna by the above gentlemen and several others (*Zeitschrift für Parapsychologie*, April 1928). Rosenbusch countered by attacking the claims and competence of Price and Kröner (*Zeitschrift für kritischen Okkultismus*, vol. 3, 1928). Other well-known parapsychologists took sides. I have rather the impression that by this time the whole issue was becoming clouded by warfare between rival factions of German-speaking parapsychologists.

It is difficult to see anything very clearly through all this dust. But one thing is obvious. It was agreed by almost everyone that at this period Eleonora would sometimes attempt to 'assist' the phenomena. In fact the Countess claimed that she had warned Rosenbusch about this beforehand. There have, of course, been many other poltergeist agents apparently capable of producing genuine phenomena who sometimes cheat. The fact therefore that Rosenbusch and his colleagues stated that they had several times seen Eleonora cheat does not introduce any fresh element into one's assessment of the case. What does introduce a new element is the alleged discovery that the Countess Wassilko-Serecki was participating in the fraud. Evidence of the Countess's complicity would undermine or enormously complicate any evidence for paranormal phenomena which the Zugun case might be thought to provide in the period after January 1926.

Rosenbusch's allegations against the Countess are based on observations or supposed observations such as the following:

1 An operator of the Eku film company said that while the film of Eleonora was being made he saw the Countess, during a pause in the shooting, scratch Eleonora's left cheek through her hair, with the remark: 'Tidy your hair'. The next phenomenon was a scratch on the left cheek.

2 During the sitting of 10 February, at 6.55 p.m., the Countess stood up, looked at Eleonora's recently scratched left forefinger, and felt it with her left hand. Rosenbusch and a colleague, however, watched what the Countess did with her right hand, which held Eleonora's left hand. The Countess, they claimed, pressed her fingers into the back of Eleonora's upturned hand (her thumb was in sight on the palm). Three minutes later Eleonora winced and showed a curved indentation on the back of her hand (according to the Countess's notes this was a bite mark).

3 At 8.03 p.m. in the same sitting Rosenbusch and a colleague both saw the Countess, who was examining Eleonora's arm, make a cross-shaped movement with her finger on Eleonora's lower arm while the company was engaged in examining a mark made on Eleonora's hand at 7.50 p.m.

The Countess's replies to these accusations are in essence as follows:

1 She often tidied Eleonora's hair during breaks in the filming. In any case this accusation is at third hand.

2 How could Rosenbusch see through Eleonora's hand to discover precisely what was going on on its underside? Furthermore marks *never* appeared on the palmar side of Eleonora's hands and fingers. Therefore to examine any marking she (the Countess) would have held Eleonora's hand back uppermost, and her thumb would have lain on the *back* of the hand. Did Rosenbusch suppose that her fingers made the bite marks

through the thickness of Eleonora's hand or that her thumb suddenly sprouted eight teeth?

3 Her own notes mention no impression on the lower arm at 8.03 p.m., so she could not at the time have regarded it as a phenomenon (Rosenbusch's notes do not make it clear whether a phenomenon was claimed). Perhaps some unexpected movement of Eleonora's led her incautiously to grasp the arm. In that case she would certainly have said that it was a mistake and that any mark which had appeared should be discounted. But she could recall no such incident. She was, moreover, only sitting close to Eleonora because Rosenbusch had insisted that she did.

On the whole it seems to me that Rosenbusch's allegations must be set aside as not proved. His notes are far from clear and his observations, when examined carefully, are ambiguous. One must remember that the Countess was at this period in effect Eleonora's foster-mother, and was obviously accustomed to fuss over her a little, as any other mother of a teenage daughter might do. The movements and manipulations which a fussing mother carries out without thinking might very easily in a seance room setting confirm the worst suspicions of a man with Rosenbusch's powerful preconceived ideas (cf. the section on 'motivated seeing' in chapter 13). It is worth noting, as the Countess pointed out, that Rosenbusch has nothing to say about those occasions on which phenomena took place without any suspicious manoeuvres being observed by the attentive witnesses. He simply passes them by. He was pretty clearly one of those dedicated but tiresome persons, to be found alike amongst the sceptics and the credulous, who constantly chop and distort phenomena to fit them upon some preferred Procrustean bed. It is easy for such persons to convince themselves that they know all the answers; and they are not hesitant in attempting to convince others. They are, however, rarely to be relied upon in matters of fact; especially where the facts concerned come from that treacherous borderland where observation and inference meet and are prone to mingle.

Eleonora Zugun lost her powers, whatever they may have been, with the onset of the menses in the early summer of 1927. When last heard of, in the 1930s, she was running a successful hairdressing establishment in Czernowitz, Rumania.

In discussing these cases of poltergeist 'assault' I have more or less explicitly adopted a framework of thought which sees the phenomena, however obscure the mechanics of their production, as originating within the poltergeist agent, and as reflecting, therefore, emotions and ideas from some level of the agent's own personality. Harry Price discussed the bite and scratch marks in the Zugun case in this kind of way, comparing them to the 'stigmata' mirroring the marks of Christ's sufferings on the cross which have appeared on various holy persons, and to the blisters, reddenings of the skin, etc., said to have been produced in good hypnotic subjects by appropriate suggestions. The Countess Wassilko-Serecki, who was much influenced by psychoanalytic doctrines, went even further. She regarded the 'assaults' upon Eleonora as a form of self-punishment, due to a conflict between 'a very strongly developed sexual need', partly centred on her father, and an equally strong self-condemnation for these feelings. 'These psychic relations,' she says, 'exactly correspond to the typical examples of hysteria according to the psychoanalytical doctrine of Professor Freud, except one further step which would have to be taken: that under certain circumstances hysterical symptoms not only act within the organism of the subject but that they can also attain an activity in the objective outer world' (*British Journal of Psychical Research*, vol. 1, 1927, p. 149).

Mr George Zorab engages in analogous speculations with regard to the case of poltergeist assault at Sitoebondo in 1893, which had many features in common with the other cases discussed here.

Such interpretations of certain poltergeist cases are tempting and can be made to sound plausible. We shall have to consider them again later on. Meanwhile perhaps we should ask what findings can be advanced against them? Could 'Dracu' after all have been an entity independent of Eleonora, or the 'witch's spirit' an entity independent of Molly and Dobby Giles? No doubt something could be made here of the ability apparently possessed by the 'spirit' in the Giles case to scratch out answers questions posed in classical languages which the girls did not understand, and of the ESP which it was supposed to have exhibited. However, the latter finding would obviously tend to lessen the value of the former. In any case the scratching entity (whether incarnate or discarnate) could no doubt have picked up clues from the reactions of persons present. In both the Giles and the Zugun cases there are (as I have pointed out) serious difficulties in regarding the bite and scratch marks as internally generated stigmata. Perhaps it is possible to conceive mechanical forces centring on the organism of a medium or poltergeist agent but capable of acting at a distance from it or of turning back upon it from the outside. Sometimes, however, in the Zugun case physical effects (the removal or delivery of apported objects) ostensibly took place at some distance from Eleonora's body, several rooms away, past several locked doors, etc., and it is not easy to think here in terms of a mechanical force centring on her body. In fact if truth were told we hardly have the terms in which to think at all.

8 Poltergeists and the dead

In previous chapters I have described a number of poltergeist cases in which the phenomena seemed as though directed or stage-managed by an intelligence, often a mischievous or somewhat malicious one. Not infrequently some kind of communication has been established with this intelligence, which responds to requests, raps out answers to questions, etc., and occasionally even produces an articulate voice. When the phenomena, or alleged phenomena, are in these ways more or less intelligent and responsive, it is only natural that persons whose curiosity overcomes their fear should invite the communicating intelligence to give an account of itself; occasionally, indeed, that intelligence has seemed to press such an account upon the reluctant spectators. I have already set before the reader cases in which the intelligence claimed to be that of a deceased person and cases in which it claimed to be that of an evil spirit or non-human entity. There have also been one or two cases in which the intelligence was ostensibly that of a living person or of some dissociated part of the agent's personality.

In this chapter I shall outline a few further cases in which the operative intelligence has claimed, or appeared, to be that of a deceased person, and in the next chapter I shall deal with various cases in which it has claimed to be that of a demon or other non-human entity. The correctness or otherwise of these claims is not currently our concern – this half of the book is largely illustrative. But it must be borne in mind that the bizarre stories we are about to embark upon are not here just for their entertainment value. They have theoretical interest for at least three reasons: first, because certain of the stories in these categories are *prima facie* so preposterous that they raise in a specially acute form important questions about the reliability of human testimony concerning unusual or alarming events; second because some people have made serious attempts to advance one or other form of the discarnate spirit hypothesis as a general explanation of poltergeist phenomena; and thirdly because other theorists have argued that the fact, or supposed fact, that poltergeists in one historical or cultural setting will claim to be demons, and in another will claim to be deceased persons, suggests that we must turn for an explanation to the agency, conscious or otherwise, of living human beings.

Under what circumstances, then, might one say that poltergeist phenomena claimed, or ostensibly indicated, an origin from some still surviving defunct human being? I can think of at least five possible sorts of cases of which this might be said. All of them have been more or less exemplified in practice. They are as follows:

1 In a few cases, one or more of the persons present (but usually not all the persons present) have stated that they saw the recognized phantasm of a deceased person perpetrating the phenomena, i.e. throwing the stones which actually were thrown, moving furniture which actually was moved, etc. The Poona case described in chapter 6 may perhaps serve as an example.

2 Most frequent have been cases in which the poltergeist has, as it were, established ostensible communication by means of the phenomena themselves, and directly stated its identity with some deceased person. The commonest means of communication has been a code of raps or scratches, as in the Lyons (1526) case, the Bristol (1761–2) case and the Hydesville (1848) case. In a smaller number of cases, ranging from that at Lagny (1210) to that at Kuala Kangsar (about 1955), the vehicle of communication has been an articulate voice. Among such cases is the most famous of all medieval ghost stories, that of the 'grisly ghost of Guy' (Alais, 1324), for which see Thurston's *Ghosts and Poltergeists* (London, 1953).

3 It is possible to imagine that the phenomena might indicate a certain deceased person as their source in ways less direct than the foregoing. For instance it might be that a poltergeist disturbed only the belongings of a certain deceased person, or other objects of interest and importance to him; or that it imitated his special knock, or other sounds characteristic of him; and so forth. There have been one or two cases approximating to this kind. In the Cambridge (1966) case objects of interest to a certain deceased person were interfered with; in a case at Leipzig (1931) the characteristic footsteps of a certain deceased person were heard; in a case in London, St Pancras (1846), was heard the characteristic knocking of a deceased lady's leather-padded stick.

4   One might suppose that a connection was indicated between poltergeist phenomena and a certain deceased person if those phenomena appeared to manifest desires, purposes and interests characteristic of a certain deceased person, and not especially characteristic of anyone still alive and present at the scene. It is not easy to find candidates for inclusion under this heading. Most of the ones I have come across are far from clear-cut, and belong in that dubious borderland where cases of poltergeists merge into cases of haunted houses. In one or two instances, the phenomena have shown what could be interpreted as resentment at changes made in the dwelling of a deceased person since his death (Oberbayern, 1928), and occasionally one reads of a case in which it is as though a particular deceased person has exhibited concern over the disposal of his former belongings (London, St Pancras, 1846; Little Minories, 1679), or has besought religious ceremonies of a sort which he favoured when alive (Vöst, 1932). None of the cases concerned is very strong.

5   If a case has one or more of the features listed under headings 1–4 above, one might reasonably say that the spook claims to be, or indicates or implies or inadvertently reveals that it is, some surviving portion or aspect of a deceased human being. (I am of course here referring only to the 'externals' of the phenomena, the form that they take; I am not expressing an opinion as to the reality which may be behind the externals.) Now the impressiveness of any such claim or indication is in many cases considerably dented by the following circumstance. Although the intelligence 'behind' the phenomena purports to be that of a deceased person, the actual occurrence of the phenomena seems to depend largely or entirely upon the presence of a particular living agent or 'medium'. In fact the phenomena follow that person from place to place, as they did in for instance the Lyons (1526) case which I outlined in chapter 2. This makes it plausible to propose that the phenomena, whatever the immediate mechanism by which they are produced, do not really originate from a deceased person, but rather have the appearance of such an origin stamped upon them by the agent or medium for obscure and probably unconscious psychological reasons. If, therefore, we can show with respect to some case which exhibits one or more of the features listed under 1–4 above that the phenomena are, additionally, to a greater or lesser

extent independent of the organism or mind of a single central agent or medium, we shall both greatly strengthen the superficial impression which the phenomena create of originating from a deceased person, and, of course, make it more arguable that they do in fact have a cause independent or partially independent of any living person. *Prima facie* this independence of an agent could be suggested in one or more of three ways:

(a) The phenomena might be totally independent of the presence or absence of any individual agent or medium.

(b) The phenomena, whilst maintaining a certain consistency in respect of features 1–4 above, might manifest now through the agency of one person, now through that of another person, and so on.

(c) The phenomena might appear to originate from an intelligence capable of communicating information in some way or another, and the information thus communicated might significantly exceed the stock of information possessed by any supposed agent, especially about the doings, circumstances and life history of the deceased person supposed to be communicating.

Cases exhibiting at least one of features 1–4 above are relatively common; it is, however, not at all easy to find cases which exhibit at least one of features 1–4 above *together with* at least one of features 5(a)–(c). So far as most early cases are concerned we do not have enough details to tell whether or not they exhibited any of features 5(a)–(c). However, on the face of it, a case which took place at Oppenheim in West Germany in 1620 possesses features 2, 4 and 5(a). The case is scarcely a strong one; but since various brief and totally garbled accounts appeared in the literature of nineteenth-century Spiritualism, and passed thence into Conan Doyle's *History of Spiritualism* (London, 1926), I shall briefly describe it. Its source is a Latin manuscript of the 1620s, composed by a Premonstratensian Father of the Abbey of Toussaints in the Black Forest – presumably the *curé* who appears in the story. I have so far been unable to trace a copy of this manuscript (though one may well still exist). It is, however, translated or paraphrased in the later editions of Dom Augustin Calmet's *Traité sur les apparitions des anges* . . . (3rd edn, Paris, 1751; English translation, sometimes inaccurate, as *The Phantom*

World, London, 1850). In his day Calmet was a noted scholar, and it is reasonable to suppose that he has given an accurate account of the contents of the manuscript. (Incidentally, Calmet's book, just mentioned, was chiefly instrumental in acquainting Western Europe with Eastern European superstitions concerning vampires; it is quite possible that but for Calmet, who took, however, a rationalistic viewpoint about vampire stories, the screen would not have known Count Dracula and his successors and imitators.) The story is as follows.

In November 1620 there died near the city of Oppenheim a wealthy burgess named Humbert Birck. On the Saturday after his funeral, 'certain noises' were heard in the house where he had lived with his first wife (this lady had died, and he had re-married). The master of this house was now Birck's brother-in-law. Suspecting the origin of the sounds, he said 'If you are Humbert, my brother-in-law, rap three times on the wall'. There came three raps and no more. The noises were also heard at the local fountain, and frightened the neighbourhood. They consisted of raps, whistles, groans, and sounds as of a person in lamentation. An articulate voice was also, it appears, sometimes heard. After about six months, these disturbances suddenly ceased; but when the anniversary of Birck's death had come and gone, they were resumed more strongly than before. Birck's brother-in-law then plucked up courage to ask the *soi-disant* Birck what he wanted. A hoarse and low voice replied 'Bring the *curé* and my children on Saturday'. The *curé*, who was ill, could not come until the Monday, when he arrived with a considerable number of people. The entity, speaking intelligibly, asked for masses, and that alms should be given in his name, and expressed a wish to alter some of the arrangements made for the distribution of his property. Asked why he haunted that particular house, he replied that he was constrained to do so by sorcery and maledictions. He repeated with difficulty the *Pater Noster* and the *Ave Maria*, attributing the difficulty to the presence of an evil spirit who prevented him from telling the *curé* many other things.

The *curé*, a Premonstratensian canon (the Premonstratensians did a good deal of pastoral work) went to his Abbey of Toussaints on 22 January 1622 to obtain the opinion of his superior. He came back with three assistants and went to the house, which was thronged with people. The master of the house asked the spirit to rap on the wall. He rapped rather gently. The master then requested him to fetch a stone and knock louder. There was a pause, as if a stone were being fetched, and louder raps were heard. Then the master whispered in his neighbour's ear that the spirit should rap seven times. Immediately seven raps were heard. Next day three masses which the spirit had asked for were said, and his other requests were undertaken. The phenomena ceased.

Even this distant and dubious tale has some characteristic points. However, my professed aim in this part of the book is to illustrate the various kinds and aspects of poltergeist phenomena so far as possible from diaries, court records and other contemporary and detailed documents. For our present purpose the best we can do here is perhaps the exceedingly curious Charlottenburg case of 1929. This case, of which we have a rather detailed day by day account, exhibits features 2, 3 and 5(b) of my list above. It took place in the early months of 1929 in Charlottenburg, near Berlin. The principal investigator was a Berlin medical man, Dr Paul Sünner, who was at that time editor of the *Zeitschrift für Parapsychologie*. His account of the case was published in the October 1929 issue of that periodical, and was followed in 1932 by two further articles of a more theoretical and reflective kind. I should suppose that Sünner was a man of Spiritualistic inclinations. He does not, however, adopt in his record of the phenomena any particular standpoint, Spiritualist or other.

Sünner's account, though pretty full, requires a little disentangling. It takes the form of a day by day narrative of his own activities whilst investigating the case. Since he kept a number of balls simultaneously in the air, the effect is somewhat confusing. I shall abandon a strict chronology of events and separate out the major themes. They appear to be these:

1 The setting of the major events; and the people involved in them.
2 Phenomena witnessed in a certain flat by the occupants thereof.
3 Phenomena witnessed in that flat by outsiders.
4 Phenomena observed by Sünner and his colleagues.
5 Apparently related phenomena which happened in other places.

6 Unrelated psychic experiences had by members of the families involved.

I shall say nothing about theme 6 – the unrelated psychic experiences – except to remark that the families concerned seem to have been more than usually prone to spontaneous psychic experiences, a fact which might by some be thought to have a bearing on certain aspects of the case. The remaining themes I shall treat as follows. First of all I shall describe the setting and the people especially involved; then I shall describe the phenomena alleged to have taken place in that setting (2, 3 and 4 lumped together); and lastly I shall mention certain curious but ostensibly related events said to have happened in other places (theme 5).

The main setting, then, of this peculiar case was a third-floor tenement flat in what seems to have been a fairly poor quarter of Berlin. The flat contained a kitchen, a toilet, a bedroom, and a living room, all opening, in that order, from a single corridor. The occupants were Albert Regulski, a linoleum layer by trade, his wife, and their three children, Walter, aged nineteen, Lucie, aged eleven (felicitously described by Sünner as the *Spukmädchen*), and Stanislaus, aged eight. They were devout Catholics, and Sünner, who got to know them well, formed a very favourable impression of their uprightness and love of truth.

Little Lucie, said to be rather weak for her age, was much attached to her uncle, Hans Regulski, Albert's brother. On New Year's Day 1929, Hans Regulski fell ill with a severe bout of influenza; and on 8 January he died. When Lucie heard the news, she wept a great deal; and that night came the first poltergeist phenomena. Herr Regulski and Walter three times heard a whistling in the corridor, and also a rapping on the toilet wall. When Lucie went to the toilet she saw standing there the phantasm of her late uncle. He carried a glittering scythe. She saw no head, but where the face would have been were two gleaming fiery eyes. Not, one would suppose, every little girl's vision of her favourite uncle.

During the next four weeks rappings on walls and doors were frequent and powerful, and took place by day and by night. Frau Regulski tried to establish communication with them. She named various names, and when she got to Hans Regulski's, confirmation of his presence was given by particularly strong raps. Objects in the house were also moved. For example, shortly before Sünner's first visit, a tin box containing curtain rings, which stood in the wardrobe in the bedroom, was shaken, and was transported through the air to the floor, where it moved as if dancing.

Sünner learned of the case through the family's priest, Pfarrer Hillebrandt, and went to the flat for the first time on the afternoon of 2 February 1929. Present were Frau Regulski, Herr Kruswicki (Frau Regulski's brother-in-law) and the three children. Lucie was in bed with a cold. At 2.30 p.m. Sünner moved the rest of the family out of the bedroom into the kitchen, and himself watched Lucie from the corridor through the half-open door. He kept up a conversation with those in the kitchen. When he turned his head away for a moment, Lucie gave a shriek and, running in, he discovered that various small objects within her reach had been disturbed. He felt sure that she had moved them herself. She was taken from her cot into her mother's big bed, and Sünner resumed his vigil as before. Suddenly Lucie shrieked and called for her mother. Raps, as if made by a hand, were coming from the wooden bedstead on which she lay. Sünner and the others went into the room. The raps continued for several minutes. The sounds came from the footboard, which Lucie, who lay with her legs under cover, could by no means reach. Also she remained visibly still for the duration of the rappings. Sünner left about 3.00 p.m.

He returned on Monday 4 February, shortly after 4.30 p.m., to hear great tales of what had happened in the interim. The drawer and little door of a night-table at the bedhead had been opened, and their contents scattered, before the very eyes of the parents. On the Sunday afternoon, when Lucie was alone in the bedroom, two chairs had sprung onto her parents' beds and danced there. Lucie had called her parents into the room and 'the phenomenon was unimpeachably seen by them. It seemed as though a hand held the chairleg through the bed-cover of the empty bed and moved the chair'. The parents had three times seen a chair move through the living room with a loud noise. A metal ashtray had fallen to the kitchen floor when Lucie was not in the room.

On Tuesday 5 February, Sünner went to the Regulskis' flat again at 7.30 p.m., accompanied by his wife and a lawyer friend. They heard various stories of events earlier in the day, and learned of a new, and peculiar, phenomenon. Over the head end of the cot or child's bed in which Lucie ordinarily slept was an iron bar, bent into a right angle (it was meant to support a canopy). From this bar there hung a little, furry ape-doll. During the whole day this little doll had made dancing movements, all its limbs going strongly. It had also nodded its head. It seemed especially to stir when music was played on a mouth organ.

Sünner and his party at once attempted to verify this phenomenon. They stood in the bedroom, which was lit by a petroleum lamp, whilst the members of the family – except Lucie, who was in the little cot – stood back towards the door. They established beforehand that treading on the floor did not cause any strong movements of the doll. Walter and his father summoned Hans to dance, and then Walter began to play on the mouth organ. Gradually the doll set itself in motion, and danced in a more and more lively fashion, up and down, this way and that, until the movements became positively violent. The movements

> did not cease, although Herr Dr B. assured himself, by holding it with his hand, that the bar on which the doll hung was absolutely still. Meanwhile the child lay quiet and motionless throughout; indeed from time to time I uncovered the bed-cushion to check the stillness of her legs and feet. Her hands were in sight throughout . . . . The movements were not broken off when the doll was lifted down from its frame for a while to show that no thread ran from it to the bedstead or the girl; it was taken down before our eyes, and the thread on which it hung exhibited.

Later on the lamp was put out in the corridor so that only a diffused light entered the room. Under these conditions they heard raps and cracks, and a long-drawn-out light whistling at the child's bedhead. When they left the room they heard a noise and, returning, found that a chair near Lucie had been moved.

On Thursday 7 February, Sünner went to see Pfarrer Hillebrandt's cousin, Fraulein Margarethe Anders, who had visited the Regulskis' flat with a friend, Fraulein Martha Brewka, on the evening of 1 February. These ladies, looking into the bedroom, saw various small objects thrown off a table at the foot of Lucie's bed. They included two books. As one of these lay on the floor, its pages were turned over as if by a hand. Their most impressive experience was this. The child was in her mother's bed, and the two ladies stood at the foot. Suddenly the bedcover lifted itself up in the air as though a force were active beneath it. It assumed somewhat the shape of a head. Pressed down, it many times reared up again (there are seventeenth-century parallels for this phenomenon). The child could not have produced this effect, for the spot was out of reach of her feet, which were occasionally held through the bedclothes. Suddenly the big coverlet was dragged off the bed from the foot end. They replaced it, and Fraulein Brewka sat on the bed near the child's breast, with the remark that now it could not be pulled away again. Suddenly it was dragged towards the bed end with such violence that the lady came too and was catapulted off the bed. Fraulein Anders, who had at first been highly sceptical, guaranteed that neither the child nor members of her family could have produced these phenomena. She was not prepared to say the same of some rather suspicious object-movements which took place as soon as Lucie was left alone. However, she thought Lucie to be honest.

Leaving Fraulein Anders, Sünner went back to the Regulskis' flat, where he heard tell of further disturbances of doors, cupboards and drawers. It appeared, furthermore, that Fraulein Brewka had the previous evening spent four hours there, and had for a long time watched the movements of the little ape-doll. Someone had lifted it down and laid it on Lucie's bedcover, where it had made clear movements as if to creep under and join her. This must surely be one of the most grotesque phenomena ever alleged to have happened in a poltergeist case!

Sünner himself observed no phenomena on this visit. However, he and his wife and various colleagues whom he brought with him witnessed phenomena on four subsequent occasions, viz. 11 February, 27 February, 7 March and 11 March. Since the raps, movements of the ape-doll, and movements of the bed and other furniture were very similar on all these occasions, I shall describe only the most interesting evening, that of 7 March. It should also be said that throughout the whole of this period the Regulskis themselves continued to report poltergeist phenomena – raps, object-movements, movements of the bedclothes, sounds like groaning, the actuation of the miaowing mechanism of a clockwork cat.

On 7 March at 7.30 p.m. there assembled at the Regulskis' a party of five members of the 'Berlin Medical Society for Parapsychic Investigation', viz. Drs Sünner, Neugarten, Schwab and Schmidt, and Fräulein Dr Wygodzinski. Frau Regulski was alone with Lucie and the little Stanislaus. Presents of storybooks and chocolate put Lucie in a good mood, and she lay down on the child's bed in the bedroom. Rappings began almost immediately on the wall by this bed – it was the wall which separated the bedroom from the living room. The new visitors went into the living room and examined the wall from that side by the light of a petroleum lamp. They also attempted, unsuccessfully, to imitate the sounds by striking both sides of the wall with their hands. While they hit the wall from the far side, spook rappings were now and then heard.

After this the bedroom lamp was taken out and placed in the corridor, as before, leaving a diffused light, which, however, reached throughout the room. The visitors gathered round the bed, and phenomena set in in good earnest. Powerful blows and joltings came against the head and foot ends of the bed. When 'Hans' was spoken to, the dangling ape-doll began lively rocking movements. These were unimpeachably seen by all present. Fräulein Dr Wygodzinski sat on a chair at the head end of the child's bed, and assured herself by manual control that Lucie did not move – as could indeed be observed by all. Various curious sounds were repeatedly heard – a metallic clanging from the foot of the bed; a sound of planing from the space between wall and bed (Hans had been a carpenter); and the long-drawn-out whispering whistle, which had been heard before. When Walter arrived, and played on the harmonica, the swinging and shaking of the doll worked up to a new and wild momentum.

Particularly impressive to all present was the displacement of the foot end of the bed away from the wall. The movement was seen by Dr Schmidt, who was sitting at a table by the foot of the bed, as a jump-like uplifting of the white bedstead. It happened very quickly, and with a noise as the castors scraped over the floor, leaving marks. All those present convinced themselves of the bed's weightiness by pushing it back again. It had moved 40 cm away from the wall.

From time to time were heard rappings and blows on the wall and the iron part of the bedstead. Occasionally they would come in immediate response to questions. 'All convinced themselves of the unimpeachable reality of these spook-phenomena, which throughout could undoubtedly not have been produced by the child with her hands or feet or in some other way.'

There was yet another curious and novel phenomenon that evening. Dr Schmidt had brought with him a table bell, which he put under the foot end of the bed. Sünner likewise put a slate and a piece of chalk there. They asked 'Hans' to move the bell and write on the slate, and Lucie lent her voice to their requests. After a while they clearly heard the bell, and Sünner drew out the slate. On the upper side was a large chalked cross. Sünner replaced the slate with the blank side (which had been shown to everyone) uppermost. All present were unanimous that the child could not have reached the floor at the foot end by thrusting a hand or foot through the lattice of her bed, which had again been pushed right up against the wall. Sünner writes

> I stood next to Fraulein Dr Wygodzinski [who was at the bedhead], next me on my right were Dr Neugarten and Dr Schwab, whilst Dr Schmidt sat at the table [which was at the foot of the bed]. Frau Regulski, who only came in now and then, and was mostly busy in the kitchen, remained, when she came into the room, standing by the stove or by the door, which was half open. After a short while the bell rang clearly, as a sign that our wish had been fulfilled. I drew the slate carefully out. The second side was covered in jumbled lines, which were interpreted by several persons present as an attempted 'H'. Below is a photograph of this rare phenomenon of direct writing.

At 9.30 p.m. the party made ready to go. While Dr Schwab and Dr Neugarten were standing by Lucie's bed, taking their leave, an object dropped on the bed before their very eyes. It was Sünner's tape measure, in a metal case, which had previously been lying on the table.

From this time onward, the phenomena in the Regulskis' flat, purportedly caused by uncle Hans, seem to have gradually declined. Sünner took Lucie to other houses and sittings were held, but without result, except that on one occasion she passed into a sleep-like state from which she could not be awakened, and in which she seemed to converse with her dead uncle. On 1 April Lucie attended her first communion and was confirmed, and after that the phenomena pretty well ceased. Later in the year, the Regulskis' landlord, who feared for the value of his property, tried, but failed to have them evicted from their flat.

Lucie was never detected in fraud, but the circumstances of some of the phenomena were such as to arouse one's keenest suspicions. It was very noticeable that small objects were prone to be moved or flung the moment observers looked away. On the other hand, if Sünner and his colleagues are to be believed they had her under close observation during several series of sufficiently peculiar events. To have deceived them under these conditions she would have had to have been a very clever little thing indeed, or to have been in collusion with others of her family (of which there is no hint). If genuine and fraudulent phenomena were here mixed, it would not be the first case in which that has apparently happened. The state of mind of the poltergeist agent during outbursts of phenomena has been insufficiently explored, and Lucie had, of course, recently received a profound emotional shock. In at least one recent case (Newark, New Jersey, 1961) in which certain phenomena seem to have been genuine, the agent also perpetrated fraudulent phenomena of which he did not seem to be fully aware.

But Lucie Regulski was not the only member of uncle Hans's family circle to whom or through whom he ostensibly manifested after his death, nor was the Regulskis' flat the only scene of his supposed *post mortem* activities. A total of no less than seven persons, excluding Frau Regulski and Walter, and Hans's four-year-old daughter, witnessed what they regarded as phenomena produced by the deceased Hans, in five separate locations other than the Regulskis' flat. Sünner, whose persistence was perhaps more notable than his scepticism, himself interviewed six of these seven persons; and he records the results of these interviews in due sequence in his chronological account.

On 27 February 1929, he went to visit Hans Regulski's widow, who had a little girl aged four, and a little girl of one. Staying in her small flat were her brother and sister, Hans and Elisabeth Pischkowski, who were also present at the interview. Since Hans's death, his widow had observed various strange happenings in the flat. For instance, about ten days after Hans's death, towards 2.00 a.m., she heard a sound as if the key of the flat door had been turned. Then she heard steps move along the corridor, and someone came into her bedroom. A hollow voice said 'Dear wife, only look carefully after the children and give them plenty of milk to drink'. She saw nothing, having pulled the bedclothes over her face, but a cold hand was placed on her brow. She thought she recognized her husband's characteristic footstep. She heard the steps and voice again on another night, when she was lying on the sofa in the living room. Her brother and sister claimed that they had often heard voices and footsteps like Hans's. They had also heard the rattling of a bunch of keys. The brother, sleeping on the living room sofa, was awakened by a repeated rushing and roaring. The little girl of four maintained that at nights she had from time to time seen and heard her father. Sporadic odd happenings – raps, rattlings, cold breezes, a luminous appearance, the movement of a match-box – apparently continued in the widow's flat until at least July, when Sünner paid another visit.

Sünner was also told that Hans had manifested at the home of a married sister a day or two after his death. In bright daylight a kitchen chair was raised into the air and beaten three times on the floor.

After leaving the widow's flat on 27 February, Sünner called on Hans's cousin and good friend, Frau Hackenberg, another pious Catholic. Early one morning, shortly after Hans's death while she was lying in bed, she heard footsteps in the corridor outside. Shortly afterwards she clearly felt one of her feet lifted up and dropped again. She had once done the same thing to Hans with a joking remark, and the action was one calculated to recall him to her memory. On another occasion, when she was lying on the sofa, someone pulled the coverlet over her feet.

On 21 March, Sünner went to see Albert Regulski's wife's sister, Frau Kruswicki, who told him that when Walter Regulski, Albert's eldest son, was with her shortly after Hans's death, they both saw a matchbox fly from outside against the window of the room. It made a loud noise, and stayed there a moment as though held by a hand.

From Frau Kruswicki's, Sünner went to visit the wife of a nephew of Hans Regulski. Soon after uncle Hans's death, this young Frau Regulski had seen a handkerchief, which was lying on a flower box made by him, float to the ground. There it was spread out as if by a hand. Furthermore their dog's chain was more than once broken or cut through during the night, and the dog himself was greatly alarmed.

What we are to make of cases such as this is a topic for later discussion. Here it may simply be remarked that when a number of persons, several of whom were clearly of a 'psychic' predisposition, separately have after the death of someone known to them all odd experiences which they attribute to the deceased, we are not driven very far towards having to accept this explanation. The case would have been notably stronger if 'uncle Hans' had exhibited a common purpose in his various manifestations.

9 Poltergeists and daemons

In this chapter I have adopted the archaic spelling 'daemon' instead of the more conventional 'demon'. I have done so because in popular thought 'demons' are quintessentially evil, whereas according to older traditions the term 'daemon' (δαιμων) may be used of any discarnate non-human intelligence or agency. The latter usage is preferable for our purposes, for in this age the primary question is as to the existence of discarnate non-human intelligences of whatever kind; the question of whether or not some among these putative beings are sufficiently wicked to fulfil the specifications laid down by Christian demonologists is obviously secondary. Though indeed, it might be observed that whilst Christians of many denominations have believed that we live surrounded by invisible hordes of sly demons continually prompting us to evil

> Christian, dost thou feel them,
> How they work within?

not a few Christians have thought it probable that there are differing degrees of turpitude even among demons. The thirteenth-century satirist Walter Map (quoted in Lea's *Materials towards a History of Witchcraft*, vol. I, pp. 104–5) represents a fallen angel as speaking thus:

> Far from us are robberies of property, the overthrowings of cities, the thirst of blood, and the greed for souls, and to desire more than we are able to perform. We are quite satisfied to indulge our lawlessness without occasioning death. We are (I confess) suited for jests and mockery, we arrange illusions, manufacture imagings, create phantasms, so that the truth having been hidden, a vain and ridiculous quarrel may spring up. We can do everything which tends towards laughter, and nothing which tends towards tears. For I am among those exiles from heaven, who without coadjutor or agreement to the sin of Lucifer drifted foolishly after the supporters of the crime.

If poltergeist phenomena are the work of discarnate non-human spirits, those spirits must surely be ones thus lukewarm in wickedness. In fact a recent Catholic writer, Sir Shane Leslie, offers the following explanation of why exorcisms so often fail to subdue poltergeists: 'Exorcism is aimed at Satan and a poltergeist is on a lower or say less sinister level'. Christian views with regard to discarnate non-human intelligences have thus been fairly accommodating, and some writers (of whom Defoe is perhaps the most famous) have combined Christian belief with the opinion that apparitions, poltergeists, premonitory dreams, etc., are the work of spirits neither angelic nor demonic, but as it were morally neutral. At least one talking poltergeist (the famous but implausible 'Bell witch', Adams, 1817–21) has given such an account of its own status; which brings me back to my original point – that the term 'daemon', being of wider scope, is preferable for most purposes to the term 'demon'.

It might reasonably be asked at this point why I am bothering with these absurd issues. For it is widely agreed by rational persons today that daemons, good, bad, or morally indifferent, do not exist. It is true, of course, that the last few decades have seen the revival of various superstitions, and that certain clergymen have managed to obtain publicity, and to convince themselves that there remains a job for them to do, by becoming almost professional exorcists (I use this term loosely) of mentally disturbed persons who believe themselves possessed or obsessed, or of houses which the nervous occupants suppose haunted by discarnate entities of malicious bent. But when one investigates the evidence which these clergymen advance in support of the view that daemons indeed exist, one finds not a clear statement of what would constitute such evidence, and why, followed by quantities of evidence of this kind, but simply interpretations of, or ways of looking at, phenomena which could be interpreted or looked at in many other kinds of ways, including ways that have the advantage of according with the general drift of modern science. The same criticisms could, of course, be levelled at psychoanalysis; but that is of itself sufficient to put the exorcists out of court – or so the argument might run.

My reply here is that there are at least two good reasons for looking at the supposed connection between daemons and certain poltergeist cases. The first is that there have undoubtedly been some poltergeist cases in which the phenomena have presented what may be called the facade or outward form of daemonic agency, and that since our concern is with all aspects of the ostensible phenomena that have been labelled 'poltergeists', and not with some subset of them selected for reasons of easier credibility or of theoretical convenience, these cases must be looked at and their possible significance considered. The second is one that I have already mentioned, namely that some authorities have attached significance to the fact or supposed fact that since the beginning of the Spiritualist movement in the middle of the last century, poltergeists which have 'communicated' by raps and so forth, have mostly done so in the guise of deceased human beings, whereas in earlier centuries, when the religious climate was different, the communications have more often purported to come from daemons. I shall take up each of these matters in turn.

First of all, then, let us examine some sample poltergeist cases in which the phenomena present the outward appearance of being daemonically inspired. Now a preliminary problem here is obviously that of deciding when we shall and shall not say that a case presents this sort of 'outward form'. It is, at a certain level, not too difficult (as we saw in the last chapter) to lay down criteria of when a case might reasonably be said to have the appearance of originating from a particular deceased person. But these criteria do not, for the most part, have analogues which could be applied to cases in which a daemon is supposedly at work. We might, perhaps, with Christian notions about devils in mind, look for indications of superhuman wickedness; but it is difficult to imagine any degree of wickedness which could truly be rated beyond human capacity, and it is certain that no poltergeist, daemonic or otherwise, has ever attained it. All in all, I can think of no better criteria than the following decidedly inadequate ones. We may say that in any poltergeist case the phenomena present the 'outward form' of daemonic origin if (a) 'communication' is established with the phenomena, and the communicating intelligence claims to be that of a daemon, and (b) the phenomena seem to be at least to some extent independent of any particular living person. Such independence could be manifested either through the phenomena taking place without regard to the presence or absence of particular individuals; or through their exhibiting in some direction or another (e.g. ESP, knowledge of foreign languages) powers greatly transcending those of any person on the scene; or, best of all, both.

There is no doubt that in a few poltergeist cases – not as many, however, as has been sometimes supposed – these criteria have been fulfilled. I have selected one case for detailed description. It might, perhaps, be more nearly correct to say that it has selected itself, since in no other case have I found anything even approximating to the contemporary diaries and court records upon which I have been endeavouring to concentrate in this survey. And 'approximating' is perhaps the operative word. By a fortunate chance, however, this case is very little known, and is, in addition, one of the most bizarre and the most violent in the literature. Even persons richly endowed with credulity concerning such matters may find that it taxes their resources. It is perhaps the most implausible of the many implausible stories with which we have to deal.

The case in question took place in a Neapolitan monastery, that of the Hieronymites (an ascetic order of hermits), between 4 May 1696 and 30 March 1697. The phenomena centred around a young novice named Carlo Maria Vulcano. He was, we learn from surviving records, of good family, and had entered the monastery aged sixteen, on 22 December 1693. The case was recorded by one of the brothers (we do not know which) who seems to have kept notes of the occurrences, and his account survives (or survived) in two identical contemporary manuscripts, entitled *Caso successo in Napoli, nell'anno 1696 a 4 maggio nella casa dei P.P. Gerolomini* (Case which happened in Naples, in the year 1696 on the 4th of May in the house of the Hieronymite Fathers). One of these manuscripts was obtained by a well-known Italian writer on psychic subjects, Francesco Zingaropoli, and was published by him with introduction and notes in a small and extremely rare book *Gesta di uno 'spirito' nel monastero dei P.P. Gerolomini in Napoli* (Naples, 1904).

The first stirrings of trouble in this case were heard on the night of 4 May 1696 when some stones were thrown in a corridor from which opened the sleeping chambers of Carlo Maria and other novices. The next night Carlo had no sooner retired than there came from the corridor a great commotion of falling stones. Carlo, his fellow novices, and *maestro* Squillante, the master of the novices, left their rooms, and searched the corridor. They found nothing but the stones on the ground.

However, as soon as they returned to their rooms they heard stones rain down once more. A little later Carlo, by that time in bed, heard movements in his room, and then a plaintive voice that said 'Give me a *Pater Noster* for the love of God'. Terrified, he rushed out, screaming 'Jesus, Jesus, help me, help me'. The other novices, with *maestro* Squillante, came to his rescue. Eventually the *maestro* told him not to be frightened, and went to bless the room. Carlo lay down again in his clothes, with the door open and with a light. However

> although he wished to go to sleep he saw enter through the door a [figure wearing the] habit of a Benedictine monk, which went through the room with a dreadful voice crying 'Help, help', and approaching the bed said 'Carluccio, Carluccio, give me a *de profundis*, give me a *de profundis*'. The young man, terrified but taking courage, came out shouting, and going into the room of the maestro, told him all; with the others they said the *de profundis* and then all the Rosary for that soul, and at this moment everyone heard [so] great a disturbance that the corridor seemed to have collapsed. After a little nothing more was heard.

Next day, 6 May, stones fell during the morning, 'now in one room, now in another', but nothing more was heard until the evening, when the brethren were again trying to go to sleep. Once again Carlo Maria heard a voice calling 'Carluccio, Carluccio'. He thought his nerves, disturbed by the previous night's events, were playing him a trick; but then he heard it say 'you do not want to reply?' As it spoke his bedclothes flew into the air and his bed fell; and he saw at the foot of the bed a figure dressed in white with a face the colour of fire, that said 'you do not know me, nor even will you know me'. Carlo ran to leave the room, and in leaving heard the words 'listen, listen'. The furniture of his room began to fall over with a great noise, the window flew open, a basin and ewer full of water were broken, without a drop of water falling to the ground.

During the next few days, stones were thrown continually, and the *demonio* considerably extended the range of his activities. He beat on doors with great cries; threw around mattresses, sheets and pillows, and flung them down the well; he interfered with divers sacred objects, putting, for example, chamber pots full of excrement before the image of S. Anastasio; he locked doors, and was only by the strongest invocations of God and the Virgin Mary prevailed upon to return the keys; he spattered the unfortunate Carlo with stinking excrement; he took pieces of paving stone and threw them outside at persons taking water from the well, breaking the jugs which they carried; he wrote on walls or pieces of paper whimsical or minatory messages in dubious Latin (which the master of the novices took it upon himself to correct).

On 11 May, in the evening, the master of the novices retired, as the manuscript puts it, 'to perform his necessity in the communal places'. The demon.

> there began to shout loudly. Taking heart [the master] asked who it might be. A smothered voice replied 'It is I'. 'Who are you?' answered the master, and received the reply 'I am the devil of the inferno'. Said [the master]: 'You are he? You are he? Filthy beast'. The demon replied, 'It is not I who am the beast, it is you', which gave the master courage to discourse longer, and among other things he asked him
>
> *Master.* What do you want of this place?
> *Demon.* I want nothing but to do what God has ordained for me.
> *Master.* And what has God ordained for you?
> *Demon.* To ceaselessly torment that novice.

There followed a long and tedious exchange of theologically toned insults, recorded in detail by the anonymous scribe, who must, one can only suppose, have chanced to be himself in the 'communal places' at the time, with writing materials to hand.

On 13 May, after a particularly unpleasant day, Carlo retired for the night to his room and

> there appeared at the door two brothers, and there placed the relic of the bindings of the cross and of the thorns. That night he saw in the seat near the bed a figure dressed in black with a fiery face, who shouted 'Now I will make you know who I am.' Unafraid the novice answered him 'You can be the Devil himself, but with the help of God I will have no fear of you.' Carrying the image of Christ, and saying 'see this Christ, filthy beast' he threw it in his face. [The demon] gave a frightful burst of activity, which not only made the two brethren flee, but made the other novices and fathers emerge from their rooms. The young man wishing to come out, the demon pulled him back by the cassock. When the names of Jesus and of Mary were called upon, he released him, but left in the cassock the print of a hand. Although great efforts were made to remove this mark, up to the point of cutting the cloth, it proved impossible . . . . In the morning there was found impressed in that room a dreadful

figure in one part and another in another part. They could not be erased; it was necessary to remove the plaster.

The Fathers could stand no more, and sent the lad with his uncle, Padre Pietro Galisio, to Capri, to the house of another uncle, D. Domenico Galisio, where they remained eight days without incident. On 22 May they went to Sorrento to visit the remains of S. Antonio, and while they were there, trouble broke out again. To avoid embarrassing the monks who were their hosts they returned to Naples, and the phenomena at once resumed with even greater violence and malice. Rooms were shaken as if by an earthquake, and structural damage was done. On one occasion the ceiling of a room in which were Carlo, his uncle, and many Fathers, crashed down amongst them, without, however, hurting anyone. The master of the novices

> made a command that he should replace the ceiling that he had caused to fall. Then was seen by all (a stupendous thing) the stones and wood of the ceiling to unite themselves and go up in the air like something carried, and to unite with the remainder that had not fallen, leaving, however, a sign of the junction.

Neither an exorcism performed by the most excellent Cardinal Ursini, nor the approach of a rib of S. Felippe succeeded in quieting this intransigent demon. He went into the refectory and broke the dishes. He removed the soft part of the bread and replaced it with horse dung, which some unobservant Fathers attempted to put in their mouths. He tormented Carlo in church, and sometimes when the populace crowded in to see the spectacle, he bound their legs to the balusters, so that when they wished to leave they fell on their faces.

Not knowing what to do the Fathers sent the lad back to Capri on 11 July. All was quiet until 2 August, when the boy and his uncle paid a visit to the monastery. Phenomena broke out again, and followed them on their return to Capri the next day. Stones were thrown, doors closed fast, furniture set fire to. They returned to Naples on 4 September, and Carlo was sent there to another house of D. Domenico Galisio's, in which were living his mother and his brother D. Domenico Vulcano. However, the phenomena continued unabated. Like *maestro* Squillante, Don Domenico Galisio engaged in a long verbal battle with the demon, which is transcribed word for word in the manuscript.

Between September and December, Carlo was shunted from

one refuge to another around the Bay of Naples, without enjoying freedom from the disturbances for more than a week or two at a time. For the most part the phenomena – stone-throwing, loud noises, the speaking of articulate sentences, the writing of inscriptions, the throwing of objects, the breaking of crockery, the locking of doors, damage to clothing, furniture and bedding – were of kinds which had already taken place, though assault in the shape of blows (directed mainly at visitors and bystanders) and the production of filth became commoner. I shall confine myself, therefore, to describing some of the more extraordinary and unusual incidents that are said to have taken place.

On 3 October, Carlo and his uncle attended mass in the church of the monastery in which they were staying. Various untoward incidents took place, but

> the most prodigious thing was that when Mass was finished, in making the genuflection with his nephew, the evil spirit stitched both of them to the cloth of the altar-step – he sewed the part of the lad's cassock below the knee, and the part of the uncle's surplice beneath both knees. In rising they carried away the said altar cloth to the amusement of all those monks and others in the church.

The clothes were so well sewn together that they were difficult to separate. At some unspecified date after this, a visitor to Capri, Father D. Felippo Pisani, found that some pouches in the clothes which he had left in his room had been torn open and money removed from them. He could not find the money anywhere. However,

> Towards evening they all went for a walk outside. They saw outside a certain beautiful peach-tree. Father Felippo pulled down four peaches. Cutting one open he found inside one of those [missing] dubloons. He opened another and found another, but he did not find the silver. Afterwards in the house, cutting a water melon, he found [the silver coins] there, but less five.

A few days afterwards

> Father Pietro, wishing to perform an exorcism, found that he had left his book in Naples, which greatly vexed him; he commenced to pray, and while he was so doing, [the demon] flung the book at his feet, saying: 'to my great confusion, I am obliged by that accursed name of that lad to bring you this book'.

On 18 October, when the boy was staying at the house of his uncle, D. Domenico Galisio, in Naples

There was then heard a great noise in a room where there was a janitor who did not see very well. Summoning up courage, they went to investigate, and found a black robe with a sheet over the shoulder, which moved. It was nothing other than a man, made up of pieces of cloth – this was what presented itself. By means of exorcism they made it disintegrate. But after some time it re-assembled, and turned over the table with its hands. A prayer on behalf of God brought it on its knees in the middle of the room . . . . It was a miraculous and frightful thing to see that man of cloth, having travelled a considerable distance, then fall upon its knees in the middle of the room, as though it had been ordained, and finally disintegrate. Inside the room they found only those pieces of cloth and the sheet of which it was composed.

The nearest parallel which I can recall to this extraordinary and implausible story, comes from the case at Orton (1849), in which hanging coats and cloaks are said to have 'come alive'

> Fifteen apparitions have I seen;
> The worst a coat upon a coat-hanger.

From 19 November until 10 December, all remained quiet, and on 17 December they ventured to return to the house of the Hieronymites in Naples. Again, all remained quiet until 2 January 1697, when phenomena of the usual kinds broke out again, and also one or two less usual ones. For instance, the demon is said to have thrown a book which broke as though made of glass. On 12 January the boy was sent back to his home, but the troublesome happenings continued. Fumigations were tried; and the demon countered with a chamber pot full of stinking excrement, above which was the inscription 'For such a deity, such a perfume'. The demon also several times showed himself in the house in the shape of the lad, who was at mass. In that guise he beat Carlo's brother and vexed his mother.

There ensued a period of quiet from 18 January to 29 March, at which point Carlo returned to the monastery. At once the phenomena broke out again with all their old force. On 30 March a decision was taken that Carlo should give up all thought of the monastic life. The demon disappeared for ever.

It is extremely difficult to know what to say of this singular tale. The first reaction of many even among those parapsychologists who accept the genuineness of certain poltergeist cases will be to reject it *in toto*. The narrative has many shortcomings – we do not know who the author was, or what were his immediate sources, and he quite commonly fails to give details which we should dearly like to have. Again some of the phenomena – the reuniting of fragmented objects, the moving cloth figure, the breaking of a book 'like glass', the manifestation of the agent's double – have, so far as I am aware, no parallels from other cases, and this is bound to lessen the credibility of the whole tale. On the other hand, Mr George Zorab, the only writer I know of who has described the case in English (*Journal of the American SPR*, vol. 67, 1973, pp. 404–5), thinks that one can plausibly assimilate it to other cases in which a poltergeist agent's inner conflicts work themselves out in the form of physical phenomena external to his body. He supposes, of course, that Carlo's problems arose over his projected future as a monk. Again, it might reasonably be remarked that while certain phenomena in this case are without parallel, most of them have many analogues. In fact it is not at all difficult to find cases which have nearly all the features of the Naples one, even though in the latter the phenomena seem to have been usually well developed.

To illustrate this point, let us briefly consider the leading features of a much better known Scottish case, the Rerrick case of 1695. Though this case is nearly contemporary with the one I have just described, it contrasts interestingly with it in cultural and religious setting, and is evidentially much stronger. It is described in a pamphlet by one of the principal witnesses, Alexander Telfair, the minister of Rerrick (a parish abutting on the sea, immediately to the east of the town of Kirkcudbright on the northern shore of the Solway Firth). This pamphlet was published at Edinburgh in 1696 and is entitled *A True Relation of an Apparition, Expressions and Actings of a Spirit, which Infested the House of* Andrew Mackie *in* Ring-Croft *of* Stocking, *In the Paroch of* Rerrick . . . . It is, of course, extremely scarce, but has been several times reprinted – as an appendix to Robert Law's *Memorialls* (Edinburgh, 1818), in the appendix to C. K. Sharpe's *A Historical Account of the Belief in Witchcraft in Scotland* (London, 1884), and, perhaps most conveniently, in the supplement to G. Sinclar's *Satan's Invisible World Discovered* (Edinburgh, 1871). A summary and extracts are given in the third volume of Robert Chamber's *The Domestic Annals of*

Scotland (London, 1861). An anglicized version of the pamphlet appeared in London in 1696, and is utilized by Harry Price for the account of the case in his popular *Poltergeist over England* (London, 1945).

Mr Telfair, the author, presents his account in the form of a diary or chronological record of events, and we can safely assume, though it is not explicitly stated, that it is based upon contemporary notes. The report of each leading incident is accompanied by the names of the witnesses who 'attest' it, and at the end comes a statement by fourteen of these witnesses (they include five ministers and several local landowners), who 'attest' the relation 'as to what they particularly saw, heard, and felt'.

The occupant of the troubled house, a small farm-house named Ringcroft, on the estate of Collin, in Rerrick, was Andrew Mackie, a married man with children, and a mason by trade. He is spoken of as a man 'honest, civil, and harmless beyond many of his neighbours'; and yet from mid-February 1695 to 1 May of the same year his house was the scene of terrifying and even dangerous poltergeist phenomena.

I shall not narrate these happenings in detail, partly because the story is well-known and easily accessible, but partly also because, for reasons which will shortly be touched upon, the case does not properly belong in this chapter. Instead I will simply tabulate the principal kinds of phenomena which took place, and beside them will set comparison data from the Naples case. By this means the similarities and differences between the two cases will be brought out.

Rerrick (1695)	*Naples (1696–7)*
Duration ten weeks	Duration ten months
—	Phenomena centre round young man of nineteen
Phenomena indoors and outdoors	Phenomena indoors and outdoors
'Busiest at night'	Busiest at night
Stones and other small objects thrown	Stones and other small objects thrown
Stones land gently	An object lands gently
Persons struck and hurt by thrown objects	Person struck and hurt by thrown object

Large objects lifted or thrown	Furniture overthrown
—	Crockery, windows, smashed
—	Book breaks like glass
—	Broken objects (including ceiling) reunited
—	Filth thrown, spread around, etc.
—	Doors locked, keys removed, etc.
'Whole house' shaken	Room shaken as if by earthquake
Structural damage	Structural damage
Bedclothes pulled off	Bedding, mattresses, pillows, removed, flung around
—	Clothes cut, sewn together, etc.
Apport phenomena	Apport phenomena of divers kinds
Raps on furniture	Blows on doors, general racketing
Animals disturbed, overthrown	—
Persons struck, gripped, scratched, hair pulled, etc.	Persons pinched, pushed, struck, hair pulled, etc.
Animals tied, untied	People bound, tied to objects, etc.
Incendiary phenomena	Incendiary phenomena
Hot or burning objects thrown	—
Luminous effects	—
—	Print of hand left on clothing
Phantasms seen	Phantasms seen
—	Phantasm of agent seen
—	Allegedly phantasmal small animals seen
'Black cloud' seen	—
Human shape made out of cloth	Human shape made out of cloth
—	This becomes animated
Inarticulate human sounds, whistles	Cries, laughter
Articulate voice converses	Articulate voice converses
—	Voice claims to be demon

Voice talks of 'God's commission'	Demon talks of what God has ordained for it to do
Written message found	Written messages and pictures found
Especial disturbances during prayers	Especial disturbances during religious services
Attempts at 'exorcism' fail	Attempts at exorcism fail

It can, I think, hardly be denied that there are somewhat striking similarities between these two cases. It is almost as though the same demon, having completed his commission in Rerrick, and improved his skills in the process, then undertook a fresh assignment in Italy. At any rate one cannot plausibly suppose that in the four months which elapsed between the publication at Edinburgh of Telfair's (highly idiomatic) pamphlet, and the commencement of satanic hostilities at Naples, a copy of the pamphlet reached Naples and was studied by the hoaxing Hieronymites of that city. Furthermore, I do not see any firm grounds upon which one could accept the Rerrick case, whilst refusing to consider the Naples one; or any firm grounds upon which one could accept some of the 'fantastical' and 'assault' cases discussed earlier in this book whilst refusing to consider the Rerrick case. This, of course, brings us to the brink of wider issues which will be taken up later.

The Rerrick case does, however, differ from the Naples one in a respect which, strictly speaking, should put it outside the confines of this chapter. The 'evil spirit' which plagued Andrew Mackie and his household made no claim to be a 'daemon', i.e. a discarnate non-human spirit. Although it very readily assumed the role for which the local ministers cast it, it made no claims as to its own nature and status. Thus, according to the criteria adopted in this chapter, the 'outward form' of the phenomena in this case was not 'daemonic'. And this is true of several other cases which are often talked of as though they were daemonic or diabolical in outward form. The famous 'Divell of Mascon' (Mâcon, 1612), for example, which, in addition to producing standard poltergeist phenomena, talked and conversed fluently, sang songs, etc., made no claim to be a daemon; in fact one of its statements might be interpreted as implying that it was the spirit of a deceased human being. The 'Demon Drummer' of Tidworth gave, as we have seen, no account of itself, beyond alleging that the drummer set it to work. These cases belong to a small but curious group, including, for example, the Kempten case of 856-8, the 'Bell Witch' (Adams, 1817-21), and the Clarendon case (1889), in which a clever but capricious intelligence manifests, communicates, often fluently, and seems happy to assume any role which the audience or the whim of the moment suggests to it. Such intelligences are equally ready to represent themselves as angels, devils, or deceased persons; no doubt one will eventually arise which claims to come from a flying saucer.

This brings us conveniently to a point at which we can tackle the second issue mentioned above as lending importance to the subject matter of this chapter. A commonly heard argument runs as follows. In former ages, when people were more apt to believe in daemonic (especially diabolical) agency than they are now, poltergeists, or rather such of them as could establish a mode of communication with incarnate human beings, often represented themselves as being daemons (devils). Nowadays, in the wake of the modern Spiritualist movement, whose beliefs and practices are well-known, poltergeists tend to represent themselves as the spirits of deceased human beings. These intelligences, which so clearly reflect prevailing folk-lore and religious beliefs, must simply be aspects of the minds of living people (particularly, of course, the minds of so-called 'poltergeist agents') acting in ways that as yet we do not understand.

This argument cannot be accepted without some reservations. For, as I have just noted, in several of the supposedly 'daemonic' cases most commonly cited, the intelligence 'behind' the phenomena, though capable of changing its complexion like a chameleon, made no special claims to be a daemon. In fact cases in which such a claim has been made are surprisingly rare. To anticipate by a little the results of an analysis of 500 cases presented in chapter 12, I may say that I have come across only eleven cases in which such a claim has been made. This contrasts with forty-six cases in which either a communicating intelligence has claimed to be that of a deceased person, or (much less frequently) the recognized phantasm of a deceased person has been observed apparently producing the phenomena. If we arrange the 500 cases in chronological order, and compare the first half (up to 1873) with the second half (1873-1975) we find the following:

	soi-disant daemon	soi-disant deceased person
1–250	7	20
250–500	4	26

There has thus been some change in the direction predicted by the argument we are considering – but hardly enough to be anything like conclusive. What is true is first that the hundred years or so following the Reformation saw a marked drop in the percentage of reported cases in which the phenomena were ostensibly linked to a deceased person (the idea of return from the dead was anathema to early Protestant theological writers), and second that in a number of cases a lively but mercurial communicating intelligence has shown a perfect willingness to play any part, daemonic or otherwise, directly or indirectly suggested to it. But both these findings can readily be squared with any view whatsoever of the alleged phenomena.

The figures just given include as 'daemonic' only cases in which a claim to daemonic origin is made through the phenomena themselves, for instance by raps or scratching (as in the case at Bristol in 1761-2) or by an articulate but ostensibly paranormal voice (as in the cases at Glenluce in 1654-6, and at Naples in 1696-7). There are, however, a few poltergeist cases in which a claim to daemonic origin is made not through the actual poltergeist phenomena, but by, or through the organism of, the presumed poltergeist agent. I refer, of course, to cases in which poltergeist phenomena have apparently accompanied an ostensible demoniacal obsession or possession. Many records of ostensible obsession have come down to us from the European witch-craze of the sixteenth and seventeenth centuries. In a typical case the victim would have visions of the witches, demons, or familiar spirits who assailed him, and would suffer from bodily convulsions, strangulation, fainting fits, swelling of the abdomen, and so forth, all supposedly the work of demons. There seems to have been a tradition that paranormal physical phenomena might accompany demoniacal obsession. Thus in 1597 the imposter William Somers, of Nottingham, thought it appropriate to accompany his convulsions with rappings upon the bedstead where he lay. The cases at Newbury, Massachusetts (1679), and Bargarran (1696) which I have already described, are essentially cases of ostensible obsession accompanied by poltergeist phenomena, and the case at Bristol in 1761-2 (chapter 7) verges upon being another. Closely similar are certain cases in which saints and other holy persons have ostensibly been beleaguered by devils, often visible to them, which have added divers poltergeist phenomena, generally of the more unpleasant sort, to their repertoire of annoyances. The histories (already referred to) of Christina of Stommeln, and of St J.-B. Vianney, provide examples. A good many further examples might be disinterred, but in most the details given are scanty. We learn, for example, from the biography of the eighteenth-century Italian saint, St Paul of the Cross (1694–1775), that he was assailed by explosions like pieces of artillery being discharged, by visions of grotesque animals, and by the opening and shutting of the warming pan in his room. Furthermore he was struck and bruised by the devil, who also twisted his gouty toe, causing him exquisite agony.

The borderline between obsession and possession is a fairly hazy one, but most authorities in these matters seem to agree that obsession has passed over into demonic possession when the organism of the afflicted person is more or less completely controlled by some demonic agency, which can then speak through it, work mischief with it, etc. The diagnosis is confirmed if the ostensibly controlling agency claims to be a demon, shuns holy objects, shows peculiar malignity, blasphemes, exhibits a knowledge of languages unknown to the victim, shows ESP, performs unusual feats of physical strength, or otherwise exhibits abnormal or paranormal powers. In such a context, the occurrence of poltergeist phenomena would probably be held to strengthen the hypothesis of demonic possession.

A few cases of ostensible demonic possession are said to have been accompanied by poltergeist phenomena. I have notes of cases in Württemberg (1844), Coullons (1850) and Alsace (1865–9), but details of the actual poltergeist phenomena are so scanty that I have not included these cases in the 500 subjected to analysis in chapter 12. In an article on 'Possession and parapsychology' published in the *Parapsychology Review*, vol. 5, 1974, Mr D. Scott Rogo cites modern cases at Earling, Iowa, in 1928, and Georgetown, a suburb of Washington, D.C. in 1949, of which detailed accounts have been printed. I have unfortunately been unable to obtain copies of them.

Whether or not we should class cases of poltergeist obsession and of poltergeist possession with the other cases discussed in this chapter is a debatable matter. I am inclined to think that we should do so only when certain conditions are fulfilled. If a poltergeist agent claims to see and to be persecuted by demons, or if a voice speaking through his vocal apparatus purports to be that of a demon, this hardly so much as suggests that the poltergeist effects are of demonic origin. It only suggests that he has mental problems, to which the poltergeist phenomena may also be related. Only where, in addition, the possessed person and the poltergeist phenomena alike exhibit knowledge, motives, purposes, and capacities, quite different from those ordinarily characteristic of that person, and where the possessed person and the poltergeist phenomena actively co-operate in the apparent pursuit of these uncharacteristic motives and purposes, could we reasonably begin to say that here too the poltergeist phenomena had the 'outward form' of demoniacal inspiration, instead of being merely adjunct to some disturbance of the agent's mental balance. I do not know of any case that completely answers this description.

The conventional explanation of cases of apparent possession has been in terms of 'hysterical pseudo-possession'. The general idea is that a person who has done something for which he feels guilty, or has even entertained desires which conflict with his moral ideals, may, through largely unconscious psychological processes which we do not fully understand, come to imagine himself a moral leper and a likely target for diabolical molestation. The delusion gradually or suddenly takes over the victim's mind, and a case of pseudo-possession is born. Now since some writers have regarded poltergeist phenomena as analogous to hysterical symptoms, as representing so to speak the conversion of inner conflicts into outer symptoms, it might not be difficult to give some account of the occasional association of poltergeist phenomena with cases of hysterical pseudo-possession. Such an explanation could perhaps be supplemented by citing cases, e.g. Boston, Mass. (1867), Amherst (1878), Molignon (1914), Rosenheim (1967–8), in which poltergeist agents have suffered 'hysterical' bodily afflictions, e.g. convulsions or swelling of the body, stopping short, however, of actual obsession or possession.

In the article just mentioned, Mr Rogo rejects this explanation. He states that in both the Earling and Georgetown cases 'psychodynamic evaluations of the victims were made, and in each case no hysterical tendencies were found'. Second, and more importantly, 'hysteria is projected inward. The victim wishes to punish himself and no one else. Yet diabolical possession cases are vicious, even murderous and there have been deaths recorded during them'. Third, he argues that modern experiments in psychokinesis do not show hysterics to have greater gifts in that direction than anyone else. Mr Rogo, who is inclined to hold that some unpleasant entity foreign to the poltergeist agent may be at work in these cases, suggests that the possession poltergeist is to be distinguished from the classical poltergeist, especially on the grounds of the frequency in the former of '(1) The agent understanding or using unlearned languages, this being one of the major points for diagnosing demoniacal possession. (2) The levitation of the human body.'

With regard to the second of these suggestions the following information may be of use. My collection of 500 cases contains fourteen in which there was ostensible obsession or possession of a poltergeist agent; in at least four, however, the obsessing or possessing entity either purported to be a deceased human being, or else was indeterminate. In thirty-three cases levitation, transportation, or projection out of bed, of the human body was reported (not always the body of the supposed agent). In five cases obsession or possession and levitation were conjoined (a figure which would be increased to seven on somewhat more liberal criteria of obsession than the ones I actually adopted) It appears, therefore, that Mr Rogo is *prima facie* right in his proposal about the frequency of levitation phenomena in cases of poltergeist-possession. He is, however, not altogether correct when he claims, following A. R. G. Owen, that 'levitation of the human body is found infrequently in classical poltergeist outbreaks'.

I have no information bearing upon Mr Rogo's first proposal, but the number of potentially relevant cases in my collection is very small. It will be recollected that in the Bristol case of 1761–2 the ostensibly diabolical intelligence which communicated through scratchings showed signs of understanding classical languages unknown to the poltergeist agents. But cases of apparent 'xenoglossy', no matter how the linguistic knowledge is displayed, are extremely difficult to assess, and require the most detailed scrutiny.

10 Hauntings

I want next to consider briefly a sort of phenomenon which is, on the face of it, rather different from the poltergeist, and would be held by many parapsychologists to be another kind of thing entirely. I refer to the haunting ghost, or recurrent localized apparition. There are many stories, more or less legendary, of phantasmal figures, usually human but sometimes animal, which from time to time reappear in a certain room, house or locality to astonish or affright some unsuspecting victim, generally during the hours of darkness. Not all these tales are totally legendary. In a small number of cases – a few dozen at most – parapsychologists have been able to collect the first-hand testimony of the various independent witnesses; and in a still smaller number, they have been able to visit the scene during the period within which phenomena were still being reported.

Parapsychologists have very commonly, though not invariably, regarded such phenomena as belonging in the realm of *hallucinations*. They have held, that is, that although the witnesses of haunting apparitions have generally supposed themselves to be seeing some kind of object, however extraordinary, in the world external to themselves, they have one and all been mistaken in this belief. Nothing was objectively present before them where the apparition seemed to be, nothing that would have affected a photographic emulsion or a photo-electric cell. The reasons for saying this are complicated and I cannot go into them in detail here. They include such facts as these: not everyone in a position to see the figure on a given occasion will be able to see it; apparitions by and large leave no physical traces behind them; apparitions have been seen, for example, to open locked doors which on subsequent investigation have been found to be still locked – the apparition and the opening of the door were seemingly *both* part of the same hallucinatory scene.

Now of course classifying haunting ghosts as hallucinations does not by any means resolve all problems concerning them. If they are hallucinations, they are none the less in some sense *veridical* hallucinations. They coincide or correspond with other events in ways which still seem to require explanation. When two or more people, ignorant of each other's experiences, successively see similar phantasms in the same spot, we must ask how these unlikely similarities come about. Sometimes more than one person may simultaneously see the same figure in the same spot; and then we have to explain why their hallucinations are thus correspondent. Very occasionally an apparition may bear a marked or distinctive resemblance to some person who formerly lived in or was connected with the locality where it appears, and if the resemblance can be established, it presents us with yet another kind of puzzle.

In an attempt to resolve these problems, parapsychologists who are convinced of the hallucinatory nature of haunting ghosts have developed some extremely involved hypotheses. They have supposed that the later percipients of a recurrent apparition must be in telepathic contact with the first percipient, presumably because a rapport is established amongst persons who visit the same scene. Somehow the shock and fear of the first percipient (who must have generated the phantasm out of his own imagination) reverberate through the later percipients and cause them to share in the former's experience. Comparable suggestions can be made when the phantasm is simultaneously perceived by more than one person. Where the apparition resembles someone who formerly lived at the place concerned, it had additionally to be supposed that the witnesses, or at any rate the first and catalytic witness, have obtained the information with which the hallucinatory figure has been constructed by ESP directed upon living persons or upon surviving records; or even that they have obtained it through telepathic contact with some surviving portion of the deceased person concerned.

These speculations may seem tortuous and incredible. None the less haunting ghosts have been widely regarded by parapsychologists as being hallucinations into whose content has been injected material which the witnesses have, unconsciously, acquired by ESP (telepathy or clairvoyance). If this view is correct, poltergeist phenomena which, whatever their causes, are undoubtedly physical, are altogether different from recurrent localized apparitions. Indeed, I have even seen it proposed that the alleged occurrence of poltergeist phenomena as it were alongside a recurrent localized apparition is so unlikely a concatenation as to give strong grounds for doubting the whole case. Where, on the other hand, the occasional glimpsing of an apparition comes as an adjunct or addition to an established poltergeist case, the apparitions are usually regarded as hallucinations due to the overwrought nerves of the persons plagued by the poltergeist.

Unfortunately for this simple, black or white, classification of the phenomena, there are quite a lot of cases in the literature, and even more which fail to reach the literature, that on the face of it seem to fall somewhere between poltergeists and recurrent localized apparitions, and to constitute a bridging category which abuts on both. These are cases which are generally called just 'hauntings'. The leading characteristics of hauntings are these: the phenomena centre round a place, usually a house, rather than round a person, and often continue off and on for several years (which is not generally so with poltergeists). The phenomena take place mainly at night, and prominent amongst them are what may be called imitative noises – sounds resembling those which normally accompany people treading on the floorboards or opening doors or breaking crockery or dropping heavy weights or banging walls, but to which no observable breakages, displacements, marks, etc., correspond; or sounds like human whispers, groans, distant conversations or articulate phrases. Other phenomena not infrequently reported in such cases include the appearance of luminosities and balls of light; disturbance of and tugging at bedclothes; and the actual opening of room and wardrobe doors with visible turning of handles or lifting of latches.

Now it is quite clear that cases of hauntings shade by imperceptible degrees into cases of recurrent localized apparitions (haunting ghosts). In some hauntings, apparitions of a transient and nondescript kind may be seen; in others what is seemingly the same distinctive figure may be repeatedly seen; and conversely in all but the very purest examples of recurrent localized apparitions (a small percentage of the total) there is a greater or less admixture of characteristic 'haunting' phenomena. Even in that most famous of all cases of a recurrent localized apparition, the 'Cheltenham Ghost' of 1880 to 1889 (and perhaps later) there was such an admixture. The ghost – the figure of a lady wearing widow's weeds – was seen in that period by at least a dozen persons, sometimes for more than half an hour at a time. But in addition to the visual apparitions, there were also certain characteristic haunting phenomena – footsteps, bumps on doors, cold winds, small flame-like lights, the turning of door-handles.

The continuity between hauntings and haunting ghosts makes it very tempting to assimilate these two classes of phenomena, and to say that just as the phantasms which are repeatedly seen in cases of the latter sort must be regarded as hallucinations, so the imitative noises, lights, cold breezes, and so forth, which figure in cases of the former sort, are likewise hallucinatory. If that is true, then of course the sort of problems which arise in connection with haunting ghosts will also arise in connection with hauntings, and parallel explanations are likely to be advanced. There is at least one occasionally reported fact (mentioned in the sixteenth century by Petrus Thyraeus, a Jesuit writer on these topics) which is often cited as evidence that the rappings and imitative noises said to occur in cases of haunting are hallucinatory. It is that just as sometimes not all of the persons in a position to see a certain apparition are able to see it, so, sometimes, not all of the persons in a position to hear a certain rapping or imitative noise will actually hear it.

The most obvious objection to this attempt to assimilate the phenomena of hauntings to those of recurrent localized apparitions (these last being regarded as hallucinatory) is that in an appreciable percentage of hauntings, phenomena which seem undoubtedly to be physical and hence non-hallucinatory have been reported. I mentioned above the tugging at bedclothes and turning of door-handles which are so often described; and ostensible examples of object-movements are by no means uncommon. Indeed it is not easy to make an hallucination-theory of the rappings and imitative noises so characteristic of hauntings appear plausible. Although these sounds are sometimes not heard by persons in a position to hear them, the same is true of many other, more ordinary sounds; and it is undoubtedly much more commonly the case that the sounds in hauntings *are* heard by all those whom one would expect to have heard them if they had an external, physical cause.

Those parapsychologists who wish *both* to regard haunting ghosts as hallucinations *and* to assimilate the phenomena of 'hauntings' to them are accordingly in a dilemma. For if they are right in assimilating the two classes of phenomena (as they surely must be) then the theory that haunting ghosts are pure hallucinations is bound to be endangered by the minor but persistent physical phenomena which seem to be an integral part of so many hauntings. Their response to this dilemma has very often been to attempt in one way or another to eliminate the alleged physical component from hauntings. Those supposedly physical phenomena which cannot be dismissed as hallucinatory are set down to ordinary physical causes of an obscure kind working upon persons whose critical faculties are as limited as their imaginations are strong, or who are incapable of remembering and accurately reporting the circumstances of the case. Now of course ordinary but obscure natural causes, malobservation and misremembering are all possible factors in stories of hauntings and poltergeists (see chapter 13); but one must be very careful that one does not fall into the trap of supposing these factors always to operate in just the ways which will make one's own favourite hypothesis continue to seem plausible.

When the physical phenomena in a case of haunting are too marked or too violent to admit of this treatment, a favourite ploy has been to say that after all the case must have been one of an ordinary person-centred poltergeist. Speculations are then engaged in as to who the supposed poltergeist agent could have been; and of course it is usually not difficult to find a candidate despite the fact that a link between the presence of this person and the occurrence of the phenomena was not noticed at the time.

In this chapter I shall briefly describe some cases of haunting. From what I have so far said it will be apparent that for our purposes the most important questions to bear in mind are the following. Are some at least of the phenomena reported in cases of haunting physical in nature? If so are they paranormal, i.e. of a kind for which no ordinary explanation presents itself? And if so again, is there a continuity or affinity or underlying relationship between cases of hauntings and cases of poltergeists?

There are cases of hauntings – with which I will not weary the reader – in the literature of classical antiquity, and certain tales from one or two of the (surprisingly large) medieval collections of ghost stories perhaps qualify. The first printed book which, so far as I know, treats of such matters – Alphonsus de Spina's *Fortalicium Fidei* (Strasbourg, 1467) – sets the phenomena of hauntings down to the *duen de casa*, or household goblin, of which the author claims personal experience. The characteristic

1 Melchior Joller and his family (see chapter 1)

2 Melchior Joller's house in Stans (see chapter 1)

3 Title-page of the North Aston pamphlet (see chapter 2). This is probably the first English pamphlet about a poltergeist case

A TRVE DISCOVRSE of such straunge and woonderfull *accidents, as hapned in the house of M.* George Lee of North-Aston, in the countie of Oxford, being in truth and matter of such speciall weight and consequence, as sildome hath the like bene heard of before. Which begun the 19. of November 1591. and continued vntill Easter even last past 1592.

Iustified by the credit of Gentlemen of worship, and others of the Countrey.

¶ Imprinted at London for Edward White, dwelling at the little North doore of S. Paules Church at the signe of the Gunne. 1592.

4 The Gerstmanns' house at Dortmund, scene of a particularly unpleasant poltergeist (see chapter 3)

5 The poltergeist house at Newbury, Massachusetts (see chapter 3)

6 Swinging lamps in the Rosenheim case (see chapter 5)

7 Title-page of the Sandfeldt pamphlet (see chapter 6)

8 Eleonora Zugun, with scratch-marks on face (see chapter 7)

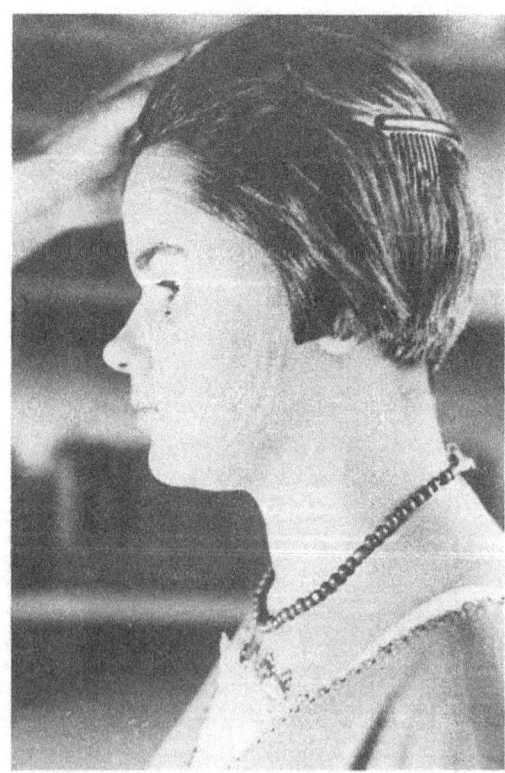

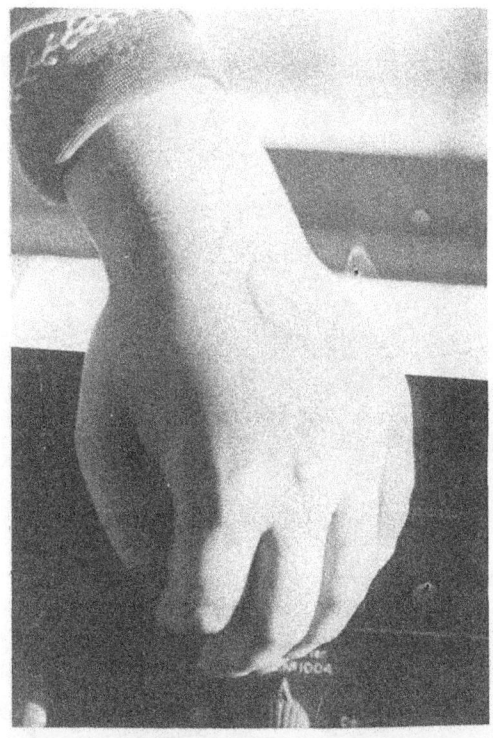

9 Hand of Eleonora Zugun, showing bite-mark (see chapter 7)

10 The 'haunted house' at Cheltenham (see chapter 10)

11 'Beth-oni', Tackley, Oxon., view from garden (see chapter 10)

12 Willington Mill about 1890 (see chapter 10)

13 The 'haunted house' on Canvey Island towards the end of the last century (see chapter 11). The original pamphlet, however, seems to indicate a somewhat larger building

14 The dressing-table which was overturned by the 'East Midlands' poltergeist (see chapter 14)

15 Hannath Hall (see chapter 16)

16 The 'house-shaking apparatus' (see chapter 17)

phenomena are noted by such sixteenth-century writers as Thyraeus, Taillepied and Lavater, and are thus described in Pierre Le Loyer's *Discours, et histoires des spectres* (Paris, 1605):

> I will say to Lucian, and to his like, as sceptical as he, that there are plenty of houses haunted by these spirits and goblins, which ceaselessly disturb the sleep of those who dwell in them; for now they will stir and overturn the utensils, vessels, tables, boards, dishes, bowls, and now they will draw the water from a well, or make the pulley squeak, the slates and tiles fall from the roof, throw stones, enter chambers, imitate now a cat, now a mouse, now other animals, lift up persons lying asleep in their beds, pull the curtains or coverlets, and perpetrate a thousand tricks. These Folets do not bring any other nuisance to the people than disturbing them, oppressing them, or hindering their sleep; for the household vessels all of which they seem to have smashed and broken, are found the next morning to be intact.

Since the characteristic phenomena were even then so clearly recognized, it is perhaps surprising that there seem to be few, if any, detailed accounts of hauntings prior to the eighteenth century. The earliest account I have come across which gives more than perfunctory details of the phenomena is contained in a booklet by a Dominican professor of theology, Father C. K. Richard. It was published at Amiens in 1746 under the title *Dissertation sur la possession des corps*, and was reprinted by Lenglet Dufresnoy in his *Recueil de dissertations* (Avignon and Paris, 1751-2). Richard cites the testimony of some twenty witnesses, including himself, to the haunting since 1732 of a certain house in Amiens. The phenomena which he cites are, for the most part, quite characteristic, and took place at night. They included footsteps, raps, imitative noises (as of the floor being swept, planks being thrown around, heavy bodies being dragged, steps being torn up – nothing was in fact disturbed), lights, oppression of a person lying in bed, the sound of whirring in the air. However, witnesses also reported such presumably physical effects as the dancing of furniture, a general shaking of the house, and blows leaving bruises.

From the same century we have accounts of the famous haunting of Hinton Ampner in Hampshire (1765-71), and a German case (1794-1815), collected by the famous poet, physician and occultist, Justinus Kerner (1786-1862). Kerner does not reveal the location of this case, which he gives as 'the former monastery of N —— g', but he prints a long account of the phenomena, written, however, a good few years afterwards, by the principal witness, the very tough-minded wife of an ecclesiastical administrator. This lady, and other members of her household, were plagued at night by a variety of bewildering and unpleasant events – footsteps; sounds as of heavy objects being thrown around (nothing was disturbed); noises like musket shots; violent explosions, which made the walls shake and once lifted her up in the chair on which she sat; a flame which made her think for a moment that her bedroom curtains were on fire; raps on the bed canopy; a feeling as if a cat were curling round her feet. Going to the cellar one night she saw a huge coal-black man's shape floating across it. It disappeared at the opposite side of the cellar. The lady was not thereby deterred from fetching the wine for which she had come! Most dreadful of all was a phenomenon which occurred many times after she had lain down to sleep:

> A frightful howl gushed downwards from the ceiling of the room, passed near me, and at last died away against the floor of the room . . . it seemed to me a pitiable sign of the state of the poor wretch. O God! how miserable must such a creature be . . . . Often it twittered by our bed in a vicious way, as if many quarrelling people talked with each other, which disturbed our sleep.

It is, however, not my purpose, or at least not my principal purpose, to recite narratives merely because they may chill the blood. I am after cases in which we have detailed contemporary records in the shape of diaries, notes, sworn testimony, tape recordings, etc. And here again, despite the fact that reports of hauntings are relatively common, the field is not large. The earliest diary record of a haunting which I have so far unearthed is again one published by Kerner. The haunting in question was of the parsonage at Klefersulzbach, Württemberg, and lasted through four successive incumbencies (1811–41). The diarist was the fourth of these incumbents, Pfarrer Möricke, and his diary describes only phenomena which occurred between August and November 1834, during which period there seems to have been an unusual burst of activity. Nights were disturbed by footsteps, rappings, round luminous appearances, sighs, noises as of pistol shots, sounds as though tiles had been flung off the roof, and sounds like a heavy ball rolling. Many of the phenomena which Möricke relates were, however, witnessed not by himself but by the members of his family, so I shall pass on to discuss some other cases of haunting of which we have diary records.

I shall begin with two cases where the leading phenomena were what I have called imitative noises. Object-movements and other undeniably physical disturbances, though not absent, were less in evidence. I shall first discuss a case which took place in the village of Tackley, Oxfordshire, in the period 1905-8; then I shall deal with an earlier case, which took place at Brighton from 1882 to 1889.

The Tackley case is set forth in a scarce little pamphlet by the principal witness, Miss Ada M. Sharpe. It was published at Oxford in 1914 as *A Disturbed House and its Relief*. The 'disturbed house' of the title belonged to Miss Sharpe, a lady of independent means and charitable disposition. It was a substantial building, in part 300 years old, with five bedrooms and assorted attics. The phenomena began in April 1905, occurred sporadically throughout that year and the next, and became suddenly more marked in January 1907. In July 1907, a religious ceremony was held in the house – Miss Sharpe was a strong High Churchwoman. After this, things were much quieter until January 1908, when the phenomena picked up again. In February another religious ceremony was held in the house and there was no more trouble.

According to Miss Sharpe's pamphlet, at least twenty-two people experienced the disturbances. There was no one person whose presence was essential to them – they even occurred whilst she herself was away. Most of the pamphlet is in the form of a diary taken from contemporary notes which she wrote in a book kept for the purpose. She says of these notes (p. 39).

> It will be noticed . . . that I have mainly copied from my brief notes made *about* the time of the occurrences. I say 'about' because I want it clearly understood that the frequent shocks to one's nerves, and the awful strain upon them, was so intense, that it was not easy to bring oneself to write down anything. Moreover, from time to time, and partly in concession to various given opinions and suggestions, one tried to believe in natural, though inexplicable, causes, for fear of lending one's imagination and losing control of it.

Though Miss Sharpe speaks of the strain on her nerves, it is apparent that her nerves were in fact of the hardiest. Her niece, Miss Florence M. Sharpe, described her to Harry Price, whose *Poltergeist over England* (London, 1945) first brought the story to a wider audience, as an iron-willed old lady, not given to imagining things. In the pamphlet Miss Sharpe says (p. 43)

> Lest, having mentioned these facts [that she had in 1903 and 1904 nursed two persons who died in the house], it may be surmised that my nerves had been overwrought and imaginative, I will just mention that on both occasions I slept – the sole occupant of the house, save the maid shut off in the little attic – alone, with my bedroom door as usual wide open, next to the 'Blue' room, in which lay the remains of the departed, which I visited before going to my room.

One suspects that not every modern parapsychologist would show such steadiness of nerve and purpose! Another perhaps relevant circumstance is the following. Miss Sharpe moved into the house, 'Beth-oni', in June 1900, and, with the doubtful exception of some door-opening about 1904, all was absolutely quiet until April 1905. Then a family named Chaundry moved from the far end of the village to a house next door but one to Miss Sharpe's. In June 1875, a member of this family, Bart Chaundry, a farmer, had died in Beth-oni after falling down the stairs in a state of drunkenness. Soon after the Chaundrys moved into the neighbourhood of Beth-oni, phenomena began there in earnest, and continued with intermissions until the final religious ceremony in February 1908. 'From that day to this,' said Miss Sharpe in 1914, 'there has been absolute peace.'

It would, I think, be fair to remark that the house was not normally a noisy one, and that Miss Sharpe does not seem to have been at all the sort of person whose perfervid imagination would have magnified ordinary household creaks and groans into the nocturnal wanderings of an unquiet ghost.

The list of the phenomena which Miss Sharpe records as having taken place in Beth-oni, almost always at night, is long and variegated. By far the commonest phenomenon was what I have called 'imitative noises'. These included footsteps, raps, explosions, the rustling of clothes, the sound of locks clicking, the sound of doors closing, noises like a mason at work with his tools, sounds like furniture being removed from the house, noises like several men fighting, the sound of a fall, the dragging of a weight across the floor. There were also various visual phenomena. The phantasm of a man was seen by several different persons – whether or not it could have been the same figure on each occasion is not clear. Starry lights and dark clouds were seen in the air. There were also various ostensible effects on physical objects. A candle was several times extinguished; two persons witnessed the levitation of a bed in which one of them was lying; bedclothes were 'clawed at' and disturbed; doors were found to have been opened; a book which a phantasm, seen by two persons, had pulled out of a bookcase, left behind a furrow in the dust. However, when, on two successive nights, Willie, the gardener, fastened threads across a staircase on which footsteps were heard, the threads remained unbroken.

I shall now give a few representative extracts from Miss Sharpe's diary notes, so that readers may make up their own minds to what extent imagination or ordinary physical causes may have lain behind the phenomena. It will be observed that Miss Sharpe sometimes recounts her own experiences, sometimes those of her friends, her servants, and the recipients of her charity (three classes of people not, I suspect, in practice always distinct from each other). Thus the testimony is sometimes first-hand and sometimes second-hand.

> *January 16 [1907], Wednesday.* – I sat on Florrie's bed in the dark at 11 p.m., and punctually at 11.10 sounds began, faint at first and growing louder behind her bed in the wall – skipping the corner of the room – then about a foot along, scratching a moment, then beginning work as with a stonemason's hammer and trowel. Florrie went down in the hall with a lighted candle, where it sounded louder.
>
> *January 17, Thursday.* – Willie slept in the house. He and I sat on Florrie's bed till 11.15 p.m., when the same sounds occurred again, and he and I searched about the house with a lantern. We stood in the side passage downstairs near the kitchen, where furious sounds as of a mason using a pick-axe were to be heard. We had previously, from the landing by the bedroom door, heard sounds as though a 'clinker' was being furiously rolled along the tiles in the hall. For hours after we got to bed the sound of mason's work continued in all directions.
>
> *April 17, Wednesday.* – . . . I kept my candle burning all night. I was awakened at 2.30 a.m. by a tremendous noise sounding like two or three people wrestling desperately on the

bathroom landing. I called to Agnes [a companion-help], whom it had also awakened, and asked her what it sounded like: she said 'like something falling'. Willie and Miss Bevan were also soon awake, but heard nothing . . . .

July 5, Friday. – Alice [a former maid, staying in the house with her three-year-old niece, Amy] had not been to sleep when she heard two taps at her open door, and while she was vainly trying to answer a man came in, tapping the door as he came, walked to the book-shelves, snatched a book with both hands from the middle shelf, carried it to the dressing-table, laid it down while he looked at Alice's watch lying there, picked up the book, replaced it on the shelf, and seemed to go out at the door. Alice got up and looked outside the door, but saw no more. She had not known that the child was awake till he had vanished, when the child said: 'Didn't that man snatch the books? and he "tiggled" me in the back. He hadn't half got cheek!' The book was called 'In Strange Company', and a distinct mark where it was drawn out was noticeable in the dust on the shelf next day, also two finger-marks on the top of the book . . .

July 11th, Thursday. – Annie [a friend of Alice's, sharing her room] went to bed about 8.30, and almost immediately called to Alice, saying the bed was being lifted from the floor. Alice lay down on the bed at once, and felt the bed being lifted from the floor, and heard noises all round – then as if someone was violently tearing down wallpaper in the room, and then on the staircase. I went up, but could hear nothing . . . .

January 29 [1908], Wednesday. – From 9.50 p.m. till 12.15 a.m. I heard sounds as if heavy furniture was being removed from every room in the house, without five minutes' cessation. I distinctly heard footsteps in the big attic as well as on the tiles in the hall. I heard a heavy van draw up outside the front windows and men talking and loading. They seemed to come in at my side window instead of passing Batter [a dog] at my door, to fetch a chest of drawers which I was watching and which they seemed to take quite easily through the window, which by the way, looks out on the glass top of the greenhouse. When they had finished loading, the van moved off and all was silent.

The second of my imitative-noise hauntings disturbed a small house at Brighton (Prestonville Road) from 1882 to 1889. The principal witnesses were interviewed by two of the leading psychical researchers of that time, Edmund Gurney and Frank Podmore, and the case was first published by Podmore (with the location and real names withheld) in the *Proceedings of the*

SPR, vol. 6, 1889. The original documents are still in the SPR archives.

The house concerned was part of a terrace. It had railings in front, three or four steps up to the front door, and steps down to a basement area. The basement had a breakfast room at the front, and at the back a kitchen, with a wash-house leading from it and opening into a small, square garden. On the ground floor was a sitting room at the front; a back bedroom overlooking the garden, and a small spare room. There was a servant's room on the first-floor landing, and on the first floor were a front bedroom, a 'small slip room just over front door', and a back bedroom overlooking the garden.

The case is noteworthy for at least the following reasons. First of all it is one of the eerier cases of which we have records. A leading member of the SPR once remarked of the ghost stories collected by that staid Society that they would be more likely to induce sleep in the reading than to banish it afterwards. This story, I am quite sure, is an exception. Second, we have on record the testimony of no less than five groups of witnesses, the second of which was for an appreciable time ignorant of the first's experiences. And third we have two diary records of the phenomena, one very partial, the other quite detailed.

Before I proceed to give some extracts from the testimony, it will perhaps be helpful if I list the five groups of witnesses, and tabulate the principal kinds of phenomena which each experienced. I cannot quote the somewhat lengthy records in full, but the extracts will be easier to assess if they are placed in the context of a general outline of events. Since the testimony of the last group of witnesses, or rather witness, was simply to the effect that there had been no phenomena in the house between September 1889 and March 1890, it will not be included.

It will be noted that the phenomena experienced by the first, third and fourth groups of percipients are for the most part simply selections of the phenomena experienced by the second group, during whose tenancy the occurrences reached their height. Details concerning the phantasms allegedly seen are too scanty for us to be able to say whether the 'little woman', 'pale woman's face' peeping around the door, etc., seen during Mrs Gilby's tenancy could have represented the woman in black with a pale sad face seen by Miss Morris. Both Miss Morris and Mrs Gilby were told that a woman had a few years before hanged

Miss L. Morris and family (Oct. 1882–Dec. 1886)	Mrs Gilby and family (Nov. 1887–May 1888)	Mr W. O. Dawson etc. (May 1888)	Mr G. A. Smith and family (17 Aug. 1888–27 Sep. 1889)
—	Taps	—	Taps
Knocks on doors	Knocks on doors	—	—
—	Thumps as if things thrown around	—	Bumps as if brick being bounced
—	Crashes	Crash	Crashes
—	—	—	Sound of zinc pail rattling
Footsteps	Footsteps	—	Footsteps
—	—	—	Dress rustling
—	Sounds as of paper being screwed up	—	Sounds as of paper rustling
—	Sounds as of paper being thrown	—	—
Sounds as of door banging	Sounds as of door banging	—	—
—	Sounds as of furniture moving	—	—
Ringing of front-door bell	Ringing of front-door bell	Ringing of front-door bell	Ringing of front-door bell
—	Notes played on piano	—	Guitar strings plucked
—	Sound of musical box	—	—
—	Deep sobs and moans	—	Groans
—	Screaming	—	—
—	Articulate voice	—	—
Door-handle turned	Door-handle turned	—	—
Door opens	Doors open and shut	—	—

Miss L. Morris and family (Oct. 1882– Dec. 1886)	Mrs Gilby and family (Nov. 1887– May 1888)	Mr W. O. Dawson etc. (May 1888)	Mr G. A. Smith and family (17 Aug. 1888– 27 Sep. 1889)
—	Bed shaken	—	—
—	Lights seen	—	—
Phantasm of woman with pale, sad face	—	—	—
—	Phantasm of a little woman	—	—
—	White face peeping round door (woman)	—	—
—	A white figure	—	—
—	Phantasm of a man	—	—
—	Two human faces	—	—
—	A shadow	—	—
—	—	A misty vapour	—
—	—	A 'form'	—

herself in the upstairs back bedroom; and to this they were both disposed to attribute the phenomena. The story was discovered, from reports of the inquest, to be true; but no clear connection, e.g. in the characteristics of the figures seen, was ever established between the woman who committed suicide and the phenomena.

The first person whose testimony we have is a Miss L. Morris. Miss Morris and her aunt, who died towards the end of the tenancy, rented the house from October 1882 to December 1886. (The previous tenant told Miss Morris that nothing abnormal happened during her tenancy.) They had one maidservant, and two of Miss Morris's sisters stayed there from time to time. Miss Morris's statement is dated June 1888. She and one of her sisters were interviewed by Frank Podmore on 9 July 1888. She emerges from her statement as a fairly strong-minded person, who did not hesitate to search the house, poker in hand, to discover the source of persistent heavy footsteps and banging. Here is what she has to say about the mysterious ringing of the front-door bell (an old-fashioned wire bell, of the kind so much favoured by poltergeists):

> It was in June 1884, that our hall-door bell began to ring incessantly and violently. We had frequently heard at intervals a ring, and discovered no one was at the door, but this especially annoyed us, and puzzled everyone inside and outside the house by the noise repeatedly made. We had always put it down to a 'runaway ring' and took no notice, but for three weeks, at intervals of a quarter of an hour or half an hour, it rang incessantly, and such peals, it electrified us. We put ourselves on guard and carefully watched, believing it a trick. We had everyone up from the basement, out of connection with the wire, in the front drawing-room, and placed the hall door and our doors wide open; it was the same result: loud and piercing peals from the bell, which, at last, after three weeks, we had taken off, when we saw the wire in connection with it vibrated as if the bell was attached to it.

Miss Morris left in December 1886, and the house remained empty until November 1887, when it was taken by a Mrs Clara Gilby, the widow of an army officer. Mrs Gilby had two childen, girls of eleven and nine, and kept one maidservant. Incessant noises and other phenomena drove her out of the house in May 1888, and she wrote an account of her experiences for Edmund Gurney who visited her at Brighton on 13 June 1888 (shortly before his own death). Her maid likewise wrote an account. Mrs Gilby's account is based on diary notes some of which are also printed. Gurney thought highly of her and says

> She struck me as an excellent witness. I have never received an account in which the words and manner of telling were less suggestive of exaggeration or superstition. There is no doubt that she was simply turned out of a house which otherwise exactly suited her, at very serious expense and inconvenience.

It is apparent, however, that by the time a few months had elapsed Mrs Gilby, her maid, and especially the children, were in a very nervous state – quite understandably in view of what was going on around them – and to this we may perhaps attribute the superfluity of phantasmal figures which members of the family began to see.

When the first phenomena of her tenancy took place, Mrs Gilby had no idea that there was anything amiss with the house:

> We had not been more than a fortnight in our new home . . . when I was aroused by a deep sob and moan. 'Oh,' I thought, 'what has happened to the children?' I rushed in, their room being at the back of mine; found them sleeping soundly. So back to bed I went, when again another sob, and such a thump of somebody or something very heavy. I sat up in bed, looked all round the room, then to my horror a voice (and a very sweet one) said, 'Oh, do forgive me!' three times. I could stand no more; I always kept the gas burning, turned it up, and went to the maid's room. She was fast asleep, so I shook her well, and asked her to come into my room. Then in five minutes the sobs and moans recommenced, and the heavy tramping of feet, and such thumps, like heavy boxes of plate being thrown about. She suggested I should ring the big bell I always keep in my room, but I did not like to alarm the neighbourhood . . . . I told her to go to bed, and hearing nothing for half-an-hour, I got into mine, nearly frozen with cold and fright. But no sooner had I got warm than the sobs, moans, and noises commenced again. Three times I called Anne in, and then in the morning it all died away in a low moan.

Like Miss Morris, Mrs Gilby had trouble with the front-door bell.

> March 3rd I was writing in the drawing-room, when the front door bell rang violently. I asked who it was; 'No one, ma'am'. I thought I would stand by the window, and presently it rang again; down the servant came, no one there, and after the third time I told her not to go to the door unless she heard a knock as well. I knew no one had pulled the bell, as I was standing by the window. [Mrs G.'s diary entry for that day runs simply: – Heard the bell about 11. No one at the door.]

Space does not permit me to give further extracts from Mrs Gilby's statement and diary. The next occupants of the house, if such they can be called, were four gentlemen interested in psychic matters, who obtained access to the house on 23 May and again on 28 May. They had various exciting experiences, but were clearly such dedicated believers in the supernatural that their evidence is of very little value. The house thereafter remained empty until 17 August 1888, when there moved into it Mr G. A. Smith, an associate member of the SPR, and his wife. They were shortly joined by a maidservant, and during the next thirteen months (Smith left on 27 September 1889) 137 visitors, many of them members of the SPR, which was I presume subsidizing the tenancy, slept in the house. Smith maintained a diary of occurrences, from which I shall shortly give some extracts.

Smith himself was an interesting and very able man, who later became a pioneer in the field of cinematography. He died as recently as 1961, having been a member and life associate of the SPR for no less than seventy-three years. In the early 1880s his powers as a hypnotist and as an ostensible telepathic agent attracted the notice of Edmund Gurney, a leading member of the SPR. He became Gurney's secretary until the latter's death in 1888, and continued to assist other leading members of the SPR for several years thereafter. He is cast by Mr Trevor Hall in *The Strange Case of Edmund Gurney* (London, 1964) as the villain of the piece, the clever charlatan who fed his patrons with exactly the sorts of evidence for paranormal phenomena which they wished to hear, and the supposed discovery of whose duplicity led to Gurney's (alleged) suicide. Here I can only say that it does not seem to me that Mr Hall's arguments will stand examination (he relies for instance upon the 'confessions of Smith's former partner in telepathy experiments, Douglas Blackburn, a man we now know to have been almost incapable of telling the truth about anything), and that I have read several other reports on haunted houses by Smith, which seem to me workmanlike and level-headed, and to exhibit no tendency at all to favour the paranormality of the alleged happenings.

Here, then, are some extracts from Smith's diary:

> August 27th [1888]. – On two occasions today the front door bell rang violently. The first time no one was found at the door; the second time my wife was quick enough to detect two children in the act of running away.
>
> September 21st. – I, writing at my desk, heard noise overhead (apparently in front bedroom) like a person tapping upon the floor with a hammer, using about enough force to drive tacks in. Eight or ten knocks, and then silence. I at once got a light and went up. Could find no explanation. Wife out. Girl in kitchen in basement. Time, 8.5 p.m.
>
> October 10th. – My wife and I were taking tea in sitting room. Time, 5.38. Front door bell rang. I at once went to window to find out who visitor was, but could see no one. While I stood at window, thinking visitor must be standing in recess of doorway,

servant opened door. No one was there. I therefore went out and looked up and down the street. Two lamp-lighters on the other side were the only persons about, and they assured me that they had not observed anybody come up our steps.

December 9th. – . . . I was in the house alone, writing at my desk. Time 8.30. Suddenly I heard a noise which seemed to come from the hall, outside my room door. I can only compare the sound to that which would be made if half a brick were tied to a piece of string and jerked about over the linoleum – as one might jerk a reel to make a kitten playful. The bumping noise seemed to commence close to the door of the room in which I was sitting; it appeared to proceed along the passage to the top of the kitchen stairs – traversing a distance of some 15 ft in about half a dozen jumps – and then it seemed to turn the staircase corner and to jump down three or four stairs, one at a time. I went out, carrying my reading lamp with me, but nothing could I find, either in the passage or down the kitchen stairs. So, much puzzled, I returned and resumed my writing. In about five minutes the bumps began again, seeming to me to come from the part of the kitchen stairs where they had previously left off. This time I ran out too quickly to take the lamp with me. Just as I reached the head of the stairs the knocks stopped again. All was now dark, but fearing to lose time by returning for the lamp I went downstairs backwards, feeling along each stair with my hands as I proceeded. Reaching the bottom, I stepped into the kitchen and turned up the gas there, but nowhere was anything to be seen that could have caused these curious sounds. More perplexed still, I returned once more to my writing, but had scarcely shut the sitting-room door and settled myself at the desk when three sharp thumps sounded on the floor just outside the door. I sprang across the room and threw the door open. Nothing was to be seen. Again I searched in all directions – without getting the slightest hint of an explanation. The thing was inexplicable, and it has remained so to me ever since. At any rate, there are the facts. I can suggest no explanation. The idea that the noises really occurred in the next (empty) house does not commend itself to me for the simple reason that they seemed to be so distinctly in the places referred to. I was the only person in the house. We had no cat at that time; and we never at any time found any indications of mice in the place.

December 15th. – A most remarkable and inexplicable noise occurred at 11.35 p.m. on this date.

Our bedroom adjoined the sitting-room, and was separated

from it by curtains. Across one corner of the sitting-room (one of the corners adjoining the bedroom) a piano was placed, and over this instrument, upon the wall, hung a guitar. The guitar, as most people are aware, has six strings – three silver and three gut. On this night I had retired before my wife, and had been in bed about five minutes; she remained in the sitting-room in order to say her prayers by the fire, as it was a very cold night. In the midst of the quietness which ensued I suddenly heard the guitar play – *pung, pang, ping* – *pung, pang, ping* – here my wife called out in a loud, awe-struck whisper, 'Did you hear that?' whilst even as she spoke a third *pung, pang, ping*, sounded clearly through the rooms. I immediately sprang out of bed and rushed in to her, finding her kneeling upon the hearth-rug by an arm-chair, staring with astonishment at the guitar upon the wall. No more sounds were heard, though we sat waiting by the fire for over half an hour. My wife . . . said that when the guitar sounded its chords (in *arpeggio*) for the second and third time she was looking straight at the instrument, and such critical observation as she had at command under the surprise of the thing satisfied her that there was nothing visible near it, and that it made no perceptible movement. Well, that is all. The three gut strings of the guitar unmistakably sounded three times in succession (making nine notes altogether) when no person was touching it, and no thing was touching it as far as we could discover. The first explanation that suggests itself is that the pegs slipped round slightly and so caused the strings to vibrate and emit sounds . . . . But the answer to that suggestion is, 1st, the sounds were not of that sort – they were more clear and musical than the result of slipping pegs would be; 2nd, it is extremely improbable that three pegs would each slip just enough to produce the corresponding chord in a lower key; 3rd, if this improbable thing had happened *once* it could scarcely happen three times in succession, and without the changes of pitch being noticed; 4th, *all six strings of the guitar were perfectly in tune next day*! So slipping down is out of the question. How to account for the fact I do not know. I can only record it as it occurred, and leave it to others to estimate the probability of such a feat being accomplished by mice (in a house where mice were unknown), or by a moth (in December), or by something similar which escaped our observation.

June 29th [1889]. – Mrs. V. reported that when alone in the sitting-room, between seven and eight this evening, she heard a note from the guitar. Subsequently Mrs. V. stated that the note heard was somewhere about 'A above middle C' . . . . Mrs. V.

had no idea that the guitar had ever done this sort of thing. My wife and I were out at the time, and the servant was downstairs.

There are various other cases of hauntings of which contemporary diaries or notes have been kept and published. I shall briefly deal with two of these. Both are well-known, and both repeat many features of the cases just described, so I shall not go into too much detail. They have, however, some points of interest; and are richer in distinctively physical phenomena (object-movements) than the previous cases.

The first is the famous story of the haunting from 1834 to 1847 (and occasionally thereafter) at the Mill House, Willington Quay, near Wallsend, Northumberland. The case is commonly, but somewhat misleadingly, referred to as that of 'Willington Mill'. A casual reader might be led to cherish visions of sails, waterwheels and rural peace. Nothing could be further from the truth. The afflicted building was the substantial dwelling house attached to a steam-driven corn mill of factory proportions. The mill was built about 1800 (no doubt the power unit was one of James Watt's rotative beam engines) and was owned by two Quaker families, the Unthanks and the Procters. In later photographs (see W. T. Stead's *More Ghost Stories*, London, 1892, p. 62) house and mill stand gaunt and hideous; and even in their heyday, when the house had stables, and a garden with flowers and pear-trees, the buildings can have had little appeal.

The occupants of the Mill House during the main period of haunting were Joseph Procter, one of the partners in the firm, and his wife, children and servants. Even before the Procters left, stories of the haunting were in print, most, but not all, at second-hand. The early material may conveniently be read in that delightful (and erudite) early classic of popular parapsychology, Catherine Crowe's *The Night-Side of Nature* (London, 1849). Joseph Procter, a man whose probity and sobriety were above suspicion, kept what has been called a 'diary' of the phenomena. Many years after his death this was edited by his son Edmund for the *Journal of the SPR*, vol. 5, 1892, from which it has several times been reprinted. It is not strictly a diary, but rather a series of memoranda, some dated and contemporary with the events they describe, some not, of the strange happenings which puzzled and frightened his family for lengthy periods. Many of the phenomena which Procter notes were experienced by persons other than himself. I do not regard this as a serious disadvantage, since he undoubtedly recorded their stories with care; we know, however, that his own experiences were more numerous than would appear from his 'diary', of which parts seem to have been lost. Some additional particulars of the haunting come from the reminiscences of Mrs Mary Davidson (*née* Mary Young) who was employed for eight years as cook at the Mill House (she is mentioned in Procter's diary). These are contained in a series of articles which her son, Robert Davidson, wrote for the *Newcastle Weekly Leader*. The articles are utilized in the account of the haunting in Stead's *More Ghost Stories*, mentioned above.

The Mill House was the scene of a considerable number and diversity of odd events. These are concisely categorized by Procter himself in a letter of 1853, which I take from *The Spiritual Magazine*, vol. 4, 1863, pp. 31-2.

> Simulations of ordinary sounds but for which there was no natural cause, were frequently heard equally by all persons within hearing of them, and often by day as well as in the night, with occasional intervals of absence, for a series of years, such sounds as shutting and opening of doors and windows, bolts and bars, setting down and moving about of chairs, boxes, etc., stirring the fire, ringing a small bell, winding up a clock, the noise of a carriage on the floor and driving up outside, a chirrup like a bird, and the rattle of a storm of rain, stepping, stamping, thumping and walking in a rustling gown, add to all these coughing, moaning, and articulate sounds, add to all these additional testimony from the sense of touch, and from that of sight by occasional apparitions both in the house and its vicinity, altogether afford a superabundance of proof as to the nature of these visitations such as no ingenuity could counterfeit, and no scepticism invalidate.

The phantasms which Procter here mentions very briefly were numerous and diverse; they included a figure like a transparent and luminous priest in a white surplice; the head and hands of an old woman; a boy in a drab suit; a man with grey hair; a figure in a shroud; a girl in a lavender dress; a monkey (seen collectively by several children); and several other small animals. With such an *embarras de richesse* in the matter of apparitions, one is tempted to revert to seventeenth-century modes of thought, and suppose the poltergeist to be an entity capable of assuming divers visible forms; or else to dismiss the whole tale as

> Cobwebs, fit for scull
> That's empty when the Moon is full;
> Such as take Lodgings in a Head
> That's to be let unfurnished.

But the latter course would be premature. This case has so much in common with so many others. It will be observed, for instance, that many of the noises were imitative. Procter himself remarks on the fact. He could hardly have failed to do so after some of his own experiences. On the last night on which he and his wife slept in the house, the rest of the family having preceded them to a new one,

> there were continuous noises during the night, boxes being apparently dragged with heavy thuds down the now carpetless stairs, non-human footsteps stumped on the floors, doors were, or seemed to be, clashed, and impossible furniture corded at random or dragged hither and thither by inscrutable agency; in short, a pantomimic or spiritualistic repetition of all the noises incident to a household flitting.

It will be remembered that Miss Sharpe had a very similar experience in her house at Tackley. An even more remarkable instance of imitative noises is this. One night early in 1835, Thomas Mann, the foreman of the Mill – described by Procter as 'a man of strict veracity and integrity' – went into the Mill yard to fetch coals for the engine. In this yard there stood a moveable wooden water cistern on iron wheels. When this cistern was drawn by a horse to be filled it made a loud, and absolutely characteristic, sound, especially when the wheels creaked through lack of grease. This sound Thomas Mann now heard as though the cistern were being dragged towards the yard gates. Afraid that it was being stolen, he set off in pursuit – only to find that it had never stirred from its place.

In the following most curious incident the imitative sounds had concordant visual and tactile accompaniments:

> On 2nd mo., 5th, between 11 and 12 at night, Jane C. [Jane Carr, Procter's sister-in-law] heard a thump on the landing near the bedroom door, upon which she awoke her companion, Mary Young [the cook mentioned above – 'a most respectable and intelligent woman']. Mary Young heard the slot in the door apparently slide back, the handle to turn and the door to open. A rushlight was burning in the dressing table, but the bed was an old four-poster, and the curtains being drawn, nothing could be seen. A

step then went to the rushlight and appeared by the sound to snuff it and then lay down the snuffers. In the act of snuffing the light was transiently obscured, as when that act is customarily performed. Jane C. then felt it raise up the clothes over her twice; then they both heard something rustle the curtains as it went round the bed; on getting to Mary Young's side she distinctly saw a dark shadow on the curtain. On getting to the bed-board where Jane C. lay a loud thump as with a fist was heard on it; something was then felt to press on the counterpane on M. Young's side of the bed, the bed curtain being pushed in but nothing more seen. Whatever the visitor might be was then heard to go out, seeming to leave the door open. In the morning they found the door still bolted as it was left when they went to bed.

This last circumstance – that the door which had seemed to open was all the time bolted – might well make one suppose that the noises and tactile impressions, as well as their visual accompaniments, were one and all hallucinatory, and lead one to speculate about the scope of hallucination in the case as a whole. Yet the same Mary Young who on this occasion found the door still bolted, stated (so her son says) that sometimes doors in the Mill House were actually unbolted and opened, and that once a table moved on its own right across her room. She also described how John Richardson, an old and trusted servant of the Procters, sat up one night with an elderly Quaker gentleman. Whilst the latter was trying to read the Bible the candle began to jump and oscillate in its holder so that he could not see to read. This performance was repeated every time the Quaker resumed his Bible.

Several instances of apparently paranormal object-movements are recorded in Procter's diary. The most elementary are the perceptible vibrations which sometimes accompanied the raps and thumps which were at times a prominent feature of the haunting. 'I heard a tap on the cradle leg,' wrote Procter in February 1835, 'as with a piece of steel, and distinctly felt the vibration of the wood in my hand from the blow.' Was the vibration also hallucinatory? I do not know, but at least it seems unlikely that the unaccountable bed shakings which disturbed the rest of various persons in the house could have been; still less does this seem likely where the beds were actually raised up with persons in them, a phenomenon of which Procter mentions several examples.

About the 21 inst. [December, probably 1835] E.P. [Mrs Procter] and nurse Pollard both felt themselves raised up and let down three times. [Note by Edmund Procter: My mother has described this experience to me; she said the bed was lifted up as if a man were underneath pushing it up with his back. She did not speak to nurse Pollard, nor the nurse to her, each thinking that the other was asleep; this not being disclosed until breakfast time.] On the 15th, about 8 p.m., J.P., jun., who had been in bed about half an hour, called of [*sic*] someone to come to him and begged for a light; he said that something under the crib raised him up very quickly many times, and wished to know what it could be. On the 11th of 1st mo., whilst the servants were at dinner, E.P. was lying on the sofa in her lodging-room when she felt the floor to vibrate as from a heavy foot in an adjoining room; in the writing room underneath J.C. at the same time heard the sound of a person walking backwards and forwards in the room above.

A story repeated by several writers does not occur in Procter's diary, but comes from M. A. Richardson's *The Local Historian's Table Book* ('Legendary and Divine', vol. 1, London, 1843, pp. 299–304):

> The two young ladies, who on a visit there, had also been annoyed by this invisible agent, gave me this account of it: The first night, as they were sleeping in the same bed, they felt the bed lifted up beneath them. Of course, they were much alarmed. They feared lest some one had concealed himself there for the purpose of robbery. They gave an alarm, search was made, but nothing was found. On another night, their bed was violently shaken, and the curtains suddenly hoisted up all round to the very tester [i.e. canopy over the bed], as if pulled by cords, and as rapidly let down again, several times. Search again produced no evidence of the cause.

Physical phenomena, in the form of ostensibly paranormal object-movements, were still more marked and definite in the last case of haunting upon which I shall touch, that of the Chateau de T—— in Normandy (apparently near Bayeux) in 1867, and again in 1875–6. The chateau was built about 1835 near the site of an old castle. The original account of the haunting comes from two articles by Dr J. Morice, a French lawyer, in the *Annales des sciences psychiques*, vols 2 and 3, 1892 and 1893. It is largely translated in the English edition of Camille Flammarion's *Haunted Houses* (London, 1924) and was reprinted thence in

Sacheverell Sitwell's *Poltergeists* (London, 1940). The story is thus pretty well known, and I shall not dwell upon it in detail.

The records in this case may be put into two categories. Firstly, we have the diary of the owner of the chateau, 'M. de X.' from 13 October 1875 to 29 January 1876. Then we have letters, all, seemingly of the year 1893, from various surviving witnesses to Morice and to Dr Dariex, the editor of the *Annales des sciences psychiques* (who, we may note, vouches for the honesty and intelligence of 'M. de X.') M. de X.'s diary is sometimes of considerable interest; but very often it fails to report details which one would wish to know, such as which phenomenon was observed by which witness, and of course pseudonyms, which so far no-one has managed to break, are used throughout. Quite commonly it is not clear whether the author is reporting his own experiences or those of other members of his household.

That household consisted of M. and Mme de X. and their young son, Maurice; the Abbé Y., Maurice's tutor; a coachman (Émile), a gardener (Auguste), a housemaid (Amélina) and a cook (Célina). In addition various visitors came to help in the investigation of the phenomena.

Those phenomena were singularly violent and macabre; and I recommend this case with confidence to anyone whose scientific detachment is not so rigorous as to preclude his enjoying the occasional midnight *frisson*. Few stories can match the dramatic impact of the knocks, raps, and long-drawn-out cries, which rose one November night above the wind, thunder and lightning of a frightful storm, and few can offer an effect so sinister as the 'loud noise of tread' with 'nothing human about it' which a few nights before had rushed up the stairs from the entrance hall to the first floor, along the passage and up to the second floor 'like two legs deprived of their feet and walking on the stumps'. None the less much about this case conforms to the pattern of many other hauntings. The phenomena were largely, though not always, nocturnal, and imitative noises were prominent amongst them. These included footsteps, blows, sounds as of heavy objects being thrown down, sobs and cries, a rolling noise as of a heavy ball, a stampeding or galloping sound, laughing and coughing, and sounds like the playing of the harmonium. Sometimes the imitative nature of the sounds was made directly apparent. Thus on 15 October 1875, the Abbé and Amélina 'clearly heard steps imitating my wife's and mine, as well as our conversation. It sounded to them as if we were going along the passage into our room. Amélina maintains that she heard both our voices.' Once when M. de X. had been playing on his harmonium, and had finally closed the instrument, 'some of the airs he had been playing were repeated in the opposite corner of the drawing-room for a considerable time'.

It is, however, the alleged examples of paranormal object-movements which I particularly wish to mention. Once again we may note that some of the noises just mentioned are said to have produced perceptible vibrations. Thus M. de X.'s diary record of the night of 1–2 January 1876 runs: 'At 1.5 a.m. hard blows were struck on the door of the green room, and we all awoke . . . . A violent blow fell on the door of the green room, and three more inside. Eight muffled blows seemed to come from the second floor. The taper beside me shook at each blow'.

As in so many examples of hauntings, bedclothes were pulled off persons in bed, and doors were opened and closed. The door openings were not hallucinatory, the doors concerned being sometimes left open. Door-handles were seen to turn, and once one was torn off. Doors were locked and unlocked, and on one occasion (29 December 1875)

> Mme de X., hearing a noise in the Abbé's room, goes up there, followed by the latter. She heard a movement in the room, and put out her right hand to open the latch of the door. Before she could touch it she saw the key turn quickly in the lock and detach itself, hitting her left hand. The Abbé witnessed this. The blow was so strong that the place was sensitive and visible two days afterwards.

At least once Mme de X. heard the sound of the bolt on her door being withdrawn. And it had been drawn. Ornaments, books and heavy items of furniture were not infrequently displaced, even inside locked rooms. Sometimes furniture was found arranged 'as for a council meeting' or in other ways. Occasionally objects were *seen* to move. A favourite site for such disturbances was the Abbé's room (or the room or rooms occupied by the two successive Abbés who acted as young Maurice's tutor). This room seems also to have served as a schoolroom, which may give some encouragement to those who would like to cast Maurice in the role of orthodox poltergeist agent. M. de X.'s diary for 13 October 1875 runs as follows:

> The Abbé Y. having told us that his armchair changed its place,

my wife and I accompanied him to his room, and we minutely observed the place of every object. We attached gummed paper to the foot of the armchair, and so fixed it to the floor. We left him then, asking him to call me should anything extraordinary happen. At a quarter to ten the Abbé heard on the wall of his room a series of slight raps, which, however, were loud enough to be also heard by Amélina, who slept in the opposite room. He then heard in a corner of the room a noise as of the winding of a big clock. Then a candlestick on his mantelpiece was moved with a grating noise, and finally he heard and thought he saw his armchair move. As he durst not get up, he rang the bell, and I went up. On entering the room I found the armchair had moved over a yard and was turned towards the fireplace. An extinguisher placed on the base of the candlestick was put on the candle; the other candlestick had been moved into a position where it overhung the mantelpiece by about an inch. A statuette placed against the mirror had been advanced 8 inches.

Noises like the winding of a big clock, the winding of a jack (i.e. a mechanical turn-spit), etc. have been reported with curious frequency in cases of haunting (e.g. Epworth, 1716; Willington, 1834–47). The Abbé wrote to Dr Morice in 1893, confirming M. de X.'s account of the phenomena at the Chateau de T——, which he, the Abbé, now a parish priest, continued to ascribe to the Devil. His successor as Maurice's tutor also witnessed inexplicable object-movements in his room. A cupboard (he wrote in a letter to Morice in 1893) laden with books and linen rose in broad daylight twenty inches off the ground and remained up for some time. He pressed on the cupboard but it did not yield. It descended afterwards of its own accord.

The phenomena in the Chateau de T—— appeared to be temporarily subdued by the presence of a Premonstratensian canon in the house, and also by a novena of masses said at Lourdes towards the end of January 1876. They were, however, resumed again as strongly as before in August and September 1876; and the despairing owner eventually sold the house and went to live elsewhere.

So much, then, by way of a few sample cases of hauntings, selected primarily because contemporary diary records of the phenomena have come down to us. Further and more recent cases of hauntings will be discussed in the next chapter, and in

Part II. Accounts of hauntings do not, even where we have diary records, generally reach the same evidential standard and the same degree of detail, as the best documented poltergeist stories. No doubt this is in part because classic person-centred poltergeists tend to be over in a few eventful days, or weeks, so that outside investigators have sometimes been able to arrive on the scene and devote their whole time to the case; whereas hauntings are long-drawn-out, and the phenomena intermittent, and such records as we have come from residents on the spot who have commonly many other tasks to occupy their minds. None the less it seems to me that in the cases described in this chapter we have no reason to doubt that the principal phenomena occurred as narrated. Details may sometimes be sparse – so sparse that it is difficult to make up one's mind about the hypotheses of trickery, natural causes, etc. – but the chief recorders appear to have been persons of integrity with no particular axes to grind. Furthermore the existence of contemporary diaries is some kind of insurance against the possibility of retrospective exaggeration and distortion. The questions which require discussion at this point are therefore the ones which I posed at the outset, viz. to what extent are the odd happenings reported in cases of hauntings physical? Do they transcend the boundaries of ordinary natural explanation (including trickery)? And can 'hauntings' be clearly separated from poltergeists?

At first glance one might well say that in most cases of hauntings there are among the reported phenomena plenty that are incontestably physical. Objects have been displaced, beds levitated, bedclothes pulled away, wire bells rung with appropriate movements of the cranks, door-handles turned, doors opened or unbolted, floors heavily tramped upon, walls, doors, tables, etc., quite distinctly rapped. All these sorts of events can be illustrated from the cases discussed in this chapter. But of course nothing in this field is ever as simple as it appears at first sight. Those who wish to sunder cases of hauntings from cases of poltergeists and assimilate them to certain cases of veridical hallucinations (recurrent localized apparitions) will certainly argue that since the standard 'haunting' phenomena are so often associated with recurrent phantasmal figures, the former as well as the latter must be regarded as hallucinatory. In support of this view they adduce occasional examples of imitative noises heard by person A but not by his companion, person B; or of doors heard to open, but afterwards found to be shut; and so on. There are, however, three lines of argument which incline me against such a position. The first is that in at any rate some cases of hauntings – for instance the Chateau de T——, and perhaps also Willington, and others which I shall discuss later – ostensibly physical phenomena have taken place that have in fact left a clear trace behind them: objects have been in reality displaced, bolts drawn, doors opened, objects smashed, etc. The second is that if normal human beings together or in succession see door-handles turn, feel beds rise under them or bedclothes pulled off them, hear bells jangle (with attendant movements of wires and cranks), and so on and so forth, then *we have evidence that certain sorts of physical events occurred;* and if one dismisses this evidence for reasons of theoretical tidiness related to one's views about certain sorts of visual hallucinations (recurrent apparitions) one is in danger of insulating one's theoretical position from any modifications by the facts – a tendency which, carried to extremes, lands people in lunatic asylums. The third is as follows. Those phenomena of hauntings which it is easiest to reconcile with the hallucination theory are without doubt what I have called the 'imitative sounds' – sounds as of footsteps, heavy objects falling, voices, groans, raps and taps, rustling as of dresses, and so forth (I have already cited many examples). Now these sounds, generally speaking, do not seem to be caused by any such physical event as would ordinarily produce noises of the kinds in question. This certainly makes it tempting to regard them as hallucinatory. But I cannot help thinking that, while they may indeed possess acoustic peculiarities, it is more probable than not that they are physical in origin. Several witnesses have noticed the vibrations which may accompany raps and blows (I gave two examples above). Even if these vibrations be set aside as themselves hallucinatory, other considerations remain. Although there are occasional examples of persons whom one would have expected to hear a certain 'imitative sound' had it been objective and physical, not hearing it, such examples are not all that common – and of course we have no data as to how the people concerned would have fared with ordinary noises. I have not found a clear instance of such a failure to hear in any of the cases discussed in this chapter. In fact Procter says (in the letter of 1853 quoted above) that at

Willington everyone who was in a position to hear, heard; a statement that is backed up by his diary, which, indeed, contains examples of persons in separate rooms having heard the same sounds from the same direction at the same time. Now auditory hallucinations are not uncommon, and shared auditory hallucinations are not unknown; but that the members of a household should have frequent auditory hallucinations nearly all of which are shared by nearly all of the persons who could appropriately share them is a phenomenon quite without parallel in the annals of auditory hallucination. The only relevant statistics come from the so-called 'Census of Hallucinations' conducted by the Society for Psychical Research in the period 1889–94 (the results are published in volume 10 of the *Proceedings of the SPR*). This census (of 17 000 persons) obtained 493 examples of auditory hallucinations (only hallucinatory voices were considered). Of these 34 were shared and 459 unshared. In 60 of the 459 unshared cases, the experient had a waking companion. In other words, about a third of the experiences which should have been shared in the case of real sounds were shared in the case of auditory hallucinations. This figure is much too low to fulfil our present requirement.

There are also, it is perhaps worth noting, several alleged tape recordings of imitative sounds in ostensible hauntings. One of them was in the Scarborough, Ontario, case of 1968–71, with which may be compared the curious but second-hand story in case 456 (see Appendix). A great deal more technical and acoustic information would be required before we could fully assess these recordings; none the less I would lay odds of two to one, or three to one at dead of night, that if a tape recording were made during the production of imitative sounds, these sounds would register.

This brings us to my second question – given that the phenomena of hauntings are for the most part objective and physical, can we find natural causes, albeit of a disguised kind, in terms of which to explain them? It is pretty clear that, generally speaking, *if the phenomena are as reported*, they are beyond the reach of any ordinary explanation. Beds do not rise in the air under their own steam, nor do voices speak out of mid-air, door-handles turn untouched, or raps resound in fusillades from walls and doors in the absence of knuckles, stick or central heating. Those who wish to deny the occurrence of paranormal physical phenomena in hauntings have to supplement their 'natural cause' explanation by invoking such further factors as misperception, misremembering and trickery. And here we run upon general issues which are reserved for later discussion (chapter 13). It is, however, worth noting at this point that misremembering is not a strong card to play in cases where our chief sources of information are contemporary diaries. Misperception and trickery are rather harder possibilities to assess; and it is here that one particularly regrets that the diaries did not go into far greater detail. However, in three of our four main cases trickery and misperception hardly seem plausible explanations of all or many of the reported occurrences. One needs to read the original documents in full to appreciate just how complex, sustained and ingenious the trickery would have had to have been, and how preposterous the misperceptions. Perhaps Joseph Procter, M. de X., Miss Sharpe or G. A. Smith were hapless fools, easily deceived or illuded; but that is by no means the reputation they enjoyed among those who knew them; and if, in the interests of scientific tidy-mindedness, one retrospectively imputes idiocy to them, one is again unhealthily protecting one's opinions from the facts.

One of our main cases, however, presents some especial difficulties of assessment. The Brighton house was in a terrace, and it can (as I know from personal experience) be exceptionally tricky to work out what may or may not be going on in such a house. According to an unpublished note in the SPR archives, the second tenant to be troubled by the spook, Mrs Gilby, became very suspicious of two elderly and eccentric ladies (they were about 80!) who shared an adjoining house. She discovered some holes in the wall which separated her loft from theirs, and formed the notion that the old ladies had manipulated the bell wires, which ran through the loft, via these holes. However, the bell-ringings did not cease when the holes were blocked up. Mrs Gilby's suspicions increased after she had been out of the house a few months (she came to believe that blocking the holes *had* in fact ended the bell-ringing), and she proposed to Mr G. A. Smith, the new tenant, that he should set a trap. All this strikes me as mere wishful seeking for a scapegoat, a phenomenon which I have frequently encountered. A more serious possibility is that some of the noises which upset Mrs Gilby may have been misperceptions of sounds from the next-door house. Her maid,

Anne Holden, thought that the frightful sobs and cries which so terrified Mrs Gilby on the occasion I described above originated there. She did not, however, think the same about other strange sounds which she heard, and Mrs Gilby was adamant that the sweet and clear woman's voice which she heard appeal for help was not that of either of the old dames. G. A. Smith specifically states, in a passage from his diary which I quoted above, that he did not think that sounds which he heard came from next door. Certainly the acoustics of terraced houses may take a bit of getting used to; but generally speaking getting used to them is only a matter of time.

The last of my three questions – that of the continuity or otherwise between hauntings and poltergeists – will be taken up in the succeeding chapters. Here I will only comment upon attempts to maintain a clear and complete distinction between hauntings and poltergeists by trying to force all cases of hauntings in which paranormal physical phenomena have apparently taken place into the mould of person-centred poltergeists. Although in all four of the main cases described in this chapter there were on the scene young people (maids, daughters, young Maurice) whom many parapsychologists might regard as possible poltergeist agents, in no instance was there any very evident tendency for the phenomena to centre round a particular person, nor was the presence in the house of any particular person essential to their continuance. In fact in three of the cases (Brighton, Willington, the Chateau de T——), the phenomena seem to have survived complete changes of personnel.

11 Some intermediate cases

I talked in the last chapter as though we had to deal with two, and only two, major classes of phenomena, which, whatever lies behind them, are on the surface markedly different. These classes were 'hauntings', centred on a place, and poltergeists, centred on a person. This division of cases is one commonly, if tacitly, accepted, and I questioned it only by doubting whether one should build into it the assumption that the principal phenomena of 'hauntings' are hallucinatory in nature. But even among the limited number of cases described in this book are several which do not fit very readily into this simplistic dichotomy. For example the very first case I discussed, the Stans case of 1860–2, exhibited many of the leading features of *both* hauntings *and* poltergeists, yet without the clear link to a place generally thought symptomatic of a haunting or the clear link to a person generally thought symptomatic of a poltergeist. In it there were on the one hand such characteristic haunting phenomena as footsteps, imitative noises, phantasms, voices, luminous appearances, and the opening and closing of doors and windows, and on the other hand such typical poltergeist effects as raps, stone-throwing, and object-movements. Very similar remarks might be made about, for instance, the Epworth case of 1716 or the Tidworth case of 1662–3. Despite the fact that it was not clearly person-centred, the Epworth case is commonly presented as a poltergeist case, the most famous of its kind. It had, however, many of the classic features of 'hauntings' – footsteps, imitative noises, animal phantasms, a preference for the hours of darkness – without, however, being undeniably linked to a particular house regardless of changes of occupant. Several writers have tried to retain cases such as these in the ranks of orthodox poltergeists by finding in them candidates for the role of poltergeist agent; but it would be at least as plausible to classify them as somewhat short-lived hauntings, provided, of course, one admits that paranormal physical events may happen in cases of haunting.

There have, however, also been some cases in which the phenomena have been of kinds generally thought typical of poltergeists rather than of hauntings, but in which there have been no clear indications of either a person link or a place link. Consider, for example, the exceptionally violent disturbances which astounded and terrified the occupants of a lodging house in Oakland, California, for three successive nights in April 1874. Of these disturbances we have very full records – so full that I cannot attempt to do justice to them here. Immediately after the disturbances had ceased a committee of three prominent local persons was appointed to enquire into them. The committee took statements, cross-examined the witnesses, and issued a report; and the owner of the house, Mr T. B. Clarke, later wrote a pamphlet on the happenings there. Report, minutes of cross-examinations, and pamphlet, with introduction and commentary by Professor J. H. Hyslop, occupy no less than 232 pages of volume 7 of the *Proceedings of the American SPR* (1913). The most frequent occurrences were object-movements. These included a good many movements of heavy items of furniture. Several witnesses stated that they had seen chairs flung across the room, or rise into the air when no one was near enough to have touched them. Sometimes the chairs were whirled round in the air or otherwise apparently manipulated rather than simply raised or thrown. The members of the committee were highly sceptical, and their suspicions, though not directly stated, fell somewhat markedly upon one particular person in the household. It is not abundantly clear why he was thus singled out – possibly factors not directly related to the poltergeist had something to do with it. At any rate, the depositions of the witnesses, if we are to accept them more or less as they stand, show that he could not have produced all, or anything like all, of the phenomena. It may of course be the case that those depositions are riddled with errors of observation and of memory; but it must be remembered that all the principal depositions were taken down within a very few days of the events concerned. Furthermore, if there were such errors, the errors of the different witnesses were curiously concordant – enough so for the concordances themselves to constitute an odd phenomenon. In short, there is no very conclusive evidence that the gentleman concerned was either the perpetrator of fraud or a poltergeist 'agent', and quite a lot that he was neither. Nor – despite the fact that there was a teenage girl in the house – is there much that tends to incriminate anybody else. We have here a case with many of the marks of a poltergeist, but lacking either a clear person link or a clear place link.

Cases like this are by no means uncommon. I select, almost at random, an American example almost a hundred years later than the Oakland case. The phenomena concerned took place in a house in New Jersey from early 1972 until at least 1974, and are reported (*Theta*, winter/spring 1974) by an investigator, R. Rosenberg, who witnessed some of them. They included apports (the removal of pills from a bottle), movements of small objects, the swinging of a lamp, the unlocking of doors, writing on walls with a crayon. Rosenberg succeeded in recording the swinging of the lamp on cine-film (there were no draughts or other obvious natural causes). There was nothing to link the happenings decisively either with the house or with one or more of the occupants.

Some parapsychologists try to assimilate cases such as these to simple categories e.g. by thrusting poltergeist agenthood upon one person on the scene, or by supposing some kind of collective agency. Another possibility – one with which quite a lot of the data can be plausibly squared – is that there may be among the causes of poltergeist phenomena both person-linked factors and place-linked factors, each tending in isolation to produce somewhat, but not completely, different parts of the spectrum of phenomena with which we are concerned, but capable when occurring together of summating or interacting to produce unusual effects or cases. We might further suppose that in certain cases *both* factors are necessary for the occurrence of phenomena. In such cases there will be no immediately evident place link, for the phenomena will not occur in the absence of the agent or agents; and there may likewise be no immediately obvious person link, for the phenomena will not follow the agent to other places.

It is, at a certain level, easy enough to fit quite a number of cases into this scheme of things, including, of course, the ones I have just been talking about. We have, for example, a small number of cases in which a person-centred poltergeist is as it were superimposed upon an established haunting of the classic kind, and interacts with it to a limited extent. As an example I shall describe, in some detail since it is little-known, an old but none the less interesting case, of which we have a contemporary record, namely the Canvey Island case of 1709.

The record is contained in an anonymous pamphlet of 1709, *An Exact Narrative of Many Surprizing* Matters of Fact *uncontestably wrought by an Evil Spirit* . . . , and has in part the form of a day by day narrative of occurrences. The narrative is not, however, a diary. The author came over from Maldon very shortly after the disturbances ceased (he dates his pamphlet 'St. Michael and all angels', i.e. 29 September, 1709, thirteen days after the last phenomena) and collected the eyewitness testimony of various witnesses. He sets out the results in a lucid and literate manner, and I should suppose him to have been a person of some education. The fact that we do not know his name detracts of course from the value of his account, though it might be possible to hazard a guess at his identity. Be that as it may, I do not think that there can be any question of his having invented the story; for, quite apart from the mass of extremely convincing local detail, which Defoe himself could hardly have surpassed in a work of fiction, and the conformity of many occurrences to patterns common in hauntings and poltergeists, there is no doubt that the principal *dramatis personae* really existed. Jan Smagge, for example, the occupant of the troubled house, is known to have died at a fair age about the year 1720 – his will is preserved in the Essex County Record Office. Mr Lord, the minister, was the recently appointed Church of England curate-in-charge of Canvey Island (Marston Acres, *Canvey Island and its Churches*, n.d., n.p., p. 3). I have come across references to several other persons mentioned in the pamphlet, and no doubt a fuller search than I have had time for would unearth many more. Another suggestion (A. A. Daly, *The History of Canvey Island*, London, 1902, pp. 24–6), is that the whole affair was got up by the islanders to lure Mr Lord away from the previously untenanted church while smuggled goods were removed from it. This proposal (smugglers have also been mentioned in connection with the Sampford Peverell case of 1810–12) exemplifies a not uncommon variety of hard-headed approach to spook stories – think of someone, even just of a possible someone, who could have had a motive for perpetrating the phenomena, and then assume that he must have perpetrated them. Do not worry at all over *how* he perpetrated them, or over whether a way of perpetrating them is even conceivable.

The setting, then, of this little drama, is the substantial farmhouse of Jan Smagge, a member of the small Dutch community which had held lands on Canvey Island for nearly a century in consequence of land reclamation which they had undertaken there. Canvey Island, it will be recalled, is a small, flat island, about four miles by two, on the north bank of the Thames, and separated from the Essex coast by a narrow creek. In the early eighteenth century it was a remote and lonely spot, reclaimed from the estuarine marshes, and occupied only by a few hardy farmers and their dependants. Ghosts must have been easy to imagine when the river mists crept over the quiet land; and for living persons it was not a healthy place. The peculiar terrain had, however, its advantages from our point of view, for, according to the author of our pamphlet, Smagge's house (which lay in the small part of Canvey Island then annexed to the Parish of Laindon)

> by its standing alone and on a plain and open Ground, without Lane or Hedge about it, is so situate, and the prospect on all sides free, that 'tis impossible any cloathed with material Bodies, cou'd be able to conceal themselves in staying; or considering the continual quick pursuits were made after a disturbance given, to carry themselves off, without discovery.

It seems that Smagge's house had been built, and for a considerable while occupied, by a certain man who, with his wife, 'was lookt upon in their life-time, jointly to have scraped together in the said House, by Fraudulent and Oppressive means, a considerable lump of Pelf'. The husband had survived his wife by a number of years, and had apparently died in the late 1670s. For some years after his death, so 'neighbours yet living' affirmed, unaccountable noises were heard about the house, and doors were inexplicably and violently opened and shut. These molestations continually increasing, a cunning man was called in to lay the spectre, 'some saying they knew the Man by whom it was done; remember the Time, and have seen the Book with which he did it: And farther tell, That most horrible Noises and Distractions fill'd the House whilst the Work was about'.

The endeavours of the cunning man were not, however, completely successful. For

> Noises have still from time to time been heard; though all say not with that Terror and Loudness as before: To wit, since that a Woman hath been heard to come up Stairs, and at the top to

vanish. The Latch of a Door to be lifted up. A great Light seen in the Hall, in the Night by the Master, when none have been up, and neither Candle nor Fire in the House. A Servant-man of Probity, and a conscientious Principle, ... does aver, He hath divers times heard, seemingly, the chinking of Money at his Bed-side; and one time, a Woman, as he supposed, by the ruffling of her petticoats, to walk about his Bed the whole Night, till towards Day-Break, and then in appearance to go away, clapping the Door with a great force after her. The Appearance of the aforesaid Deceased Person, as having on a Grey-Coat, such as he used to wear in his Life-time, hath been twice seen standing at an old Barn in the Fields, that formerly was his.

Various further instances are given of the appearance of this phantasm, and also of the figure of a woman, to particular persons. It will be noted how characteristic of hauntings in general are all these phenomena. Not without parallel, too, are the whistles (said to resemble those of the 'deceased person') which several witnesses said they had heard outside the house when no one was about.

We come now to Saturday 10 September 1709. About four o'clock that afternoon a maid of sixteen, named Mary Moss (she had previously seen both the apparitions mentioned above), was working in the kitchen. She saw a shadow at the door as though a man were coming up to it, and immediately a dead but still twitching chicken was thrown into the room. She and another person who was nearby at once ran out and searched round the house and barn, but could find no-one. In the evening a post mortem was conducted on the chicken, with curious results:

> And the Mouth being first open'd there were found cram'd into the entrance of the Throat 76 Barly-Corns; then feeling the Neck as it were broke, the Feathers being first pluckt, they slit the skin of the Neck up to see that, and instead of broken, found it nicely cut Flesh and Bone together as with a keen Knife, without the least roughness, but as absolutely smooth as a Radish can be cut, and the two ends when put together to join as compleatly as two Parts of a Radish can do, which as the Head was on, and not the least scratch or impression on the out side of the Neck, and the whole Body entire, exceeds without farther Proof, all the moral Causes and Operations in the World.

Killing of, or injury or annoyance to animals has been reported in quite a number of poltergeist cases; but of course such stories are extremely hard to assess. The poltergeist proper began on the afternoon of Tuesday 13 September 1709, with a repeated jarring of one of the outer doors. It appears that Mary Moss, the maid, and a lady who is referred to throughout the narrative as 'the Person' or 'that Other Person' or 'one other' (appellations which make one wonder about Mr Smagge's domestic arrangements) were alone in the house with a neighbour's child of three and a half, Mary and the child in the kitchen, the Person in the parlour. A particularly loud bounce on the door caused Mary to open it, and the Person to look through the parlour window at it. No one was to be seen. The Person then returned to the parlour, and shortly heard a bounce as of a stone against the weatherboards beneath the window where she sat. She called Mary, and both went out; but they saw nothing. The Person, 'beginning now to apprehend there to be some of the old usual Disturbances', returned to the parlour to put by her work, but immediately

> she heard the Glass break in the Hall; which Room lyes between the Parlour and the Kitchen; and the Maid skreeking, she then went back, and they found three Panes broken in the middle Window: then not having dispatch'd in the Parlour, she returned again thither, but presently she heard more Glass break in the Hall, and the Maid to scream as before; they then found two Panes more broken.

At this the Person went into the harvest field to inform Mr Smagge and his work-folk what had passed. On her return she found the maid and the child sitting by a gate. Mary said that, being afraid, she had gone outside with the child and sat upon the threshold of the door. Immediately all the hall windows were broken with a terrible clatter. A later count showed that no less than nineteen panes had been broken (the windows were clearly leaded ones with small panes).

The next day, Wednesday 14 September, about seven or eight o'clock in the morning, a great stone was thrown in through the 'fore door'. It went across a short passage and into the hall. The fore door was closed behind it. Shortly after this Mr Lord, the minister, arrived. While he was walking and talking in the hall, apparently with the Person,

> a great knock was given upon the Table close by them, and immediately following it, a noise of breaking of Glass in the Parlour; Mr. *Lord*, and that other Person, instantly ran into the

Parlour, and found three Panes broken and a large piece of Pantile sticking in the window; after they had view'd it with Wonder on the inside, they went to see it without. Mr. *Lord* observing the place where the Tile stuck to be above the reach of any ordinary Man; and the Tile to hang in such a strange Geometrick Manner, betwixt the broken Lead and Glass, that one can scarcely think a less artist than he that cut the Chicken's Neck cou'd so place it.

After this Mr Lord had to leave. The maid and the Person were soon afterwards alarmed by repeated rattlings on the pantiles of the beer-room. Even when one remained in the beer-room and the other went outside to look at the roof nothing could be seen, though the sounds continued. During a brief visit from 'Master *Smagge*' glass was broken in the kitchen window. When he left, the maid and the Person were again left alone.

> As they were standing in the Kitchen, looking towards the back door, the Door open, and the Coast clear, they saw a piece of Tile come in of the said Door, about two Foot from the Ground, but very leasurely; and yet so strait, as though it had moved on a Line; and then, in a languid manner, after its creeping thus five or six yards in her sight, touching against the Gown of one of them, (who but the Arch-Juggler could so throw it?) fell down near her Feet; the other, who was the Maid, ran to catch it up; but let it fall, crying, It burnt her; and a little Blister, in touching it, was raised on her Fore-finger. The other Person then put the Tile into her Apron, and carry'd it over a long Field to show it the Master and Work-folks, who all felt it yet warm. The Windows of the Beer-Room were broke again after this; and it now drawing towards Noon, all was quiet till five or six of the Clock in the Evening.

Many parallels can be found both for the slow and erratic movement of objects and for objects being found warm when picked up. I have already cited several examples. So far as the slow movement of objects is concerned, a particularly close parallel is presented by the Durweston case of 1894. The principal witness, a gamekeeper named Newman, declared that sitting in a cottage in full daylight, and looking at the open garden door,

> I saw coming from behind the door a quantity of little shells. They came round the door from a height of about five feet. They came one at a time.... They came very slowly, and when they hit me I could hardly feel them. They came so slowly, that in

the ordinary way they would have dropped long before they reached me.

To return, however, to the Canvey Island case, and the events of 14 September. In the early evening the maid was milking just in front of the house, several other persons being with her. Suddenly the parlour window, within three or four yards of them, was smashed. 'No body was then in the House, and none but the Invisibles could do it from without, and not be seen.' After this, as Mr Smagge was talking with several neighbours, part within and part without the kitchen fore door, two or three violent knocks were given upon the wall, between, and close by them.

The following day, Thursday 15 September, Mr Lord, the minister, decided to spend all day in the house. He sat in the hall to study. A window in the parlour was broken, and then in a little while

> the Windows of the Hall, against his back as he sat, were, with a more forcible Dash and Clatter than ever, broken; tho' the other Person, that stood right against the Window, that very interim, saw nothing strike against it; and the Glass not to shatter out, but fall down on the Ledge. At this Mr. *Lord* immediately rose up, and adjured it a third time, saying, *In the name of God, what is it? If it be the Pleasure of God that we may know what it is?* But no answer was made.

There ensued a good deal of sporadic breaking of glass, and knocking, and the rumours which by now were circulating freely began to bring neighbours and even strangers to the house. One further curious incident of this day deserves quoting in full:

> Two of the Company, standing in the Kitchen, the others in the Hall and elsewhere, they saw a Stone with some Dirt and Straws upon it, the bigness of a Turkey-Egg, come as from the Crevice of the fore Door, which as the Door was close shut, one cou'd not thrust a small Hazel-Nut thro'. I say, come as from, not in of the Crevice, because one of the Persons, who was not above half a Yard from it, and looking that way, discern'd it not till 'twas an inch within side (so that how it came there we have no Account) but closely observing its Progress afterwards clearly saw it to take a kind of half Circle, but so slow, as tho' its Motion had proceeded from a regular Piece of Clock-work; and then gently, as if let down by a Spring, descend to the Ground, about a Foot and half from the said Crevice. This stone was also hot, and

being presently taken up, by the Person next to it, in her apron, she call'd Mr. *Lord* who, with the other Company, came, and all feeling it, found it too hot to grasp in the Hand. Mr. *Lord* then said, consider this Stone: this is enough to convince anyone; for besides the amazing Circumstance how it came in, and its being hot, this Straw and Dirt upon it, cou'd not be in the form you see it, had it been heated by a material Fire.

The apparent passage of stones, and other small objects, through crevices too small to admit them, or even through walls and ceilings with no crevices at all, is a poltergeist phenomenon on whose frequency I have already commented.

The next day, Friday 16 September, saw the end of the phenomena, though there was at first little to indicate that an end was likely. In the afternoon, Mr Lord was at the house with seven or eight persons, mostly neighbours of Smagge's. A window of the 'little Parlour' was broken, and the party went to the outside to inspect it.

Whilst all were looking here and no body within, the Window of the other Parlour that in like manner faced them as they stood, was with a furious loud dash broken as from the inside, in the sight of them all; the pieces of Glass not flying out, but gradually falling down on the Ledge, as usual. One there cry'd she saw somewhat white strike against it, which by the rest though the breaking was seen and blow heard by all, was not observed. Mr. *Lord* that moment rush'd into the Room . . . Which was of the passage Door, that by its standing and nearness so favour'd their speed, that had a Bird broken the window, it cou'dn't, by the help of its Wings have escaped without their seeing it.

At this point Mr Lord left, being, we are told, 'obliged to go and bury a Corps', and the company for a time dispersed. However

New Spectators quickly came, *viz.* Mr. *Bell*, Mr. *Weakling*, and his daughter, Mrs. *Cooper*, Mrs. *James* and her son, &c. These took their seats in the Hall, and having staid a little while, Knocks, the usual warning, before breaking of Glass, were heard. Presently upon it a most amazing blow was given against the Hall-Window, That greatly scared all there. Mr. *Weakling* sitting directly over against it, said he saw somewhat, but cou'd not describe it. Mrs. *James*'s Son said he plainly discern'd a white Stick; the rest did not apprehend anything it was done with, only heard the blow, and saw the Glass broken: All in the Hall instantly ran out, some of one Door, and the rest of the

other, which Doors, as if they were contriv'd on purpose, open so opportunely on both sides the said Window, (and the situation of the House in general as is before described) there was no place of concealment near enough for any Mortal to have recourse to, in ten times the space the People were getting out
 . . . . Every one now again are out of the House, and whilst 3 or 4 of them stood gazing just against the Hall-Windows, at the shatter'd Glass, and astonishing form thereof, which all round the House is now much the same, they plainly saw the Glass broken, as before, from within, and a piece of Stone or Brick to come thro' and fall down on the outside.

The end of the disturbances came later in the day when all save Mary Moss and a boy had left the house. Mary, looking through the kitchen door at the parlour door across the hall, saw the parlour door open, and a man come out, putting it half-to behind him. He wore a grey coat, and a whitish hat, and carried a white stick. His countenance was 'pale and ghastful' and he looked sharply about him. When this figure moved towards the milk-house, Mary was seized with such terror that she ran shrieking to Mr Lord's house, resolving never to enter Mr Smagge's house again. The next morning she was taken with such a miserable fit, as none thought she could ever come out of alive. She vomited blood and foamed at the mouth and nose. However, with God's blessing, and the ministrations of Mr Lord, in two or three hours the fit went off; and, says our author, 'by my spy, sent thither the 15th instant, I hear she is indifferent well, and that the House, unto that Day, has not afterwards been disturb'd'. He goes on:

There is one odd Passage I had almost forgot, but which you may depend upon for Truth, *viz.* That it was generally reported, among the People of the Island, for some Months before these last Molestations began, that the 21 years were this Summer expired, for which the Spirit was said to be laid.

It seems quite clear that in this case Mary Moss, the sixteen-year-old maid, was the poltergeist agent. In fact of some of the phenomena she was the only witness, so that she might well fall under suspicion of having produced them herself. There were, however, other happenings which one could not pin upon her without making some entirely ad hoc assumptions, and others of which it is, *prima facie*, not easy to imagine any ordinary explanation. Do we then have here simply the superposition of a person-centred poltergeist on an established haunting? Or was there perhaps some interaction of a place-linked factor with a person-linked one? It seems fairly clear that the two sets of phenomena were in *some* way connected. The poltergeist began with a shadowy apparition, or rather the apparition of a shadow, and ended with the fully formed manifestation of the house ghost, complete with truncheon suitable for smashing windows. But the connection between the poltergeist and the haunting may well have been quite indirect. Perhaps, for instance, the girl was intensely frightened by the haunting, and the poltergeist phenomena represented an unconscious expression of the conflict thus stirred up in her. I have previously mentioned several cases in which poltergeist phenomena began after the agent had received a severe fright.

One of the chief problems, in fact, in assessing the hypothesis we are toying with – the hypothesis that there may in some poltergeist cases be summation or interaction of place-linked with person-linked factors, so that both the form of the phenomena and their very occurrence may initially depend upon the presence and operation of both kinds of factor – is just this difficulty in determining whether a supposed place factor interacts directly with a person factor, or whether the setting of the case exercises its influence indirectly, through affecting the mind and outlook of the poltergeist agent. Most cases in which the phenomena are both place-bound and person-linked could be interpreted either way. There are, however, just a few cases in which the evidence for the direct interaction of a place factor and a person factor seems a little more compelling. These are cases in which phenomena seem as it were to be triggered off by the presence in or near a certain fairly sharply-defined locality of a particular individual, but in which the phenomena, once initiated, will continue for a while in that locality, even though the triggering agent is no longer actually in it. Furthermore the agent does not similarly trigger-off phenomena in every other place which he regularly visits. Under these circumstances both the function of agent as catalyst and the role of the place as container of that which is thus catalysed seem clear. It might, of course, still be possible for some highly ingenious person to advance reasons for supposing that the agent's mind had become fixated upon that particular spot and to propose mechanisms by which under these circumstances his paranormal gifts would be exercised there even when he himself was absent; but all such suggestions would, of course, be totally ad hoc unless based upon supporting evidence (of what kind it is not easy to imagine).

Cases meeting these specifications, or even approximating to them, are fairly uncommon. I know of no case which completely fulfils all the requirements. One which I myself had a share in investigating comes close. It will be described in chapter 14. Other cases which possess some at least of the required features are the cases at Guillonville (1848) and Appleby (1887).

What would be the ideal evidence that place and person factors may interact in poltergeist cases? It would, I think, be something like this. Find a moderate number of haunted houses (say half a dozen); find also a small collection of poltergeist agents (say half a dozen again); let the poltergeist agents each take a turn living in each haunted house, and also in each of a 'control' group of houses not thought to be haunted. If there can be in poltergeist cases an interaction of place-linked with person-linked factors, we might expect something like the following. In a 'control' house, each poltergeist agent will produce either no phenomena, or his own basic repertoire of phenomena, whatever that may consist in. In a haunted house, each agent will produce phenomena, and the phenomena he produces may be influenced in a certain direction by the house in which he is currently living. The direction will remain relatively constant across agents, but the results of each agent–house interaction will not be predictable in detail. (It would of course be crucially important that the agents should know nothing in advance of the reputation of the houses concerned.)

So much by way of fantasy. In fact, of course, no such experiment has been carried out, nor will one ever be practicable. The case which approximates to it most closely (and the approximation is still pretty distant) is the one which I have somewhat misleadingly listed in the Appendix as Montclair (1918–25). This case was reported by perhaps the most capable American parapsychologist of his day, Walter Franklin Prince (1863–1934) in his *The Psychic in the House*, published by the Boston Society for Psychic Research, of which he was research officer, in 1926. Like the Oakland (1874) case, this deserves much fuller consideration than I can give it here – Prince's book is 284 pages long, and I cannot in the space available adequately subdue the mass of detailed contemporary records which it contains.

The background to the case is as follows. Prince, a graduate and doctor of philosophy of Yale University, was for much of his life an Episcopalian clergyman. In 1909 there came to his church in New York a young woman of twenty, in a state of severe mental and physical disturbance. He undertook to help her, and was ultimately successful in doing so. His studies of her mental problems appeared in the *Proceedings of the American* SPR as 'The Doris Fischer case of multiple personality'. During his treatment of 'Doris', he observed various examples of apparent extrasensory perception, and it was this that first turned his interests in the direction of parapsychology. He and his wife adopted 'Doris', who became known as Theodosia Prince. After her cure, Theodosia began to develop as a medium of more or less the orthodox spiritualist kind. She produced automatic writing, saw clairvoyant visions in a crystal, and so forth. (It may be remarked parenthetically that the effect on her mental and physical well-being seems to have been entirely for the good.) She also became the focus of some minor poltergeist effects – chiefly raps, which ultimately developed to the point at which they could be communicated with, but also, apparently, the shaking of beds and the rocking of rocking chairs – whilst phenomena of a more characteristically 'haunting' kind – footsteps and imitative noises – were occasionally heard in the houses where she lived. Prince, a man of great acumen, who had had unrivalled opportunities of observing the agent and the phenomena, made these remarks (pp. 2–3) about the interaction of person and place factors in the case.

> I have hinted at the possibility, if not probability, that the something in the psychic and the something in the house react upon each other. It is well known that the something in the psychic may undergo development. It may be that the something in the house may also undergo development as a reaction to the presence of the psychic. This would be intelligible and plausible if that something consists in the presence of discarnate intelligences who either are interested in manifesting their existence and find at last an instrumentality reacting like a sounding board to their efforts, or whose activity is automatically made, as it were, resonant, by the presence of the psychic.
>
> Take the psychic of this volume and the various houses in which she has lived. She has lived in seven houses, and spent periods in others, without hearing mysterious sounds. But in

the subsequent three residences she has heard them. It is highly improbable that say ten houses should successively have utterly lacked a quality which the next three possessed. It is intelligible that something in her developed to the point that henceforth she is capable of stimulating activity on the part of the something in the house, or possibly of becoming aware, and somehow of causing others near her, to be aware, of it in part.

That the something is not all in the psychic, but one factor is in the house, is indicated by a number of considerations connected with this narrative. The three last residences in chronological order are the one on Bellevue Avenue, Montclair, New Jersey, 27 Forest Street in the same place, and our present residence on Beacon Street, Boston. The first named manifested by far the greatest number and variety of peculiar happenings, and the reason for diminution is not traceable to the psychic. But, more important, the character of the phenomena in the three houses, respectively, has been individual and characteristic. In spite of the fact that strong expectations had been raised in her mind that the most striking group of the Bellevue Avenue phenomena would be continued at Forest Street, it utterly ceased there. And although there was no particular expectation of anything in this general nature occurring at Beacon Street, curious things are happening, but with new characteristics.

It would, I think, be fair to summarize the situation with regard to what may be called the two-factor theory as follows. We may, at a certain level, plausibly interpret cases in which there is neither a clear place link, nor an obvious poltergeist agent, by supposing that there may sometimes lie behind the phenomena a place-linked factor and a person-linked factor, which separately may be inadequate to produce phenomena, or to produce a striking phenomenon, but which summating and perhaps interacting may cause various kinds of peculiar events, including perhaps events not characteristic of 'simple' hauntings, or of 'simple' poltergeists. But when we look for actual evidence that interactions of the postulated kinds might take place, and not just for cases that may be interpreted in terms of such interactions, we can come up with very little. There is perhaps about enough evidence to justify us in bearing the hypothesis in mind; but no more than that.

Some cases, of course, are pretty resistant to interpretation within even the most vaguely worded versions of the two-factor theory. For example, there are on the list in the Appendix at least two cases (West Brompton, 1871-7, and Worcestershire, 1914) in which phenomena of the classical haunting kind seem to have followed a person rather than to have remained centred on a place. Enough well-authenticated cases of this kind would completely undermine the commonly-made distinction which I have been discussing in this chapter, and would return the whole issue to the melting-pot – which may, indeed, be where it properly belongs.

Since this chapter was written there have appeared accounts by F. M. Mathews and G. F. Solfvin (J. D. Morris, W. G. Roll and R. L. Morris, eds, *Research in Parapsychology 1976*, Metuchen, N.J., 1977, pp. 219–27) of a case which has certain analogies with the Canvey Island case described above. In 1974 the lower storey of a house in New Bedford, Mass., was occupied by a certain Mr C., and the upper story by a Mrs S. and her three young great-grandsons. Mr C. and Mrs S. disliked each other intensely. In August 1974 Mr C. died, and both the upstairs and the downstairs of the house shortly became the scene of a characteristic imitative-noise haunting. There were also object-movements of various kinds. At the end of January 1975 Mrs S. and her great-grandsons moved into a new apartment, which was soon afterwards disturbed by violent poltergeist phenomena centring round the two elder boys. Two striking incidents were witnessed by Mathews. However, the haunting continued in the original house throughout 1975. The phenomena included raps, footsteps, muffled voices, the sound of breathing, pinches, and apparitions. Solfvin and Mathews conclude:

> the facts that the RSPK followed the family to their new residence and that the haunting manifestations continued to disturb the new occupants of the former home provide us with a clue that there may be an interaction between the two kinds of events. Further, because of the sequence of the activity, there is an implication that the RSPK was initiated by the haunting.

12 Poltergeists and the computer

In this chapter I propose to attack from another angle the problem of whether or not there is a clear distinction to be made between hauntings and poltergeists. I shall do so by attempting a statistical analysis of the characteristics of a sample of 500 cases of poltergeists and hauntings in the hope of throwing light upon the natural groups (if any) into which those cases fall. The cases (which are listed with details and sources in the Appendix) have all been drawn from printed sources. The sources cover a fairly wide range, and some would not be thought 'reputable' by the majority of parapsychologists. I have paltered with disreputability in order to reduce the likelihood that the overall shape of the collection will be distorted by the preconceptions of 'reputable' editors and case investigators; for the former may be reluctant to publish, and the latter slow to investigate, cases which do not quite harmonize with prevailing doctrines. It is reasonable to hope that any spurious features thus introduced will be diluted into insignificance.

My method of collecting cases has simply been to follow well-trodden paths through the literature, and, whenever I ran across a path less well-trodden, to enter that also. My explorations, being determined simply by the avenues I happened to come across, may well not have fully sampled the terrain, but at any rate they have not consciously been biased to favour any particular outcome, indeed could not have been, since I had not formed the idea of a statistical analysis when I began them. It was not difficult to find 500 cases; in fact the chief problem was to stop the accumulation becoming unmanageably larger than that. In order to keep the numbers within bounds, I have, with a very few exceptions, cut out all cases for which the sole sources were newspapers and magazines, and all European and American cases later than the year 1800 of which the reports did not reach level 2 on the scale of detail (see next paragraph). This means that my samples of early cases, and of non-Euroamerican cases (I was, for reasons explained above, pp. 18–20, particularly anxious to build up such samples), are not comparable in respect of amount of detail to the main collection of post-1800 cases. However, anyone who wishes to correct for this may easily do so by using the Appendix.

Each case report was broken down in the following manner. First of all the value of the testimony was rated on a scale from 1 to 10. Ratings were based primarily on such points as whether the testimony was first-hand or second-hand; whether there was more than one witness; how soon after the events the testimony was set down; whether or not there was instrumental recording. Thus a case report which consisted merely of a distant recollection of a second-hand story would be rated 1; a case report which consisted of, incorporated or was immediately based upon continuous instrumental recordings by competent persons would have rated 10 (had there been one). It is important to note here first that the rating of the testimony does not represent a guess as to whether or not the phenomena were paranormal (it is perfectly possible that a case should be rated 10, and yet be known to be entirely fraudulent), and second that the rating is of the *best* of the testimony in such reports of the case *as I have myself been able to read*. Next, each case report was rated for amount of detail given, on a scale from 1, very little, to 5, minute by minute logging of events. Again it is important to note that the rating is of the *best* of the testimony rather than the whole of it.

Finally each case was assigned a 1 for the occurrence or a 0 for the non-occurrence of each of sixty-three kinds of characteristics. They are listed in Table I below, but certain preliminary clarifications seem desirable, as follows:

For all characteristics: absence of information concerning the occurrence or non-occurrence of a given characteristic in a given case has been treated as implying its non-occurrence.

Characteristics 1 and 2: 'American' includes 'Latin American'.

Characteristic 5: Any investigation by any moderately competent outsider, e.g. clergyman, police, parapsychologist, has been counted; also a few cases in which the investigation was by a relatively detached and competent insider.

Characteristics 8 and 9: These two characteristics are not meant to exclude each other. 'Nocturnal' implies that an appreciable percentage of the phenomena took place at night, 'diurnal' that an appreciable percentage took place during the day. A case can thus be both nocturnal and diurnal, and calling a case

Table I

1 Characteristic	2 Cases 1–500		3 Cases 1–250		4 Cases 251–500		5 Testimony below 3 (253)		6 Testimony 4 & above (247)		7 Eur.+ Amer. (460)		8 Non-Eur. + Amer. (40)	
	N	%	N	%	N	%	N	%	N	%	N	%	N	%
1 Eur.+Amer.	460	92	242	97	218	87								
2 Non-Eur.+Amer.	40	8	8	3	32	13								
3 Trickery, total or partial	41	8	15	6	26	10	12	5	29	12	41	9	0	0
4 Natural cause discovered	5	1	1	0	4	2	1	0	4	2	5	1	0	0
5 Investigation	117	23	39	16	78	31	27	11	90	36	111	24	6	15
6 Lasting less than year	281	56	128	51	153	61	133	53	148	59	252	55	29	73
7 Lasts year or more	118	24	52	21	66	26	45	18	73	29	113	25	5	13
8 Diurnal	182	36	81	32	101	40	64	26	118	47	166	36	16	40
9 Nocturnal	288	58	141	56	147	59	120	48	168	67	271	59	17	43
10 Male agent	54	11	18	7	36	14	24	10	30	12	48	10	6	15
11 Female agent	143	29	66	26	77	31	58	23	85	34	137	30	6	15
12 Agent under 20	152	30	60	24	92	37	60	24	92	37	142	31	10	25
13 Agent 20 or more	42	8	19	8	23	9	19	8	23	9	40	9	2	5
14 Agent disturbed	30	6	15	6	15	6	10	4	20	8	29	6	1	3
15 House-centred	61	12	28	11	33	13	32	13	29	12	57	12	4	10
16 Small objects moved	320	64	153	61	167	67	153	61	167	67	287	62	33	83
17 Large objects moved, e.g. chairs tables	181	36	82	33	99	40	71	28	110	44	169	37	12	30
18 Objects move as if carried	94	19	36	14	58	23	33	13	61	24	85	18	9	23
19 Apports	112	22	57	23	55	22	48	19	64	26	100	22	12	30
20 Objects appear in mid-air, seem to pass through ceilings, etc.	25	5	13	5	12	5	9	4	16	6	19	4	6	15
21 Raps etc.	241	48	117	47	124	50	100	40	141	56	236	51	5	13
22 Imitative and miscellaneous noises	217	43	111	44	106	42	100	40	117	47	211	46	6	15
23 Voices, groans whistles, etc.	130	26	74	29	56	22	59	23	71	28	127	27	3	8
24 Phantasms (human)	143	29	81	32	62	25	48	19	95	38	135	29	8	20
25 Small animals seen, heard, felt	33	6	18	7	15	6	17	7	16	6	32	7	1	3

POLTERGEISTS AND THE COMPUTER

1	2		3		4		5		6		7		8	
	N	%	N	%	N	%	N	%	N	%	N	%	N	%
26 Misty figures etc. seen	12	2	3	1	9	4	3	1	9	4	12	3	0	0
27 Luminous effects	49	10	23	9	26	10	16	6	33	13	49	11	0	0
28 Incendiary effects	53	11	28	11	25	10	25	10	28	11	47	10	6	15
29 Objects thrown or transported found hot	18	4	7	3	11	4	4	2	14	6	17	4	1	3
30 Inundations of water etc., cold water etc. 'boils over'	26	5	7	3	19	8	5	2	21	8	23	5	3	8
31 Electrical installations, switches, tampered with	14	3	0	0	14	6	3	1	11	4	14	3	0	0
32 Spontaneous breakages	24	5	11	4	13	5	8	3	16	6	24	5	0	0
33 Objects arranged	22	4	15	6	7	3	11	4	11	4	21	5	1	3
34 Objects animated	15	3	7	3	8	3	6	2	9	4	15	3	0	0
35 Bedclothes, pillows, etc. disturbed	66	13	30	12	36	14	27	11	39	16	63	14	3	8
36 Cloth, clothes, etc. cut, torn, etc.	30	6	24	10	6	2	19	8	11	4	28	6	2	5
37 Hair cut	2	0	0	0	2	1	0	0	2	1	2	0	0	0
38 Persons in bed oppressed	12	2	5	2	7	3	4	2	8	3	12	3	0	0
39 Assault—pinches, blows, scratches, etc.	77	15	46	18	31	12	34	14	43	17	71	15	6	15
40 Animals attacked, annoyed	28	6	13	5	15	6	7	3	21	8	28	6	0	0
41 Possession, obsession	14	3	10	4	4	2	5	2	9	4	11	2	3	8
42 Levitation etc. of human body	33	7	25	10	8	3	15	6	18	7	31	7	2	5
43 Phenomena manifest ESP	17	3	12	5	5	2	6	2	11	4	17	4	0	0
44 Communication through phenomena	79	16	44	18	35	14	35	14	44	18	74	16	5	13
45 'Daemon' communicates	11	2	7	3	4	2	5	2	6	2	10	2	1	3
46 'Deceased person' communicates	46	9	20	8	26	10	21	8	25	10	40	9	6	15
47 Witch etc. blamed	36	7	26	10	10	4	14	6	22	9	32	7	4	10
48 'Exorcism' works	34	7	20	8	14	6	21	8	13	5	28	6	6	15

1	2		3		4		5		6		7		8	
	N	%	N	%	N	%	N	%	N	%	N	%	N	%
49 'Exorcism' fails	16	3	12	5	4	2	10	4	6	2	14	3	2	5
50 'Exorcism' transiently successful	9	2	6	2	3	1	2	1	7	3	8	2	1	3
51 Cold breeze, air movement etc. reported	18	4	6	2	12	5	7	3	11	4	16	3	2	5
52 Metal bent, broken	6	1	3	1	3	1	2	1	4	2	5	1	1	3
53 Doors, windows, opened, shut, resist	59	12	26	10	33	13	15	6	44	18	58	13	1	3
54 Latches, door-handles seen to move, locks turned, keys moved	25	5	11	4	14	6	5	2	20	8	24	5	1	3
55 Direct writing, painting, drawing, etc.	23	5	9	4	14	6	3	1	20	8	21	5	2	5
56 Marked stones etc. thrown away and returned	9	2	5	2	4	2	5	2	4	2	5	1	4	10
57 Candles, lamps, put out, burn low, burn blue	22	4	10	4	12	5	9	4	13	5	22	5	0	0
58 Wire bells, other bells, rung	29	6	12	5	17	7	9	4	20	8	28	6	1	3
59 Plants uprooted, damaged	5	1	3	1	2	1	2	1	3	1	5	1	0	0
60 Structural damage	18	4	9	4	9	4	6	2	12	5	17	4	1	3
61 Hand seen, felt	35	7	18	7	17	7	7	3	28	11	35	8	0	0
62 Filth, excrement thrown, spread, etc.	18	4	13	5	5	2	11	4	7	3	14	3	4	10
63 Offensive smells	9	2	4	2	5	2	2	1	7	3	9	2	0	0

nocturnal does not imply that there were no phenomena at all during the day, and vice versa.

Characteristics 10–13: I have included as person-centred only cases in which there was clear evidence that the phenomena centred round a particular person, only cases in which, for example, the phenomena followed a particular person, or were closely connected with his comings and goings. One or two cases of dual agency are disguised by this way of dividing things up.

Characteristic 14: I have counted agents as 'disturbed' only if *prior to the onset of the phenomena* they already suffered from a mental or emotional problem, or were in a state of physical distress likely to have emotional consequences. I have not counted agents as disturbed if the disturbance is not known to have set in until after the onset of the phenomena.

Characteristic 15: Cases are not counted as centring on a house unless there is some evidence that they survived at least one complete change of occupancy.

Characteristic 21: I have included under this heading all kinds of raps, bangs, thuds, cracks, explosions, scratchings and percussive noises.

Characteristic 42: Under 'Levitation' are included examples of all kinds of ostensible transportation of the human body, and of its projection out of bed.

I may say that if I were to undertake the analysis again I would use a somewhat different set of characteristics. I would omit 5, which is not properly a case characteristic, and also such infrequently occurring characteristics as 37 (hair cut), 52 (metal bent) and 59 (plants uprooted), and might subdivide 16 (movements of small objects), 21 (raps), 22 (imitative noises), 23 (human voices, whistles, etc.) and 39 (assault).

Table I, which has been prepared from a computer print-out, is to be read as follows. Column 1 lists and describes the sixty-three kinds of characteristic in respect of which each case was analysed. Column 2 lists with respect to each characteristic the number and percentage of the total 500 cases which possessed it. Columns 3 and 4 give the same information for the first 250 cases (up to the year 1873) and the second 250 cases (1873–1945), thus yielding some information as to whether or not the leading characteristics of poltergeists and hauntings have changed over the centuries. Similarly columns 5 and 6 permit a comparison of the characteristics of 253 cases in which the testimony is rated at 3 or below in the 1–10 scale, with 247 cases in which it is rated at 4 or above, and columns 7 and 8 permit the comparison of 460 American and European cases with forty non-American, non-European cases.

Comparison of the older with the newer cases (columns 3 and 4) reveals only a little that is of interest. A chi-squared analysis involving characteristics 6 to 56 (omitting 31) suggests that these characteristics are differently distributed in the two sets of cases ($P = 0.0001$), but this method of analysis is not really appropriate in view of the large number of characteristics in the second half of the list which are rarely found. A chi-squared analysis of characteristics 6 to 32 (omitting 31) – these are the central and frequently observed ones – does not reveal a conventionally significant difference in the distribution of case characteristics ($P = 0.0851$). Examination of the particular characteristics in respect of which marked differences of distribution are found brings little to light that seems of interest. The fact that since 1873 objects have more commonly been reported to have moved through the air as if carried or guided rather than as if thrown has probably to do with fuller recording and more careful observation. If inundations of water have been more frequent, and the flinging or spreading of excrement less frequent, in the later period than in the earlier, that is no doubt because water-pipes have become common, and cess-pits rare, during the last 100 years. Very possibly a further analysis of the kinds of small objects thrown by poltergeists would reveal analogous changes. The two most interesting areas of difference have to do with the sorts of persons who become poltergeist agents, and with matters related to poltergeist assaults. There has been a noticeable increase in the percentage of poltergeist cases which centre round male agents, and in the percentage of cases which centre round agents under the age of twenty. One might – after taking a pinch of salt – perhaps try to relate these changes to changes in the social situation of women and of young people. These days there are hardly any frustrated maidservants, indeed hardly any maidservants, frustrated or otherwise. Cases characterized by poltergeist assault have also declined in numbers somewhat steeply in the last century, and with them have gone cases in which the presumed agent has been the victim of an apparent possession or obsession, cases in which a human being (usually the agent) has been levitated, cases in which the phenomena (or communicating intelligences) have exhibited apparent ESP, and cases in which a witch or cunning man has ostensibly occasioned the happenings. It seems likely that these changes are all related, and reflect an influence upon the form of the phenomena of changes in the folk-beliefs in which potential poltergeist agents are likely to be brought up. But further data and further analysis would be required to establish the point with certainty (cf. chapter 9).

Comparison of the 253 cases in which the testimony is weaker with the 247 cases in which it is stronger reveals nothing of any interest, except indeed the fact that there is nothing of any interest. A chi-squared analysis of the twenty-five leading characteristics mentioned in the last paragraph yields a marginally significant difference in the distribution of case characteristics in the two groups of cases ($P = 0.0259$). This kind of analysis allows for the fact that the less well-evidenced cases are also the cases which are reported in less detail, so that the sum of all entries in column 5 is considerably less than the sum of all the entries in column 6. It is concerned only with the pattern of distribution of the entries in the two columns. The chief point of interest that seems to emerge is that it is not just 'simple' poltergeist phenomena, like raps and object-movements, that have been more frequently reported in the better-evidenced cases, but the more complex and bizarre phenomena too – for instance, objects appearing in mid-air, apparitions of all kinds, objects moving slowly through the air, objects being found to be hot when picked up, poltergeist assault in all its forms, ESP, 'communication' with the phenomena, voices, direct writing, hands seen or felt, the appearance of clouds of mist, possession or obsession, levitation of the human body. This suggests two important things. The first is that no 'theory' of poltergeist phenomena can be satisfactory which confines itself only to 'simple' phenomena. The complex phenomena are no less well, or not much less well, attested than the simple ones. The second is that there is little to suggest that poltergeist stories grow in the retelling – even in second-hand retelling. This finding is of relevance to matters discussed in the next chapter.

The number of cases from which the data presented in column 8 is derived is so small that I have to omit the cross-cultural comparison upon which I had originally hoped to embark.

To return now to the problem of whether or not poltergeists and hauntings constitute two distinct categories of phenomena, or whether the field would be better divided along different lines entirely. In the hope rather than the expectation of making progress with this problem I submitted my 500 cases, each broken down in terms of the sixty-three binary characteristics (i.e. present/absent) listed above, to examination by the statistical technique known as cluster analysis. This is a technique (or rather group of techniques) for sorting cases into groups or 'clusters' on the basis of number of shared characteristics or of degree of similarity in shared characteristics. The present analysis was carried out by means of the CARM (Cluster Analysis by Relocation Methods) program of the Cripps Computing Centre of the University of Nottingham (a program from a suite developed by M. Youngman; see his *PMMD: Programmed Methods for Multivariate Data*, Nottingham, 1975). The method followed by this program is (very roughly) as follows. Each case in the sample under scrutiny is given on the basis of its listed characteristics a place in an (imaginary) space of as many dimensions as there are characteristics on the list. Suppose, for example, that there are only two characteristics on the list, let us say rapping and stone-throwing, and that each of these characteristics is treated as being either present or absent, and not as being present to a greater or lesser degree. Each case will be assigned a position with respect to each of two intersecting axes, one symbolizing rapping and the other stone-throwing, and in the two-dimensional space thus defined any possible case may be represented by a point whose co-ordinates completely specify its characteristics. For instance a case which combined the characteristic of rapping with the characteristic of stone-throwing would be represented as in Figure 1.

If we were to throw in another characteristic – say person-centredness – we should have to construct another dimension at

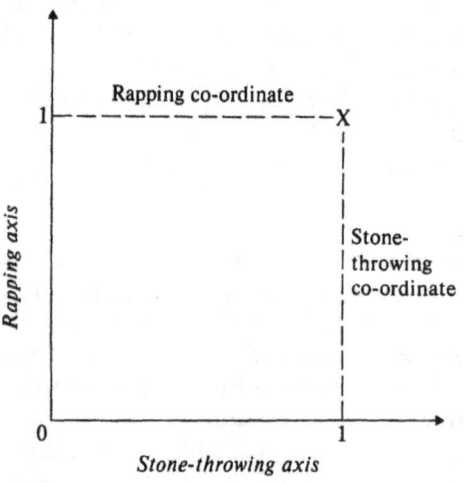

Figure 1.

right-angles to the present two. In other words, if cases are to be assigned a spatial position which completely specifies them in terms of the presence or absence of three characteristics, they will have to be represented by points located at the eight corners of a cube (if simply presence or absence is considered) or throughout the interior and exterior of a cube (if characteristics are permitted to have degrees). When we pass beyond three characteristics – as for instance to the sixty-three of the present analysis – we pass beyond the limits of what we can represent pictorially, but it is still possible to pinpoint each case in terms of its characteristics by finding it co-ordinates which define a particular point within a hypothetical space of as many dimensions as the case has possible characteristics.

Having thus pinpointed each case in an n-dimensional space by reference to its characteristics, the program then arbitrarily assigns each of the cases on the list to one of a specified number (in the present instance fifteen) of initial 'clusters'. For each cluster what may be called a central point or 'centre of gravity' within the n-dimensional space is computed. The program then embarks on a 'relocation cycle'. Each case on the list is scanned in turn, and if any case is found to be closer to the central point of a cluster other than its parent cluster, then it is moved from its parent cluster to the other cluster. At the same time the central points of both clusters, which will have been altered by the changes, are recomputed. Since the central points of the clusters may be radically different at the end of the cycle from what they were at the beginning, a case which was properly a member of one cluster at the beginning may now properly belong to another cluster (i.e. will be closer to the central point of that cluster than to the central point of its parent cluster). Accordingly the program reiterates the relocation scan up to ten times, or until no case has been relocated during one complete scan, when the clusters are said to be 'stable'.

At this point useful pieces of information about the clusters ('cluster diagnostics') are computed. We will return to these in a moment. Finally the program fuses the two most similar clusters (i.e. the two whose 'centres of gravity' are closest), thereby reducing the total number of clusters by one. The processes of relocation, diagnosis and fusion are then repeated until all the clusters have been fused into one, or until some prescribed number of clusters has been reached.

Among the valuable pieces of information which this program prints out for one are the following:

1 Which cases were in which cluster at the termination of each stage in the running of the program.

2 (In effect) what percentage of cases in each cluster at each stage possessed any given characteristic.

3 How close each case was to the central point of each cluster at any selected stage or stages.

4 How great was the 'stress' involved in the fusion of each pair of clusters that was fused.

I shall concern myself for the moment only with 2 and 4. (Some details of 1 and 3 may be gleaned from the Appendix.) I shall begin with 4. The degree of 'stress' involved in the fusion of each pair of clusters is shown by a so-called 'fusion plot', which charts the increase with each successive fusion of an 'error coefficient' which rises progressively with the fusion of increasingly dissimilar clusters. Sudden jumps in the error coefficient signify a particularly 'stressful' fusion, i.e. the fusion of two clusters whose members differ markedly in respect of many of the listed characteristics.

In the present analysis the first ten fusions, which reduced the number of clusters from fifteen to five, caused the error coefficent to increase by 1.59, from 0.63 to 2.22, an average increase of 0.16 per fusion. But on and after the eleventh fusion the error coefficient began to increase much more sharply, and on the fourteenth and final fusion, which reduced the number of clusters to one, it increased by 3.55 in one bound.

Table II

Fusion	Clusters	Error coefficient
10	5	2.22
11	4	3.05
12	3	4.00
13	2	4.61
14	1	8.16

I must emphasize at this point that the error coefficient is not a statistic which one can simply transform into a measure of the probability that the clusters just fused correspond to genuine 'natural groups' of cases. It is better regarded simply as an aid to one's assessment of the classifications which the program has set up for one. Another fact of relevance is whether or not the clusters consequent upon a given fusion are 'stable' in the sense defined above. 'Instability' may be a sign of a forced and artificial classification of cases. The five clusters resulting from fusion 10 above were stable. So were the two clusters resulting from fusion 13. The intervening sets of 4 and 3 clusters were not stable. Accordingly I shall concentrate upon the five clusters resulting from fusion 10, and the two clusters resulting from fusion 13. In Table III I tabulate for each of these seven clusters the numbers of cases in each cluster, the average coefficient (AC) of each cluster, and the percentages of cases in each cluster which exhibited each of the listed characteristics 1–63. Where a percentage figure is marked with asterisks it means that the number of cases in that cluster which exhibited the characteristic concerned differed significantly on a chi-squared test from the number of cases exhibiting that characteristic in all the other clusters of the group. In short these are the characteristics to examine particularly when seeking to define the differences between the clusters of the group. (Two asterisks indicate significance at the 0.01 level, one asterisk significance at the 0.05 level, and a dagger significance at the 0.10 level.) It should be noted that clusters 1 and 2 of the post-fusion 10 group are not to be identified with clusters 1 and 2 of the post-fusion 13 group. The average coefficient (AC) for each cluster is the average distance of that cluster's members from its 'centre of gravity'. In effect it is an index of the cluster's 'cohesiveness' relative to that of the other clusters – the smaller the coefficient, the more cohesive the cluster.

It is immediately obvious at even a casual glance that cluster 1 and cluster 2 of the post-fusion 13 group – in other words the two surviving clusters whose final fusion into a single grand cluster caused such a marked jump in the error coefficient – correspond quite closely to the traditional categories of poltergeists (cluster 1) and hauntings (cluster 2). Cluster 2 is rich relatively to cluster 1 in long-lasting and primarily nocturnal cases, in cases centring on a house, in cases characterized by raps, imitative noises, voices, phantasms, luminous effects, and in cases in which doors are opened and door-handles seen to move. Cluster 1 is rich in short-lived person-centred (especially young-person-centred) cases, and in cases in which objects are displaced, thrown, or even carried through the air. In fact the traditional distinctions could hardly have been more decisively

Table III

Characteristic	Post-fusion 10 group Clusters					Post-fusion 13 group Clusters	
	1	2	3	4	5	1	2
	$N=158$ $AC=0.1291$	$N=91$ $AC=0.1231$	$N=63$ $AC=0.2594$	$N=86$ $AC=0.1338$	$N=102$ $AC=0.1362$	$N=328$ $AC=0.1712$	$N=172$ $AC=0.1558$
1 Eur.+Amer.	83**	97	95	98†	95	89**	98**
2 Non-Eur.+Amer.	17**	03	05	02†	05	11**	02**
3 Trickery	07	05	11	00**	18**	12**	01**
4 Natural cause	00	03†	02	01	00	00†	02†
5 Investigation	22	16	46**	06**	33*	30**	12**
6 Less than year	60	80**	49	01**	79**	71**	28**
7 Year or more	08**	00**	35*	90**	06**	09**	52**
8 Diurnal	35	14**	83**	10**	51**	49**	13**
9 Nocturnal	25**	85**	89**	79**	46*	47**	78**
10 Male agent	20**	04*	17	02**	06	15**	03**
11 Female agent	04**	07**	40†	07**	97**	38**	10**
12 Agent under 20	15**	03**	40	03**	96**	44**	04**
13 Agent 20 or over	09	08	13	06	08	08	09
14 Agent disturbed	03	01†	11	02	15**	08†	03†
15 House-centred	03**	09	05†	49**	04**	03**	30**
16 Small objects thrown	86**	31**	95**	30**	69	80**	33**
17 Larger objects thrown	22**	35	78**	35	34	38	34
18 Objects 'carried'	20	04**	62**	06**	13	25**	06**
19 Apports	22	13*	63**	07**	19	27**	15**
20 Mid-air	07	00*	16**	00*	04	07**	01**
21 Raps etc.	18**	68**	65**	76**	43	36**	72**
22 Imitative noises	09**	75**	52	99**	17**	18**	92**
23 Voices etc.	13**	31	38*	53**	10**	15**	47**
24 Phantasms	11**	22	44**	71**	17**	16**	52**
25 Small animals	01**	04	17**	12†	06	04*	10*
26 Misty figures	01	04	06†	02	00	02	03
27 Luminous effects	01**	11	14	30**	03*	03**	22**
28 Incendiary effects	12	03*	32**	06	06	13*	06*
29 Objects hot	04	00†	13**	02	02	04	02
30 Inundations etc.	03	01†	17**	05	06	06	04

Charactertistic	Post-fusion 10 group					Post-fusion 13 group	
	1	2	3	4	5	1	2
31 Electrical equipment	02	03	05	01	04	03	02
32 Spontaneous breakages	03	03	17**	01	04	06	03
33 Objects arranged	05	04	13**	02	00*	05	03
34 Objects animated	02	01	11**	01	02	04	01
35 Bedclothes disturbed	08*	09	35**	20†	06*	10*	19*
36 Clothes, etc. cut	07	01†	19**	02	04	08†	03†
37 Hair cut	00	00	03**	00	00	00	01
38 Oppression in bed	00*	01	03	10**	00	01**	06**
39 Assault	07**	11	52**	10	13	16	15
40 Animals attacked	02*	04	21**	03	05	06	05
41 Possession or obsession	02	00	02	01	08**	03	01
42 Levitation	04	03	21**	02	09	07	05
43 ESP	03	02	14**	00	02	04	02
44 Communication	07**	24*	44**	08*	11	16	15
45 Communication with 'daemon'	00*	03	11**	00	01	02	02
46 Communication with deceased person	06	15*	17*	05	07	09	09
47 Link with witch	04	04	21**	02†	10	08	05
48 Exorcism successful	11**	01*	10	02	07	08	04
49 Exorcism unsuccessful	05	00	08†	00	03	04	01
50 Exorcism temporarily successful	00†	02	08**	02	00	02	01
51 Cold breeze etc.	01*	03	02	15**	00†	01**	09**
52 Metal bent etc.	01	00	06**	00	00	02	01
53 Doors, etc. opened	03**	05†	24**	29**	10	08**	20**
54 Handles, etc. move	03	04	05	15**	01†	02**	10**
55 Direct writing	03	00*	17**	02	05	05	03
56 Marked objects returned	03	00	05	00	02	02	01
57 Candles etc. extinguished	03	05	05	09*	02	03*	08*
58 Bells rung	05	08	05	10†	02	05	08

Characteristic	Post-fusion 10 group					Post-fusion 13 group	
	1	2	3	4	5	1	2
59 Plants uprooted	01	01	03	00	01	01	01
60 Structural damage	03	03	11**	01	03	05	02
61 Hands seen, felt	01**	05	16**	19**	03	04**	13**
62 Filth thrown etc.	03	02	13**	02	01	03	04
63 Smells	01	03	02	05†	00	01*	04*

brought out. Furthermore these two clusters are so much more distinct from each other than were the members of the groups of clusters which existed at earlier stages that even though there may be cases 'intermediate' between the two classes, we should not expect such cases to be particularly numerous or to fall into clearly defined categories. With regard to the 'two-factor' hypothesis which I touched upon in chapter 12 – the possibility that in some cases the occurrence of phenomena may depend upon the conjunction of a person possessing some unknown special factor with a place possessing some unknown special factor – the data do not tell us much one way or the other. There are indications of a person factor at work in some cases from cluster 2, but virtually no indications of a place influence at work in cases of cluster 1. However, my criteria for admitting a case to be person-centred or place-centred were fairly strict; and of course many poltergeist cases are so short-lived that a place influence might well pass unnoticed.

Is the upshot of the analysis, then, to tell us nothing that we did not already know? Not quite. For in the first place it is worth noting that certain cases that have commonly been talked of as poltergeists, and which one might therefore expect to end up in cluster 1, actually end up in cluster 2. This reinforces the contention, for which I argued in chapter 10 (before seeing the results of the present analysis), that in many cases of haunting, despite what the pundits have said to the contrary, paranormal physical phenomena do take place, and that some well-known 'poltergeist' cases really belong in the ranks of 'hauntings'. I instanced such cases as Tidworth (1662-3), Epworth (1716), Stans (1860-2), Willington (1834-47), and Normandy (1867, 1875-6), and I might equally well have added the famous Slawensik (1806) and Sampford (1810-12) spooks. I am pleased to report that the programme assigned every single one of these cases to cluster 2. We may therefore reasonably suggest that the conventional distinction between poltergeists and hauntings, though probably valid in a general way, has been in important respects misdrawn. Certain cases of which ostensibly paranormal physical happenings have been a marked feature should none the less be classed with 'hauntings'.

In the second place there remains the interesting question of whether and to what extent clusters 1 and 2 are themselves composite. The 'fusion plot' jumps markedly at each of fusions 11, 12 and 13, which suggests that clusters 1 and 2 may at any rate contain within themselves what could be described as recognizable sub-clusters. Let us go back to the state of clustering as it was after fusion 10. Of the five clusters then existing (see Table III), two (clusters 2 and 4) were finally (with some 'stress') fused by fusion 11 to form a new cluster substantially identical with cluster 2 of the penultimate stage (i.e. the 'hauntings' cluster), whilst clusters 1, 3 and 5 were fused (again with some 'stress') in fusions 12 and 13 to yield cluster 1 (the 'poltergeists' cluster) of the penultimate stage. Let us look in turn at each of the five clusters produced by fusion 10, starting with clusters 2 and 4, the ones which combined to yield the final 'hauntings' cluster.

It will be apparent from Table III that there are some fairly marked differences between cluster 2 and cluster 4. Cluster 4 contains most of the hauntings of the 'traditional' type, cases like those at Cheltenham (1880-9) and Brighton (1882-7) which are advanced in chapter 10. Cluster 2 contains a notable proportion of cases that are short-lived in comparison with the traditional haunting, and also a fair sprinkling of cases in which the traditional phenomena of haunting — voices, noises, phantasms, luminous effects, door-opening — are less in evidence than in the cases of cluster 4. Cluster 2 contains, however, a notably higher percentage than cluster 4 of cases in which there was 'communication' with the phenomena. Sample cluster 2 cases are: Woodstock (1649), Epworth (1716), Slawensik (1806), Oakland (1874), Glasgow (1907), Worcester (1914), Ardachie (1957), Tydd (1957) and Pittsburgh (1971), several of which are described elsewhere in this book.

Of clusters 1, 3 and 5 — those which ultimately merged into the final 'poltergeist' cluster — cluster 3 seems to be the odd one out (clusters 1 and 5 were shortly fused by fusion 12). It contains a relatively low percentage of clearly person-centred cases, and high percentages of cases exhibiting the more bizarre and exciting kinds of poltergeist phenomena – the 'carrying' of objects through the air, assault, ESP, raps, 'communication', ostensible intervention by a deceased person, voices, phantasms, arrangements of objects, 'animated' objects, ostensible link with a witch. Here if anywhere among poltergeist cases we find the manifestation of discarnate entities. Sample cases from this cluster are: North Aston (1591–2) Mâcon (1612), Rerrick (1695), Naples (1696), Canvey Island (1709), Sandfeldt (1722), Bristol (1761), Stratford (1850), Amherst (1878), Ylöjärvi (1885), Paris (1888), Clarendon (1889), Poona (1920), Buhai (1925) and Charlottenburg (1929). However, cluster 3 is less 'cohesive' than the other clusters, and it is perhaps worth noting that one or two cases from it – e.g. Tidworth (1662–3) and Sampford (1810–12) – ended up after fusion 13 classified as 'hauntings' (i.e. in the post-fusion 13 cluster 2).

A little more will be said about clusters 2 and 3 in chapter 18 below. My own view is that the present analysis has unearthed some indications, neither very strong, nor completely negligible, that the classes of 'poltergeists' and of 'hauntings' may be composite rather than unitary. It would, I think, be appropriate to examine the question further by at least two methods. Another cluster analysis might be undertaken in which a smaller number of case characteristics were rated as absent or as present to a quantified degree, rather than as simply present or absent. Such an analysis might very well arrive at clusters differing from those reached by the present one. The quantitative rating of the variables would, however, be an exceedingly arduous task, and would probably involve a large number of quite arbitrary decisions. (I may say that even with the binary variables of the present analysis some of my decisions have been pretty arbitrary.) My suspicion is that this fuller kind of analysis will have to await an accumulation of case reports of a moment-to-moment detail so far almost without precedent in the literature.

It might also be appropriate to identify the distinctive characteristics of each cluster by a more rigorous statistical analysis, e.g. by the techniques of discriminant function analysis.

Part II Some personal investigations and conclusions

by Alan Gauld and A. D. Cornell

13 Explaining away the poltergeist

Few would dispute, and least of all the present writers, that before one invokes the preternatural one should exhaust the natural. To put it more carefully: if one is confronted with some phenomenon which at first sight appears inexplicable, one must try very hard to explain it in terms of factors that we already understand, before one begins to suppose that there may be involved factors which we do not yet understand. So far as poltergeists are concerned, many people – including both those who have and those who have not thought about the question – would take the view that there is no need to look for new kinds of explanations. Old and well-tried ones can be stretched to do the job. These old and obvious explanations, however, do not so much explain the phenomena as explain them away. For they all involve the assumption, or else seek to demonstrate, that the phenomena were not what they appeared to be. The plate did not really fly through the air untouched by human hand; the eerie sound which broke the stillness of the night did not really have the acoustic properties of the human voice; the raps that answered questions intelligently were merely random – the questioner read the answers into them. We shall begin Part II of this book by asking how far it is possible thus to explain poltergeist phenomena away.

The simplest, most obvious, and most popular of all such explanations is fraud. It fits happily with the undisputed fact that many poltergeist cases centre around children, and also with the alleged fact that it is very uncommon in poltergeist cases for objects which are being directly looked at to move. And one can say this much in its favour: in 41 of the 500 cases (8 per cent) whose characteristics were analysed in the last chapter fraud was detected. This is a percentage to be reckoned with, and an adherent of the view we are discussing might well propose that many further instances of fraud have remained undetected. However, one might with equal readiness advance reasons for supposing that the figure is too high. In many cases the kind of trickery detected could not possibly have accounted for all the phenomena reported; in some the evidence for trickery is a 'confession' which may have been extracted by explicit or implicit threats.

Like most people who have investigated an appreciable number of poltergeist cases, we have ourselves come across occasional instances of almost undoubted fraud. Out of about fifty cases investigated by us which we have selected as a basis for this part of the book, we estimate that fraud was either undoubted or else very probable in seven or eight; but in at least two of the cases the fraud seems to have been only partial. In no case was more than one person involved in the fraud, though in one case it was probably being connived at by at least one other person. The case concerned was one of a stone-throwing poltergeist which centred round a boy of twelve. The flying stones had broken window-panes, small ornaments, and the glass of a picture frame. The local vicar had come to read prayers in the house, and had been struck by a stone, an event which had greatly impressed him. However, we learned from neighbours that while the vicar was in the house, they had seen the lad emerge into the front garden, stoop, pick something up, put his hand in through the letter box, and twist his arm sharply. The house concerned was a council house, which was basically a pleasant one, but had been allowed to lapse into a state of such filthiness that the family was intensely disliked in the vicinity. After some talk with the father we concluded that he was aware of what was going on, but was conniving at it because he felt the 'spook' would improve the family's chances of being rehoused elsewhere. We have come across one or two other cases in which we suspected a similar motive.

In the great majority of poltergeist cases in which fraud has been detected, the fraud concerned has been of a simple, though sometimes skilfully executed, sort; it has involved, for example, manual and psychological dexterity in throwing objects or oversetting them, and in choosing the moment at which to do so, together perhaps with a certain ingenuity in obtaining and resourcefulness in concealing potential missiles or apports. (An entertaining and illuminating account of a battle of wits between an investigator – a member of the Magic Circle – and a crafty child will be found in Ian Fletcher's article 'A poltergeist case' in the *Journal of the SPR*, vol. 33, 1946.) Only rarely does one hear of a case, such as that at Windsor, Nova Scotia (1906–7), in which there has been conspiracy and the use of mechanical aids. In this case the conspiracy, which was by way of a joke played upon a particularly gullible local Spiritualist, was at once detected by a competent investigator sent to the spot.

It might well be remarked at this point that to hint that fraud occurs only in some 8 per cent of cases, and to claim that it is generally of a simple kind, may be quite misleading. It is only the least efficient tricksters who will get caught; fraud of a more complex and sophisticated kind may well have gone on undetected in an appreciable proportion of the remaining 92 per cent of cases. A skilful conjurer could have done it, the argument might continue, and since we are sure that conjurers exist, whereas poltergeists are ephemeral and debatable, it is both more prudent and more logical to ascribe all the phenomena, or at any rate all for which no ordinary natural causes can be found, to adept conjuring.

Conjurers themselves have not discouraged this line of thinking; like many wonder-workers, they often exhibit a certain reluctance to admit that they cannot duplicate the feats of others whom they regard as being in the same line of business. Now at first sight a claim by a clever and baffling conjurer that he can duplicate certain poltergeist phenomena is very difficult to assess, especially if, as commonly happens, he refuses under the (frequently preposterous) pretext of keeping professional secrets, to tell us how. We suggest that any such claim by a conjurer must be assessed by the following criteria:

1 The method of trickery that is suggested, or the effect allegedly produced, must be within the reach of the known conjuring technology of the period concerned. It is, for example, no good suggesting that the glass which in 1762 Henry Durbin saw rise vertically in the air before his eyes and then fly across the room (see chapter 7) was levitated and projected by ultrasonics. Such issues are in general not too difficult to resolve. The secrets of one generation's conjurers are commonly to be found in the next generation's conjuring literature. Sometimes an interested individual makes it his business to subject the performance of a master to detailed study in an attempt to reveal his methods to the world, as Decremps did with Pinetti (Decremp's *La magie blanche dévoilé*, Paris, 1784, and *Testament de Jérome Sharpe*, Paris, 1793, are a mine of information about eighteenth-century conjuring in general); sometimes a great conjurer in his later years writes on the subject seriously and in detail, as Robert-Houdin did in his *Secrets de la prestidigitation et de la magie* (Paris, 1868). At any rate the materials are there, for all but the very

latest developments; and it seems most unlikely that the very latest developments will be known to and utilized by the average teenage poltergeist agent.

2 We cannot assume without evidence, or at any rate we usually cannot assume, that a given poltergeist effect was brought about by complex and weighty offstage machinery concealed about the house. In most poltergeist cases there is no offstage to conceal machinery in, still less assistants to operate it. We cannot, for instance, suppose that in the Sauchie case of 1960–1 11-year-old Virginia Campbell concealed in the fairly crowded house where she lived a sophisticated specially made mechanism capable of rocking, lifting, dragging along, and raising the lid of, a full linen chest weighing 50 lbs, and that she also concealed a confederate to operate it when she (Virginia) was closely watched. The levitation of a bed with occupants – a phenomenon which supposedly happened in, for instance, cases at Woodstock (1649), Tidworth (1662–3), St Maur (1706), Epworth (1716), Cambridge (1718), Sandfeldt (1722), Willington (1834–47), Strathtay (1878–98), Cronheim (1899), and Tackley (1905–8) – would require something like an offstage fork-lift truck (of course modern ones are fairly compact). As for the transportation through the air of a coach (Schkeitbar, 1738–9) or a two and a half ton Jeep (Ponta Porã 1969–73), nothing less than an offstage crane would suffice; but we do not put these last two cases in evidence.

3 We cannot assume, in order to explain away some poltergeist phenomenon, that the poltergeist agent, or some other person on the spot, is secretly a master conjurer (or a master mechanic – great conjurers have tended to be both). People do not become master conjurers overnight, or through being (like the present writers) amateurs of conjuring literature. What is needed – in addition to knowledge and natural gifts – is practice, hours and hours and hours of it. We have heard of only one case (and that at second-hand) in which a poltergeist agent is said to have shown an interest in conjuring prior to the outbreak; and we know of no case in which a poltergeist agent has afterwards gone on to establish himself as a skilled stage conjurer.

If these criteria are applied, the proposal that poltergeist phenomena have in most cases been produced by clever conjuring is bound, in the great majority of cases, to collapse. And these criteria – or ones very like them – *must* be applied. For if they are not applied, the issue of whether or not there was conjuring is placed beyond the jurisdiction of observed fact; the hypothesis can be maintained in the absence of any positive evidence at all and despite all indications to the contrary. This is a situation upon whose absurdity and unhealthiness we shall comment at the end of the chapter.

It remains true, of course, that trickery in the form of distraction, followed by some surreptitious quick movement, has been detected in an appreciable percentage of poltergeist cases. Trickery of this kind is in no case ruled out by the above criteria. But neither will it suffice to explain more than a small percentage of the phenomena *if the phenomena were as reported*. It will not explain, for example, Mr Durbin's experience with the levitated and then projected glass, which is no doubt why one often meets the suggestion that it is very rare indeed for a witness in a poltergeist case to see an object begin to move. But perhaps it is not all that rare an occurrence when one considers that one's eyes cannot at any given moment be resting upon more than one of the objects in a room. In Part I of this book there were cited several examples of objects seen to start moving – e.g. Gröben (1718), Boston (1867), Buhai (1925), Miami (1966–7) – and similar observations have been claimed in quite a few other cases, for example (and these are only cases which happen to come to mind), Slawensik (1806), Munchhof (1818), Philadelphia (1866), Oakland (1874), Amherst (1878), Worksop (1883), Cheriton (1917), England (c. 1920, case 371), Mauritius (1937), France (1940), Olive Hill (1968) and USA (1974, case 499). In a recent article, 'Experimenting with the poltergeist', *European Journal of Parapsychology*, vol. 1, 1977, Mr W. G. Roll claims that of 105 cases involving object-movements, visual fixation seemed to have an inhibiting effect in 47 and to have no effect in 43.

All in all the simple trickery hypothesis does not seem to have much to recommend it. Nor will it explain those very commonly observed phenomena, the slow flight of objects through the air, and their movement in a curved or erratic path. To fit reports like these, and reports of quite a lot of other kinds of phenomena too, into the trickery hypothesis, we have to assume that the witness was *not* looking at the object when it moved, that it did *not* pursue a slow and curved path through the air, etc. We have, in other words, once again to assume that *the phenomena were not* as they were reported to have been. Now some people are prepared to adopt this extreme assumption as a working hypothesis; and they do so upon the grounds of certain general and factually based doubts about the reliability of human testimony concerning transient and startling occurrences. We shall consider the factual basis for such doubts in a moment.

So much for fraud as an explanation of the occurrence of supposed poltergeist phenomena. Another popular tactic for explaining away such phenomena is to represent them as misinterpretations or misunderstandings by nervous or imaginative people of happenings, perhaps slightly unusual ones, which would prove susceptible of perfectly commonplace natural explanations if anyone bothered to investigate carefully. The sample of 500 cases, whose characteristics were discussed in the last chapter, contains only a very few cases in which a commonplace natural cause was shown to lie behind the phenomena reported. We suspect, however, that there is a simple explanation for this shortfall. Most of the cases susceptible of such explanations are tedious and trivial and have not found their way into print. In our own experience of case investigation, however, they far outnumber cases in which the phenomena are attributable to fraud. It will perhaps be of some interest if we give a few examples of some of the kinds of 'normal causes' of poltergeist effects which we have ourselves come across, or concerning which we have first-hand information. We shall do so under the headings of the kinds of 'phenomena' concerned rather than of the kinds of causes at work. It will be noticed that the kinds of phenomena concerned are ones more characteristic of what we have called hauntings than of poltergeists proper.

1 Whispers, muffled voices, spoken words, groans, laughter, etc.

Most people do not realize how easy it is to misinterpret indistinct noises, especially if they at all resemble the human voice. One 'reads' meaningful content into obscure noises just as readily as one 'sees' it in the Rorschach inkblots. The sources of such sounds may be difficult to locate, thus giving imaginative persons scope to exercise their talents. Sounds from neighbouring houses may sometimes be reflected so as to seem to come from near at hand, and sounds may also be carried from one room to another of the same house along pipes and other hollow cavities. The wind in certain chimneys or through television aerials may give rise to curious hummings, whispers, or howls. The escape of air in double-glazed windows can also cause peculiar noises. Certain common animals – in Britain especially owls and hedgehogs – at times produce the most alarming groans, screeches, snorts, snufflings and sounds of heavy breathing. One of the writers (AG) once had a singular experience in this last connection. When he was a small boy, during the war of 1939–1945, he was alone with his mother one dark evening. From the garden there suddenly began a prolonged series of the most anguished gaspings and groanings. His mother became understandably convinced that these were the death-rattles of a wounded enemy airman, and proceeded into the garden with a heavy stick, ready to do battle. AG followed at a safe distance. It was, however, no airman, but two hedgehogs on the lawn.

2 Raps, creaks, knocks, scratches, etc.

Causes at work here may include such things as: house subsidence, branches tapping on windows, moths flying into windows, rats or mice behind skirting boards or in the loft, nesting birds, owls 'dancing', death-watch beetles in woodwork, plaster crumbling and dropping away, waterhammers, noises in central heating pipes and drips from overflow pipes. These causes may seem trivial and obvious, but it is remarkable what an imaginative person can make of them. AG once ran across a case in which an entire household was being alarmed by an ordinary waterhammer.

When the operative causes are slightly more obscure than these, even quite prosaic people can be frightened and mystified. A case in point was investigated by ADC in 1957. In this case the occupants of a remote Cambridgeshire house were being terrified by eerie and four-dimensional thudding noises (we call them four-dimensional because they seemed to come from all around one rather than from a particular place). It was not until the family was on the verge of quitting the house that the explanation was discovered. It was this. Apples had been stored in the loft. Rats had found them there. Now apples are difficult for rats to transport, rats being constructed as they are. However, these wily beasts had evolved the following stratagem. They would roll a small apple to the edge of the loft and push it down the hollow of a cavity wall. At the bottom they made off with it or disposed of it. The falling of the apples had produced the spooky sounds.

3 The opening or closing of doors

This phenomenon, which is quite commonly reported, may sometimes be traced to such obvious natural causes as warped door-frames, improperly hung doors, or a build-up of air pressure due to wind or to the sharp closing of a door in another part of the house. A not-uninteresting case of ostensibly paranormal door-opening at Poole in Dorset was investigated by one of the writers (ADC) in January 1960. The house concerned was a fairly new, semi-detached one, built on a slight rise overlooking the town. It was occupied by a married couple with two children aged seven and five. The husband worked mainly on night shifts, and it was at night, when the wife was left alone with the children, that most of the phenomena had occurred. The phenomenon that had principally alarmed her was this. About three to five times over the preceding few months, the following sequence of events had taken place: the front door had rattled and the knocker sounded; then the door between the lounge and the hall (this door was close to the front door and opened into the lounge) had opened, the handle being sometimes seen to turn; and then (after 5–10 seconds) the door from the lounge into the kitchen (at the opposite end of the lounge) would open. ADC discovered that this sequence of events could be produced if air pressure were built up in the hall by vigorously swinging the bedroom doors in the upstairs corridor. The lounge door-catches had very weak springs and would open at a light touch. The windows of the bedrooms were so situated that the south or south-east winds played upon them, and the bedroom doors fitted very poorly into their frames. It seemed very likely that a strong wind from the appropriate quarter would similarly cause a build-up of air pressure in the hall and set off the sequence of door openings. This diagnosis was confirmed by the fact that neighbouring houses of like design proved to have been similarly afflicted, and by the fact that the phenomenon had been particularly in evidence on a windy day a few weeks previously. As for the door-handle turning: the wife was the only person who claimed to have seen this; and ADC came to the conclusion that the effect was purely subjective – an interesting example of the power which the context of a phenomenon may exercise upon one's perception of it.

4 Switching on and off of lights and other electrical appliances

This is an effect which seems to be becoming increasingly common. It is possible that in some cases weak springs may allow a switch to remain at a point of balance from which a very slight jar may disturb it. Sometimes, however, more obscure causes are at work. A colleague of ours once investigated a case in which a lady claimed that the spirit of her deceased husband would switch her bedside lamp on or off at request. They went into the bedroom and the lady switched on the lamp. After a pause she invited her late husband to switch it off. It duly went off. Another pause, and she asked him to switch it on. It went on again. Our colleague was naturally taken aback. Investigation of the flex, plug and socket revealed nothing amiss. It was not until he dismantled the lamp and found that a thermal switch had accidentally been incorporated into the circuit near the bulb that the explanation became apparent. The lady had presumably learned to time her requests to accord with the workings of the switch.

In a case which came to the notice of one of the writers (ADC) a house had acquired the reputation of being haunted because an escaped convict was living there and switching the lights on and off from time to time.

It goes without saying that a crucial factor in whether or not causes such as the ones we have just been considering give rise to stories of hauntings and poltergeists is the personality and intelligence of the various witnesses. Events which may frighten a nervous or imaginative person into fits will not make a steadier man so much as look up from his newspaper. Furthermore some people, principally ones whose lives are so dreary that any kind of excitement is a welcome relief, desperately want the phenomena to be genuine. Such people very often convince themselves that they are the centres of paranormal happenings without there being in reality any special events at all to which the supposed happenings correspond. In a case in Nottinghamshire investigated by AG, a kindly but not very bright *paterfamilias* had come to believe that spirits were responsible for certain small markings which he thought appeared in his very depressing little cottage when his back was turned. In reality the markings, or such of them as AG saw at the time when they 'appeared', had been there all along. The householder simply noticed them for the first time when he made a search. In a case which we investigated jointly, a middle-aged lady, whose artistic impulses struggled vainly in the net of her colourless domestic routine, became convinced that, amidst other psychic phenomena centring on herself, the end of her bed was regularly lifted up and dropped during the night, waking her up. To her annoyance this had so far escaped the observation of her husband, who slumbered soundly in a separate bed. We went along one night to see if we could witness the phenomenon. The lady lay down on her bed. Nothing happened; and after a while she fell asleep, snoring loudly. The tedium of this performance became unbearable, and in despair ADC several times lifted up and dropped the end of her bed as the spirits were said to do. She did not even stir.

As we said above, phenomena of the four illustrative classes which we have been considering are more characteristic of hauntings (and mild ones at that) than of poltergeists. The gap between trivial events like these, and some of the alleged feats of even quite unexceptional poltergeists, is enormous, and we cannot see any way of crossing it. There are no 'ordinary causes' of objects rising slowly upwards and then shooting off sideways, or of their suddenly appearing inside closed spaces, or of their moving slowly and erratically through the air; nor are there any 'ordinary causes' of rappings responding intelligently to questions or following a particular person around the house. If one wants to make 'ordinary causes' explanations cover all the phenomena, one has again to assume that *the phenomena cannot in fact have been as they are reported to have been*. Once more we are confronted with questions about the reliability of eyewitness testimony; and this time we must come to grips with them.

The position which we have just reached has been reached many times before. It was reached long ago by Frank Podmore, one of the Society for Psychical Research's most hard-bitten professional doubters. Podmore had at least studied some of the relevant literature, and investigated some poltergeist cases himself, which is more than can be said for most of those who advance views like his today. In his *The Naturalisation of the Supernatural* (London, 1908) he says of poltergeist phenomena (p. 162): 'Many of them, *as described*, are quite inexplicable; especially is this true of the movements of objects, which are frequently spoken of as hovering, floating, or as being gently wafted by an invisible agency'. His conclusion is that the phenomena could not have been as described. Neither human observation nor human memory is to be relied upon under such circumstances:

> we may see from the account given by the untrained observer of a conjuring trick how widely the thing described may differ from the thing done. . . . It is difficult, without long training, to realise how small is the part played in general perception by actual sensation, especially in the case of retinal impressions, and how largely those retinal impressions are interpreted and supplemented by immediate and unconscious inference. When we are dealing with familiar matters the inference is generally correct; but the conjurer induces us to adopt a wrong inference – we 'see' in a conjuring trick something which does not really take place. Again, when, as happens in many cases, the account is not written down until some time after the events, errors of memory, may distort the facts . . . . That such errors, of observation or of memory, are responsible for a great part at any rate of the marvels reported in Poltergeist cases, we can often find out by comparison of the accounts given by different witnesses of the same incident, or by the same witness at different times; or, more generally, by a comparison of the evidence given by educated and uneducated witnesses. (*Ibid.*, pp. 162–4)

Having said all this, however, Podmore obviously feels he has still not done quite enough to dispose of the numerous reports of hovering, floating, or slow-moving objects. To account for them he develops a supplementary hypothesis:

> Such an appearance would be caused by any temporary aberration in the estimation of time; and we know that such erroneous estimates occur in delusion, and under the influence of haschish, and other drugs, and apparently in the partial dissociation of

consciousness which accompanies many waking hallucinations. (*Ibid.*, pp. 168–9)

He rather noticeably fails to support this view with any evidence that haschish users are apt to see objects 'fall slowly'; but perhaps his hypothesis has more to recommend it than that of a recent proponent of the 'geophysical' theory of poltergeists, who suggests that poltergeist missiles may appear to travel in a wavering path because the observers are themselves being moved up and down by localized earth tremors.

Podmore supports his arguments entirely by a discussion of anecdotal material. However, we now have a good many ostensibly relevant experimental findings. In fact even in Podmore's day not a few such findings had been obtained. The experiments concerned may for the most part be regarded as falling within the sphere of applied psychology – they have been particularly aimed at throwing light on the validity of testimony put before law courts in criminal trials. It is, however, not difficult to see their possible relevance to the problems we are here discussing. Anyone who wants to look further into the relevant literature might usefully begin with J. Marshall's *Law and Psychology in Conflict* (New York, 1966), A. Trankell's *Reliability of Evidence* (Stockholm, 1972), G. Williams's *The Proof of Guilt* (London, 1955), and an article by D. S. Greer, 'Anything but the truth? The reliability of testimony in criminal trials', in *The British Journal of Criminology*, vol. 11, 1971. On the parapsychological side the most valuable single source is I. Stevenson's 'The substantiality of spontaneous cases' in *Proceedings of the Parapsychological Association*, no. 5, 1968. It will be convenient to consider some aspects of these findings under the three headings of memory, observation, and motivated seeing.

1 Memory

A good many psychological experiments have been carried out which have had the following general form. Subjects have been read a story, or shown slides, a film or a playlet. Subsequently – after intervals of time which have varied from a few minutes to several years – they have been asked to reproduce the story, or describe the contents of the slides, film or playlet. (Classic early accounts of work of this kind are F. C. Bartlett's *Remembering*

(Cambridge, 1932), and W. Stern's article 'The psychology of testimony' in *The Journal of Abnormal and Social Psychology*, vol. 34, 1939.) Such experiments have very commonly found that subjects tend not just (as might be expected) to omit material, including sometimes even important material, but that they are quite likely to import material which was not contained in the original. The general setting of a story or scene is remembered, and so are certain 'dominant details'; but in between the dominant details imagination and plausible reconstruction get to work, and departures from the original are common.

The possible applications of such findings to the issues with which we are here concerned are obvious. A large element of imaginative reconstruction enters into one's 'memory' even of material that has been presented to one quite recently. An even greater degree of 'imaginative reconstruction' may be expected to vitiate one's memory when the events 'recollected' were themselves sufficiently exciting and dramatic to stir the imagination.

This line of argument accords well with the views which, as we saw a moment ago, Frank Podmore arrived at long ago on the basis of anecdotal material and educated common sense. However, we do not think that the argument can be sustained, at least if it is carried to the point where we are invited to reject the alleged evidence for poltergeist phenomena in a wholesale and indiscriminate fashion.

To start with, we may note that the results of these experiments do not suggest that persons in our culture have any general tendency to make tales retrospectively taller in the telling, so long, that is, as the recall situation is one which demands reproduction rather than active embroidery. Rather the contrary – the tendency is more commonly for subjects to eliminate or tone down the odd or the bizarre or the culturally anomalous. What is more, when witnesses are put on oath, or are otherwise placed under pressure to be scrupulously accurate, the number of errors made is substantially reduced. Nor is there much to suggest that tales grow progressively taller with the passage of time. If errors and changes are made, they are made at the first telling, and do not change much in subsequent re-tellings even over a period of years.

Podmore, as we have seen, thought that the inadequacies of one's power to observe and to remember accurately, together with the lapse of time between the events observed and the testimony being set down, were in most poltergeist cases quite sufficient to discredit the alleged phenomena. For him it was enough to point out (as he often did) that a few weeks had passed between the poltergeist outbreak and the recording of the testimony, and that there were assorted minor discrepancies between the accounts of the various witnesses. So far as his argument has to do with the fallibility of memory, it does not appear to be strongly supported by the experimental evidence.

In fact there is quite a lot to suggest that peoples' memories for events which, like many apparently paranormal happenings, interest and impress them, may be very good. Stevenson, in the article just referred to, cites a number of cases in which witnesses of ostensibly paranormal occurrences wrote two accounts of their experiences, one at the time, and another many years afterwards. Despite the fact that the first accounts were not consulted before the second ones were written, the discrepancies were neither numerous nor serious. We can support Stevenson here, from the results of similar trials which were carried out by the witnesses at the case at Tydd St Mary (1957) three years after the events. In the *Journal of the SPR*, vol. 10, 1902, pp. 308–20, and vol. 11, 1903, pp. 25–36, 113–16, will be found the documents of a case of haunting (Clough House, Sheffield) in which, by chance, two separate sets of accounts by the same witnesses, given some years apart, came into the SPR's possession.

It might further be said that Podmore's position is in any case outdated, for we now have quite a few case reports in which the time interval between the occurrence of the phenomena and their being recorded was so brief that the question of retrospective errors and exaggerations can hardly be raised. In fact more such reports were extant even in his own time than he seems to have realized. If the witnesses in these cases made crucial errors, they must have been errors of observation rather than errors of memory. So it is to the possibilities with regard to errors of observation that we now turn.

2 Observation

It is, of course, in a sense impossible to make an absolute distinction between errors of observation and errors of memory.

Some period of time, however brief, is bound to elapse under even the most ideal conditions between a witness's observing something, and his being able to record it. So we shall talk of 'observation' and of 'errors of observation' when this lapse of time appears to have been as short as was possible under the circumstances.

Quite a lot of experiments of the 'staged incident' kind have been conducted by lawyers and by forensic psychologists. As a typical example we may take one cited by Greer in the article mentioned above. A class in a law school witnessed a carefully arranged 'row' enacted between four students. The class then adjourned to the law school courtroom. A jury of law students who had not witnessed the row was empanelled. Thirteen arbitrarily selected witnesses of the class-room incident were each asked nine questions about what had happened. On the basis of this evidence the jurors arrived at a version of the row – their 'verdict'. This version was then compared with the pre-arranged version, and the following were some of the discrepancies noted:

(a) The person found by the 'jury' to have made the first move did not in fact make it.

(b) Several relevant 'facts' were not mentioned in the jury's version – e.g. that one of the participants had shouted 'That is an insult and I shall here resent it.'

(c) The jury's version of another statement uttered during the incident differed from what was actually said.

Numerous comparable findings could be cited, and the question arises, what bearing, if any, do they have upon one's assessment of observations of alleged poltergeist phenomena? The answer, we think, is very little. The errors made by eyewitnesses of staged 'crimes', though perhaps important in a legal context, fall far short in magnitude of the errors of which eyewitnesses of poltergeist phenomena would have to be held guilty in order to explain away their observations. Eyewitnesses who have watched a staged crime from near at hand may be mistaken as to who said what or as to who drew a gun first; but they are not mistaken in supposing that they saw someone 'shot'. Eyewitnesses who have observed poltergeist phenomena from near at hand may be mistaken as to whether person A or person B was standing beside them, or whether person C was present or not (which may certainly be important matters in some cases), but can we really suppose them mistaken when they say that they saw, quite possibly that they *collectively* saw, an object rise into the air untouched by anyone, or fly from a corner where no-one was lurking? There is nothing in the experimental findings that remotely justifies this conclusion.

One might at this point cite various recent cases – a slowly growing number – in which we have instrumental recordings of ostensible poltergeist phenomena. Of course instrumental recordings are not *per se* evidence that genuine phenomena took place – there still remain questions as to the reliability of the investigators, and as to the general context within which the alleged phenomena took place. But they *are*, or at least *can be*, evidence against the hypothesis that we are now considering, namely that reports of allegedly paranormal happenings in poltergeist cases are to be ascribed to malobservation, sometimes amounting to actual illusion. Photographs have occasionally been taken of poltergeist objects in motion – the earliest case we know of in which this was done was at Eggenberg (1929). A cine-film of a swinging lamp was taken in the case at New Jersey in 1972, and a video-recording of the rotation of a picture in the Rosenheim case of 1967. A more extensive cine-film of poltergeist phenomena is said to have been made in Brazil. In the Nicklheim case of 1968–9, investigated, like the Rosenheim case, by Professor Hans Bender, objects seemed to have been transported out of closed and empty rooms and cupboards. Accordingly various little objects were placed in a small box, the open front of which was controlled by a photo-electric light curtain such as those used by jewellers to protect their shop windows. The objects placed inside the box were controlled by light-responsive photo-electric switches, activation of which triggered two still cameras and a cine-camera. On one occasion a figurine fell over triggering the cameras. The light curtain had not been penetrated, and the cameras recorded no cause for the movement. Tape-recordings of ostensibly paranormal rappings have been made in several poltergeist cases, and we have already mentioned (chapter 10) certain tape recordings of supposed imitative noises in cases of haunting. We have little doubt but that the tally of instrumental recordings will increase significantly in the next few years.

3 Motivated seeing

Another cliché of popular psychology is that we have a tendency to observe not what really is there, but what we expect or would like to be there. A classic example that ended in the law courts is a Canadian case in which a hunter was mistaken for a deer, and shot by his companions. Greer, in the article cited above, gives the following account (p. 143):

> The hunters, who were eagerly scanning the landscape for deer, perceived the moving object (the victim) as a deer. Before the trial, the police re-created the scene under the same conditions, using another man in the place of the deceased. They reported at the trial that the object was clearly visible as a man. But the important psychological difference between the first and second 'shooting' was that the hunters, expecting to see a deer, 'saw' a deer; the police expected to see a man and therefore 'saw' a man.

Many reports of ostensibly paranormal phenomena without doubt belong in this category. It has been the good fortune of the writers to have had (separately and in different places) a number of experiences of the following kind. We have sat in dimly lit, but not blacked out, seance rooms, in or through which we thought we saw prance a somewhat portly middle-aged gentleman draped in a sheet of butter muslin or of nylon net curtaining. Others (the majority) in the room did not see this at all. They saw the ethereal forms of departed spirits, some of whom they recognized. One man even tenderly embraced what he took to be the materialized form of his late wife; and we are absolutely certain that he would not have embraced it had he supposed it to be that of the medium in question. In these situations, either our seeing, or that of the other people, or both, was undoubtedly influenced by antecedent hopes or expectations. Now if this is possible with one sort of ostensibly paranormal phenomenon, why not with another? Why not with poltergeist phenomena? Why should not witnesses, desiring and expecting marvels, 'see' objects, which have been thrown into the air by deceitful hands, move in a trajectory not originating from those hands, and perhaps appear to move slowly or erratically through the air? Why should they not hear random crepitations produced by thermal changes or by house subsidence as intelligent answers to questions? Why, indeed, should there not be 'motivated failure to see', a tendency to overlook suspicious circumstances, or to misinterpret them in a favourable manner? It could be added that it is far from difficult to demonstrate 'motivated seeing' and 'motivated hearing' in the psychological laboratory, and that what might be called evidence of motivated 'failure to see' has also been obtained.

We are far from saying that 'motivated seeing' and 'motivated hearing' do not play a part in generating reports of poltergeist phenomena and of hauntings. In fact we are sure from personal experience that they sometimes do. But it seems to us quite certain that they are not the whole story, or anything like it. Why on earth should it be supposed that all, or most, persons who claim to have seen poltergeist phenomena hoped or expected to do so? In numerous cases it seems quite certain that the witnesses did not previously believe in poltergeist phenomena, and that a poltergeist phenomenon was almost the last thing that they wished to see. And in some cases at least the presuppositions of the witnesses were divergent whilst their observations were in accord. Furthermore it is abundantly clear from both the anecdotal and the experimental material that motivated seeing has scope to operate only in proportion as the viewing conditions are poor. Where light is dim, or the object distant or seen out of the corner of the eye, or a quick glimpse only is obtained, desire and expectation may determine what is 'seen'. But where light is good, and the object is near at hand and closely observed, reality predominates and hope and expectancy lose their grip. And there are plenty of examples of poltergeist phenomena which have been observed from close at hand by apparently unprejudiced witnesses, in good light, and sometimes collectively. We quote two examples of such observations, selected almost at random.

Here is how J. G. Pratt, whose observations of phenomena in the Miami poltergeist of 1966–7 have already been quoted, describes what he saw in another American case (location not given) in 1974. (The extract is from J. D. Morris, W. G. Roll and R. L. Morris, eds, *Research in Parapsychology 1975*, Metuchen, N.J., 1976, p. 111.)

> I was looking directly toward an upholstered swivel chair from a distance of 10 feet when the person nearest to the chair, the grandmother, was three feet from it. She was sitting on the floor facing me, with the chair to her right and slightly behind her. I saw the chair tilt backward, gathering speed as it went, and slam

its back against the wall. It then fell, apparently normally, onto the floor in essentially its original position.

The following is from an article by Sir Ernest Bennett entitled 'A modern poltergeist' in the *Journal of the SPR*, vol. 33, 1946. The poltergeist, which took place in 1942, centred around an adult kitchen maid in a Malvern nursing home. (The matron of the home, Miss Julia Clancy, one of the principal witnesses, has furnished some further details in correspondence with AG.)

> On the last week of January 1942, about 2.30 p.m. in good light, we, the undersigned, were present in the kitchen of Clarence Nursing Home, Graham Road, Malvern, Worcs. While we were all facing the kitchen range, the poker, suspended from a nail at the side of the range, detached itself from the nail, and passed over the suspended electric lamp. It struck the kitchen table point downwards near to Mrs Collins, and made a clearly visible dent in the top of the table. It then fell down to the floor.

This statement is signed by Miss Clancy, and identical statements were signed by four of the six other persons concerned. The remaining two witnesses signed an earlier report of Sir Ernest's, which was apparently mislaid; they could not, however, be traced to sign the above statement.

Various explanations might be offered of observation-reports such as these; but we do not think that motivated seeing is amongst them.

We have now successively dismissed trickery, ordinary natural causes, and errors of observation and memory, as satisfactory means of 'explaining away' all the peculiar phenomena reported in poltergeist cases. We must emphasize the word 'all'. We are far from denying that such factors are responsible for *some* of the reports; indeed we have supplied instances from our own case investigations.

At this point certain writers on these subjects would probably argue as follows. Of course there are reports which cannot be explained away in terms of trickery, reports that cannot be explained away in terms of commonplace natural causes, reports that cannot be explained away in terms of malobservation and errors of memory. But if we are prepared to suppose that in outstanding cases two or more of these factors were simultaneously operative, and are prepared also perhaps to suppose a fair admixture of lying and conspiracy by the witnesses, and of exaggeration and suppression by publicity-hungry investigators, all may yet be explained away.

Such a position is, in a sense, quite impregnable. But, paradoxically, it is its very impregnability which undermines it. One cannot deny that, logically speaking, undetected trickery, undetected natural causes, undetected malobservation and undetected lying *may* lie behind all reports of poltergeist phenomena. But to assume without supporting evidence, and despite numerous considerations (such as we have advanced above) to the contrary, that they *do* lie behind them, is to insulate one's beliefs in this sphere from all possibility of modification from the cold contact of chastening facts. It is to adopt the paranoid stance of the flat-earther or the religious fanatic, who can 'explain away' all the awkward facts which threaten his system of delusions. At its worst, such a stance borders on insanity; at best it constitutes an unhealthy and unprofitable turning away from the realities of the world.

14 Some poltergeist cases

In this chapter, and in the next two, we shall straightforwardly describe some of the cases of ostensible poltergeists and hauntings which we have ourselves investigated. We shall do so under headings which will facilitate a comparison with cases of comparable kinds discussed in Part I. Accordingly, this chapter will contain accounts of two poltergeist cases in which the alleged phenomena were relatively simple; chapter 15 will be concerned with cases of haunting; and chapter 16 will deal with some cases of more complex or unusual kinds.

The cases which we treat in these chapters are exclusively ones in which we think that genuine phenomena *may* have taken place; in two or three we witnessed ostensibly paranormal phenomena ourselves. These cases are a selection from a much larger number of cases which we have investigated either separately or together. For the purpose of writing this book we have been through and selected from our notes of some fifty case investigations; and these in turn represent perhaps only half the cases we have looked into. It must be emphasized that in many instances (only a few of which were mentioned in the previous chapter) our findings were wholly negative. The would-be investigator is warned that what he is presented with in the next three chapters is the rather small yield of a large number of often tedious excursions.

The first of the two cases which we shall deal with in this chapter is that of a poltergeist which took place in a large East Midlands town in the summer of 1967. It has certain affinities with the Sauchie (1960) case (see chapter 4). The present case is described at considerable length in two articles by the present writers and Mr C. Lamb in the *Journal of the SPR*, vol. 47, 1973. Here it will only be possible to give a much briefer and less formal account. Pseudonyms will be used to protect the persons principally involved; copies of all relevant statements and documents have, however, been deposited with the SPR.

The scene of this case was the southernmost of a row of

terraced cottages which we shall refer to as numbers 13–16 Carey Street. These houses, of a conventional 'two up, two down' design, shared a communal yard, in which stood like sentry boxes a lavatory for each house. In number 16, with which we shall be principally concerned, lived Mrs Mary Connolly, a hard-working widow in her fifties, her son Brian, aged twelve, and an elderly friend, Mrs Revill, generally referred to as 'Grannie', although she was not a relation. Next door, at number 15, were a Mr and Mrs Harper, their daughter Sonia, aged about 22, and their son, Frank, aged 15; and at number 14 lived Mr and Mrs Lockwood, a young couple with a baby.

The Connollys moved into number 16 during the Whit weekend of 1967 (27–29 May). The first poltergeist phenomena took place on Monday, 5 June. According to a statement signed by Mrs Connolly on 14 June, they began about 11.15 p.m., shortly after the family had gone to bed – Mrs Connolly and Mrs Revill to the upstairs front bedroom, Brian to the upstairs back bedroom. Brian's light remained on, as it usually did. From the floor of Brian's room, or the ceiling of the kitchen below, there commenced a series of extremely powerful pounding noises, not unlike those which might have been made with a heavy hammer. Mrs Connolly thought someone was trying to break in. She got up, got the others up, and searched the house. They found nothing; but the noises continued unabated. Eventually all three congregated in the kitchen, and remained there until about 2.00 a.m., when the sounds stopped rather abruptly.

Next day, Tuesday 6 June, the noises again started about 11.15 p.m., immediately after they had retired for the night. Mrs Connolly got up, went to bed again, and got up again while the noises still continued. She got up again and hammered on the wall of the back room, and after a couple more thumps the noises stopped. On the following day, Wednesday 7 June, a rather similar performance was gone through. The poundings lasted about an hour, and then suddenly stopped. They did not get faint and die away.

This brings us to Thursday 8 June and the most remarkable night in the whole case. On the other side of number 16 Carey Street from number 15 stood a house, number 17, which did not share in the communal yard. The ground floor of this building was occupied, during the daytime only, by a ladies' hairdressing establishment; on the first floor was a flat, then occupied by Mr

C. Lamb. Mr Lamb, a quantity surveyor of great practical intelligence, had heard the poundings of the three preceding nights through the wall of his flat. At first he thought they were intended to get him to turn down his radio, which he did. When they still continued he set them down to some private eccentricity of the occupants of number 16, and thought no more about them. On the Thursday evening, however, he became personally involved in the happenings, and from notes which he wrote the following day, together with a very full statement dictated to AG on 14 June by Mr Lockwood of number 14, and Mrs Connolly's statement, mentioned above, we have a fairly complete picture of that night's events.

The noises began again about a quarter to eleven, just after the Connollys had gone to bed. The previous night Mr Lockwood had promised Mrs Connolly that he would go round if the trouble started up again. Hearing the sounds, he did so. Mrs Connolly and Brian had got up, and Mr Lockwood found them downstairs. The bangings still continued from the upstairs back bedroom. Mr Lockwood developed the suspicion that the noises might be being produced from number 17. Together with Mrs Connolly he went to Mr Lamb's door (sounds continuing from number 16 meanwhile) but received no reply. Seeing a light in number 15, they went there. Sonia Harper and her boy-friend, Mr Alan Kirk, came out, and, after another abortive attempt to get a reply from number 17, they all went into number 16, where the poundings were still going on. By this time Mrs Revill ('Grannie') had also come downstairs. Representatives of numbers 14, 15 and 16 were all present, so suspicion was naturally directed once more to number 17. A delegation once again proceeded to Mr Lamb's door, only to meet him coming up the road. He went back with them into number 16. Brian was standing at the foot of the stairs, and the poundings were still coming from upstairs. Mr Lamb described the noises as follows:

> The noises were not low-pitched or thuds, but very loud, sharp and staccato and intense. They came in bursts both short and long. As far as I could tell, there was no vibration on the ceiling, and most certainly there was no 'flicker' or vibration on the electric light hanging down from the ceiling. The noises seemed most definitely to come from above the kitchen. They were loud enough to be heard in the front street with Mrs Connolly's front door open.

There was now no-one upstairs. Mr Lamb went out to fetch the police. While he was absent, the thuds reached a new crescendo of violence, pounding continuously for three or four minutes. Then they stopped. Shortly afterwards Mr Lamb returned with a policeman. While the policeman questioned Mrs Connolly, Mr Lockwood went with Brian into the upstairs back bedroom; however, there were no sounds.

At this point a somewhat bumptious police sergeant arrived with two more policemen. They searched the house and the loft, which opened from Brian's room. They found nothing and no-one to account for the happenings. The sergeant gave vent to some sarcastic remarks, and departed with his flock.

All remained quiet, and the company dispersed. The Connolly family went upstairs again. Mr Lamb and Mr Lockwood remained downstairs. After a while there were several more thuds. During these thuds Mrs Connolly was sitting on Brian's bed. Mr Lamb went upstairs, but the sounds had ceased. After everyone had settled down again, there was one more burst of two or three bangs. Mr Lamb and Mr Lockwood left between one and one-thirty.

There were no phenomena on the Friday and Saturday. On the Sunday night thumpings again broke out in the upstairs back bedroom after the Connollys had gone to bed. They lasted for about quarter of an hour.

Mr Lamb had rung Nottingham University on Friday 9 June in the hope of finding a psychical research society there. AG received his message on Monday 12 June, and he and a colleague, Mr J. D. Shotter, called at Mr Lamb's flat the same evening. Mr Lamb described the events of the preceding nights, and we then all went to talk to Mr Kirk and Miss Harper. Finally we called on the Connollys, heard their story, and obtained permission to remain in the house while they went to bed.

We explored the house and its surroundings, and set up a tape recorder in the kitchen with the microphone on a 6'6"-high shelf by the door into the lounge. The microphone was thus close to the floor of Brian's bedroom. The Connollys retired to bed about quarter past eleven. Our log from 11.15 p.m. to 11.46 p.m. – it was written by Mr Lamb and AG in turns – runs as follows:

> 11.15 p.m. Started tape in kitchen, mike on mantelpiece, dog and cat in lounge.

SOME POLTERGEIST CASES 267

11.19 p.m. Mike on shelf 6'6" up on wall with door to lounge. JDS and CL and AG in kitchen. Mrs C. and G[rannie] in front bedroom. B. in back bedroom.

11.21 p.m. A series of heavy bumps or bangs from upstairs – 6–8. AG proceeded upstairs. Could see Brian in mirror [through the open door] of room. Breathing heavily and restlessly turning in bed.

11.25 p.m. Brian upstairs asks if cat was in attic tonight. Asks if mother there. Then if man was here. AG returns downstairs.

11.26 p.m. 4 knocks. All party downstairs.

11.32 p.m. JDS creeps up stairs with battery TR to watch in mirror.

11.35 p.m. Brian sighs.

11.37 p.m. CL goes home for a while.

11.39 p.m. 2 raps. JDS by bedroom door, AG in kitchen, CL next door. [Note added by AG later in evening. JDS could see B in mirror – he moved restlessly, but nothing to account for bumps which were hard to localize and like kid bouncing on bed.]

11.44 p.m. 2 or 3 sounds as of bedsprings. B yawns.

11.46 p.m. AG changes places with JDS.

Mr Shotter wrote and signed (17 June 1967) the following account of his experience on the landing:

> After the first series of raps (which turned out to be eight in number) I made my way slowly up the stairs. I could hear the boy making noises as if laughing or giggling to himself. From my position at the top of the stairs I could see the end and one side of the bed through the crack between the door and the door frame and the boy's head and shoulders via a dressing table mirror. The boy was restless, almost asleep. I think we must have disturbed him by our movements on the stairs because he got obviously less sleepy as I was observing him.
>
> The bed moved slightly as he moved and there were very slight noises but none at all like the raps that we had heard or which occurred later. I had not been at the top of the stairs for more than a couple of minutes when two more raps occured. I had been observing the boy through the crack in the door. [Mr Shotter does not make clear in his statement how much he could see through the crack in the door. However, a sketch subsequently drawn by him shows that his field of view included Brian's head and shoulders and the line of his body under the blankets to the level of the waist or a little below. Brian was lying on his back towards the right of the bed, the foot of which

was close to the open door. His bedroom light was on, and the landing light off.] Nothing occurred that could be a preliminary to the raps nor, as far as I could see, during the raps. The boy did not seem to react to them at all. The mother, from the next room, commented to the grandmother, also sleeping in that room, '*He's* only giving short ones tonight' (or something to that effect). The boy continued lying restlessly in his bed, following the patterns on the bedhead with his finger and nothing further happened.

The sound seemed to come from the hatched area of the floor [sketch omitted]. It had the quality of the sound made by jumping very hard on a bed with a spring and wire mesh base – a rap or thud of some quite definite duration with some variation of quality during its occurrence.

It will be apparent from what Mr Shotter says that the thuds had lost the staccato quality on which Mr Lamb had earlier commented; in fact they now sounded double – 'ker-blunk' – and could be approximated to by raising and dropping the end of the empty bed, the 'double' effect being contributed by the slap of the mattress on the bedstead. (However, ADC later established that Brian had considerable difficulty in raising the end of the rather heavy bed, and he could certainly not have done it several times in quick succession.) We remained in number 16 until nearly 1.00 a.m., one or other member of the party being on the landing outside Brian's room for a good part of the time, but nothing else of note took place.

On the next two evenings AG was joined in Carey Street by ADC, who came over from Cambridge. Short bursts of thumpings took place in Brian's room on both evenings soon after the family had retired to bed. We tape recorded some of these with a microphone placed in Brian's room. The tape recordings revealed that prior to the sounds Brian had been stirring restlessly; but there was nothing to indicate that he made any sudden or violent movement. However, the poundings somewhat noticeably failed to take place during periods when we had Brian under direct observation. They came when we were downstairs or on the stairs; but not when we were in Brian's room, or watching his reflection in the dressing-table mirror.

Reviewing the situation at this point, we concluded that it was impossible to doubt the connection between Brian's getting into bed in the upstairs back bedroom and the occurrence there of quite violent noises. At the same time the evidence that he had not himself directly produced *all* the noises was very strong. For he (and also the other members of his family) had been seen downstairs by a number of witnesses whilst the noises continued upstairs; in fact he had even been seen outside the house in the same circumstances. Furthermore Mr Shotter had had him in partial view during the occurrence of one set of thumpings, and his mother had signed a statement that she was seated on his bed during the occurrence of another.

It accordingly seemed to us that we should consider more carefully the possibility that someone outside the Connolly family was fraudulently producing the phenomena. We decided that our best policy would probably be to keep the presence of all outside investigators so far as possible unknown to the Connollys and to the neighbourhood, and to see what we might be able to observe in those circumstances.

A further consideration which weighed with us was that the overt presence of investigators seemed to have a noticeably inhibiting effect on the phenomena. There could have been any number of reasons for this, including of course, that the noises were fraudulently produced; but we were inclined at this stage to suppose that the phenomena were genuine and focused round Brian, and that our presence had for various reasons an inhibiting psychological effect on him. It also struck us that the noises were becoming rather weaker, and much less frequent, and we wondered whether the long talks, climbing into the loft, etc., which he had had with ADC, might have provided some element in his rather restricted life which had hitherto been missing.

The plan just outlined was put into practice from 15 June to 25 June. Mr Lamb had already obtained from Mrs Connolly *carte blanche* to take whatever steps he thought proper in the investigation of the phenomena, and she had arranged to leave the front door open for him every night on condition that he locked it before finally departing. AG and ADC would arrive as darkness was falling, park their cars in another street, and turn into Mr Lamb's flat from the alley on the corner of which number 17 stood. Only twice was there reason to suppose that their presence was suspected. Mr Lamb conducted all overt commerce with the Connollys and their neighbours, and AG and ADC would slip into the yard or into number 16 only when phenomena had begun or were anticipated.

Our belief that phenomena might pick up again when investigators were no longer in evidence proved justified. The noises occurred, generally soon after Brian had got into bed, on eight of the eleven nights in this period, and they increased in number and intensity. On the night of Sunday 18 June they were especially loud and sustained. Brian went to bed at 11.30 p.m., and his mother put the downstairs light out at 11.38 p.m. The landing light remained on and filtered into Brian's bedroom. Mr Lamb and AG were in the yard. They could hear Brian talking to his mother. At 11.41 p.m. he said 'Goodnight, Mum', and there immediately came three thumps from the direction of his bedroom. Between then and 12.32 a.m. AG, who remained in the yard the whole time, apart from two intervals of a minute or so when he went round to check the front of number 16 and the shop beneath Mr Lamb's flat, noted altogether some two hundred thumps. They sounded exactly as they had done on previous nights. Some of them were very meaty, and AG could hear the furniture or the window frame in Brian's bedroom vibrating with each blow. The thumps came in bursts, most commonly of five or six, each thump within a burst succeeding the next after an interval of approximately half a second. At 11.47 p.m. Mr Lamb let himself into number 16 through the front door. Mrs Connolly came down to the kitchen, and at 11.49 p.m. there came the longest series of thumps of the evening, nineteen in all (this series was also counted by Mr Kirk, who was in number 15 with Sonia Harper). Mr Lamb began to creep up the stairs in his stockinged feet, but the noises ceased before he reached the top. He found Brian in bed with the bedclothes tucked in round him right the way up to the pillow. Mr Lamb waited upstairs until 11.57 p.m., and then came down again. Immediately there was a burst of eleven thumps. He crept up the stairs twice more, and each time the same thing happened. On the last occasion he remained upstairs from 12.12 a.m. to 12.31 a.m. without any thumps occurring. The moment he came down there were four and then twelve. After that peace reigned.

By about 20 June we had become at any rate very nearly convinced that the occupants of the neighbouring houses could not have had a hand in the production of the phenomena. The facts which brought us to this conclusion with respect to the occupants of number 15 were these:

1 From whatever vantage point one listened to the sounds

they were definitely localized in number 16 rather than in number 15. There was nothing to suggest that sounds made in number 15 were being carried through the wall or along a joist into number 16. Nor did we detect any signs of activity, unaccountable noises, and so on, from number 15, such as might have occurred had the blows been somehow engineered there.

2 Although Mr and Mrs Harper were totally unco-operative, we were able to interview their daughter Sonia and Mr A. Kirk, both of whom were present in number 15 while the noises were in progress. Sonia could not have been the culprit since on 8 June she was seen by several persons during the occurrence of the phenomena. She occupied the upstairs back bedroom adjacent to Brian's (apparently she shared it with her young brother) and was kept awake by the thumpings. We may assume that trickery could not have gone on without her knowledge. Much later, on 21 March 1969, Mr Lamb was able to interview her brother, who had also heard the noises, and was favourably impressed by him.

3 The occurrence of the thumpings was closely tied in not just with Brian's retiring to bed for the night, but with the comings and goings of investigators on the staircase and landing. The investigators concerned were endeavouring to make as little noise as possible, and were sometimes in their stockinged feet. It seems most improbable that their movements could have been detected from number 15, especially since the staircase of number 16 is adjacent to number 17.

4 On the afternoon of 19 June 1967 AG visited the house with a surveyor colleague of Mr Lamb's. They conducted a detailed structural examination of the floor of Brian's bedroom, and also investigated the loft. It was quite apparent that no machinery of any kind had ever been laid under the floorboards (five of which were removed) and that none could have been operated from number 15. Number 16 was separated from number 15 not merely by a stout wall but by an old and very large chimney breast rising from the kitchen below. This came up to the level of the underneath of the joists in the back bedroom floor and was filled with bricks and other rubble (it was open at the top). We searched it thoroughly.

We also satisfied ourselves that the noises did not come from number 17, where, of course, we had our base in Mr Lamb's flat.

Our endeavours during this period were thus to a fair extent successful in achieving their main aim, that of eliminating the Connollys' neighbours as sources of the phenomena. On the other hand we had learned nothing further about the actual nature of the phenomena or about Brian's possible role in producing them. We did not succeed in observing him during the occurrence of the thumps, and to have kept a sustained covert watch on him at night would have been very difficult – someone sitting on a tennis umpire's ladder outside his window might have done it, but the yard was a communal one and not suitable for such a stratagem. ADC had toyed with the possibility of setting up a TV or cine camera in the loft, but it did not seem practicable. It seemed as though concealing the investigators' presence would serve no further useful purpose.

Our decision to reappear overtly on the scene was precipitated by the following incident. On the evening of 21 June 1967, a party consisting of AG, Mr Shotter and Dr G. M. Stephenson assembled in Mr Lamb's flat. At 11.26 p.m., shortly after the Connollys had gone to bed, we heard the noises begin. Mr Shotter climbed out of Mr Lamb's kitchen window on to the roof of a shed. From this vantage point he was, by standing on tiptoe, just able to peer in through the window of Brian's bedroom. He saw Brian standing in the middle of the room, apparently stamping on the floor (Mr Shotter could only see the upper half of his body). His mother came into the room and Brian returned to bed. After a few minutes he flung back the bedcovers and kicked the edge of the bed with his stockinged heel.

Questioned shortly afterwards by Mr Lamb, Brian denied that he had been 'mucking about'. His story was that while he was undressing and immediately after he got into bed he heard various poundings from the floor. His bedroom door flew back and forward, striking the end of the bed. Then he was thrown, or fell, out of bed, hitting his head. His mother came in and put him back to bed. It is hard to say whether or not Brian was attempting to cheat. We already knew that both he and his mother were in the habit of shouting at the thumpings and banging back at them in the hope of making them stop. But the door movements and the projection from bed represented, if they really occurred, a new development in the phenomena, and we were rather inclined to regard the story as a cover-up. In the following few nights, also, there was a change in the quality of

SOME POLTERGEIST CASES 273

the noises; they sounded sharper, and, as Mrs Connolly put it, 'more like someone banging on the floor with a shoe'. From 26 June until 1 August (after which the Connollys left Carey Street) we once more appeared openly on the scene.

Unfortunately none of the happenings of this period took place whilst any member of our various parties was actually in number 16. During the first two weeks or so our suspicions that Brian was perpetrating some of the phenomena and inventing or imagining others grew stronger. He claimed that while he was lying in bed on the night of 2 July the wardrobe in his room, after some heavy poundings, had pitched forward from its separate framed base and fallen across him, hurting his shoulder. Similarly, on the night of 10 July, after further banging sounds, he saw from his bed (the bedroom light being as usual on) his heavy dressing-table lift off the floor some four inches, move towards the door, turn at an angle, land on the floor, and fall heavily forward against the foot of his bed. After this Mrs Connolly went to Mr Lamb's door for help; not finding him in she went to a local pub and came back with an acquaintance who lived further down Carey Street, Mrs Ella Clarke.

Owing to a series of oversights, we did not succeed in contacting Mrs Clarke until November 1972. She then gave us the following statement:

> The following is an account of what happened on my first and only visit to Mrs Connolly's house at No. 16 Carey Street. (I cannot recollect the date but understand from a Mr Lamb that this would be on the night of Monday 10th July 1967.)
>
> I was in conversation with a Mrs Whitehead at her residence, the 'Green Man' Public House, when Mrs Connolly re-arrived (having left the premises earlier) asking if someone could help her as some furniture had fallen across her son's bed. (Mrs Connolly had intimated in previous statements that there had been some strange noises and happenings in the house. From what she had related, I was inclined to believe that her son Brian was probably responsible as he may have been wanting to dodge school or for some similar reason.)
>
> I accompanied Mrs Connolly back to her house and as far as I can remember the time would probably be sometime after 11 p.m. On arriving at Mrs Connolly's, I found Mrs Connolly's aunt ['Grannie'] and Brian together with their dog in the downstairs front room. Mrs Connolly's aunt appeared to be quite distressed. Together with Mrs Connolly and Brian [I] proceeded

upstairs into the back bedroom. There were very loud heavy noises ringing around the bedroom as if someone was using a cudgel. The noises were all around the room and not appearing to come from one particular place. The wardrobe was lying across the foot of the bed – the bed being against the wall opposite from the door.

There was also a hole on the wall opposite the bed [this had appeared on the night of 24–25 June]. I put my head into the hole as far as I could. A noise (as loud as the other bangings) came from the hole. I jumped back, away from the hole. It was a noise like someone very enraged. It was a venomous noise, very belligerent and with animosity. I thought it was evil. I told Mrs Connolly that there was nothing I could do and suggested to her that she should leave the house. Also I offered to Mrs Connolly that she and her family could stay at my house for the night, if she preferred to. However, Mrs Connolly decided they would stay at home. I then left to go home, by which time it was probably around midnight or possibly later.

Mrs Clarke amplified this statement somewhat in response to questions put to her by AG and Mr Lamb on 27 November 1972. She told us that she thinks she was in the house for perhaps an hour, and in Brian's bedroom for a fair part of that time. Whilst in his room she thinks she heard perhaps four bursts of four to six thumps. The noise was so considerable that the thumps were hard to localize – they might even have come from the walls or ceiling. She had her eye well and truly on Brian during the noises. He was scared – quiet, but white and frightened. He would gladly have gone downstairs to join 'Grannie'. He was certainly not responsible for the noises. The sound from the hole in the wall lasted a few seconds, like an ordinary human roar of rage. It appeared to come from inside the wall. She stood back and said 'That wouldn't do for me. My God, I'd be out of this house – it's an evil place'.

We asked Mrs Clarke whether she was certain it was a wardrobe which was lying against the bed. She replied (unprompted) that at any rate it was a large piece of furniture – 'it might have been a big, old dressing-table'. We asked her how clear was her memory of the events concerned. She answered that it was very clear. 'You don't forget that sort of thing in a life-time. Not until you die.' Her memory of that evening undoubtedly corresponds with Mr Lamb's contemporary notes, and with what we know about the case in general, in a considerable number of respects. She impressed us as an excellent and absolutely honest witness. She is a lively and intelligent person of middle age. She and her husband were publicans for some fourteen years and her experience of human nature and its vagaries has been wide. We are inclined to accept her story as being substantially accurate.

There is thus some evidence that whether or not Brian had himself 'got up' the stories about the wardrobe and the dressing-table, pounding noises of no obvious origin still periodically resounded from his bedroom. And that there may have been some truth in his stories about the wardrobe and the dressing-table is suggested by the fact that the dressing-table – which was extremely heavy and required two adults to carry it – was thrown over in the back bedroom with a mighty crash on two occasions (16 July and 29 July) when Brian was in the upstairs *front* bedroom in bed or preparing for bed. On the first occasion Mrs Connolly and Mrs Revill were with him; on the second occasion Mrs Revill only. Both signed statements testifying that Brian was with them when the incident occurred. AG had left the house immediately before the former of these incidents; Mr Lamb arrived during or immediately after the latter, and was the first person to enter the back bedroom and see the damage.

On 21–23 July ADC brought Brian to Cambridge with him for the weekend. He was kept under unobtrusive observation, but there were no phenomena of any kind, either at Cambridge or in Carey Street.

Our conclusions with regard to this case up to that point may be summarized as follows:

1 Brian could not have executed all the reported phenomena himself.

2 No-one else in number 16 could have been responsible for all or anything like all of them.

3 There was no-one in the neighbourhood who seemed likely to have been Brian's confederate.

4 There was no plausible means by which the phenomena could have been perpetrated from either of the neighbouring houses.

5 No such ordinary causes as waterhammers, house subsidence or sounds reflected from elsewhere could have been responsible.

The Connollys left Carey Street at the beginning of August

1967. Between then and 13 March 1969, a number of the subsequent occupants of number 16 Carey Street reported unaccountable noises in the house. We were unable to determine with any confidence how much their imaginations had been influenced by local gossip, but felt that there was just sufficient of interest in their stories to warrant our taking the house ourselves. In collaboration with Mr Lamb we arranged a tenancy of four weeks, starting on 14 March 1969. Unfortunately our tenancy coincided with university vacation time, and it was not possible to provide observers on more than eleven of the twenty-two nights which remained after the house had been made habitable. The only event requiring note was a visit to the house on the evening of 9 April by a party of mediums from a Nottingham Spiritualist Church. AG, who arranged this visit at very short notice, had planned on only one medium. The others were a bonus, but made recording difficult, since the three mediums wandered round the house independently of each other. At 10.15 p.m. occurred one rather curious incident. All the party was downstairs. AG was in the kitchen with two other persons. All three heard a faint but distinct thump apparently from the bedroom overhead, which of course had formerly been Brian's. The thump was very similar in quality, though not in loudness, to the 'double' thumpings of June 1967. Immediate investigation revealed nothing to account for the noise.

While in the upstairs back bedroom one of the mediums, Mrs Ruth Johnson, now Mrs Lewis, 'saw' a small old man in the bed. She also 'saw' a younger man and woman in the room, and gave the names 'Ted Turner' and 'Annie'. She also said that the police had made enquiries at the time of the old man's death, probably on suspicion that he had been poisoned.

Subsequently we discovered from electoral registers and street directories in the local library that number 16 had been occupied from 1916 to 1931 by not an Edward but an Ernest Turner, and his wife Annie. This was certainly curious, for the party of mediums had had only a few hours' notice of their destination, and we ascertained from the librarian that in the preceding few months no-one had asked to examine the registers or the past street directories, all of which were kept in his office. The most extensive enquiries in the neighbourhood and from local Turners failed to uncover anyone who had heard of Ernest and Annie. Some years later AG met in Nottingham a person who had lived a few doors down from them and could just recall them; but he could remember nothing of relevance to the case.

Although we reached the conclusion that some at least of the phenomena were genuine, the case remains a disappointing one in some ways. There is a considerable need for physical experimentation on the nature of the forces operative in poltergeist phenomena. Unfortunately in the present case the phenomena showed marked signs of being inhibited by the presence of observers so that most of our time had to be devoted to trying to find out whether or not they were genuine. On the psychological side also, though for different reasons, we found out very little. At first sight the case might seem to provide strongish support for the school of thought which regards poltergeist phenomena centring on adolescent subjects as being akin to hysterical symptoms. At the time of the first phenomena Brian was a boy, verging on adolescence, who had long ago lost his father and until the preceding month had shared a room with his mother. The phenomena would begin only after Brian had got into bed. However, although all three of us, and especially ADC, got to know Brian fairly well, he did not strike us as being in any way psychologically abnormal, unless indeed the mere occurrence of poltergeist phenomena in his vicinity is to be reckoned a sign of abnormality. He was, perhaps, somewhat on the dreamy and lazy side, and may have been over-indulged in this respect by his exceptionally industrious mother. We found no evidence that his family life was not happy and he himself well-adjusted to it. We did not feel inclined to plant in his or his mother's mind the idea that he might not be quite normal by suddenly subjecting him to a battery of psychological tests (in the value of which we had in any case little faith).

None the less the case had some interesting features:

1 In this case the phenomena all occurred in one *place*, to wit Brian's bedroom, but they seemed to be triggered off only by the presence there or in the immediate vicinity of a particular *person*, viz. Brian himself.

2 Once the phenomena had been triggered off in that place by Brian's presence they might continue there even when Brian himself was under observation elsewhere.

3 A medium brought to the house succeeded in obtaining the (not especially common) surname, and one of the Christian names, of two persons who had lived there many years before. It

does not seem likely that she could have obtained the names by prior enquiries in the neighbourhood. That there was any connection between the persons whose names were given and the phenomena which occurred in the house remains of course unproved; but it must certainly be asked *why* the upstairs back room of number 16 Carey Street became a focus for the poltergeist effects which centred round Brian Connolly. Is the answer to be sought in some property of the room or aspect of its history, or in some feature of Brian's psychological make-up? These questions remain to puzzle us.

The second case which we shall describe in this chapter likewise centred around a young person; the phenomena were, however, very different. It took place in 1968 in a three-bedroomed, semi-detached house on the outskirts of a largish Lancashire town. The house was about twelve years old, and for much of its existence had been occupied by a youngish married couple whom we shall here refer to as Mr and Mrs S. They had two children, a daughter, Elizabeth, aged thirteen and a half, and a boy, John, aged ten. Elizabeth, we may say at the outset, was the undoubted focus of the phenomena. She was a bright and intelligent child, just reaching the age of puberty, who sometimes felt (as both she and her mother said) that her brother received a disproportionately large share of attention in the family. There was some suggestion that phenomena were particularly liable to occur when she was asked to do something she did not wish to do.

The phenomena in the case had principally, though not exclusively, to do with water. They began about the beginning of March 1968, when three rubber hot water bottles, two of them new, burst within the space of a few days. (Subsequent examination of one of the bottles by ADC revealed a small slit in it such as might have been made with the point of a pair of scissors.) A few days later, on 13 March, some rather odder happenings began. The brief account that follows is based on data collected by ADC, and a colleague, Dr C. J. Stephenson, during a visit that will be described shortly. On a very high proportion of evenings in the subsequent ten weeks, especially around the children's bed-time, considerable quantities of water started to appear in the house. At first the beds, carpets and soft furnishings were chiefly affected. The amounts of water which appeared were sometimes very large. The mattresses were so wet that, even after drying in front of the fire, a pool of water appeared when they were sat upon. And on one occasion the water that came down over the stairs was *swept* out of the door over the threshold. Sometimes water was flung against the walls. The ceilings, however, generally remained dry, as did the loft. Later on clothes were also saturated, including even ones in closed wardrobes. The children – especially John – were splashed with water whilst lying in bed, even after they had been reduced to sleeping on camp beds owing to the condition of their mattresses. On a few occasions spurts of water – about a cupful – were seen flying through the air. Later still the water supposedly started to cause damage in another way. It knocked several vases on the floor, breaking them, and caused a watch and a ring to be 'washed' from the mantelpiece into the fire below. Clocks and watches in the house lost and gained time substantially, and this was also attributed to the poltergeist. Once when the S.s were visiting another house in the vicinity, various garments there spontaneously caught fire. No periodicities could be detected in a chronological list of the occurrences compiled by ADC from conversations with Mrs S. and Elizabeth. A visit from a plumber had disclosed nothing to account for the inundations.

The case was brought to ADC's attention when a neighbour of the S.s telephoned and then wrote to the SPR in London. In consequence ADC and Dr Stephenson visited the S. family in their home on Friday 17 May and Saturday 18 May 1968, staying overnight. The data which they obtained (notes and tape recordings) are too bulky to be given here. The summary account above is based on them. ADC's unedited notes of the actual visit, written immediately on his return, are as follows:

After spending Thursday night at Cambridge to pick up test tubes, photographic film and recorder tape C.J.S. and myself arrived at —— about 8 o'clock in the evening. Only Mrs S. and her daughter Elizabeth aged 13½ were at home. Mr S. and the 10 year old son were away on a camping excursion in the Lake district, having left that afternoon. The house was in a considerable state of upheaval. All the mattresses and damp bed linen were stored in the garage at the side of the house. The downstairs hall, stairs, upstairs landing, back bedroom and small front bedroom were without carpet or linoleum. These had been removed to (a) facilitate drying out . . . and (b) to allow the plumber access to the central heating pipes in the back bedroom and the front bedroom. Mrs S. described the various incidents that had happened, showed us the collection of glass and porcelain vases that had been smashed in the front and back downstairs rooms and in the wood and glass porch built on to the back of the house.

I drew up a plan of the house, after which CJS and myself sat in the front downstairs room talking to Mrs S. about the various incidents while her daughter Elizabeth sat in the same room doing her Latin translation homework.

In the account Mrs S. gave of the various incidents that had happened since the 3rd of April [= March] 1968 . . . she appeared to be convinced that the appearance of the water was in some way connected with the plumbing. From her account of the incidents involved it was quite obvious that the central heating system could in no way be held responsible for the amount of water and its location. The fact that the whole plumbing system had been thoroughly inspected by local experts and pronounced in order tended to rule out anything but the slightest amount of the water involved being contributed to from this source.

From quite early in the account given by Mrs S it also became obvious that the daughter Elizabeth was always in near proximity to the area affected by water, whether it involved a small amount splashed on the ceiling, large quantities found on the mattress, poured on John the son's head while he was asleep or saturation of the carpets of the stair well immediately outside the upstairs bathroom.

Only on two occasions was water actually seen in flight through the air by the members of the family, once by Mrs S. whilst she was ironing in the back sitting room, and by both Mr and Mrs S from their position at the bottom of the stairs when it was splashing down the stairs off the wall with Elizabeth behind in the bathroom at the top of the stairs. At no time, according to Mrs S, did either she or her husband attempt to track down the source of the water immediately it was noticed. During the recording of all the events by Mrs S., and in response to my questions as to where different members of the family were at the time of the incidents Elizabeth frequently asserted that she had not been responsible for the incidents when her mother observed that Elizabeth was near the area affected or was not in sight at the time. While CJS was out purchasing sandwiches I jokingly charged Elizabeth with having thrown too much water about – which she denied and remonstrated with her mother when Mrs S. agreed that they (she and her husband) had noticed that Elizabeth was always near the area affected when water had been found.

Mrs S. recounted numerous incidents appearing only too pleased to tax someone else with the problem of the cause. In order to determine the existence of any periodicity of the events and get a clearer understanding of the various incidents and command an overview of the events in chronological order, aided by Elizabeth's memory of the events a schedule of the events of the last 11 weeks was slowly compiled but not finished by 1 o'clock due to constant diversions in the conversation of one sort and another. Elizabeth was by this time dressed in her pyjamas and resting in a sleeping bag by or on a camp bed. Some bits of the conversation were tape recorded.

CJS and myself retired to the back room bringing our own sleeping bags, while Mrs S. slept in the front room with Elizabeth. We arose at 10.30 next morning and while Elizabeth went out shopping with a friend the completion of the history of events in chronological order was commenced for another 1½ hours.

CJS and myself left at 1 o'clock to get some lunch in ——, spent the afternoon in the town, and came back at 7 o'clock in the evening. While CJS spoke to Mrs S. and Elizabeth in the front room I called next door and spoke to Mrs —— regarding what had been going on at No. –. She knew all the details but thought that Elizabeth was not intentionally producing the effects in spite of the fact that they always occurred when she was around. When asked if she could throw any light on the affair she said that she doubted if the central party could be held responsible, knew of no explanation for the watches varying in time and when asked about the general day to day life of the S.'s thought that the children were not very well disciplined. Mr S. believed in free expression by his children. Having obtained these views I returned to No. – and found that CJS was testing Elizabeth for telepathy and PK.

We omit ADC's remarks on the PK experiments, to which we shall return in a moment.

As was stated in ADC's notes, it quickly emerged that all the mysterious incidents had occurred when Elizabeth, who was at the age of puberty, was at home. She was a bright and intelligent child, who, as noted before, sometimes felt that her brother received an unfairly large share of attention. Both Mrs S. and Elizabeth were easy to talk to and communicate with. They both seemed quite eager to recount incidents and discuss the case.

They gave the impression of being completely honest. Elizabeth constantly said that she did not know anything about the causes of the phenomena. On several occasions ADC placed Elizabeth in a position where she might have been tempted to cheat if that way disposed. She did not cheat. She was also asked a number of questions designed to trick her into giving away her game. On no occasion did she admit anything suspicious, or even look uncomfortable about the questions.

Elizabeth also denied that she was always in a position to have caused the effects. This claim was not specifically supported by Mrs S. Dr Stephenson and ADC thought from the descriptions given that it would in all cases have been physically possible for Elizabeth to have produced the phenomena by normal means, though sometimes this would have involved creeping about the house with the risk of getting caught.

No phenomena occurred during the visit of ADC and Dr Stephenson; and none occurred thereafter. The visit itself seemed somehow to have suppressed them. We therefore simply cannot say whether the phenomena in this case were genuine or not. We can, however, add the following curious tail-piece. Late on the Saturday evening, Dr Stephenson tried both ESP tests and PK tests with Elizabeth. She had no success with the former, but her scores in the latter were quite striking. The procedure was as follows. Two dice were procured. Elizabeth was asked to throw for a high score. After a run of thirteen trials had been completed, she was asked to throw for a low score for a further run of thirteen. The whole procedure was then repeated. She threw the dice from her hand, at her own speed, but no sign was detected of her trying to influence the fall of the dice by the way she threw them. ADC then took over as experimenter and two more runs of seventeen throws were similarly recorded. When aiming high Elizabeth scored a total of 329 where chance would have been 301; and when aiming low she scored 279 where chance would have been 301. The total deviation was +50, yielding odds against chance of about 75 to 1. A number of poltergeist agents have undergone laboratory PK tests, but it is unusual for them to score significantly. These preliminary trials with Elizabeth were at least interesting; and it is a pity that distance and shortage of time prevented their being carried further.

15 Some cases of haunting

Cases of really pronounced haunting (we are here, of course, using the word in the restricted sense of chapter 10) – cases in which the phenomena were as sustained and as definite as in, say, the cases at Willington or at the Chateau de T —— – are fairly infrequent. We have not ourselves come across a case which we would place on a par with these. Yet in our experience of case investigation, the commonest of all kinds of case – far commoner, for instance, than clearly person-centred poltergeists of the rapping and stone-throwing sort, or than haunting apparitions – have been cases which are perhaps best described as 'minor hauntings'. In them are especially reported footsteps, voices and other imitative noises, together with occasional movements or displacements of small objects, the switching on and off of lights, and now and again some peculiar visual appearance such as a cloud or ball of mist. Such cases – at least these days – very rarely find their way into the leading parapsychological journals (an exception is perhaps the Maryland case of 1973-4). We suspect that this is not because our experience of their frequency is atypical, but because they are so very difficult to assess. How easy it is to postulate natural causes for the alleged phenomena, or to ascribe them to imagination and wishful thinking! We talked about such sources of error in chapter 13, and there is no doubt at all that they account for the reported phenomena in many cases. Yet when one is actually engaged in investigating a case, things do not always seem so straightforward. Sometimes cases which would appear quite convincing if one merely read about them will lose all credibility after one has talked to the witnesses for a few minutes; sometimes, however, reports which from one's armchair one would dismiss without a second thought, appear much more impressive when one hears them at the scene of the events concerned from the persons involved. We have, for example, talked to several persons who claim to have seen, in the context of a minor haunting, small objects rise a foot or two in the air and descend again, or jump for no apparent reason from a shelf or television top. These persons saw what they saw in good light, and were, on the face of it, neither unintelligent nor mentally disturbed. They told us of the happenings soon after they occurred. It is far from clear that such observations, made quite independently by apparently sincere witnesses, should be set aside without further consideration.

We have (with one debatable exception) never ourselves succeeded in witnessing any of the phenomena in a case of this kind, though AG, sometimes accompanied by ADC or other investigators, once spent the best part of three weeks waiting, with a tape recorder, near the foot of a staircase down which loud ghostly footsteps had been regularly heard to pass. All we have been able to do is collect and scrutinize the testimony of others, and examine the locations involved.

We shall give here the results of one such investigation. The case concerned is a particularly good example of what a moment age we called a 'minor haunting' – good because the principal witnesses gave careful and articulate accounts, and because one of them made some brief contemporary jottings about the phenomena in his diary.

The case took place during 1971 and 1972 in a fair-sized, detached, two-storey house (built in 1929) of which the only feature requiring mention is that its five bedrooms (assigned in the statement below numbers referring to a plan not here reproduced), together with bathroom and W.C., open from, and completely surround, the upstairs landing. The house is occupied by a Mr and Mrs J. and family. Both Mr and Mrs J. are lecturers at a local technical college. The account printed below was given to AG by Mr J. during two sessions on 15 May and 28 June 1973. It was taken down in semi-note form, expanded, and typed out. Mr J. then went through it and made some corrections. It was also read by Mrs J., who added some notes which are given in square brackets. Appended to the statement are two letters from other witnesses.

Mr J. struck AG as a meticulous person, careful to state neither more nor less than he could remember. Some extracts from his diary jottings concerning the phenomena have been inserted in square brackets into his statement.

The case has many of the classical features of the 'hauntings' discussed in chapter 10 above. Footsteps, voices, luminous phenomena, raps, small object-movements, above all imitative noises of various kinds, were all reported. It is unusual perhaps (if we set aside the 'column' of hot air mentioned at its beginning) only in that a rather unusually high percentage of the phenomena occurred during the day time. It is to be noted that the phenomena did not seem in any way related to the comings and goings of any particular member or members of the family.

The occupants of my house are, besides myself, my wife M., and my children Kathleen (b. Aug 1971), Jill (b. 1961), Robert (b. 1960) and Peter (b. 1952) [these are not the actual names].

We bought our present house about April 1971 and moved in in August 1971. The house was built in 1929 and was originally owned by a Mr and Mrs G. Mr G. died about 1946, Mrs G. on Xmas Eve 1970. I believe that between Mr G.'s death and the death of Mrs G., Mrs G.'s four sisters lived with her one by one, and that some of them died in the house. Our then next-door neighbour, Mrs F., had never seen Mr G., and neither had the lady from the paper-shop below, who used, when a girl, to deliver newspapers to the house. This was strange in view of the time he had lived there. Mr G. was an ex-colliery manager who set up a business in Nottingham . . . . He supplied equipment to the local collieries.

Some incidents happened while we were decorating the house prior to moving in. One evening I turned up at the house and felt there was something wrong with the house. I went home (i.e. without doing any decorating). The same thing happened again in the morning about fourteen days later. It was nothing one could put one's finger on. Something was not right. I felt as if a hostile presence was pervading the house.

Once when I was working in the pantry I heard a creaking noise like someone moving on the stairs. However I assumed at the time that the sound was due to the wood warping with changes in humidity and this in fact could have been the case.

The first inexplicable phenomenon took place when I was decorating upstairs. My father was with me on the landing. For no apparent reason I suddenly felt hot all over for a few seconds. I moved further along the landing in the course of my work and felt very hot again. Within a few seconds my temperature went back to normal. The process was repeated a third time. It seemed as though there were a moving column of hot air – 15° to 20° warmer than the surrounding air. It caught up with me as I was working and moved on past me. I caught up with it, it moved on again and I caught up with it again. I said to my father 'What do you make of this?' I think he felt with his hand and agreed that he could feel the temperature difference. I tracked the column for about five minutes and then returned to work. It was moving at a slow walking pace clockwise round the perimeter of the landing. My father tracked it also for part of the time. It has not been encountered since. I would have said it was about the thickness of a man's body. I did not check the height.

We moved in early in August 1971. On 25th August 1971 my daughter Kathleen was born in hospital. The children had been sent to stay with their grandparents for a week (except for Peter, who was out at work). I was about to visit my wife, and was in the kitchen washing up after a makeshift meal. There was no one else in the house. I heard a sharp metallic rap behind me and turned round. Then there came another rap on my left. I turned to face that, but could see nothing to account for it. A similar sound then came from behind me. The sounds had about the quality and intensity of a spoon being rapped sharply on the melamine worktop and seemed to come from that sort of level. I turned round to face the third noise and saw a teaspoon suspended in mid-air about a foot from the end of my nose. The cup part was uppermost and the handle hanging down. It is difficult to say how long the spoon remained poised there, but I would have said it was somewhere between half a second and a second. It then fell on the floor at my feet. It was one of our best teaspoons and had not been in use. It was early afternoon, between 1.15 and 1.30 p.m., and I was perfectly sober. I was not afraid at the time of this or the other things that happened. I did not tell my wife or family about the incident at the time. My wife and I were both experiencing things, but we did not mention them to each other as each thought it was our imagination playing tricks on us. It was only when we had a common experience [the sound of a trunk being dragged, mentioned below] that we told each other all we knew.

[An entry in Mr J.'s diary for 1971 seen by me reads as follows: '25th August: M. went into hospital 5.30 a.m. Kathleen born 1.30 p.m. Spoon materialized in kitchen (after bangings)'. AG.]

The next thing that happened (I only found this out afterwards) was two or three days later when my wife came back from hospital. She had a ring with a clasp from which the stone had become detached and which she had put in a jewel box for safety prior to having it re-set. On three consecutive mornings she found the loose jewel lying on the bed when she came to make it. The jewel box was not locked. The children were not in the house, as they were staying with relatives.

[Mr J. has shown me an entry from his diary in a space for

notes at the foot of the page for 26–28 August 1971. He says that this entry was filled in afterwards – about a month later. Mrs J. returned from hospital on 26 August, so the events concerned were probably on 27, 28 and 29 August 1971. The entry is as follows; 'About this time M. discovered the jewel from a ring (kept in a jewel box on the dressing table) in three different places on three separate occasions'. AG.]

It was after that I think that we heard a sound which we subsequently often heard, as of a trunk being dragged across the top landing. This sound was often followed by the sound of drawers, from a chest of drawers in bedroom 5, being opened. One lunch time, I remember, my wife and I were together. The children were out at school, the eldest boy at work. We were alone in the house. We both heard the trunk movement. It was sustained as though it had been dragged in one continuous movement. Then we heard several drawers of the chest of drawers opened – or the same drawer moving several times. It was a double movement, in and out, and was quite plain and unmistakable. We could even hear the distinctive sound of the ring-shaped metal drawer handles flapping against their metal base-plates as if they had been lifted and dropped again. We went straight upstairs to investigate, but nothing had been disturbed. The trunk was still in its place in bedroom 3.

We subsequently heard the same sounds on numerous occasions. On each occasion that I can recollect it happening, we investigated – except sometimes when we would hear them early in the morning, about 5.00 a.m., and would not bother to investigate. One or other or both of us heard them perhaps two dozen times. They would occur at any time of day. Sometimes we heard the sound of the trunk or the sound of the drawers on their own. The children also heard these noises but we told them that they were mistaken. When the trunk and drawers were both heard it was in that order.

The next thing was in September 1971. My wife's sister came down from Burnley with her five children. They asked if they could bring tents and sleep on the lawn. Jill, who was then nine, and one of our nieces, aged six, were in a tent just outside the French windows of the lounge. I came down about 7.00 a.m. to let them in. They said we had burglars in the night. They said they had seen a man standing by the mantelpiece in the lounge leaning his head on his elbow. [Note by Mrs J.: 'The man was leaning with his elbows on either side of the clock on the mantelpiece. Interesting because we had previously lowered the level of the mantelpiece about 1½'. Also the clock on the mantelpiece was permanently stopped at 3.15'. See also the letters printed at the end of this statement.] Later in the day we questioned each of them separately and their stories tallied. Jill said that when they saw the man she looked at her watch and saw that it was half past five. They watched the figure for a few minutes. I don't know how it disappeared. The figure was dressed in a suit. They slept out one more night but didn't see the 'man' again.

[An entry in Mr J.'s diary dated 17 September 1971 seen by me runs: 'Jill saw figure of man in lounge approx 5.00 a.m. from tent on lawn'. AG.]

I am a little vague as to the precise order of events after this. One thing that happened soon afterwards was that a book borrowed by my wife out of the College Library disappeared for a week or so and reappeared on a cushion on one of the chairs of a three-piece suite in the lounge. The book was an essential textbook and we had carefully searched the house for it. We had looked on the lounge chairs and sofa. A number of things disappeared and suddenly reappeared in our house. A tea strainer disappeared from the kitchen and reappeared there some days later.

On a number of occasions in the lounge (four or at most five times) I have heard the sound of slow and rhythmic heavy breathing. So far as I know no one else in the family has experienced it. On each occasion I was sitting reading either in an armchair or on the settee. When I was in an armchair the sound seemed to come from the direction of the settee. When I was on the settee it appeared to come from an armchair. On each occasion it sounded about six feet away from me. When I heard it I got up to switch the TV on after two or three minutes to drown it. It was a pronounced and definite sound, and I made no attempt to investigate it further. I got up only to switch on the TV.

Another odd thing happened on two consecutive nights at Xmas 1971. I switched off the television in the lounge at about half-past midnight. Immediately we (myself, my wife, my father and perhaps Peter) heard the sound of singing. The children were in bed. The singing appeared to come out of the television set. It sounded in the room. It was like three children carol singing. What was sung was the first line of *While Shepherds Watched*. The sound stopped after the first line. I dashed outside to make sure that there were no carol singers there. This happened on two consecutive nights, Xmas night and Boxing Day night. The same song was heard on both nights. It was as

SOME CASES OF HAUNTING

loud as you would have expected from three people just outside the door. However the TV set is opposite the door. The singing began instantly when I switched off the television.

Several dozen times between August 1971 and August 1972 we heard the sound of the front door chimes. This occurred usually about 5.00–5.30 a.m. when we were in bed, though often awake listening to the odd sounds. We did not go to the door. Once, at the same sort of time, we heard a sound as of saucepan lids being clashed very loudly like cymbals outside our door. The children did not say whether they heard any of these sounds.

On a number of occasions during the daytime we heard the sound of the telephone from the breakfast room. When we picked up the phone we would get the dialling tone, but the whistling sound of the Trimphone would continue. The imitation was perfect. It would continue only for a few seconds after the phone had been picked up. This happened at least ten times. Sometimes I was in the house on my own, sometimes we were both in the house and one or other of us would come down to answer the phone. It happened more during the daytime than at night. So far as I know the children have never heard this. The sound was quite characteristic, and not at all like, e.g., a whistle from the gas-fire.

[Note by AG: Mrs J. told me that on one occasion when her husband was at the College, she heard him come in through the front door, and then in through the next (i.e. inner) door. Then he whistled in his characteristic way. He did not in fact come in until half an hour later.

Entries from Mr J.'s diary seen by me:

26 September 1971 'I heard sound of footsteps on landing and door opening and closing in early hours. During afternoon 3 p.m. we both heard footsteps above breakfast room. On investigation M. heard a door closing.' (They were in the breakfast room and the sounds came from the landing. Mrs J. was on the stairs when the drawer closed in bedroom No. 5 where the chest of drawers with the ring handles was.)

27 September 1971 'We both heard footsteps again and door opening and closing around early breakfast time.' (Mr and Mrs J. were in bedroom No. 2. The footsteps were on the landing. Mr J. would not like to say which door it was that opened and closed.)

26 October 1971 'Robert (11) heard voice with Scottish accent on upstairs landing.' (Robert was in bedroom No. 3. He was not in bed but was doing his homework. It was roughly seven o'clock in the evening. Robert was too terrified to know what

the voice said. Everyone was in, downstairs. Mr J. thinks he was in the breakfast room and the others in the lounge. Robert rushed downstairs. He'd heard about a couple of sentences before he came downstairs. At this time the children did not know there was anything amiss. Mr and Mrs J. pooh-poohed anything that happened. A few days later, after he was in bed one night, Robert shouted out in terror at about 11.00 p.m. Mr and Mrs J. went up and he said that his bedcover was rippling like the waves of an ocean. They told him he must be having a nightmare. Mr J. thinks that it could have been a nightmare. Robert said that at the same time he had heard footsteps in the bedroom. These things stopped as soon as his parents came upstairs to him.)

26 October 1971 'M. saw figure standing over bed during night.' (Mrs J. woke up out of a dream, and would not like to be definite whether it was indeed an actual figure or the finale of the dream. It was dark.) AG.]

Events built up to a crescendo in July and August 1972. I went away in mid July 1972. One evening whilst I was away my wife was putting the children to bed about 9.00 p.m. when they heard the front door open and footsteps in the hall. My wife thought it was Peter, called out and didn't get a reply. She called again, and there was still no reply. She looked out of the window to see if Peter's car was in the drive. It wasn't. She became afraid and came downstairs accompanied by two of the children (Robert and Jill) and they all three heard footsteps in the breakfast room. The breakfast room has a tiled floor. The footsteps were going from the breakfast room into the kitchen and back again. The sounds were as of footsteps on tiles. One of the tiles in the breakfast room clicked, which it normally does when trodden on. My wife and the children were in the doorway of the breakfast room. When they heard the footsteps coming back again my wife retreated upstairs, put the children to bed, and phoned her parents. The children were uneasy rather than frightened. My wife was terribly frightened but didn't let it show more than she could. Her father came over and stayed until Peter came home about half-past eleven. [Note by Mrs J.: 'Not only were there footsteps but muted men's voices heard by children and myself. We armed ourselves with heavy toys to hit the intruders (Robert's suggestion). No-one there. We were very frightened.']

After I returned (middle to end of July) there was a lot of activity in Jill's bedroom. One night when Jill was in bed (bedroom No. 4) after 9.00 p.m. she heard what she thought were footsteps walking round the bedroom. She buried herself under the bedclothes and tried to ignore them. She eventually fell asleep. The next morning we discovered that a picture had been moved from her wall. The picture had been hanging on the wall . . . and was found lying on its face in the doorway (undamaged). She told us the next morning. The following night she heard similar footsteps. Again in the morning we discovered that her radio which had been standing on the floor was lying on its face. It was a large old-fashioned radio with a broad base and could not have fallen over by its own accord. The following night (not at her request) we moved her into bedroom 5 where Kathleen sleeps. During that night my wife and I in bedroom No. 2 could hear noises from the direction of bedroom No. 4 (we could not swear that it was actually from that room). The noises were like someone moving around the room – a combination of footsteps and bumpings and bangings as though someone was moving round the room displacing things. The following morning we discovered that her reading lamp, which had been standing on the floor, had been knocked over. It has a wide base, and it would not ordinarily fall over. We had had a look round bedroom No. 4 before we went to bed to see if everything was all right.

On one occasion, in the spring of 1972, one Friday night at 6.00 p.m. Robert was preparing to go to scouts. My wife and I were in the breakfast room and he came in to say goodbye. He said 'There's someone in our orchard' (at the end of the garden). He had looked through the breakfast room window. We looked and couldn't see anything, and he said 'It's gone now'. We said 'What was it?' and he said 'A figure in red'. He wasn't clear whether it was a man or a woman. It would have been between 50 and 75 yards away. We dismissed it as his imagination, which it may well have been.

On another occasion (I can't date this one) my wife was in bed. As I came upstairs the door of bedroom No. 5 was open and so was that of our bedroom, No. 2. Kathleen was in No. 5. I went into our bedroom to ask my wife if they were open for any particular purpose. She said she'd closed the door of bedroom No. 5 as she came out (which is what she normally did) and our bedroom door after she'd gone in. It had opened and she had assumed that it was I who had opened it meaning to come into the room. She thought I must have changed my mind at the last minute. So I closed the bedroom door and then went into the bathroom and bolted the door. I started to wash and approximately two minutes later the bathroom door sprang open. I can be quite categoric about that – I had consciously and carefully bolted the door because of the earlier incidents. I would not normally have bolted it.

When events built up to their crescendo in July and August, my wife in particular was very nervous and said we couldn't go on living there. [Note by Mrs J.: 'My sister and I were sitting in the living room eating a Chinese meal. (My husband) was away. We both heard a number of very sharp raps. The noise was very near us and yet we could not place it. We dashed to the front door and then into every room. Raps still occurred near us at intervals. We slept in the same bed that night.' Mrs J.'s sister's account is given at the end.] We had still kept it from the children. I can't remember whether we had told Peter. My wife had been to the doctor for tranquillizers. [He] recommended contacting the vicar of ———. He came round to the house early in August 1972. He suggested an exorcism might be a possible solution. This was carried out at 4.00 p.m. on Saturday 19th August 1972 [date on duplicated form of service seen by me. AG.] He was assisted by [various persons].

We went away for a holiday the following day. We came back, went to Burnley on 8th September, returned on 10th September.

[Entries from Mr J.'s diary seen by me:

10 September 1972 'Whilst in bathroom at 19.30 M. heard rustling noises in bedroom 5.'

12 September 1972 'M. heard rumbling noises upstairs during morning.'

13 September 1972 'When in bathroom at 10.00 M. heard three loud raps which caused glass in shaving cabinet to vibrate.' (These raps formed a sequence.)

14 September 1972 'M. got up at 0530 to see Kath who was crying. (It was most unusual for Kath to cry.) On entering bedroom there was an intense flash of bluish light lasting about ½ second.' AG.]

These flashes were in fact seen again on entering the bedroom last thing at night on at least two subsequent nights. My wife saw them once or twice and I certainly saw them once. They appeared to be in the bedroom itself. On the one occasion on which I saw the light it just filled the bedroom with blue light. I could not pinpoint its source. There were three very quick flashes – less than half a second would have covered all three. The curtains were drawn. Next door's bathroom window, with frosted glass, faces the west window of this bedroom. The light was of uniform intensity throughout the room – about the same intensity as the diffused light from a torch. My wife saw several flashes on two subsequent occasions.

[Note by Mrs J.: 'Sept '72 I sat on the stairs listening to the noise of papers rustling in bedroom 5, I then crept upstairs to pounce on whatever was there but sounds ceased. re. blue flashes. I phoned Watnall Meteorological Centre in order to find out if the Aurora Borealis had occurred during the night.]

The final occurrence happened about November 1972. [A lady who knew about the haunting came to the house when Mrs J. was alone in it, and carried out 'some sort of service' of her own, rather to Mrs J.'s distress.] Afterwards Mrs X. left and my wife went out shopping for no more than ten minutes [leaving the house empty]. When she returned she found a small pane of glass in the staircase semi-landing window broken. It had cracks radiating out from a small central cupped indentation. When I came in at lunch time I found a round lead weight, of the type which Robert uses for his fishing line, on the carpet underneath the window. It is slightly larger than an airgun pellet. It fitted the cupped indentation on the glass. It must have been projected with some force. The house was empty during my wife's absence. She had taken Kathleen with her. When Mrs X. had been in the house my wife had been with her all the time.

[A note by Mrs J. refers to an episode that took place after this, though still in November 1972: Final episode when (my husband's) father had been with us a few days (Nov). Peg bag hanging behind kitchen door, swinging quite vigorously to and fro, both (my husband) and I noticed it. I jokingly told it to keep still and put up my hand to steady it, but it jerked out of my hand and re-commenced vigorous movement.' This was about 11.00 p.m.]

This is the text of a letter from Mr J. to AG, dated 23 October, 1973. The enclosures to which the letter refers follow.

I now enclose the statements which you requested:
(A) from my wife's sister, Mrs M.S.
and (B) from my daughter Jill

This latter statement contains discrepancies from her original account. This is hardly surprising since she was only 9 at the time and over two years have elapsed. In particular, they had been provided with a watch so that they would know the time and would have had no need to look at a clock; the breakfast room clock could not have been seen from the outside; there would have been no point in looking at the lounge clock as it was permanently stopped and Jill knew this; in the original account, the man disappeared without turning and the girls observed the figure without leaving the tent.

Despite this, I hope the statements may be of some use to you.

(A) In July of last year, when visiting my sister at [address given] I had an interesting experience.

One evening we were sitting, enjoying a Chinese meal, in a very relaxed frame of mind when we heard a sharp knocking. We immediately went to the front door but nobody was there. It was impossible for anyone to have run off without being heard as the path was gravel and therefore noisy. We then rushed to the back door – again no sign of anyone. We searched the house but it was impossible to trace the knocks which continued the entire time so we were left with no satisfactory explanation. V.M.S.

(B) I was camping in my back garden on the lawn. I was with my brother and cousins, one of my cousins were sleeping with me.

It was the morning and only my cousin and I were awake.

We decided to look at the clock in the dining room (actually breakfast room) to see what the time was. My cousin followed me up to the breakfast room window, I looked through a gap where the curtain had not quite being closed, I could see the table but not the clock so I went to the lounge to look at the clock. Luckily there was a larger gap so I could see the clock. I looked towards the mantle piece where the clock was, then I saw the shape of a man by the Mantle piece (standing) he was holding the clock. My cousin saw it as well. Then the shape turned and disappeared towards the book-case.

Concerning this case we can say no more than we said about 'minor hauntings' in general. When one investigates such cases on the spot, and meets the people concerned, the evidence even in the most superficially impressive examples tends to crumble before one's eyes; but sometimes the witnesses on better acquaintance seem so careful and so conscientious that one can neither dismiss nor yet completely explain away their stories. This was a case of the latter sort.

16 Some unusual cases

In this chapter we shall describe four relatively unusual cases. Generally speaking they cannot simply be compared with the cases set forth under the chapter headings of Part I, though the heading of chapter 11, 'Some Intermediate Cases', might perhaps be stretched to accommodate them. Some people would certainly want to classify the last two as instances of intervention by deceased persons; but neither case fulfils the criteria for tentative inclusion under that heading which were laid down in chapter 8.

The first case took place in Norfolk in a bungalow (one of two converted prefabs) occupied by a young married couple, Mr and Mrs M., with two little boys aged (in November 1967) four and three. Mr M. was employed in a responsible capacity by a local farmer. The first unexplained occurrences happened about November 1965. In November 1967 the local vicar contacted the SPR. He was referred to ADC, who paid three visits to the M.s the first on 15 November 1967, the second on 10 March 1968, and the third on 21 April 1968. He was also frequently in touch with the M.s by telephone.

The following account of the case consists essentially of an expansion of notes made by ADC on these three visits.

On his first visit, 15 November 1967, ADC received these details of the alleged phenomena down to that date. What may be called the first period of the phenomena lasted from roughly November 1965 to November 1966. In no instance during this period were things seen or heard to happen; they were found to have happened. Electric lights were turned on during the night. Objects – a wallet, beads, a watch, a corduroy cap, car keys – disappeared from various places and were never found again. A clock on the lounge mantelpiece was repeatedly turned the wrong way round. It was found like this both during the day and at night, under circumstances when it could not have been due to the children. The door of an airing cupboard was repeatedly found open both in the daytime and at night. Its bolt was six feet from the floor – too high for the children to reach. Metal coat hangers, left in drawers, were found badly bent.

The most striking event of this period took place on a summer evening when Mr and Mrs M. had gone with the children to a local shop. The windows were shut and the bungalow locked. When they returned they found all the cushions from the settee in the lounge piled up in the middle of the lounge floor. The children's toys, which had been lying in the lounge, were not touched. The cable of the vacuum clearner was found to have been tied up in knots.

As a result of these happenings Mr and Mrs M. approached the local vicar, who, according to a letter of his to ADC, 'after some enquiries, decided to exorcize the house'. The exorcism was carried out in November 1966, and was apparently successful. There were no further phenomena until the following September.

One day that September (1968), Mr M. came home about 1.00 p.m. to find the curtains in the front lounge all tied up in knots. Mrs M., who had been in the kitchen since mid-day, knew nothing about it. They both then went into the child's bedroom (the elder boy was at this period absent from the house for medical reasons), and found that a patch of wallpaper had been stripped from the wall, near to the child's bed, but too high up for the child to have reached.

On a Friday, also in September, Mr M. arrived home about 6.30 p.m. He discovered his wife standing in the middle of the lounge in a state of terror, with their younger boy. She said that she had found all the sheets and blankets pulled off the child's bed. One blanket was missing. After a search this blanket was found stuffed down between the dressing table and the wall.

Mr M. called in a friend to show him what had happened. Whilst all were in the lounge, they heard a rumbling sound, which, they discovered, had been caused by all the linen falling out of the linen cupboard. A little later, all the lights went dim for no ascertainable reason. The M.'s were so frightened that they left the bungalow and stayed away until the following Sunday.

On Thursday 26 October, Mrs M., alone in one of the bedrooms, became very nervous, feeling that there was someone behind her. The next day, Friday 27 October, Mr M. drove a friend to London, having arranged for the vicar to call on his wife. When he arrived back in the early evening, he found that the vicar had been and left, but had carried out no 'exorcism'. Mrs M. still remained very nervous about the atmosphere in the bungalow. She sat in the car outside the house with Mr M. and the little boy. At about 7.15 p.m. Mr and Mrs M. both saw the front door handle moving up and down. They drove off to the vicarage, but found the vicar out. They left a message, and returned to the bungalow. The lights in the house, which had been switched off prior to their departure, were now all on. The vicar shortly came round, and they went into the bungalow. Nothing had been disturbed. The dog had been in the kitchen all the time, but did not appear to have been upset.

The next day all was quiet, but in the evening, half an hour after the boy had been put to bed, Mr and Mrs M., who were both in the lounge, heard the front door violently thrown open. There was no wind, and no sign of anyone who could have been responsible. Mr M. closed the door, whilst his wife went in terror into the kitchen. They decided to go to Mrs M.'s mother's house some distance away.

On 31 October the vicar again exorcized the house, and the M.s resumed occupancy. But the old happenings began again the very next day. About 11.00 a.m. Mrs M. was washing up in the kitchen. She saw something fly past her to her left. She turned and saw a saucepan on the floor, still rolling. She had just placed it on the draining board. She grabbed the saucepan, and ran into the lounge where her husband was sitting. The child was not in the house. The M.'s decided to leave the house again, and stayed away until 10 November.

During their absence, the vicar wrote to ADC, with the result that on 15 November ADC visited the M.s, accompanied by Mr J. K. Farrell, then secretary of the Cambridge University SPR. The M.s appeared very upset, and wanted the matter cleared up. Mrs M., in fact, was so nervous that ADC felt it incumbent upon him to attempt to dispel the phenomena. He explained that no-one has ever been seriously hurt by a poltergeist, and that often the people involved are themselves in some unknown way responsible for the happenings. He then promised to get rid of the poltergeist. He collected some mysterious-looking odds and ends from his car, and went into one of the bedrooms, saying 'Whatever happens while I am in there, no matter what you hear, you must not come in'. It was the bedroom in which the wallpaper incident had taken place. Neither Mr nor Mrs M. would go into it. ADC sat inside smoking a cigarette. After fifteen minutes he emerged, with his jacket off and his tie pulled down, and dramatically stated that it would not come back. All were impressed. Mrs M. went into the bedroom – for the first time in weeks – with ADC, and said that it felt quite different. A few days later the vicar wrote confirming that there had been no further trouble.

All remained quiet thereafter for about three months. But on 2 March 1968 Mr M. rang ADC, who was away for a few days, to say that 'it' had started up again. On 6 March he rang again, and contacted ADC, who arranged to pay another visit on 10 March. The day before the visit ADC received yet another phone call from Mr M., who said that they were going to leave the bungalow. 'You (ADC) said when you were here that you would take it away with you. You did not do so. Please come and take it away with you. Do not say it will not come back. Take it away with you.'

When ADC arrived, he found both the M.s very disturbed. He received an account of the following incidents.

Saturday 28 January. Whilst the family was sitting in the lounge watching television, a three-shelf wood and metal decorative shelf-set fell off the wall.

Wednesday 7 February. When Mr M. had put his car away at 3.00 a.m., potatoes were thrown across the garage.

Tuesday 13 February. Coming into the house at 9.30 p.m., Mr M. found the curtains in one of the bedrooms all tied in knots. In the main bedroom he found the doors of the airing cupboard ajar with a clock balanced across them. He also found a packet of razor blades in the lounge fire. The house was empty at the time, Mrs M. and the child being with neighbours.

Friday 16 February. In the evening Mr M. went out to a shop. When he came back he saw smoke billowing out of the garage and discovered his wallet burning on top of a sack of wheat.

Saturday 2 March. Mrs M. lost a pound note out of her purse, and Mr M. lost a pound out of a pair of trousers which he had left over the settee.

Sunday 3 March. In the morning, electric light bulbs in the bathroom, all the bedrooms, the hall and the garage, were found to have burst. Mr M. procured some replacements.

Tuesday 5 March. Bulbs in the hall and one bedroom were

again found to have burst in the night, and a glass light shade in the bathroom was found shattered. During the day the teapot was found first placed on a high shelf, and then in the oven.

Friday 8 March. During the night of 7–8 March, the M.s were disturbed by thumps and bangs for which they could find no cause. In the morning, a 12-bore shotgun in the lounge was found to have been dismembered lock, stock and barrel. During the day a milk bottle, which a moment before had been clearly seen on the kitchen table, vanished and could not be found anywhere.

In the afternoon came perhaps the oddest incident of all. Mrs M. was working in the kitchen. The kitchen sponge, which had been on the draining board to Mrs. M.'s left rose in the air and began to travel slowly at shoulder height from the kitchen through the open door into the lounge. Mrs M. saw the sponge in flight, and ran after it, trying to grab it. It went past her husband, who was sitting in the lounge by the door to the kitchen, with shotgun across his knees, and fell down after travelling perhaps six or eight feet into the lounge. Mr M. too saw it in flight. The incident was too much for the M.s, and caused them to ring ADC yet again.

Sunday 10 March. In the morning, Mr M. found that the shotgun had again been dismantled into three parts. These were found in different places in the lounge and one of the bedrooms.

During the morning the clock which normally stood on the mantelpiece in the lounge was found on a window ledge in the same room. No-one moved it or saw it move.

Over the previous few days this clock had on a number of occasions been found in the lounge fire. Its wooden case had been slightly charred in consequence. The front door key had also been repeatedly found in the same fire.

ADC arrived at 4.50 p.m. on the Sunday to find Mr and Mrs M. extremely excited. They reproached him for having said in November that it would not come back. He must now take it away as promised. The bungalow was becoming impossible to live in, and it was 'not good for' the younger child (the elder one was still away).

ADC took a slightly tougher line during this visit, saying that he would not 'exorcize' the spook again, but would talk through the matter with Mr and Mrs M. to see if they were causing it unconsciously. He explained that some people try to relate the occurrence of poltergeist phenomena to the emotional state of some person or persons present at the scene of the happenings. He then discussed at length the possible emotional causes of the poltergeist activities that they, the M.s, were experiencing. Did they have serious rows? At first they both denied it. But eventually it came out that they did have rows, especially over Mrs M.s suspicions that Mr. M. might be seeing other women. Furthermore about seventy-five per cent of the poltergeist phenomena occurred during the period of silent hostility that such rows produced.

Before this admission was made, there was one interesting incident. Mr M. appeared particularly anxious that ADC should witness something to substantiate their experiences. Mr M. said that the most common recent phenomenon had been the disappearance of the front door key, and its frequent discovery in the fire grate. Perhaps it might happen now. A close watch was kept on the key, which, from the lounge, could be seen in the front door through the door between the lounge and the hall.

Meanwhile Mrs M. made some tea in the kitchen, the door to which opened from the other side of the lounge to the hall door. She produced two ordinary-sized mugs and one very large one. ADC commented on the latter. Mrs M. said it was the one from which her husband always drank.

ADC and Mr M. remained in the lounge, talking to the child. The key continued visible. After about five minutes, ADC asked to be shown one of the bedrooms. Mr M. and the little boy walked with him into the passage at the far side of the lounge. After entering the passage, ADC held back for a moment in a position from which he could glance across the lounge and see into the hall. The front door key was missing. He said nothing. Mrs M. was still in the kitchen, and at no time had ADC seen her move across the lounge to the hall. All returned to the lounge, and Mr M. said excitedly that the key was gone. He started to rake out the fire and look in the ashes under the grate; but no key was found.

Tea was then served, and ADC was given the large mug. He said that he should not have it because it was the one Mr M. always used. However, it was pressed upon him, and lo and behold, when he drank out of it he discovered the front door key at the bottom!

Mr and Mrs M. both denied responsibility. If Mrs M. in fact

surreptitiously secured the key, she must have done so in the period of 15–20 seconds whilst ADC was walking the length of the lounge and through the corridor door. She would have had to have moved both fast and silently.

ADC left the bungalow about 10.30 p.m., saying that he would take 'the thing' away with him. It has never returned.

The scene of the next case was a semi-detached council house in a small village not far from Bath. The house, it may be worth mentioning in view of certain of the phenomena alleged to have taken place there, stood on stony ground on top of a hill; not a likely site for an underground stream (there was no stream nearby) or for the accumulation of underground water. The house was forty-two years old, and was in good repair. The occupants were Mr and Mrs W. and three of their four children (boys aged thirteen, nine and eight). The children, it should be noted, figure very little in the story. Most of the phenomena took place during the daytime, when they would have been at school. Mr W. was a lorry driver, and consequently away a good deal. The person principally involved was therefore Mrs W., who was aged 32.

The phenomena in this case lasted from about March 1963 to about November 1963. They received some notice in the local and national press, and ADC took an opportunity to visit Mrs W. on 13 September 1963. He arrived about 12.30 p.m. to find Mrs W. doing her ironing some four feet outside the front door. She explained that she did not like working inside the house because of the frequency there of sudden influxes of water and outbreaks of fire. It transpired, however, that the majority of these outbreaks had occurred when she was away from the house altogether.

Mr W. was absent, but in the course of a long interview with Mrs W., ADC learned of alleged happenings of the following kinds (we give them in approximate chronological order of first occurrence):

1 Leakage of water apparently from a water pipe running across the living room ceiling. The ceiling was damaged, and water dripped in considerable quantities onto the living room floor. This took place about March 1963.

2 The appearance of pools of water on the living room floor. Investigation by a builder disclosed no leaks in pipes or moisture in the concrete. On one occasion when Mrs W. returned

home to find the room flooded, the screw-in plug of the drainage cock in the hot-water system had been removed.

3 At intervals switches, especially to the cooker, would be found thrown when no-one had touched them. The lever tap on Mrs W.'s electric wash boiler would sometimes be found on. We subsequently learned that on the night of 19–20 September, six days after ADC's visit, Mr and Mrs W.'s bedroom light was repeatedly switched on and off after having been switched off. Mr W. was alone in the room at the time.

4 Over a period of several months from about March 1963, water repeatedly overflowed from the copper combination water tank which was situated in a cupboard over the hall, passing through into a bedroom over the living room. The bedroom and living room floors were repeatedly soaked and the plaster came off the hall ceiling. Prolonged investigations by plumbers and council officials failed to reveal any cause for the phenomena.

5 One afternoon in April 1963, Mrs W. returned to the empty house to find that the glass doors of the cupboard next to the kitchen fireplace had been smashed. It appeared that the glass had fallen outwards, as though the force breaking it had come from inside the cupboard.

6 Neighbours had on several occasions heard heavy thumps coming from the house when there was no-one in it. On two occasions, about June 1963, in the evening, Mr W. had heard these noises, but could find nothing which might have caused them.

7 From time to time various small objects – for instance a hairbrush, a paper weight, wooden book-ends – were found to have been displaced. Only once was an object seen to move. Mrs W., who was in the front bedroom, saw her hairbrush jump up from her dressing table (she was about six feet away) and then 'glide' perhaps six feet across towards a cupboard by which it landed.

8 In the later stages of the case – from at any rate September 1963 – incendiary effects of one kind and another became frequent. The first such effect – an armchair found on fire – seems in fact to have occurred about January 1963. But the principal concatenation of such happenings seems not to have come for another eight months or so. Mrs W. told ADC how she would find sheets or crumpled balls of newspaper smouldering in the corners of downstairs rooms – not in flames, but smouldering.

In the few weeks following ADC's visit there was an increase in frequency and a diversification of these incendiary phenomena. On 11 November Mrs W. came home at 2.30 p.m. to find a rug smouldering and a leg of the dining table badly scorched. The house was empty at the time. The following day Mrs W. came home similarly to find a tablecloth smouldering and the wallpaper scorched, and on 25 November to find the living room curtains burning.

Several unsuccessful attempts at exorcism were made during September and October; however, the phenomena seem eventually to have died away.

Mrs W., though distressed by the inexplicable outbreaks, seemed resigned to them, and struck ADC as quite a sensible person. She said that she always carefully locked the house before she went out, and latterly paid particular attention to seeing that the windows and doors were closed. She was not, however, an ideal witness, being rather vague as to dates and details; she retold the story of the hairbrush incident with some minor discrepancies.

This case is chiefly interesting for reasons other than the account given by Mrs W. to ADC. As mentioned above, about March 1963, when the inundations of water became troublesome, Mrs W. complained to the local council. The result was an investigation by experts in heating and plumbing, one of whom, Mr H. M. Popham, a representative of the company which had recently supplied a new hot water system for the house, became so intrigued by the odd happenings that he wrote an account of them, probably about the end of 1963. We give the opening sections of Mr Popham's hitherto unpublished narrative (names have been replaced by initials).

> Sometime during March 1963 Mr. K. asked me to have a look at the Hot Water System installed at [address given]. This had worked alright for 2–3 months, but he now complained that the water from the . . . recessed type direct copper rectangular Combination Tank had overflowed down through the hall ceiling into the hall.
>
> The Tank was situated in a cupboard over the hall and in a bedroom, which was over the living room. The backboiler, behind the living room fireplace, heated the water.
>
> The installation appeared to be correct and Mr K. assured me the layout was similar to those in the other houses completed

using, within a few inches, a similar amount of copper tube in the runs etc.

I asked him the normal questions and although quite happy with his replies, I was perplexed and suggested our Mr. D, a practical heating engineer, should have a look at it.

He tested the system and found everything in order and went away a puzzled man.

During the course of the next few weeks the overflowing persisted with and without a fire in the grate and always, apart from one occasion, when no-one was in the house.

Mr. K. and myself tried to think of a possible explanation, we asked other Heating and Plumbing men, but they all said it was impossible for it to happen; but it did.

We changed the Tank, the Backboiler, the Flow and Return Pipes were taken down and refitted and in the meantime we contacted Mr. G. V. of [address] who represented the R. Tank Co. He inspected the system but could find nothing wrong.

A similar Tank was put on test at the works, found to be in order and was sent down and installed as Tank No. 3. This overflowed at about 5.00 a.m. the next morning when Mr. and Mrs. W. were sleeping in the back bedroom.

The plaster now had come off the hall ceiling and Mrs W. had taken up the linoleum in the bedroom and in the living room and was using the front room.

Whilst annoyed with the whole affair, she showed much tolerance to Mr. K. and myself, although how much longer this would be the case, I did not know, but she realized we were doing our best to get to the bottom of the trouble.

I decided one day to try to find out for myself the cause of the trouble so I visited the house one Thursday about twelve noon and aiding Mr K., by a series of elimination tests cut out the various circulations etc. until we had virtually an open top cold water storage cistern, no water being allowed into the cistern or out, with the Flow and Return and hot water draw off pipes extended to run over into the small cold water feed tank, and the cold feed pipe to the hot water compartment stopped up at each end and the Ball Valve tied up and with no fire in the grate. We had found that the water surged over after being watched for approximately 1 hour 45 minutes and then being left and both Mr. K. and Mrs. W. thought the surging was becoming much stronger.

After watching the Tank for this period of time and nothing happening, I went to the local Café, for a snack and about ten minutes after I had left, with no one in the house, the water surged over.

SOME UNUSUAL CASES   305

When I returned from the Café, after an absence of approximately half an hour, Mr. K. dismantled the pipes and they were perfectly dry inside.

I then said to Mr. K. that this was like putting a Tank of water in the middle of the room, leaving it, and returning to find that the water had surged up of its own accord, and overflowed. It seemed fantastic and no-one would believe it, and I did not know whether there was a scientific explanation for this, such as an attraction of some sort or some 'pull'.

However, the fire was then lit, and I watched the tank for 3¾ hours, but apart from a few large bubbles and quite a number of small ones causing circulation, nothing happened so I left the house at 6.45 pm and the water surged over later in the evening.

A different type of Copper Combination Tank was supplied by the same manufacturers at their Representative's suggestion, the working principle was similar, as also was the size and shape, but the Hot Water compartment was a closed tank, with the open cold water compartment immediately above, with a slight gap in between, the whole giving an appearance of one unit, which in fact it was. This pattern was called a 'Cromwell' Tank. This was not a success, water surged out over the top. This was installed during the early half of June.

At this stage, Mr. C., the Housing Manager called in Messrs E. [a firm of heating engineers].

On their advice, the system was changed, the small copper cold water tank being removed from the unit, the copper hot water compartment being retained and used as a normal hot water tank, in conjunction with a galvanised open top cold water storage cistern fixed in the roof. This tank was a 40 gallon one, but was using only about 20 gallons.

Mr. K. finished the installation at approximately 8.00 pm one Saturday evening. The same evening the water came down through the bedroom ceiling. The following Saturday morning, 8th June, Mr E. phoned and told me they had put a Galvanised iron bucket of water on the slats in the airing cupboard, left it and waited outside the front door for a few minutes, returned and found water had surged over the top of the bucket, the rim of the bucket being about 1¾ inches above the water level. They marked the water line with a pencil, repeated their movements, until all the water had left the bucket, leaving four or five pencil marks, not quite evenly spaced apart on the inside of the bucket.

They had also tried a bucket of water in the opposite front bedroom, in the cupboard in the bedroom, the cupboard being on the opposite side of the wall dividing it from the airing cupboard and also on the stair landing. In the bedroom the water surged up and fell on the bedclothes, the water surged over in the cupboard but did not surge over on the landing.

This news really hit me below the belt, and we talked of 'grudges' and exorcism, but at this time I did not believe in 'grudges' and the word exorcism had only the vaguest meaning for me.

I was also told that a Water Diviner had been called in, but found no detectable springs underneath the house, i.e. the part occupied by Mrs W.

The Council then decided to take out the 2 tanks, and Mr. K. installed the original Pattern Tank in the bathroom downstairs on the ground floor. This happened during the latter part of June 1963.

The tank being put as near to the ceiling as practicable and for a while the system worked perfectly. At the same time Mrs W. could not leave water in a bucket upstairs and forget about it and leave the house, for when she returned she would find the water had come down through to her living room ceiling. Water left in the childrens' chamber suffered the same fate. In the first instance water in a plastic bucket was not so affected, but the second time it was tried, over came the water.

Mr. T., reporter for the 'Bath and Wilts Chronicle and Herald', suggested mixing up some white 'Walpamur' distemper in an empty 7lb. tin and putting it on the floor in the airing cupboard beside an electric kettle full of water.

This was done and he stepped outside the house, returned and found the 'Walpamur' wall paint had splashed up the wall approximately 9" from the floor and water had come out of the spout of the kettle on to the floor. This was reported in his paper.

Shortly after this episode, I visited Mr. K. one morning at [the house] to take an order for the goods required for the last house to be altered, which was No. – .

I found him at No. – talking to Mrs. W., who repeated to me that on her return from 'Bingo' the previous evening, she heard a noise whilst walking up the path to the back door, but as soon as she opened the door, the noise ceased.

She went upstairs to her bedroom, and found that short lengths of Copper Tube left in the small copper open top Tank in the airing cupboard had moved, and one piece had fallen out on the floor. Also she was certain that the hot water tank, which was part of the unit and measured approximately 20" long and 12" wide and 20" deep, had moved away from the right hand wall on the landing.

Mr. K. and myself then went upstairs, and re-arranged the

short lengths of copper tube in the tank, put one length size ¾" × 9" on the slats and pencilled around it, put some 2¾" lost head wire nails on a piece of newspaper inside a pencilled six inch circle and put these on the slats. We then put the large tank on the landing in the right hand corner against the wall, where it was originally and went in next door to No. – . We left Mrs W. talking to Mrs. W., her neighbour at the back door of the house. About 15 minutes later [the neighbour] told me she thought she heard something, so we went upstairs and found the tank had moved 9" to its left away from the wall. The nails had scattered, some outside the circle and some on the floor. The 9" × ¾" piece of tube was on the floor and the pieces in the tank were dis-arranged.

The tank was left where we found it, and a few days later it eventually edged itself around the landing, until a corner lodged in a doorway and finally crashed down the stairs, when no-one was in the house.

The small tank was also left on the bedroom floor and eventually this was found against the inside of the bedroom door, which barred its way to the landing and the stairs.

A corked lemonade bottle was left on this bedroom floor and was found broken in pieces. This happened when the house was empty.

We believe this to be the most expert account of a 'water poltergeist' yet published.

The curious little case which we shall describe next came to the notice of one of us (AG) in a somewhat unusual way. He received a phone call from Mrs Violet Edwards, who is a medium well-known in the Nottingham district (and also to AG). Mrs Edwards said that she herself had just had a telephone conversation with a lady from a town near Nottingham, whose house was the scene of poltergeist disturbances. This lady wanted Mrs Edwards to visit her, and Mrs Edwards wondered if AG would like to accompany her. He agreed, arranging first to visit the lady on his own, which he did on the evening of 20 April, 1977.

The house had been occupied since September 1976 by a young woman of 31, who will here be called Julie, and her children, a boy of 7 and a girl of 2. Julie was separated from her husband, but with her there was living a girl of 24, whom we will call Liz. Liz was a close friend who had been constantly in and out of the house, and had moved in temporarily when Julie became frightened by the odd happenings. Julie and Liz gave AG accounts of what they had witnessed, showed him the objects which had moved, etc., and it is upon the notes which he then took, confirmed and corrected in details during a subsequent visit and telephone calls, that the following is based.

Julie is a person who feels herself to have 'psychic' gifts – she narrated one or two quite striking examples of apparently clairvoyant experiences – and about February 1977 she and Liz began to experiment with an alphabet and upturned wine glass. They received coherent 'messages', and some regular 'communicators' began to manifest through successive sittings. One Saturday evening, however, – it was almost certainly Saturday 26 March 1977 – while they were sitting at the glass and alphabet, Julie had a curious sensation, which she described as being 'as if a vortex were coming up the glass'. She heard a ringing sound come from the glass, lasting several seconds, then as it were a voice coming up from it. The voice was very deep, and she could not tell what it said. Liz stated that she had heard the ringing sound, but not the voice.

They sat again on the evening of Monday 28 March. Nothing 'came through', but, said Julie, 'Something was there and that was when it began'. While they were still sitting at the table they heard a great outcry from the little dog, who was in the kitchen. They went to investigate. A child's clothes, which had been on the table, were now on the floor, and both clothes and dog were soaking wet with water. The dog is too small to be able to get on the table, and the amount of water involved was much greater than that in the dog's bowl. They took the dog back with them into the living room, where it calmed down. They resumed their sitting. On a small table in the living room was some crumpled newspaper, which had contained some fish and chips. On top of the paper was a table fork. The fork fell off the paper onto the table top. Then the crumpled up paper began to unscrew itself. They dismissed this as a natural phenomenon, but none the less packed up (about 11.30 p.m.) and went to bed.

From this time on Julie began to be troubled by the feeling of a 'presence', 'not a very nice person', about the house, and by a series of minor unexplained happenings of a poltergeist type. On Tuesday 29 March, in the afternoon, Julie, alone in the house but for her little girl, asleep in the kitchen, was vacuuming the living room. She was bending over the carpet, the vacuum cleaner going beside her, when she heard a loud noise from behind. Thinking that the little girl had come in to the room, she turned round. She discovered that the onyx top of a coffee table immediately behind her had been raised from its frame and twisted sideways, whilst a potted plant, which had been on the table, had fallen on the floor. The stone table top, which AG raised by way of experiment, is quite heavy, and would not have been jerked out of its frame by a casual kick or knock. At the time Julie thought the happening odd, but was not frightened. Another curious and unexplained occurrence on that day was that the brass knobs which were screwed into the ends of the living room curtain rail were found on the floor no less than three times.

That evening Julie's mother came, and the three of them had another sitting with the glass and alphabet. A good deal was written about a 'foe', together with instructions that they should 'stop calling'. Julie smashed the glass, and the sittings were terminated.

The next evening, Wednesday 30 March, Julie was sitting in the living room alone, at about 10.00 p.m. Suddenly she heard sounds 'as if the kitchen were full of people', followed by a sound as though an angry person were flapping newspapers there. There were some newspapers on the kitchen table (the kitchen is the other side of the hallway from the living room). The dog leapt up and barked. Julie ran into the hall, but was too frightened to go into the kitchen, and instead opened the front door. She stood on the doorstep dithering, the dog with her and trying to get out. She pulled the door to behind her, more or less holding it open with her bottom. After a few moments, the door was shoved firmly against her bottom, pushing her out onto the path. She rushed back through the door, calling 'it' all sorts of names, but despite this boldness continued to stand on the doorstep waiting for Liz, who arrived about 10.40 p.m. Liz went into the kitchen and found that nothing had been disturbed.

On Friday 1 April, both Julie and Liz were out, and a baby-sitter, a girl of nineteen, was left in charge. When Julie got home, she heard the following story from the babysitter. She had been sitting on the floor about 10.00 p.m. when the wine table, which was behind her and to her left, fell over, taking with it the plant in a basket which stood on it. The babysitter thought that she must have pushed back against an armchair which was between her and the wine table.

One day at about this time Julie was standing at the top of the stairs. She was doing her hair with curling tongs and comb, and dropped the comb on the top of the stairs. She thought 'I'll pick it up in a minute'. She continued work with the curling tongs, and suddenly the comb flew out and landed about half-way down the stairs. When she eventually went to get it she found that it was now right at the bottom of the stairs.

At about this period she on two occasions heard glasses chinking together in the pantry (the pantry door has been removed, so as to display the objects standing on its shelves). 'Nothing much,' said Julie, 'but off-putting.'

On Monday 4 April, in the afternoon, Julie was on the telephone in the hall, whilst Liz was in the kitchen, cleaning the floor. Liz had just gone to the sink to rinse out a cloth, when a stainless steel hot-water jug and sugar basin fell with a great clatter from a shelf in the pantry. The pantry was to Liz's left and six feet or so away from her. AG examined the jug and basin standing together in their accustomed places on the shelf. They would certainly not have fallen from this position in the ordinary run of events.

Liz claimed that when this phenomenon took place she heard a peculiar buzzing very close to her head – it was, indeed, a vibration rather than a sound. It made her run into the hall to Julie. Julie says that she too has suffered from a similar buzzing above her head when 'things' have happened.

One afternoon, soon after this, Julie, not thinking of the spook, was in the kitchen, wearing a plastic hair dryer, and making her face up in the kitchen mirror. She heard a rattling as if someone were trying the garden door, which was locked. She rushed to it, unlocked it, and went out and up the path. There was no one there. The dog barked and rushed out too.

About this time, while Julie was in the bathroom during the daytime, the heavy metal soap dish was knocked into the bath.

A few days before AG's visit Julie was in the kitchen. Just as she turned towards the sink she heard a clink from the window ledge behind it. She saw that a porcelain cockerel, one of a pair, each of which stands on a particular tile on the window ledge behind the sink, had been moved on to a neighbouring tile. AG was shown this cockerel. Its normal position is such that a shift of the kind in question would be instantly noticeable.

On Friday 22 April, AG took Mrs Edwards to visit Julie and

Liz. Mrs Edwards said that she could sense the presence of a man, now dead, whom Julie had once known. He had been attracted in the first instance by the sittings with the glass and alphabet. However, he meant no harm, only to amuse himself. He did not want to frighten the children (nothing had in fact ever happened when the children were present). Mrs Edwards gave a christian and surname which she said were those of the man in question. He was, she said, the eldest of three brothers, all of whom Julie had known. He had been a soldier and was killed in battle. Julie could in fact remember a family of that name in which there were three boys. She could not, however, remember the name of the eldest brother, and she is, for various reasons, unwilling to institute enquiries.

Both Julie and Liz struck AG as intelligent persons, and were able to give clear accounts of the phenomena which they had witnessed. AG is inclined to accept the accounts as substantially accurate, and though the phenomena were trivial, he is not able to produce any satisfactory explanation of them. Julie appears somewhat tense, partly no doubt because of her domestic situation. AG put it to her that a young woman living apart from her husband could very well begin to imagine a 'man about the house'. Julie reiterated that the phenomena were not her imagination, and that she could find no way of explaining them. Furthermore the 'person' whom she sensed around the house was not anyone she would desire to have there.

There are several other cases in the literature in which poltergeist phenomena have supervened on the sittings of a 'home circle', and some in which the 'communicators' in the sittings have explicitly claimed responsibility for the poltergeist phenomena which took place between the sittings. See, for example, the cases at Paris (1888) and New York (1907). In the former case an obliging communicator promised to shift, and ostensibly did shift, chairs in a room which had been specially sealed off by a committee of medical and professional men. By a curious chance another case of supervenient poltergeist phenomena lately came to AG's attention. In this case, ostensibly paranormal raps, which had become a feature of sittings in a certain 'home circle', were heard between sittings for several minutes in broad daylight by two members of the circle, both of whom have furnished AG with signed accounts. At the next sitting one of the regular 'communicators' claimed responsibility. There were also phenomena of other kinds between sittings. However, this case has a somewhat complex background, and we cannot discuss it adequately here.

The last case we shall deal with in this chapter is one which we looked into more than twenty years ago. It is both interesting and instructive; interesting because of the puzzling phenomena which took place, and instructive, we fear, partly at least because of certain errors and oversights on our part. We did not (which should be done as a matter of course) maintain a minute by minute log of events and of peoples' comings and goings; and above all we did not bring a tape recorder (our usual one being out of order), an omission which, as will be seen, was especially unfortunate.

The case in question took place at Hannath Hall, an attractive but dilapidated Tudor house in Tydd St Mary near Wisbech, Cambridgeshire. The tenants of the house at that time were the family of Mr Derek Page, now Lord Whaddon, then Labour candidate, later MP, for the constituency of Wisbech and the Isle of Ely. Mr Page's family consisted of himself and his wife; two children, aged at that time three and five; and Mrs Page's mother. They had moved into Hannath Hall in August 1957, and during the next few months were frequently disturbed by inexplicable happenings – mostly thumps on doors and raps, but occasionally footsteps and groans, and once a violent jolt imparted to a bed. A local journalist learned of these strange happenings, and contacted the SPR. In consequence of his action, ADC and AG visited Hannath Hall on the evening of 16 November 1957. We were accompanied by Mr D. J. Murray, secretary of the Cambridge University SPR, and Mr (now the Rev.) J. M. Brotherton, a member of the same society; and also by the journalist and two of his friends, who met us at Wisbech to guide us to the house.

We arrived about 10.30 p.m., and during the next hour and a quarter we interviewed the members of the family (apart of course from the children), and carefully examined both the outside and the inside of the house. Hannath Hall has only two floors, and all the rooms on the upper floor open from a single large gallery. The phenomena reported had all taken place on the upper floor, though they were not confined to any particular part of it. The bedroom at the northern end of the gallery had been christened 'the haunted room', but seemingly for no better reason than that a nineteenth-century owner of the house was reputed to have left the body of his deceased wife lying there for several weeks, and to have had meals sent up to her.

At about 11.45 p.m. ADC organized a ouija board (i.e. glass and alphabet) seance in the living room downstairs, chiefly to ensure that all the hands in the house were in plain view; whilst AG stationed himself in the gallery upstairs, which was somewhat dimly lit by a single bulb. At 12.08 a.m. he heard a sharp snap from the haunted room; he set this down to a drop in temperature, and did not investigate. At 12.10 he thought he heard quiet footsteps on the stairs. The steps ceased before they reached the gallery. AG went to the head of the staircase and found there was no-one on the stairs. He concluded he had probably misinterpreted some noises from below. At 12.32 he was driven downstairs by the cold; during his vigil the temperature in the gallery had dropped from 60 °F to 52 °F.

At 1.25 a.m., whilst the others continued the seance downstairs, ADC and AG went into the haunted room upstairs with a view to settling down there for the night. The room had no electricity, and we searched it again by the light of our torches. It was used as a storeroom for unwanted furniture and oddments. Across the floor lay two mattresses end to end, and on these we settled down feet to feet, with one blanket over our legs. The thermometer had by now sunk to 49 °F, at which it remained during the ensuing events. We extinguished our torches.

A few minutes later we heard gentle taps coming from the floor on AG's left and ADC's right at a point roughly equidistant from both of us and about three feet from the mattresses. Our torches showed nothing but bare boards in the region concerned. We found that we could get specific numbers of raps at request. The raps became louder and moved nearer to the wall of the room. This meant that they came from a position about three feet from ADC's right shoulder. We questioned them by means of a simple code, and found that they would answer leading questions readily, but could not spell out coherent messages. The rapper claimed to be a woman who had been murdered in the house in 1906 – a claim which we have not been able to substantiate. After a while we heard a series of six or seven knocks, growing in loudness, from the position in which the rappings had begun. The last one was of such intensity that AG flashed his torch in its direction. The raps ceased instantly, and there was nothing but bare floor in the place from which they had seemed to come.

Meanwhile the seance downstairs had broken up, and the reporter and his two friends had departed. Messrs Murray and Brotherton came up to the gallery, and heard the rappings. Mr Brotherton ran downstairs, leaving Mr Murray outside the door of the haunted room. He found the Page family sitting round the table in the living room, and then rejoined Mr Murray, who informed him that the raps had continued throughout his absence. Both then at once went downstairs and searched the room immediately below the haunted bedroom.

These activities caused a certain amount of noise, and we decided to leave the haunted room to ask the others to keep quieter. AG went to the door and ADC followed. As AG was passing through the doorway we heard a noise behind us, and found that a wooden dining-room chair, which had been stacked about five feet from the mattresses, was now lying on top of them. AG then left the room whilst ADC replaced the chair. He turned to follow AG and heard the chair drop behind him again. This time it had simply fallen down. He replaced it more firmly and left the room.

We returned to the haunted room about ten minutes later. Mr Murray went with Mrs Page into the room underneath it, and Mr Brotherton and Mr Page stood in the gallery. This left Mrs Page's mother on her own in the living room. We soon heard loud raps, but this time from a position on the other side of the mattresses and about three feet from them; that is, on AG's right and ADC's left, and again about equidistant from us. Mr Murray and Mrs Page in the room below could also hear the raps, and noted down some of the sequences. The raps confirmed, though still in reply to leading questions, some of the information previously given. We then asked the month of the supposed communicator's death, and heard eleven raps. We asked the day of the month. There commenced a series of raps which moved along the floor towards ADC's head. The sixteenth rap seemed to him to come from the air behind his head. He switched on his torch, and the raps ceased immediately. He put out his torch, and we asked the rapper to begin again after ten. The raps were much fainter, and continued up to eighteen. We then made some not very successful attempts to ascertain the rapper's age at death. The raps quite soon died away altogether, and after a few minutes we returned downstairs. It was then quarter to three.

Meanwhile, not long after we returned to the haunted room, the journalist and his two friends had come back to the house. They said that their car had broken down. Mr Page took them to Wisbech in his own car, and did not return until 2.50 a.m.

We returned to the haunted room at 3.34 a.m., this time with Mr Murray. AG walked into the room first, Mr Murray second and ADC last. ADC slammed the door, and we heard a sharp rattle. We turned, and saw by the light of our torches that a brass toasting fork with three prongs had been thrust behind the metal plate to which the door bolt was attached. One of its prongs was inserted through the staple into which the bolt normally ran, thus 'bolting' us into the room from the inside.

There were no subsequent phenomena of much interest. On our second visit (21–22 November 1957) we heard some further rappings, faint and distant-sounding, but under conditions of good 'control'. Altogether we paid between us some twenty visits to the house. On 25–26 April 1959 we brought a non-professional medium to the house, and held a seance in the haunted bedroom. A lady calling herself Eliza Cullen or Culler came through and said she had made the raps. She said she had buried her baby in the garden. But we could not trace any person of that name.

On 22 April 1959, and again in July 1959, Mrs Page, in the living room, twice thought she saw the figure of a small, fair-haired boy peering at her round the boxroom door when she was certain that there was no one there.

It is worth asking how an out-and-out sceptic might set about demolishing this case. He could hardly claim that the memories of the investigators present had retrospectively magnified the events of the evening, because all four of us wrote preliminary notes on the phenomena within a few minutes of their occurrence. These notes were shortly amplified into fuller statements (copies of all relevant documents have been deposited with the SPR). A sceptic could, however, point to various discrepancies between the statements of the different witnesses. In particular, the times of events, despite the fact that we synchronized our watches at the start of the investigation, are very imperfectly recorded, and different witnesses' guesses sometimes conflict with each other. This makes it, of course, very difficult to say with certainty whether the journalist and his friends were or were not under observation during any given set of phenomena, which is obviously an important flaw in the evidence.

Can these discrepancies be said to invalidate the case for the paranormality of the raps? We think not. It seems quite certain that the journalist and his friends left and also returned to the house while the rappings were still in progress, and so were actually observed at a critical period. In any case there are arguments against the possibility of fraud which do not depend upon showing that any given persons were under observation at a particular time.

Let us consider the hypothesis that there was a practical joker concealed somewhere in the house. Of course we measured the whole house inside and out and could detect no place where a trickster could have lurked; but even if there *had* been such a person, he would still have needed to instal rapping machinery under the floor of the haunted bedroom. Accordingly we removed all furniture from the room and examined every inch of the floorboards with a manifying glass. The boards were tongue-and-grooved together. We could detect no tool marks or splintering, and are convinced that no floorboards had ever been taken up. We removed a board that ran through the positions where we had first heard the rappings, but could see nothing suspicious under it or under the neighbouring boards. We then likewise examined the ceiling of the room below, which was also made of boards tongue-and-grooved together, and reached a similar conclusion. After examining the structure of the floor we were convinced that rapping machinery could have been installed under the floor only by removing boards from the floor of the haunted bedroom or from the ceiling of the room below; and that no boards had been removed from either of those places. It therefore does not seem that the case for the paranormality of the raps leans very heavily on proving that certain persons were under observation at given times.

Another possibility which a sceptic might explore would be that of illusions of the sense of hearing. He might suggest, for instance, that the rappings were really quite random, and produced by subsidence of the house. We were in a state of nervous expectancy due to being in a reputedly haunted house, and interpreted these random noises as intelligent responses to questions. Or else he might suppose that a practical joker was outside the house tapping on the window sills with a stick – and certainly in the still hours of the night noises in the haunted room could be clearly heard from outside the house, and of course the flashing of torches could be seen through the uncurtained windows. None the less we do not think there is much to be said in favour of either of these possibilities. All four investigators heard the raps; and all agreed they were answers to the questions. In general they did not occur whilst we were asking questions. They came in an even tempo, at a rate of one a second or somewhat faster. Immediately a question had been put, answering raps began. They were appropriate in number to the questions asked, for example one for 'Yes', eleven for 'November'; and once a question had received an appropriate answer there was nearly always silence until the next question had been posed. Nor does there seem the slightest reason for supposing that we mistook raps made by a mischief-maker on the walls, windows or window sills of the haunted room for raps made inside it. Auditory localization is an ordinary room (as distinct from localization out of doors or in an anechoic chamber) is more accurate than is commonly supposed; and we conducted extensive experiments in the haunted bedroom to ascertain whether or not we were liable to confuse rappings made from the outside of the house with rappings made inside the room itself. The answer was unequivocally that we were not.

The only remaining possibility for a sceptic to put forward is that of fraud by a member or members of the family or by the investigators themselves.

It is certainly possible that the toasting fork incident was fraudulently produced. We found that if we pushed the toasting fork behind the metal plate so that its prongs just shaved the staple when we closed the door, and then slammed the door, the fork would jump a little and 'bolt' us into the room. Almost anyone in the house could have placed the fork in position while we were absent from the room between 2.45 a.m. and 3.34 a.m. – although we should add that the journalist and his friends were definitely absent from the house during this period, and that the members of the family, apart from the children, all signed statements that they were in no way concerned in the production of the phenomena. Incidentally we are convinced that the two children were too young to have been responsible for any of the phenomena; and in any case while phenomena were actually in progress we several times checked up that they were safely asleep.

There is, we fear, no escaping the conclusion that the only persons who could have faked the remaining phenomena were ourselves. In our statements we each considered the possibility that the other had produced the phenomena fraudulently, and, while there is no doubt that ADC could have tipped over the chair without AG seeing him, we neither of us thought that the other could have faked the various series of rappings. When the rappings began we each suspected the other, and in consequence we watched each other like hawks. There were no curtains on the windows of the haunted room and so we were each able to keep a fair check on the other's position. We switched our torches on and off without warning, several times interrupting series of raps, and each of us is prepared to assert quite definitely that if the other had been making the noises with his hand or with a reaching rod he would have been detected. We are left only with the possibility that we conspired together to produce the phenomena fraudulently. To this we must confess that we cannot find a ready answer. No sceptic worth his salt would accept our avowals of honesty, even if supported by evidence as to our moral characters, as refuting the hypothesis of fraud, for he could always conceive of overriding motives which might have impelled us to throw our habitual scruples to the winds – the desire for publicity, for instance, or the sheer joy of deceiving other people. To such dedicated disbelief there is in the last resort no answer. We touched upon the issue in chapter 13.

17 The forces at work

In this chapter and the next, we shall discuss some of the main theories of the nature and causes of poltergeist phenomena. Many of the theories and relevant issues were touched on earlier, and have been left dangling. Not a few of these loose threads will, we fear, still remain untied at the end of the book.

The first problem which confronts the theorist is: to what cases should he address himself? There has been a tendency amongst theorists – quite understandable in view of the complexities and obscurities of the field – to confine their endeavours to one or a few relatively common and straightforward kinds of phenomena. But this is a short-sighted policy, against which Professor Bender, whose investigation of the Rosenheim (1967–8) case was described in chapter 5, has recently protested. It is true that such phenomena as raps and simple object-movements appear at first sight much less incredible than some of the more complicated, grotesque, and physically anomalous happenings of which ostensible examples will be found in chapters 1–3 and 6–11. But, as was pointed out with supporting statistics in chapter 12, there is little reason for regarding the occurrence of the more 'plausible' poltergeist phenomena as *much* better authenticated than the occurrence of the 'implausible' ones. Furthermore it is clear from the results of the cluster analysis presented in that chapter that different kinds of poltergeist phenomena, plausible and implausible alike, occur together and are not uncommonly associated with each other. To throw some light on the *modus operandi* of even one, relatively simple, sort of poltergeist phenomenon, would of course be an achievement; but one must ask oneself whether one is likely to progress very far in one's endeavours to throw light on it if one considers that sort of phenomenon in isolation from the other sorts with which it is so obviously associated.

The immediate answer, then, is that the theorist would do well to address himself to all the major sorts of phenomena that have been reported, and to all the major kinds of case. Does this involve his looking at hauntings as well as poltergeists? We think on the whole that it does. It is clear that by and large, the ranges of phenomena which one finds in hauntings and in poltergeists are largely coincident; the difference is that in hauntings one subgroup of these phenomena is markedly more prominent, and in poltergeists another.

Theoretical discussions of poltergeist phenomena have concerned themselves with two main issues. The first is that of the physical forces involved in the production of poltergeist phenomena. Speculations about these forces will be treated in this chapter. The second issue is that of the origin of the 'intelligence' so often manifested by the phenomena. It will be treated in the next chapter.

Theories as to the nature of the physical forces operative in producing poltergeist phenomena can be divided into two groups, according to whether the postulated forces are held to centre around the organism of a human being or not. Theories of the former sort are much the more numerous – so numerous, in fact, that we shall mention only a few leading contenders – and we shall begin with them. There is, however, one preliminary point that requires mention.

The last forty years have seen a growing body of experiments on what has been called 'psychokinesis' (PK), the alleged direct influence of mind over matter. The best-known PK experiments are those pioneered by J. B. Rhine, involving attempts to selectively influence the fall of dice, but in recent years experiments have been undertaken in which the 'targets' have ranged from the output of binary random number generators to the acceleration of enzyme reactions. Should one not look to the findings of these experiments to illuminate the forces at work in the production of poltergeist phenomena (which, as noted in chapter 1, some American researchers prefer to call RSPK – recurrent spontaneous psychokinesis)?

The answer, unfortunately, seems to be a definite 'No'. This is not the place in which to attempt a review and a criticism of modern PK experiments, but it may safely be said that, whatever the value of these experiments as evidence for paranormal physical happenings, they have yielded no clear or certain evidence as to the nature of PK. Thus to explain poltergeist phenomena by reference to PK is to explain the unknown in terms of the unknown. We might of course accept PK of the laboratory sort as a manifestation of a basic and not further analysable physical force and proceed to explain poltergeist phenomena in terms of it. But this would hardly be a legitimate move; for there is no obvious similarity between alterations in the fall of dice or in the output of electronic binary random number generators, and the sorts of happenings which are reported in poltergeist cases; nor do we know of any 'laws' of PK which would enable us to show that these seemingly different kinds of phenomena fit within a common theoretical framework. It is at least as likely that poltergeist phenomena will throw light upon the nature of PK as that the laboratory study of PK will illuminate poltergeist phenomena; and neither of these eventualities is, we feel, *very* likely.

Let us return, then, to some of the attempts which have been made to give a plausible account of the physical forces allegedly operative in the production of poltergeist phenomena. In a way, the most clear-cut of all these theories is the one that supposes the same mechanisms to function in poltergeist cases as function in certain cases of 'physical mediumship'. Some of the phenomena said to have taken place in the presence of certain 'physical mediums' – raps, including 'intelligent' ones, object-movements, the carrying of objects through the air, apports, whistles, whispers, even articulate voices (we have between us witnessed purported examples of all these) – are strikingly similar to the phenomena reported in many person-centred poltergeist cases. Several famous physical mediums – e.g. Stanislawa Tomczyk and Stella Crandon – were supposedly the focus of poltergeist-like disturbances during their adolescence or even later, whilst in a number of poltergeist cases the agents have subsequently developed, or been developed, into physical mediums. Examples are the agents in the Hydesville (1848), St Petersburg (1880), Siebenburg (1880), Güssing (1925) and Eggenberg (1929) cases. Once again it is impossible here to review the relevant literature. Our own view is that in certain instances of physical mediumship – a rather small percentage of the whole – phenomena have taken place, and in rare instances been instrumentally recorded, for which we have as yet no sort of explanation. Now of course if we have no sort of explanation for them, studying the literature about them is unlikely to further our understanding of poltergeist phenomena. However, a sort of tradition has grown up in certain circles as to the mechanisms of the physical phenomena of the seance room. Roughly speaking, the idea is this. The organisms of certain persons – 'physical mediums' – contain or can generate copious quantities of a mysterious substance commonly called 'ectoplasm'. Under certain circumstances this substance may be extruded through the orifices of the body. Though fluidic in nature, it can solidify into 'rods' of sufficient strength to move objects in the vicinity of the medium. Furthermore it is sufficiently plastic to be moulded into the 'spirit' hands, vocal organs and bodies which are supposed to manifest at 'direct voice' and 'materialization' seances. These delicate ectoplasmic structures are said to be liable to damage by exposure to light. Hence sittings for 'physical phenomena' are commonly held in darkness; and hence too, it would be said, the preference which poltergeist phenomena have frequently exhibited for the hours of darkness. 'Ectoplasm' is generally supposed to have a misty, whitish appearance, and is sometimes alleged to be slightly luminous.

Evidence that the object-movements which have occurred through certain physical mediums are in fact produced by ectoplasmic rods exhibiting many of the mechanical properties of ordinary rods and cantilevers is said to have been obtained by a number of investigators, and most notably by the Belfast engineer W. J. Crawford, in his *The Reality of Psychic Phenomena* (2nd edn., London, 1919). In a series of seances held in moderate red light with the medium Kathleen Goligher, during which tables were levitated and small objects raised and moved without any visible connection to any person present, Crawford thought that he had established, by a series of experiments *prima facie* quite carefully conducted, such facts as that when a table was levitated the weight of the medium would change appropriately, as though she were pushing downwards upon one end of a cantilever, the other end of which was correspondingly pushing upwards underneath the table.

Can we utilize this theory of Crawford's, validated as it apparently is by experiment, to account for the object-movements and related phenomena so commonly reported in poltergeist cases? We know of no positive evidence in its favour so far as poltergeist cases are concerned, and there are some observations which seem to tell against it, e.g. the removal of objects from closed boxes, and, in the Nicklheim case of 1968–9, the displacement of an object inside an open box when the light curtain that protected the opening was not obstructed. Furthermore it is impossible to look at the photographs of Miss Goligher's 'ectoplasmic rods' at the end of Crawford's *The Psychic Structures of the Goligher Circle* (London, 1921) without being irresistibly reminded of strips of cheese-cloth, sagging perceptibly between their points of attachment. Prudence suggests that one suspend judgment with regard to Crawford's claims; charity, perhaps, demands that one does not put it more strongly.

The next theory we have to consider, though superficially more respectable, is in fact much harder to get a grip on. It is what we shall call, as others have done, the electromagnetic theory, though this term is a misnomer, since there are many possible 'electromagnetic' theories, none of which has sufficient plausibility to be labelled *the* electromagnetic theory. Electromagnetic terminology was freely used in the first half of the nineteenth century in attempts to explain mesmeric and parapsychological phenomena; in most instances the theories concerned did no more than postulate unknown forces which, like 'animal magnetism', were conceived as having vague analogies to electromagnetism. Such theories rapidly fell into deserved disrepute, and little further had been heard in parapsychology of electromagnetic concepts until relatively recently. They have been revived by, for instance, Professor John Taylor, whose popular *Superminds* (London, 1975) attempts to provide an electromagnetic explanation of the 'metal-bending' phenomena which have achieved such fame through the performances of Mr Uri Geller. Taylor supposes that spoon-bending may perhaps be due to low frequency electromagnetic radiation from the human body working upon minor imperfections in the metal and causing them to coalesce.

He goes on to offer an electromagnetic explanation of poltergeist phenomena. He is much impressed by the apparent paranormal gifts of two Russian ladies, Nelya Kulagina and Alla Vinogradova. These ladies have, under relatively strict observation, been alleged simply by concentrating to make small objects, including non-magnetic objects, placed on table-tops in front of them slide towards them or away from them. Kulagina has also produced other curious effects, such as the rotation of compass needles and the marking of photographic plates. Western observers have been able to witness the phenomena for themselves, and cine-films have been taken.

Taylor says of poltergeist phenomena (pp. 151–2):
> A common feature of poltergeist phenomena is that they are usually associated with children, especially young girls. It is possible to understand the occurrences in terms of the electromagnetic hypothesis . . . . The explanation . . . is along the lines of that offered for the movement of objects achieved by Kulagina or Vinogradova . . . . In Vinogradova's case strong electrostatic fields were observed during experiments, while Kulagina had an associated low-frequency magnetic field. These fields may produce motions in light objects by a separation of positive and negative charges on the objects, in a way which may be similar to that in the Geller effect. It is still difficult to understand how enough energy can be radiated from the human brain to cause, for instance, an object to be hurled across the room. On these grounds alone one is tempted to doubt the truth of such extreme cases and to accept only those instances where gradual movements of objects with much lesser amounts of energy and without physical intervention may actually have occurred.

It is hard to know where to begin criticizing this passage. The last sentence is a classic of its kind, and requires no comment, except the remark that many other theorists in this field are forced to adopt the same tactic. Of course they do not all agree as to which phenomena can, and which cannot, 'actually have occurred'. The phenomena recently produced by Kulagina and Vinogradova and one or two other persons are indeed exceedingly curious and of absorbing interest. But we cannot discover, from the careful analysis of the phenomena by H. H. J. Keil, B. Herbert, M. Ullman and J. G. Pratt published in the *Proceedings of the SPR*, vol. 56, 1976, or from ourselves looking at cine-films of them, either that there is any definite or even substantial evidence that they are caused by electromagnetic forces, or that they exhibit any striking similarities of detail with the phenomena reported in poltergeist cases.

In hardly any poltergeist cases have observations been made which suggest even remotely that electromagnetic forces of any description have been at work. The fact that insulating the subject's bed, chair, etc., stopped the phenomena in the Boston (1867) case is more likely to have psychological than electrical causes. It is, however, somewhat surprising that investigations with electrical instruments have been carried out only in a very small number of cases. Such investigations were attempted in several nineteenth-century cases, e.g. those at Munchhof (1818), Stans (1860–2) and Iletski (1870), and also in the Seaford (1958) case. In all instances the results were negative; but few details are given in the reports, and the instruments used in the first three cases must have been exceedingly primitive. In an article entitled 'Experimenting with poltergeists' in the *European Journal of Parapsychology*, vol. 1, 1977, Mr W. G. Roll cites from *Research in Parapsychology 1974* an observation by W. Joines in a case in New York in 1971. Joines explored with a FM radio receiver the region near two objects which had just been paranormally moved. He detected a spherical region about two feet across which for about a minute emitted radiation at a frequency of 146 MHz. However, this swallow will hardly make a summer, especially in view of the facts that two feet is less than the half wavelength of radiation of that frequency, and that high frequency radio reception is extremely sensitive to all kinds of local interference effects.

The final theory in this group which we shall touch on – the 'rotating beam' theory – has been developed by a well-known investigator of American cases, Mr W. G. Roll, and several colleagues. To Mr Roll belongs the credit for having pioneered various kinds of analyses of what one might call the distribution of phenomena in poltergeist cases. Such analyses should have been begun years ago. Examining data from various recent American person-centred cases, Roll has shown that the frequency of object-movements declines with increasing distance from the poltergeist agent. In two or three cases, this 'attenuation effect' appears not to follow the inverse square law, but an exponential decay function. Roll has also presented some interesting statistics concerning the frequency with which objects of different chemical composition (metallic, plastic, etc.) have been affected; though it does not appear that anything very revealing has emerged from these statistics.

The 'rotating beam' theory of poltergeist disturbances was first presented by Roll, D. S. Burdick and W. T. Joines in a paper on 'Radial and tangential forces in the Miami poltergeist' in the *Journal of the American SPR*, vol. 67, 1973. This paper analyses statistically the characteristics of thirty-six of the object-movements which took place in the Miami (1966–7) case (see chapter 5). The 'attenuation effect' just mentioned was marked. With regard to the length and direction of movements the findings were these. Object-movements close to the agent tended to be short, radial (inwards or outwards), clockwise, outward, and to his right. Object-movements further from the agent were predominantly long, tangential (crossways), counter-clockwise, inward and to his left.

To account for these somewhat complex findings Roll and his co-authors develop a somewhat complex theory. They express the gist of it as follows:

> If a pebble is dropped in a pool of still water, waves emanate radially outward in a manner similar to the waves radiated by an electromagnetic antenna. Two pebbles, displaced in position but striking the water at the same time, will form interference patterns with peaks of reinforcement along some radial lines and nulls of cancellation along others. If the pebbles strike the water at different times the radial pattern of peaks and nulls is unchanged except for an angular rotation about an origin taken midway between impact points.
>
> This interaction between water waves is similar to the interaction between two (or more) antennae generating electromagnetic waves. For example, two antennae on a plane surface fed by identical signals (like two pebbles striking the water at the same time) will combine their radiated energies within a cigar-shaped beam perpendicular to the plane surface. However, if one signal is delayed by a specific time (like two pebbles striking the water at different times) the pattern of radiated energy is rotated about the origin, diminished in radial extent, and increased in angular extent; that is, the beam becomes shorter and fatter. Furthermore, by proper adjustment of the time delay the beam can be swept smoothly from the long skinny position to the short, fat position and back again. This is how a phased-array radar antenna works.

Roll and his co-authors do not commit themselves to saying that poltergeist agents generate electromagnetic waves; they talk more generally of an RSPK energy. Their idea is that objects caught up in this rotating and expanding and contracting beam of RSPK energy, asynchronously radiated from two different positions in an agent's body (presumably the two halves of his brain) would exhibit the peculiarities of movement noted above. The theory would also account for the fact that in the Miami case, where most of the movements originated behind the agent, they were predominantly counter-clockwise, whereas in the Seaford (1958), Newark (1961) and Indianapolis (1962) cases, the movements tended to originate at the front of the agent and to be clockwise. This apparent inconsistency disappears if we suppose that a rotating beam of RSPK energy emanates from the agent's skull moving from his left to his right. Objects in front of the agent would then be carried clockwise, and objects behind him anti-clockwise.

In a later paper (*Research in Parapsychology 1973*), Roll, Burdick and Joines apply this theory to the Olive Hill poltergeist of 1968. A group of fifteen object-movements observed by the investigators (Roll and J. P. Stump) were held to conform with the theory; though the long movements tended to be clockwise and the short movements counter-clockwise, contrary to what had been the case in Miami. However, a group of sixteen unwitnessed object-movements did not fit their hypothesis.

In recent papers (see, for example, his article 'Poltergeists' in B. B. Wolman (ed.) *Handbook of Parapsychology*, New York, 1977), Roll has tried to link the rotating beam theory to known facts about central nervous system functioning. He finds that in ninety-two cases of person-centred poltergeists which he has surveyed, there are four in which the presumed agent was a diagnosed epileptic. This figure of 4 per cent contrasts with a general incidence of only 1 per cent. Furthermore in a considerable proportion of the other cases the agent showed symptoms, e.g. hallucinations, dissociation, often associated with epilepsy. The central nervous system (CNS) outbursts characteristic of epilepsy involve a neural discharge which begins at a particular point in the CNS and rapidly 'recruits' other areas. Thus RSPK energy waves, if they are related to CNS functioning, might quickly come to radiate from two locations.

It is hard to know what to say of any theory which postulates a novel form of energy, but does not make clear how one can detect it other than through the occurrence of the phenomena it was invented to explain. Perhaps it is simplest just to say that we think it extremely unlikely that the object-movements in all or even many person-centred cases past and future, will be found to conform to Roll's proposed pattern, or indeed to any particular pattern beyond that of decline in frequency with distance from the agent. For instance, out of sixty-one object-movements recorded by Grunewald as having occurred in the presence of Eleonora Zugun (see chapter 7), thirty-one were directly towards Eleonora. Many of these objects struck her, a few dropped short, one or two missed her and went close by. Four movements were of objects near Eleonora which flew away from her, generally at the impudent herdsman, Mihai, and two were 'tangential' in Roll's sense. In twenty-four instances either the object-movement did not fit into any of Roll's categories, e.g. it simply dropped down out of the air, or else its relation to Eleonora was not completely clear. Again a number of objects in the latter class were clearly thrown at Mihai rather than at Eleonora. Grunewald gives only a few sketches of the actual trajectories of the objects, and it is not possible to make such an exact analysis as Roll has provided; but it is quite clear that the pattern of object-movements at the beginning of this 'assault' case was very different from the movement-pattern in the Miami case.

To take an even simpler example – one for which we do have a sketch – on page 318 of his *Gesammelte Aufsätze zur Parapsychologie* (Stuttgart, 1929), A. von Schrenck-Notzing prints a plan (fig. 42) showing the trajectories of three objects out of five which successively moved while the poltergeist agent, Therese Winklhofer, remained under observation standing with her back to a bookcase. Firstly, what may have been skewers (*die Spitter*) flew around the whole room; then a cup came out of the upper oven space about 3.5 metres from Therese on her right, and moved in a slightly curved path to hit a person (a police official) 2.6 metres away, standing 1.5 metres from Therese and somewhat to her right. Then a knife from the top of the bookcase suddenly fell down onto the police official's cap-badge. Then a sugar-dish, standing to Therese's left on a table at the far end of the room, flew the whole length of the room to the oven the other side, passing within a metre of her. It travelled a total distance of 6.95 metres. Finally a key, which lay on the bookcase, less than a metre to Therese's right and slightly behind her, flew past her right side, and passing in front of her at an angle of about 45°, travelled to the far left-hand corner of the room, a distance of 4.10 metres. The overall pattern of these movements does not appear to be consistent either with the theory of an energy beam rotating to Therese's right or with the theory of an energy beam rotating to Therese's left.

Again, consider these words of Mr Schschapoff, the perceptive chief witness in the Orenburg (1870) case (A. Aksakoff, *Vorläufer des Spiritismus*, Leipzig, 1898, pp. 248–9):

Our first and principal wish was to bring the phenomena under some system or known rule; however, as if in defiance (and no doubt intentionally!) they always contradicted us. For instance, right at the beginning, when we sat together at tea, we observed that various things – the teaspoon, the lid of the tea-pot, etc. – flew at random from the table, and all of them took the direction away from my wife. This made us think that some sort of repulsive power resided in her, shall we say a negative current.

However soon afterwards exactly the opposite happened: my wife went to the sideboard, and the moment she opened the door the things therein came towards her.

It may be that by adjusting the proposed time relations of the activities in the brain regions that are supposed to generate RSPK energy, Roll and his colleagues could produce an explanation of almost any pattern of object movements that may be reported in a poltergeist case, and that they could also account for sudden shifts in movement pattern by postulating sudden changes in the pattern of neural events. But such procedures would reduce the rotating beam theory to vacuousness, unless they were accompanied by concrete proposals as to how, other than through the mere occurrence of paranormal object-movements, RSPK energy, and the neural outbursts which accompany its emission, are to be detected.

In an article entitled 'Physical aspects of paranormal metal bending' (*Journal of the SPR*, vol. 49, 1977, 583–607), Professor J. B. Hasted, a physicist, of Birkbeck College, University of London, presents some speculations which bear a certain family resemblance to Roll's. Professor Hasted has carried out a series of experiments in which young persons, ostensibly gifted with 'metal bending' powers like those supposedly possessed by Mr Uri Geller, have apparently succeeded in influencing up to three pieces of metal (latch-keys untouched by the subjects) simultaneously. That the influence at work can synchronously affect the keys is demonstrated by chart recordings from strain gauges set in the keys. Synchronousness was, however, most readily achieved when the keys were so positioned that an imaginary vertical 'surface of action' extending radially outwards from the subject could simultaneously impinge on them all. Certain further observations, involving regularly recurrent peaks in chart records whilst thin strips of metal were ostensibly being paranormally bent or twisted over each other, were compatible with the view that 'part or all of the surface of action is capable of rotation at several revolutions per second about an axis in its own plane; a pair of specimen wires or metal strips caught in rotations of a sufficiently flexible surface will twist or fold, its maximum rate of twisting being that of the surface. We might suppose that a flexible surface folds so as to wrap itself around the strip' (p. 589).

We shall have to wait and see whether anything evolves from this line of work which may have a bearing upon the explanation of poltergeist phenomena. For the moment we have only two points to make. The first is that Professor Hasted does not provide sufficient details of the position of his experimental subjects in relation to the keys to enable one fully to assess his experimental findings. The second is that metal bending is so rarely reported in poltergeist cases (there are only six instances among the 500 cases listed in the Appendix) that it must remain doubtful whether studies of ostensibly paranormal metal-bending can be expected to throw any light on the mechanisms of poltergeist phenomena in general.

We turn now from theories which postulate forces emanating from the body of a poltergeist agent, to theories which make no such postulate. And here the only candidate which has been expounded at sufficient length to warrant discussion is the theory (or rather group of somewhat loosely related theories) generally termed 'the geophysical theory'. Speculations linking poltergeist phenomena to the action of underground water go back at least as far as the Dibbesdorf case of 1767–8, and speculations linking them to earthquakes at least to the Adams case of 1817–21. These ideas were, however, for the first time elaborated and provided with apparent evidential support in a series of articles by a distinguished member of the British Society for Psychical Research, Mr G. W. Lambert, in the *Journal of the SPR* between 1955 and 1964. They are also taken seriously, if not wholly accepted, by E. J. Dingwall and T. H. Hall in their *Four Modern Ghosts* (London, 1958).

Mr Lambert's version of the theory at first concentrated very much upon the possible effects of underground water. He supposes that when underground water channels – underground streams, old sewers, and so forth – run beneath or close to the foundations of a house, that house may be subjected to spasmodic upward thrusts as a head of water builds up following flooding, downpours, or abnormally high tides. The jolts thus imparted may cause objects in the house to fly in the air, whilst the general strain upon a house as it is forced upwards by this natural hydraulic jack will produce creaks, cracks, groans and all sorts of eerie sounds. Objects may also be displaced if underground water pressure, having risen sufficiently to tilt a house somewhat, suddenly subsides, causing the house to drop.

A later supplement to the theory, suggested in particular by Dingwall and Hall, is that in some cases of hauntings and poltergeists the noises and object-movements may be due to localized seismic activity, to earthquakes affecting, perhaps, too small an area to register on instruments at seismic observatories. This proposal was also taken up by Mr Lambert.

The principal kinds of evidence advanced in favour of the geophysical theory will now in turn be briefly listed and considered. We have criticized the theory in detail in the *Journal of the SPR*, vol. 41, 1961 (a reply by Mr Lambert is in the same issue), and shall here outline only the main features of the arguments. The kinds of evidence concerned are these:

1 *Reports of earthquake effects in poltergeist cases.* Many of the phenomena often or sometimes reported in poltergeist cases find parallels in accounts of earthquakes – cracking sounds, displacement of objects, stopping of clocks, breaking of windows. However, what we have in mind under this heading are reported similarities more fundamental than these. In an appreciable number of poltergeist cases – for instance Tidworth (1662-3) Amiens (1732), Belledoon (1829-31), Oakland (1874), Portland, Oregon (1909), Fougères (1913), Kecskemet (1921) – witnesses have come out with statements like 'The whole house seemed to be heaving', 'The room creaked and groaned like a ship in a gale', and so forth. Statements like these undoubtedly lend some force to the claims of the geophysical theory. One of the writers (AG) has been present in a poltergeist house when a statement of such a kind was made by the principal witness in the case; but the house was certainly not heaving about as the witness alleged. She was a trifle over-wrought. However, it would be going too far to suggest that this is a likely explanation of all such reports.

2 *Clustering of cases in tidal areas and near underground rivers.* Mr Lambert has tried to show that British and some other hauntings and poltergeists cluster especially around coastal

areas, tidal areas, and (for London) around underground rivers. We argued, with supporting statistics, in the paper mentioned above, that this is simply because population tends to cluster in such areas. Mr Lambert believes that poltergeists cluster somewhat more than does the population.

3 *Clustering of cases in earthquake areas.* The 'earthquake area' which Mr Lambert has principally considered is the Scottish central rift valley. Much the same considerations apply as in 2 above. We have come across one case – Thorney (1868) – in which the phenomena are said to have been ushered in by an earthquake. But C. Davison's *A History of British Earthquakes* (Cambridge, 1924) mentions no earthquake at the relevant place and time. Nor does it list any earthquake which demonstrably coincides with any of Mr Lambert's rift valley or other cases.

4 *Citations of coincidences in some individual cases between tides, heavy rainfalls, etc., and poltergeist phenomena.* The trouble here is that when the number of poltergeists and hauntings is so large, and heavy rains and high tides so frequent, it is no good picking upon one or two or a few cases in which such coincidences are apparent. Careful and very time-consuming statistical analysis of a large number of cases would be required before we could legitimately assume that the coincidences were more than chance ones, and such an analysis has not so far been provided. We have our own reasons, which we shall shortly make clear, for thinking that they would not come up with positive results.

We do not, of course, suggest that the geophysical theory has *nothing* to recommend it. Quite possibly (as we indicated in chapter 13) small house movements may be among the 'natural causes' of the odd noises so often reported in minor cases of alleged haunting. Mr Lambert, however, apparently believes that the geophysical theory can explain the great majority of poltergeist cases, for he said in 1959: 'I have yet to find a violent poltergeist case where the subterranean conditions make the geophysical theory manifestly inapplicable', and he has published nothing to indicate that he has since changed his views. We shall advance three quite general sets of reasons, other than the above criticisms of Mr Lambert's arguments, for rejecting the geophysical theory in this strong form. They are as follows:

1 The theory is forced to lean heavily on the crooked stick of illusion. That is to say, in order to reconcile all the phenomena

with the theory it is necessary to suppose that rappings which witnesses took to be intelligent replies to questions were really random and inconsequential; that witnesses who reported that objects were carried through the air, turned corners, etc., were suffering from some peculiar, fright-engendered affliction of the senses; that when the phenomena are thought to centre round a particular person rather than round a particular place, this is due to distortion of the judgment by superstition and to a well-known human propensity for witch-hunting; and so on. Mr Lambert produces some ingenious ideas with which to buttress these supposals. He gives, for instance, the following reason why in the nineteenth century maidservants were so often suspected of producing poltergeist phenomena. Stresses and joltings from underground water, producing noises, object-displacements, etc., would most readily be communicated to a house through the main chimney-stack. The unfortunate little maidservant would have spent her days by the kitchen fire at the base of the stack, and her nights in an attic near the top of the stack, and in both these places would have been especially liable to 'poltergeist' disturbances from underground water. We do not have any statistics as to whether kitchen maids or parlour maids were the more frequently affected; but in general terms we may say (returning to the arguments of chapter 13) that one must at all times beware of maintaining one's theory by purely ad hoc supposals, especially ones designed to eradicate just those awkward facts which apparently contradict it. We saw an egregious example earlier in the chapter. Such moves are the first steps on the road to flat-earthery.

2 Ordinary houses could not withstand geophysical forces of a magnitude which would throw objects around within them. In the article mentioned above we presented some simple calculations as to the amplitudes and accelerations of the vertical and horizontal house-movements which would be required to project small objects standing on the floor or against the walls into the air or across the room. From data supplied by the Building Research Station it is abundantly clear that no ordinary brick and timber frame house could survive repeated jolts or vibrations of the required amplitudes and accelerations without suffering serious structural damage and very probably collapse. Nor would such houses survive tilting of more than about 1 in 150. Furthermore data on human sensitivity to vibration and house-move-

ments indicate that house-movements of the kinds concerned could not take place without at once being noticed by the persons on the spot. We will, however, not elaborate the points again here, but will instead pass on to:

3 An experimental investigation of these claims. Between June and August 1961, when the geophysical theory was young and hopeful, ADC arranged a series of 'house-shaking' experiments to investigate the two questions (a) whether when a house is artificially jolted or vibrated with progressively greater violence, poltergeist-like phenomena will take place in it, and (b) whether under such circumstances poltergeist-like phenomena could conceivably take place without persons in the house becoming aware of the vibrations or joltings. Since these experiments have not previously been described in print, we will accord them a little space here. The arrangements for these experiments were as follows.

Through the courtesy of the Cambridge Borough Surveyor, several houses scheduled for demolition were put at ADC's disposal. One of these, the end and northernmost of a terrace of five, was eventually selected on account of its structural soundness and freedom from damp. It was a small building of 'two up, two down' design, with a kitchen added downstairs. Equipment was installed for both impact tests and vibration experiments. The 'vibrator' consisted of a 1" steel shaft, 16" long, running in ball bearings at each end of a reinforced steel sleeve. At each end of the shaft was a weight. The two weights were out of balance. The vibrator was cemented through the bottom of the end external wall, the thickest and most accessible in the house. It was additionally secured by metal plates at either end of the sleeve. These were bolted into the wall. It was driven from ¼ h.p. and 1 h.p. electric motors by means of a belt and wheel system, and could produce predominantly vertical vibrations of the house in the range 0–120 Hz, with maximum thrust against the walls of 892 lb. We discovered, however, that the age of the brickwork and the powdery mortar heavily damped down all vibrations above 25 Hz. It was the vibrations in this range that we were principally investigating even when we ran the vibrator up to 120 Hz to secure maximum thrust. Equipment for the impact experiments was crude but quite effective. A rope was passed around the chimney stack at the north end of the house, and a 60 lb 3 oz metal weight was secured to it. The weight hung

THE FORCES AT WORK 335

about 18″ clear of the ground, resting against the outside wall of the chimney breast. It was hauled away from the house by means of a rope and released at specified heights and distances. Some experiments were also conducted in which heavy weights were dropped close to the house from varying heights.

Preliminary trials were conducted on 30 June 1961. More sustained experiments began on 2 July. Those participating were ADC, AG, Mr D. J. Murray, Mr H. Osborne and Mr R. Brooks. Various small test objects (thirteen in all) had been placed around the house, especially in contact with the wall around the upstairs and downstairs fireplaces and mantelpieces, i.e. the wall most affected by both the impact tests and the vibrator. AG and Mr Osborne acted as observers inside the house, whilst ADC and Mr Murray operated the equipment outside, and Mr Brooks recorded the memorable scene on film. First of all we ran the vibrator for about two minutes at each of 45, 57, 75 and 95 Hz. At the lowest frequency the vibration was plainly perceptible if one placed a hand on either the upstairs or the downstairs mantelpiece or chimney, but it could not be felt through one's feet, though it could be detected by a hand placed on the floor. At the highest two levels, the whole house vibrated. The vibrations were plainly perceptible through feet on the floor. If one put an ear to the wall, the reverberation was almost painful. None of the test objects moved.

Five impact trials were then carried out with the 60 lb weight. It was drawn back to a distance of 10 feet from the wall, and a height of about 6 feet. It struck the wall at a height of a little over two feet above ground, with an impact energy of about 241 ft lb. At the second trial, the cement rendering on the outside of the wall at the point of impact was shattered and fell away, leaving the bricks and mortar exposed. AG and Mr Murray observed in the upstairs front bedroom. The jolts were not merely audible but could be felt through the feet. Dirt fell down the chimney, and small pieces of plaster fell from the ceiling. None of the test objects moved.

We then ran the motor for several minutes at maximum revolutions, and walked down the terrace of houses. Vibrations could be detected two houses away by putting one's hand on the wall.

Finally the weight was swung four more times, with AG and Mr Murray again observing in the upstairs front bedroom. This time it was hauled back to 15 feet and a height of just over 7 feet; when it struck it cleared the ground by only 8″, giving an impact energy of over 300 ft lb. This produced a big jolt, clearly perceptible through one's feet, and more plaster fell. On the third impact a detached leg of a camera tripod, which had been leant against the wall by the fireplace moved about ¾″ to the left; at the fourth impact it fell over to the left. Nothing else moved – not even a marble which was lying on the floor, or a match which was projecting almost half its length over the edge of the mantelpiece.

The next day, 3 July, similar experiments were carried out with similar results, or rather absence of results. When vibrations of 100 Hz were created by a 1 h.p. motor, a cup and saucer on the upstairs mantelpiece in contact with the wall was found by AG to have moved about ¼″ from the wall. The cup was slowly rotating in the saucer. On 8 July, the vibrator was run up to maximum under the observation of Mr P. M. Turner, an expert in vibrations from the University Engineering Department. He estimated that a thrust roughly ten times that which the vibrator produced – say 8000 lb – would produce collapse of the house. He expressed the opinion that horizontal vibrations, as opposed to the predominantly vertical ones hitherto produced by the vibrator would be more likely to set the house in a state of resonance which *might* cause movements of household objects. He advised us as to the best way in which the vibrator should be fixed to produce such vibrations. His own view, however, was that the house would collapse before any poltergeist-like effects occurred.

The vibrator was repositioned in accordance with Mr Turner's recommendations, and modified so that it now produced a maximum thrust upon the wall of 1600 lb. A final series of experiments with it was conducted on 11 August. Those present were ADC, AG and Mr Osborne. The vibrator was run up from 0 to 120 Hz, producing maximum thrust. ADC and AG observed upstairs both separately and together – quite our most terrifying experience in pursuit of the poltergeist. At maximum thrust the noise from the vibrating walls was quite loud, and the whole structure of the house shook so much that no one could possibly ignore it. Considerable amounts of plaster fell from the ceilings, and large quantities of a fine dust from the front ends of the house. A crack in the lintel over the window of the upstairs front bedroom was found to have appreciably widened. None the less there were only four insignificant movements of test objects. These were as follows:

(i) and (ii) A plastic beaker which had been placed half over the edge of the upstairs mantelpiece twice fell off.

(iii) The cup and saucer (previously mentioned) which stood on the same mantelpiece in contact with the wall vibrated down a slight slope to the edge of the mantelpiece, and fell off. It would have smashed on the floor had AG not caught it.

(iv) A small plaster of paris figure of a donkey, which had been placed on the downstairs mantelpiece on contact with the wall was found to have advanced outwards ¾" from the wall.

In this experiment the vibrator was only run at maximum thrust for a period of three minutes, due to the extra load put on its bearings. The possibility that the vibrator might disintegrate causing injury and the obvious near proximity of serious structural damage to the house led ADC to terminate the experiments at this point.

Crude though these experiments may have been – a black and white cine-film of them bears some resemblance to an early silent comedy – they were efficacious in demonstrating practically what our previous study of the relevant literature had led us to anticipate, namely, that vibrations of and sudden jolts to a house would cause serious structural damage and probably collapse well before object-movements anything like those reported in classic poltergeist cases took place, and that such vibrations and joltings would be immediately evident to persons inside the house well before the point of serious structural damage was reached. The geophysical theory of poltergeist phenomena cannot possibly be sustained.

A quick answer to the question 'What are the forces at work in the production of poltergeist phenomena?' is that we do not have the slightest idea. There are, it is true, all kinds of odd poltergeist phenomena, or odd aspects of the phenomena, which many people have supposed would, if their implications could only be drawn out and fully grasped, give us vital clues to the nature of the beast. Such are, for instance: the cold breezes and cold spots not infrequently reported in hauntings; stones (and other objects) picked up hot; the preference which, to a moderate extent, the phenomena exhibit for the hours of darkness;

supposed peculiar acoustic properties of paranormal rappings; sounds like 'the winding of a jack' sometimes said to precede phenomena; the passage of objects in and out of closed spaces, allegedly by transit through a 'fourth dimension'; luminous effects; misty ('ectoplasmic') shapes mentioned in various cases, and in a surprisingly high percentage of the cases we have ourselves investigated; and so on. But we can neither make these findings, or alleged findings, 'add up', nor derive from one or a few of them any comprehensive theory as to the forces at work in poltergeists and hauntings.

A shortcoming of all the theories discussed in this chapter is that they have confined their attention almost entirely to object-movements and to raps, and even so have had to ignore some part of the range of happenings reported. But of course many other kinds of phenomena are alleged to have occurred in poltergeist cases and in hauntings – witness the examples given in this book. We argued at the beginning of this chapter that it would be imprudent to develop a theory of the forces at work in the production of one kind of phenomenon without considering all the other sorts of phenomena to which it appears closely linked. This we remain convinced is true; but it does not follow that we must look for *just one kind of* 'force' at work in poltergeist cases. The appearance created in at least a substantial minority of cases is that there is *one agency* capable of effecting its purposes in a number of different ways. Perhaps it effects them now by a control (which we do not understand) of one natural force (which we do at least partially understand), now by control of another; and perhaps also by control of natural forces which we do not as yet understand at all. We are talking here, it must be remembered, only of the appearance created by the phenomena. The realities behind the phenomena remain to be discovered. But we can no longer avoid tackling the second major kind of theoretical issue which arises in connection with poltergeists and hauntings – that of the nature of the intelligence which, in quite a number of instances, apparently directs the phenomena.

18 Are poltergeists living or are they dead?

Finally, then, we come to what is undoubtedly the most intriguing of all the questions which arise in connection with hauntings and poltergeists: what is the nature and source of the intelligence which not infrequently seems to organize and direct the various happenings? It is not easy to say in what percentage of cases such intelligence is manifested. In seventy-nine of the 500 cases surveyed in chapter 12 (16 per cent) 'communication' took place; the phenomena were in one way or another responsive to questions, requests, etc., and perhaps 'answered back'. But this does not exhaust the range of possible ways in which a poltergeist may seem 'intelligent'. It may appear to pursue purposes of its own – e.g. to tease, annoy, persecute, even assault, a particular individual – without bothering to 'communicate'. Very often there is a 'focusing' effect; the spook will exhibit a preference for disturbing particular objects, or objects in a particular area, and this too might be held a mark of 'intelligence'. It is hard, indeed impossible, to draw a sharp line separating 'intelligent' from 'non-intelligent' poltergeists. However, for present purposes it will suffice if we agree that there are some poltergeist cases, and some hauntings too, in which the phenomena sometimes appear as if controlled by an intelligent agency. We can then ask: 'Whose is the intelligence concerned, and what kind of intelligence is it?'

Speculations about this question may be divided into two broad categories: those which propose that the intelligence is that of a living human being, and those which propose it is the intelligence of some discarnate entity, especially that of a deceased human being.

We shall begin with the living person theory. This theory supposes that the intelligence which manifests itself is that of the living human being whose organism is reckoned to provide the energy necessary for the phenomena. Of course in the great majority even of 'person-centred' cases, this person – the so-called poltergeist 'agent' – has virtually no conscious control over the phenomena. However, so far from this constituting an obstacle to the hypothesis, it is made out to be one of its cornerstones. For the theory commonly supposes that the phenomena are in some way or another the outcome of an emotional state or conflict which has been denied conscious expression and the relief it brings. Just as (it is alleged) anxieties, aggressive urges, sexual desires, etc., kept from consciousness because they conflict with the social and moral code which the agent accepts, or with his preferred image of himself, may continue a subterranean existence in the unconscious mind, and find covert expression on the 'surface' in the neurotic symptoms of whose origin he is unaware, so these same unconscious anxieties and urges may, in a suitably endowed subject, find expression in poltergeist phenomena in his vicinity without his having any clear realization that the phenomena reflect his own emotional problems.

One can make such a view sound extremely plausible from a variety of different angles. One can do so by, for instance, simply examining one individual case after another. It is hardly possible to read an account of, say, the four cases described in chapter 4 above, without supposing that there was *some* connection between the emotional or personal problems of the various agents and the outbreak of the phenomena. Sometimes a severe shock seems to precipitate an outbreak, presumably by bringing an underlying condition to the boil. This was no doubt so in the Hopfgarten case, as also in the cases mentioned at the end of chapter 3. In some cases the 'outlet' nature of the poltergeist phenomena seems particularly evident. Thus in the Sauchie case of 1960, the agent passed into 'trances' in which she talked with unusual freedom of her dissatisfactions. During these trances, there were no poltergeist phenomena – it was as though the two were alternative outlets for the same repressed emotions. (One may note, however, as a warning against hasty generalization that in the Bergzabern case of 1852 and the Hopfgarten case of 1921 phenomena took place only when the agent was in 'trance' or asleep.) Or take a United States case investigated by G. F. Solfvin and W. G. Roll in 1975 (case 498). Here the phenomena centred round a young man of twenty-one who had been an active athletic person until he sustained a back injury which incapacitated him for two years, and in addition caused acute financial worries. He began to have epileptic seizures. He also became the centre of poltergeist disturbances. The epileptic seizures were almost certainly related to his emotional problems. According to Solfvin and Roll '"Peter's" stress level appeared to correspond closely to the level of paranormal activity, while his seizures preceded the only two reported periods when paranormal events were absent while the family was at home'. It was as though the psychomotor seizures and the poltergeist phenomena alike served the purpose of 'reducing tension'. In several cases – Buhai (1925), Seyssuel (1930), and the Andover case mentioned in chapter 2 – phenomena centring round a girl have ceased with the appearance of the menses.

Another approach is statistical. In a recent article (in Wolman (ed.), *Handbook of Parapsychology*, New York, 1977) Mr W. G. Roll concludes after a survey of ninety-two person-centred cases that in forty-nine the agents appeared to have medical or psychological problems. In his *Can we explain the Poltergeist?* (New York, 1964), Dr A. R. G. Owen classifies the mental problems of twenty-four poltergeist agents as follows: anxiety reactions, one; dissociative reactions, five; conversion hysteria, nine; phobias and obsessions, three; mania, four; schizophrenia, one; 'emotional need', one. In a number of cases successful psychotherapy has supposedly been responsible for the cessation of the phenomena.

Yet another approach involves the detailed psychological investigation of the agent, especially in his family setting. Such investigations have been attempted in, for instance, the cases at Neudorf (1952), Newark (1961), Indianapolis (1962), Bremen (1965), Miami (1966–7), Rosenheim (1967–8), USA (1971, case 489), New York, Bronx (1974), USA (1974, case 498) and Rome (1975). The most common themes in the resultant diagnoses have been repressed aggression and tension within the family (the two being generally related).

If it be agreed that these considerations provide substantial support for the view that poltergeist phenomena not uncommonly express emotions and emotional conflicts denied access to the agent's ordinary stream of consciousness, the 'living person' theorist can proceed to develop his argument as follows. Consider a group of cases in which the phenomena exhibit no, or few, signs of intelligence, yet in which there are clear indications that they originate from unconscious levels of the agent's personality. The Boston (1867), Sauchie (1960) and Miami (1966–7) cases will do as examples (see chapters 4 and 5).

In such cases the emotional problems and frustrations are expressed in an unsophisticated way by the violence and peremptoriness of the phenomena. Cases like these pass by insensible degrees into cases in which the problems find expression in quite sophisticated ways. In the middle of the range we have cases such as that at Kingstown (1876), in which communicative rappings centred round a bored girl, and made the sort of spelling mistakes she made herself, that at Grenoble (1907), in which the agent's living fiancé, whom she was anxious to marry, ostensibly communicated through rappings in her vicinity, or that at Nikolsburg (1927), where communication was established through raps with an entity which claimed to 'dwell in' the agent. We end by reaching, without any clear break in the series, cases such as the Buhai (1925–7) case, in which subconscious guilt feelings found expression in phenomena shaped to resemble the activities of a punishing and persecuting devil, or the Amherst (1878) case, in which one of the communicating 'deceased persons' bore a marked resemblance to a former boy-friend of the agent. This young man, whom she apparently liked, had attempted to rape her, and the phenomena may well in part have represented a playing out of her unconscious fantasies and desires.

Now, the argument might continue, if we have, as we indeed seem to have, a number of cases in which an intelligence manifests, and manifests in the guise of a fictitious personality, and is yet demonstrably at root merely an expression of the emotional problems of the poltergeist agent, why should we ever be forced to suppose, in any case in which there is anyone who is even a candidate for the role of poltergeist agent, that the intelligence which ostensibly directs the phenomena is other than that of some part of the agent's mind? It may of course claim to be that of a daemon or a deceased person, but such claims are of no consequence once we appreciate the psychodynamics of it all; the claims merely reflect the creative and dramatizing powers which the unconscious mind can call upon in handling repressed emotions and emotional conflicts.

It is true that, as pointed out in chapter 8, there are a very few cases (significantly few some would say) in which the phenomena, in addition to announcing, or indicating, a certain deceased person as their source, exhibit a certain apparent independence of any single agent or medium. They might exhibit this independence either by not requiring the presence of any person in particular, or by giving information about the ostensible communicator which would have been known to him but could not have been known to anyone present. However, we do not know of a single poltergeist case that has convincingly fulfilled the latter requirement. And even if such a case were to turn up, it could no doubt be satisfactorily dealt with – since in several cases of the 'living agent' type the communicating intelligence has exhibited ostensible ESP – by supposing that the information concerned came not from the next world but from ESP focused upon this world. In chapter 8 were described one or two cases that apparently fulfilled the former requirement. There is perhaps no single, simple formula for sweeping all possible cases of this class into the net of the living agent theory. But even in the fairly striking case at Charlottenburg (1929) it seemed more likely that the phenomena's apparent independence of a single agent was due not to the toings and froings of a particular deceased person, but to the fact that the members of the family concerned were more than usually liable to have 'psychic' experiences. In short, there do not appear to be any cases which seriously strain the living agent theory. Or, if there are cases which engender doubt, we are led by the well-known maxim of parsimony in explanation – that one should not multiply explanatory principles unless one is forced to do so – to accept the living agent theory in preference to the deceased person or discarnate entity theory. For we know that living agents exist, whereas to postulate discarnate agents is to lumber the universe with a highly questionable and probably superfluous class of furnishings. And we might furthermore confront the discarnate entity hypothesis with such awkward questions as: when there is 'communication' by raps in a poltergeist case, and a deceased person purports to reply, with what ears does he hear the questions addressed to him? Ears or other acoustic devices are necessary for the detection of soundwaves, and no device that would stop sound-waves could possibly be discarnate. The ears that hear must be the ears of a living agent.

At this point upholders of the discarnate entity theory would probably allege that an important kind of evidence has been left out of consideration, namely evidence from what may loosely be called 'exorcisms'. We shall use, or rather misuse, this term to cover all systematic attempts of whatever kind to dispel the phenomena. Thus psychotherapy, where it has been applied to that end, will count as a form of exorcism. In fact, however, in the great majority of the fifty-nine cases from the list of 500 in the Appendix in which exorcism was attempted, the exorcist based his endeavours on the assumption that a discarnate entity of some kind or other was the source of the trouble. In thirty-four of the fifty-nine cases, or about 60 per cent, the exorcism was apparently successful. In only sixteen cases was it largely unsuccessful. Even when allowance is made for the fact that some of the thirty-four successful cases probably found their way into print simply because the exorcism worked, the success rate remains (to us) surprisingly high. Surely, it might be claimed, this shows there is *something* in the assumptions of the exorcist?

Unfortunately it does not show this at all. There is much to suggest that, as with psychotherapy, what determines the success of the operation is not the particular tenets held and applied by the exorcist, but his impact on the persons involved in the case and the conviction with which he inspires them. How else could ADC (see chapter 16) have succeeded in suppressing a poltergeist for three months by simply leading the occupants of the afflicted house to think he had done something of significance when in fact he had done nothing but smoke a cigarette? An exorcist who attributes his success to the correctness of the belief system from which his procedure arose is in effect committing what may be called the 'psychotherapist's fallacy'. He is giving to a school of thought the credit which is properly his own.

But, it will be said, what about those cases in which the 'exorcist' is a medium and has not merely 'exorcized' but given, clairvoyantly or in trance, an account of certain deceased persons allegedly responsible for the phenomena, which account has been shown upon subsequent investigation to correspond with facts – facts, that is, either about the past occupants of the afflicted house, or about the deceased relatives and friends of the present occupants? Such cases crop up from time to time in newspapers. It is, however, difficult to find instances which have been recorded in sufficient detail to allow of a proper assessment. The late Mrs Eileen Garrett, a medium who later came to occupy an uniquely respected position in the world of parapsychology, describes in her autobiographical *Many Voices* (London,

1969), how in 1927 she was taken without knowing her destination, to a house in Sussex, in which poltergeist phenomena were centring round two boys, aged thirteen and eleven. The boys' mother 'came through', and claimed that she was producing the effects because the boys' stepmother and their father were conspiring to cheat the children out of an inheritance from their real mother. It transpired that there had been such a conspiracy, and steps were taken to set matters right. Mrs Garrett, however, appears to have been writing from memory forty years after the event.

We have ourselves come across one or two similar examples. We have already described (chapter 14) a case we investigated in which a medium, brought to the scene, was able to give the surname, and one of the christian names, of two people who had lived in the house over thirty years before. Another curious case of the kind was one in which AG became involved in 1972. The setting was a substantial council house in a town some ten or fifteen miles from Nottingham. The occupants were a young married couple, their three children aged 1, 2 and 6, and the wife's mother, hereinafter referred to as 'mother-in-law'. The phenomena had focused, if at all, around the wife. They consisted of the scent (smelled by several persons) of St Bruno pipe tobacco, a brand used by mother-in-law's deceased second husband (he had never lived in the house), hereinafter referred to as 'Grandpa Jim'. There had also been a much less pleasant smell, described by mother-in-law as like that of rotting bodies. Unexplained rappings had repeatedly come at the front door. At night, members of the family had been kept awake by the sound of indistinct voices, and the wife had heard her own name called twice in succession. Once the boy, aged six, was heard talking as if to a person in his room. He said it was Grandpa Jim, and described him accurately though he had died four years previously. One evening while the wife was in the kitchen with the six-year-old at her side, she had heard a spring which was stretched across the back door to hold a towel creak in a characteristic way. She turned to see the towel sailing across the kitchen. The boy ran out of the room. She then went into the pantry, from which she had previously heard some loud cracks. She found a saucer therein had cracked in a pattern of concentric circles. It broke up in her hand as she picked it up. Then, as she came out of the pantry, two more saucers fell behind her. They had been at the back of a shelf about 4' 6" up, and she could not have accidentally dislodged them. One or two other small object movements took place, and one evening the wife three times had the match with which she was trying to light a cigarette blown out with a detectable puff of air. She was also several times overcome with the feeling of an unpleasant 'presence' at the top of the stairs.

These happenings perhaps seem trivial when merely read about, but they had reduced a family of more than averagely intelligent people to a state of chronic anxiety. Wife and mother-in-law both seemed keen that AG should bring a medium to the house in the hope of clearing up the trouble, and on 10 December 1972, AG and a colleague, Mr D. Roughton, brought over a well-known Nottingham medium, Mrs Violet Edwards (who was also mentioned in chapter 16 above). Mrs Edwards had no idea where she was being taken until she got out of the car. Only mother-in-law and the wife were present. Mrs Edwards sat quietly in the living room without passing into a trance and related what she 'sensed'. She undoubtedly seemed to those present to 'sense' correctly a great deal more than she could have known by ordinary means about the family and its concerns. Here are some brief excerpts from the transcript of the tape recording, together (in square brackets) with comments later supplied by the wife and by mother-in-law (W = wife, M = mother-in-law):

Mrs E. . . . and a gentleman that worked on the land.
W. Grandad. [Not Grandpa Jim, but M's father, who grew up in a farming family, and worked on the land till he was 30.]
M. Yes
Mrs E. . . . Farming conditions. This gentleman would be five feet ten or eleven, well made, well built, and very full-faced, you know, really fat cheeks, fresh complexion. Medium sized nose. I see him standing at a fence. He had a habit of pulling his cap over his eyes.
M. Yes. [He was full-faced and well-built. About 5'8". He had a fresh complexion, hardly a wrinkle till he died at 87. He used to wear a cap over one eye.]
Mrs. E. Now he's on a bank by a field. I could come down a high bank onto a built up area.
W. Grandad's garden. [He had a garden, or allotment, in such a position. He was a great gardener.]
Mrs. E. As I come down to this built up area there's a garage . . . I could smell the petrol you see. [There was a big railway cabin

at the top of his garden, in which was stored paraffin and oil and creosote. It had a very characteristic smell. One had to pass the shed to get down to the built-up area.] . . .

Mrs E. [after some remarks about W's fear of the stairs, which the latter acknowledges] Have you smelt anything? It's a dirty smell.

W. It's a horrible vile smell. [See above.]

Mrs E. Blood?

M. It's like blood, but it's, like, old.

Mrs E. Slimy?

M. . . . mostly it's indescribable. It's horrible.

Mrs. E. But it's the smell of blood with it. [She goes out on stairs, is 'taken over', and bursts out crying. One of her guides then 'controls' her and says a prayer. She returns to the living room.] There's a lady and a gentleman. The lady I don't think you would have felt very much – but the gentleman, yes. He was a bully and a coward.

M. Jim. [i.e. Grandpa Jim.]

Mrs. E. Also he was cruel, and this little lady he used to knock about. And he beat her and lost his temper.

M. Yes. [Grandpa Jim used to knock his first wife about.]

Mrs. E. This is where the blood was.

M. He knocked her downstairs – his first wife. [N.B. not the stairs of the present house.]

Mrs E. Did you know this?

M. Oh, yes, he was my second husband. . . .

Mrs E. Oh, don't tell me any more. Oh, she was a pathetic little soul, and oh, he was a bully. He used to get into vile tempers.

M. Yes, yes, he half-strangled me. [Grandpa Jim's first wife was a tiny woman. His sons would never forgive him for what he did to her.]

Mrs E. He was a thick-set man, not particular about the way he dressed.

M. Yes. [He was thickset in his younger days, but at that time was particular about his clothes.]

Mrs E. He couldn't always hide the horrible temper that was in his face. Oh, his eyes, his eyes. [His eyes used to stand out in his rages. He would pick the table up and throw it across the room regardless of what was on it.]

Mrs. E. [Proceeds with some advice as to how this troublesome entity may be induced to depart.] . . . [to M.] Someone linked with you who was very fond of football. Never missed a football match if they could help it. Now I'm in country surroundings, and I'm on a country football pitch.

M. My first husband. [M's first husband loved football. He liked

> *local* football, not major club football. Football and boxing were his two chief interests in life.]
> Mrs E. He was tall wasn't he?
> M. Yes. [5'11½".]
> Mrs. E. That's the gentleman I'm seeing. He didn't play but he liked to watch a match. He didn't like to miss one if there was anyone playing hereabouts. [All this is true.] . . .
> Mrs E. [out of the blue, during tea afterwards] Did he walk around with a knife?
> M. Yes, he [Grandpa Jim] used to take a knife to me. When he was kind he was the kindest man. But his two sons wouldn't come to his funeral. [The knife was used to frighten rather than stab.]

What would a supporter of the living agent theory say of cases such as this, in which a medium, brought without advance information to the scene of poltergeist disturbances, gives a plausible account of the origin of those disturbances in the malice or misery of an unmistakably described deceased person, whose former existence and connection with the place and people involved is subsequently established? He would probably see in the extracts we have just quoted the wherewithal to attack the discarnate entity theory. For the medium gave correct information not just about the deceased person ('Grandpa Jim') supposed to be responsible for the phenomena, but also about a variety of other deceased relations of the family, none of whom were said to have, or indeed would have been likely to have had, any responsibility for the disturbances. And likewise a medium brought to *any* house, haunted or otherwise, may be able to give correct information about its past occupants. For instance AG once brought a medium to a poltergeist house where the phenomena (he later concluded) were probably fraudulent. None the less the medium produced a piece of somewhat unlikely information about a past occupant of the house which it did not seem likely she could have acquired by normal means. Now if mediums can do this, it is no doubt a very interesting and peculiar fact, and one that requires close investigation. But it means that we cannot even contemplate concluding simply from the fact that a medium, taken to a supposedly haunted house, comes up with a correct description of a past occupant of that house, or of a deceased relative of its present occupants, that the deceased person described was responsible for the phenomena. For she might have done so in any house, haunted or otherwise.

Before we could draw this conclusion we should have to have reasons for taking a further step, namely that of accepting the medium's say-so that that particular deceased person caused the phenomena. But what conclusive reason could there be for taking this step? It may be that the medium obtains information about the deceased persons by exercise of her peculiar gifts (whatever they may be) and then exercises her imagination in pinning responsibility for the disturbances upon one of them. Even if the disturbances cease following her visit, that might be for psychological reasons to do with her impact upon persons present. So, at least, the argument would run.

We must now turn from an exposition of the living agent theory, and of the way in which it might be extended to swallow up the discarnate entity theory's most cherished data, to an exposition of the discarnate entity theory.

It would not be easy for the discarnate entity theory to turn the tables on the living agent theory by swallowing up all the latter's most cherished data. There are, as we have seen, some cases in which the phenomena seem quite clearly to have been expressions of a poltergeist agent's emotional problems. Still, a discarnate entity theorist might find grounds for suggesting that the role of the agent's emotional problems in the production of poltergeist phenomena has been commonly exaggerated. It is no doubt true that poltergeist agents who have subsequently come under the scrutiny of psychologists and psychiatrists have been full of suppressed aggression and of tensions in their family relationships. But we really need to know what the agents were like before the poltergeist outbreak began. Poltergeist phenomena may change the people afflicted by them. We have seen not just a family but a whole terrace of houses torn by aggressive tensions because of the activities of a poltergeist. Psychological tests given during and after the outbreak will not help us here. Furthermore in several cases it appears that the psychologist who administered and scored the tests knew that he had a poltergeist agent to deal with. This is particularly undesirable when, as has often been the case, free response tests, whose interpretation is in some ways up to the tester, were included. It is worth noting that in the survey reported in chapter 12, the agents in only thirty out of nearly two hundred person-centred cases were rated as clearly 'disturbed' prior to the onset of the phenomena.

And there was no obvious common denominator among the disturbances concerned. This figure of about 15 per cent is undoubtedly too low. Still, it is large enough to require explanation, and an underestimate is preferable to wholesale indulgence in the enjoyable but misleading game of retrospective diagnosis.

Next we must ask, what sort of basis in fact can the discarnate entity hypothesis derive from cases already in the literature? Earlier in the chapter we asked whether the literature contained any cases in which the influence of some particular deceased person seemed unequivocally indicated. We could not find any – at least, none that seemed likely to resist the arguments of the living agent theorists. However, we wish now to consider some proposals put forward by Professor I. Stevenson in an article (whose title we have borrowed for this chapter) in the *Journal of the American SPR*, vol. 66, 1972. Professor Stevenson argues that it is at least possible that some poltergeist effects are in fact caused by discarnate entities. He goes on as follows:

> The *modus operandi* for the kinetic effects of such discarnate agents might be different from that of living poltergeist agents. The existence of important differences might become manifest in analyses of the characteristics of large numbers of cases studied with minds open to the possibility of discarnate influence as a factor in some, but not necessarily all.
>
> Thinking along this line, we may try to imagine how a discarnate poltergeist agent might differ in his conduct and powers from a living one. In what respects, we should ask ourselves, would his capacities, motives, and manifestations differ from those of a living poltergeist agent?

Professor Stevenson presents his own conjectures (he regards them as nothing more) with regard to this question. They may be summarized as follows:

Living agents may: move lighter objects shorter distances; move objects in simple trajectories and frequently break them; move objects aimlessly; express destructive impulses towards other people through the phenomena produced; not 'communicate'; not generate collectively perceived phantasms; not pass into mediumistic 'trances'; be the focus of the phenomena; be young; be amenable to cure by psychotherapy.

Discarnate agents may: move heavier objects longer distances; move them as if carried or guided; move or project them as if for a purpose, e.g. at someone; not benefit, but possibly injure, the living focus, if any; communicate meaningfully by raps, etc.;

generate collectively perceived phantasms; produce mediumistic trances in the supposed living agent; be localized around a person *or* a place; centre round an adult *or* an adolescent; and be discouraged by exorcism. Having a discarnate agent in the house is thus like having an invisible person there; one can see what he does and why he does it, but not how he does it.

The main line of demarcation here is that phenomena centring around living agents are thought of as lacking in intelligence and purpose, as being a mere blind letting-off of steam; while phenomena originating from discarnate agents are thought of as being intelligent and as being purposive in characteristic ways. This appears to us a somewhat debatable way of separating the two classes of case. The totally blind and purposeless poltergeist is perhaps a rarity even among obvious 'living agent' cases. If there are indeed both living agent cases and discarnate agent cases we should surely expect, not the *absence* of intelligence and purpose in the former, but different kinds of purposes and different degrees of intelligence in the two sorts of case. To this point we will shortly revert.

For the moment we want to return to chapter 12, and consider again the five 'stable' clusters of cases which remained after fusion 10 of the cluster analysis therein described. It will be recalled that fusion of these residual clusters proved much more 'stressful' than any of the earlier fusions. Clusters 2 and 4 of the post-fusion 10 group were combined to yield a category approximating to the final cluster 2 (hauntings); clusters 1, 3 and 5 went to make up (most of) the final cluster 1 (poltergeists). A glance at Table III (pp. 236–8) will show that most of the putative 'discarnate entity' cases belong in either cluster 2 or cluster 3. These clusters are far and away the richest in cases of 'communication', and of the ostensible influence of 'daemons' and deceased persons. Curiously enough cluster 3 – relatively poor in person-centred cases, relatively rich in cases of carrying of objects through the air, of assault on the agent, of ESP, apports, 'matter through matter', raps, communication, phantasms and other manifestations of intelligence and purpose – corresponds fairly closely (but with some differences) to Stevenson's 'discarnate agent' category. It should be noted that, though Stevenson clearly thinks of deceased human beings as the only likely discarnate agents, his criteria are not such as to distinguish deceased human beings from other supposed classes of discarnate agents. Clusters 1 and 5 – the remaining 'poltergeist' clusters – together correspond to Stevenson's 'living agent' class. Both are low on 'carried objects', assault, and all forms of communication.

How simple it would be if at this point we could say: cluster 3 is a clearly marked cluster, and corresponds to Stevenson's 'discarnate agent' class; clusters 1 and 5 are clearly marked clusters and correspond to Stevenson's 'living agent' class; the problem is solved, his distinction is a valid one! Of course we cannot say anything as straightforward as this, and Stevenson would not say it either. In the first place it is extremely unlikely that our cluster distinctions are as yet properly drawn, or that all the cases which the cluster analysis of chapter 12 assigned to the various clusters have been correctly assigned. In the second place, why should one suppose that the 'intelligence' so often exhibited in the, admittedly often complex and bizarre, cases of cluster 3 is always that of some discarnate entity? There is, as we saw earlier in the chapter, a good deal of evidence that living agents can produce not just mere whirlwind-like explosions of energy around them, but, for example, communicative rappings through which pseudo-personalities manifest themselves. With such phenomena we move into the manifestations characteristic of cluster 3.

None the less we think that Stevenson's is an idea worth pursuing. For if it is possible that the purpose and intelligence apparent in so many poltergeists may in some instances be those of a living agent, probably with emotional problems, and sometimes that of a discarnate entity, perhaps with other sorts of problems, then we should expect the purposes manifested in the two sorts of case to be different, and the intelligence to be utilized differently. And we might also anticipate, as Stevenson suggests, that since, whatever may be the condition of discarnate entities, if there are such things, it will certainly be very different from our own, there may be characteristic differences in the physical effects which it is possible for living agents and for discarnate entities to produce.

We propose as a preliminary move that where poltergeists exhibit some degree of intelligence and ostensible purposiveness, it would be inappropriate to regard the intelligence as that of a living agent under the following circumstances:

1 If the phenomena appear either wholly, or failing that

partially, independent of the comings and goings of any particular individual; best of all if they occur in the absence of anyone whatsoever. What we refer to as 'partial independence' of a living agent would be shown if either

(a) The phenomena, though not demonstrably independent of a particular person, were demonstrably not strictly tied to the comings and goings of any particular person. For instance they might sometimes linger on for some while after his departure, occur in his absence, occur inside a locked empty room away from him, and so on. A particularly curious form of the latter is when 'arrangements' of objects into patterns are made inside empty rooms or in empty houses, i.e. when not just phenomena, but intelligent phenomena, take place in the absence of any putative agent. It is as though some intelligent entity is present which can store and make use of some form of energy even in the absence of those who may have generated it. At least fifty-four cases from the list of 500 in the Appendix exhibit one or more of the features listed under (a). Of these eighteen come from cluster 3, and eight from cluster 2, making altogether 50 per cent although these two clusters together account for only 154 out of 500 cases, and cluster 3 only for sixty-three. Perhaps the bringing of intelligently selected apports from a considerable distance, alleged to have happened in the Poona (1920) and Buhai (1925) cases should also be placed here. Or

(b) The phenomena, though fairly constant in form, pass as it were from agent to agent, as though something transferred itself from one to the other. The best example of what we have in mind is perhaps the case at Lading (1916). Here poltergeist phenomena of quite a complex kind, including communicative rappings ostensibly from deceased persons, and incipient assault, developed around a girl of eleven; after a year or so the spook transferred itself to a boy of the same age who had come with his family to visit the girl's house. A member of his family was foolish enough to invite it to do so! Similar but less marked transfers of a spook from one agent to another are alleged to have taken place in the cases at Schwartzbach (1749), Guillonville (1849), and France (1940), and a transfer from one family to another is said to have happened at Orielton (1184) and at Ponta Porã (1969). Unfortunately in none of these cases is the available testimony of the highest level. Certain cases of double agency – cases in which either one of two agents seems capable of maintaining the phenomena – may perhaps be grouped here.

2 If the purposes exhibited by the phenomena appear quite alien to the known aims and purposes of the poltergeist agent, or, in the absence of an obvious agent, of any other person in the household. Of course a difficulty here is the readiness with which living agent theorists are apt to postulate unconscious motives which are the reverse of any which the supposed agent is consciously aware of possessing. If the phenomena severely injure his person or property, then he must have unconscious guilt feelings and a desire for self-punishment; if the phenomena assume the personality and purposes of some deceased person, it is because the agent, for his own reasons, wishes him alive again; and so on. Resisting here the temptation to insert some unflattering remarks concerning all doctrines about the unconscious mind, we will confine ourselves to making the following point. A situation cannot be allowed to arise in which *any* proposal to the effect that in such and such a case the purposes exhibited and the intelligence deployed differed from those of any living person on the scene, is immediately countered by the assertion that someone present *must* unconsciously and unbeknown to himself, have cherished that aim and pursued it with that kind of intelligence. Such ploys at once put the living agent theory in the same class as the flat earth theory; in the category, that is, of theories which are propounded by their advocates in such a way that refutation is logically rather than empirically impossible. We have already commented several times on the vacuousness of such theories. The principle must be firmly propounded and adhered to that assertions that so-and-so entertained such-and-such unconscious wishes, etc., cannot be agreed to merely because they save a favourite theory from foundering. They must be supported by evidence or else withheld. On the face of it, for instance, it seems preposterous to suppose that the little boy who was the ostensible focus of the phenomena in the Poona case, at some level of his being wanted to undergo the sufferings and tribulations which the phenomena brought upon him. The same sort of remark might be made in connection with numerous other cases; including, for instance, the Nottinghamshire case which we described earlier in this chapter.

3 If on more than one occasion several witnesses simultaneously see, or failing that a series of separate witnesses not

ARE POLTERGEISTS LIVING OR ARE THEY DEAD?

knowing of each other's experiences see, the same phantasmal figure or figures, or similar misty shapes, etc., in association with, or better still actually bringing about, certain of the phenomena. For such repeated visions must surely count, in the absence of strong indications to the contrary, as evidence that something, some kind of agency other than that of a living person, is present on the scene and linked to the occurrence of the phenomena. We are not sure, however, that in any actual case the evidence for this sort of collective percipiency has been quite strong enough for the case to be reckoned as fulfilling this criterion.

4 If phenomena take place which have no certain parallel from cases which are undeniably and solely of the living agent sort; i.e. when phenomena take place which so far as is known exceed the capacities of any living agent, however powerful his repressed emotions and however saturated he may be with 'psychic force' or 'RSPK energy'. It may of course be doubted that there are any such phenomena, and in the present state of our knowledge it is almost impossible to say definitely whether or not a given phenomenon belongs in this category. So we note the point as being rather of theoretical than of immediate practical interest. Perhaps certain forms of 'apport' phenomena belong here, e.g. the ostensible 'eating' of fruit by invisible beings in the Poona (1920) case, or cases in which objects have 'materialized' in mid-air or in which 'direct voices' have spoken fluently or direct writing been received, or in which objects have become 'animated' in characteristic ways.

We have here, then, some crude and preliminary criteria by means of which we might sort out cases in which the intelligence at work may be presumed to be that of a discarnate entity from cases in which it must be assumed to be simply that of a living agent. The question now arises, are there in fact any cases which in terms of these criteria fall on the discarnate side of the line? There seem to us to be candidates both among the cases of cluster 3 and among the cases of cluster 2. For cases of cluster 3 the best we can do is refer to the main cases featured in chapter 6, the Sandfeldt (1722) and Poona (1920) cases. In one or both of these cases we have dual agency, or lack of obvious agent; the arrangement of objects in an empty room and the bringing of selected apports from a distance; deliberate persecution of persons who, on the face of it, cannot themselves have had the slightest desire, conscious or otherwise, for such sufferings; and a great variety of exceedingly unusual phenomena. In both cases phantasmal figures were seen by more than one person ostensibly producing the phenomena. Other cluster 3 cases worth studying in this connection are Stommeln (1260), Mâcon (1612), Tidworth (1662), Portsmouth (1682), Rerrick (1695), Stratford (1850), Oderwitz (1862), Iletski (1870), Madras (1872), Clarendon (1889), City of London (1901), Nidamangalam (1920), Nikolsburg (1927), and Eggenberg (1929).

Cluster 2 cases have been insufficiently exemplified in this book, so we shall briefly outline a case from this cluster which seems to fulfil the criteria with which we are at the moment concerned. In this case the phenomena were independent of the presence of any particular person. The happenings, which had a hint of purposiveness about them, severely upset the occupants of the house and certainly did not reflect any goals which they may reasonably be supposed to have entertained, whether consciously or unconsciously. Some of the phenomena – the misty figure and the child's voice – were also somewhat unusual. This case can be compared with such other cluster 2 cases as Epworth (1716), Appleby (1887), Paris (1888), Glasgow (1907), Cherbourg (1918), Leipzig (1931), Ardachie (1953) and Tydd (1957).

The case concerned is reported in the *Journal of the American SPR*, vol. 67, 1973, by Mr H. W. Pierce, a science writer on the *Pittsburgh Post-Gazette*. It was investigated by Pierce himself and by Dr R. A. McConnell, a well-known parapsychologist who is Professor of Biophysics at the University of Pittsburgh. They interviewed the witnesses, but did not themselves observe any of the phenomena.

The scene of the case, which lasted from about August 1971 to about April 1972, was a two-storey house (built April 1968) in Pittsburgh, Pennsylvania. The upstairs and downstairs of this house constituted two separate apartments. The upstairs one was occupied by an engineer, referred to as 'Ellsworth Cramer', his wife 'Naomi' (a former nurse), and their baby daughter (born January 1972). Downstairs lived 'Peter Henry', a nuclear training engineer, his wife, 'Clair', a son 'Sam', aged four, and a son 'Michael', aged eighteen months. All the adults in the house were young and were persons of intelligence and education.

The principal kinds of phenomena witnessed may be grouped as follows;

1 *The switching on and off of lights and radios.* A number of such incidents were reported. We shall cite one as a specimen. On 12 November 1971, Ellsworth Cramer stepped from the hall to an outside front 'stoop' to let the dog out about 11.00 p.m. As he did so the hall light went off. He stepped back in, and the light went on.

2 *Appearance of a white, misty figure.* Towards the end of January 1972, about midnight or later, Ellsworth Cramer woke up in a sitting position, and saw a greyish mist or cloud at the foot of his bed. It jumped up, moved to the closet door, and went through it. He kept this incident to himself.

During the early part of February 1972, Naomi Cramer 'for about 5 or 6 nights in a row' observed what she said looked like an oblong white cloud approximately four feet high in a chair at the dining room table. Naomi said she observed this late at night as she passed by the living room door from the bedroom to the bathroom, from a distance of about twenty feet. Initially she was not disturbed by it, although she was unable to explain it. 'But after the third or fourth night it began to bother me.'

Perhaps this effect was due to a street light shining through the curtains. However, on 22 April 1972, about 11.30 p.m., Naomi was alone in the house. She was in the bedroom but not yet in bed. Suddenly the dog jumped from under the bed and ran barking to the living room. 'Naomi followed and in full light for perhaps two minutes saw a dancing cloud in the middle of the room. The dog continued barking and there was a laugh, more eerie than childlike. Afterwards the dog trembled and panted as though frightened by a thunderstorm.' This incident was related to Pierce on 24 April.

Under this heading should perhaps also be placed the following two incidents.

In November 1971, about 6.00 p.m., Peter Henry, who was entering the building, saw what appeared to be a shadow on the landing inside the front entrance. 'I looked again . . . and saw that it was not a shadow. It had depth. It was three dimensional. It moved horizontally across the landing, went back into the lamp shadow, and disappeared. I went up to the landing and looked around the corner and there was no one there.' He saw the shadow from a distance of about ten feet. He did not mention this experience to any of the others until 7 February.

On 18 February 1972, about 1.00 p.m., Naomi Cramer was downstairs with Clair Henry, when she heard a thump from upstairs. Her baby began to scream. She ran upstairs, and going into the baby's room, saw what appeared to be 'a black-gray shadow dart into the baby's closet'. Clair, who had followed Naomi, did not see this form.

Also possibly relevant is the following experience. Sometime in January 1972, Clair Henry, sitting on the living room sofa about 5.00 p.m., saw a form out of the corner of her eye, and *only* out of the corner of her eye, made up of 'vertical waves'. Presumably the effect was something like that of heat shimmer. The form was about three feet high and one foot wide. See also the next paragraph.

3 *A child's laughter*. On 22 February 1972, about 10.45 p.m., Peter and Clair Henry, who were in bed, had the following curious experience. Clair felt 'a small body' get into bed between herself and her husband. Peter kicked in his sleep, and the small body left the bed. Then Clair became convinced she could see in the room the 'wave-body' just described. This was followed by the sound of things being moved around, apparently in another room, and a child's laughter – 'it was beautiful, but it scared me'. Peter also heard this laugh, which he was sure was a boy's giggle, but did not admit it at the time. They got up and combed the house. Nothing was amiss, and the children were sound asleep.

The following day, 23 February, about 5.30 a.m., Naomi Cramer, who was 'changing' the baby, heard what she described as 'childlike laughter'. It seemed to come from the baby's crib 'almost as if it was coming from in her or through her'. But the baby was definitely not laughing. The laughter was loud enough to waken her husband in the next room.

We have already described a later occasion (22 April) on which Naomi heard laughter in association with the 'misty figure'.

4 *Object-movements*. On the afternoon of 15 February 1972, Naomi Cramer had disassembled her salt and pepper shakers and had left them on the kitchen counter. She turned and walked to the telephone. She heard something fall behind her, and turned in time to see the remaining parts of the shakers flying directly towards her. They landed at her feet.

On 18 February, soon after 1.00 p.m., Naomi, who was in

Clair's apartment downstairs, heard noises above. Going up a couple of hours later she found that the kitchen chairs had been moved into new positions.

5 *Rockings of a rocking chair and a rocking horse.* In late December 1971, Peter and Clair Henry together observed a rocking chair in their living room rocking several inches up and down, steadily and without deceleration. A match was struck, but its flame revealed no air current. Peter put a hand on the chair, which slowed it down; but when he removed his hand, the rocking picked up its former pace. Clair had previously when on her own seen the chair rock for about a minute 'with a pronounced motion'.

Early in January 1972, while dusting in the children's bedroom, Clair Henry saw a small rocking horse rocking vigorously to and fro. The movements went on for about two minutes. The children were in the living room. About this period Peter Henry saw the same horse, now in a closet, rock pronouncedly. He could not remember where the children had been at the time; but clearly they were not in the closet.

About 20 February 1972, Naomi Cramer was in the rocking chair in Clair Henry's apartment downstairs, holding her baby. The rocking chair began to rock more strongly, as if it were being impelled. The force increased so much she became afraid that the baby would be thrown off, and got up.

Mr Pierce tentatively links the phenomena in this case to a mentally retarded child, who had been killed in an accident shortly before his mother had moved into the house subsequently occupied by the Cramers and Henrys. This child had lived in an institution, but was strongly attached to his mother. He was nine years old and 3'10" tall. He is described as hyperactive and aggressive and prone to nocturnal wanderings and mischief. But he had of course never lived in the house.

We may summarize our own, exceedingly tentative, assessment of the living agent and of the discarnate entity hypotheses as follows:

1 There is convincing evidence that in some poltergeist cases the intelligence at work is that of a living agent.

2 There are a few cases, both of poltergeists and of hauntings, which fulfil our proposed criteria for accepting the intelligence at work as that of a discarnate entity. We can see no

grounds for dismissing the evidence in such cases *en bloc*, and are therefore constrained to admit that in such cases it is appropriate to explore the discarnate entity hypothesis further and more fully. We put it no more strongly than this because of the extreme difficulty we experience in grasping or imagining what might be involved in this hypothesis and how it might be developed.

3 What we are talking about here is the discarnate entity hypothesis in its most general form; we are not attempting to decide whether or not the supposed discarnate entities are to be identified with surviving portions of formerly incarnate human beings. If cases come to hand which *in addition* to meeting several of the four criteria of discarnate origin listed above, presented the appearance of being initiated and guided by a putative deceased person (compare the criteria for this advanced in chapter 8), it would be appropriate also to take the deceased person hypothesis seriously. At least, it would be quite ad hoc to propose that some discarnate entity (nature unknown) was deliberately impersonating a deceased human being. However, we do not feel sure that there is as yet any case which completely fulfils these conditions. The Charlottenburg case (chapter 8) does no more than teeter on the brink.

We do not think that much further progress is likely with regard to these problems, or any of the other very numerous problems that arise in connection with poltergeist phenomena, until sustained and competent investigations have been conducted into the nature and point of origin of the physical force, or indeed quite certainly forces, at work in poltergeists and hauntings. It may seem surprising, in view of the growth during the last decade or two in the number of cases that parapsychologists have been able to investigate at first-hand, that such investigations have so far not been extensively undertaken. But of course part of the answer is that cases, and competent scientists interested in them, do not grow on trees, and that the cost of the investigations and of the necessary equipment would almost certainly be substantial. However, we have little doubt that these obstacles will be overcome in time, and that our knowledge in this area will gradually increase. For human curiosity is boundless; and the phenomena are perennial.

Addendum

Too late to be considered in the main body of this chapter, comes a most interesting report (J. D. Morris, W. G. Roll and R. L. Morris, eds, *Research in Parapsychology 1976*, Metuchen, N.J., 1977, pp. 13–15) by J. F. McHarg of a case in which he was called in as consultant psychiatrist. Violent poltergeist phenomena centred round two boys, aged fifteen and eleven, who lived with their parents in the upstairs part of a Glasgow house. The phenomena lasted from August or September 1974 until about May 1975. They included communicative rappings which spelled out a good deal of alleged information about the younger days of an elderly gentleman who lived in the downstairs part of the house, together with ridiculous messages of incitement to strangle him. The rappings also beat out the rhythm of the Dead March. There were no indications of fraud. The boys also exhibited certain bodily effects resembling those said to occur in cases of ostensible possession. The phenomena ceased quite abruptly about the time of the elderly gentleman's death, and it was afterwards discovered that their course had in all probability coincided quite closely with the course of a malignant tumour from which he died. Dr McHarg remarks: 'The ultimate origin and significance of the frank death wishes which were ostensibly communicated remain, so far, conjectural'. So far as the arguments of the present chapter are concerned one could look at the matter in one of two ways. One might suppose that the death wishes were those of the old gentleman, and that they simply found expression through the mediumship of the poltergeist agents who happened to be on the spot. This might be held, by showing that the intelligence exhibited in poltergeist cases may sometimes be that of a person other than the poltergeist agent, to make the discarnate agency theory seem more plausible for certain cases. Or one might suppose that the boys bore a grudge against the old gentleman (there was an antagonism between the two families), and that becoming aware that all was not well with him they unconsciously gave vent, through the poltergeist phenomena, to a crow of triumph at his imminent demise. However, Dr McHarg states: 'I did not find anything suggestive of fraud, neurosis or psychosis in the affected family'. It is to be hoped that more details of this briefly reported case will be made available.

Appendix to Part I
Chronological list of 500 cases, with sources and case characteristics

The following list is of the cases subjected to statistical analysis in chapter 12, and has to be read in the light of background information given there. It does not purport to be anything like comprehensive, or to give complete and formal bibliographical information for each case. Its aims are firstly to enable anyone interested in any particular case to find the original printed sources, and secondly to provide persons interested in doing statistical analyses of their own with data to work on. In this last connection, it should be noted that since the cluster analysis described in chapter 12 was carried out some minor corrections (too few to have any serious bearing on the outcome of the analysis) have been made. They are incorporated in the data given below, and also in table I of chapter 12. All involved errors of omission (characteristics 18, 23, 25, 34, 39 and 41 were respectively omitted from cases 114, 125, 143 and 300, 279, 460 and 96), and it is not improbable that there are other errors of omission (I did not finalize the list of characteristics to be especially noted until I had done an appreciable percentage of the reading). I hope that errors of commission, though not of course impossible, will not be too numerous.

Each case entry is laid out as follows:

Case number. Country, location of first phenomenon. Date(s), (duration). Post-fusion 10 cluster to which the case was assigned, post-fusion 13 cluster to which the case was assigned (similarity with post-fusion 13 cluster 1, similarity with post-fusion 13 cluster 2). Source(s). Rating of testimony on scale 1–10, rating of detail on scale 1–5; characteristics from list of sixty-three in chapter 12 exhibited by the case in question.

In listing sources, the following abbreviations are used:

Aksakoff = Aksakoff, A., *Vorläufer des Spiritismus* (Leipzig, 1898).
Annales = *Annales des sciences psychiques*.
Annals = *Annals of Psychical Science*.
Ashton = Ashton, J., *The Devil in Britain and America* (London, 1896).
Aubrey = Aubrey, J., *Miscellanies upon various Subjects* [1696] (London, 1890).
Baxter = Baxter, R., *The Certainty of the Worlds of Spirits* (London, 1691).
Bayless = Bayless, R., *The Enigma of the Poltergeist* (West Nyack, 1967).

Beaumont = Beaumont, J., *A Treatise of Spirits* (London, 1705).
Bender = Bender, H., *Telepathie, Hellsehen und Psychokinese* (Munich, 1972).
Blätter = *Blätter aus Prevorst.*
Bodin = Bodin, J., *De la demonomanie des sorciers* [1580] (Paris, 1582).
Bovet = Bovet, R., *Pandaemonium* [1684] (London, 1951).
Britten = Britten, Emma Hardinge, *Nineteenth Century Miracles* (New York, 1884).
Buchner = Buchner, E., *Medien, Hexen und Geisterseher* (Munich, 1926).
Burr = Burr, G. L., *Narratives of the Witchcraft Cases* (New York, 1972).
Calmet = Calmet, A., *Traité sur les apparitions des anges, des démons, et des esprits* (3rd edn, Paris, 1751), tr. by H. Christmas as *The Phantom World* (2 vols, London, 1850).
Carrington and Fodor = Carrington, H., and Fodor, N., *The Story of the Poltergeist down the Centuries* (London, 1953).
Crowe = Crowe, Catherine, *The Night Side of Nature* (2 vols, London, 1849).
De Mirville = De Mirville, J. E., *Pneumatologie: des esprits et de leurs manifestations fluidiques* (vol. I, Paris, 1854).
Dufresnoy = Dufresnoy, N. Lenglet, *Recueil de dissertations* (2 vols, Avignon and Paris, 1752–1).
Du Plessis = Du Plessis, I. D., *Poltergeists of the South* (Cape Town, 1966).
Flammarion = Flammarion, C., *Haunted Houses* (London, 1924).
Glanvill = Glanvill, J., *Saducismus Triumphatus* [1681] (London, 1682).
Görres = Görres, J. von, *Die christliche Mystik* [1836–42] (Regensburg, n.d.).
Guazzo = Guazzo, N. F., *Compendium maleficarum* [1608], tr. M. Summers (London, 1929).
Hauber = Hauber, E. D., *Bibliotheca acta et scripta magica* (3 vols, Lemgo, 1738–45).
Horst = Horst, G. C., *Zauber-Bibliothek* (6 vols, Mainz, 1821–6).
IJP = *International Journal of Parapsychology.*
JASPR = *Journal of the American Society for Psychical Research.*
JSPR = *Journal of the Society for Psychical Research.*
Kerner = Kerner, J., *Revelations of the Invisible World*, tr. C. Crowe (London, 1847).
Lambert = Lambert, R. S., *Exploring the Supernatural* (London, 1955).
Lang (*Cock Lane*) = Lang, A., *Cock Lane and Common-Sense* (new edn, London, 1896).

Lang (*Dreams and Ghosts*) = Lang, A., *The Book of Dreams and Ghosts* (London, 1897).
Lea = Lea, H. C., *Materials towards a History of Witchcraft* (3 vols, New York, 1957).
Mahan = Mahan, A., *Modern Mysteries* (Boston, 1855).
Mather = Mather, I., *An Essay for the Recording of Illustrious Providences* [1684] (London, 1890).
Moor = Moor, E., *Bealings Bells* (Woodbridge, 1841).
More = More, H., *A Continuation of the Collection*, in Glanvill, J., *Saducismus Triumphatus* (London, 1682).
Moser = Moser, Fanny, *Spuk: Irrglaube oder Wahrglaube?* (Baden bei Zürich, 1950).
Owen = Owen, A. R. G., *Can we explain the Poltergeist?* (New York, 1964).
Perty = Perty, M., *Die mystischen Erscheinungen der menschlichen Natur* (2nd edn, 2 vols, Leipzig and Heidelberg, 1872).
Playfair = Playfair, G., *The Flying Cow* (London, 1975).
Price = Price, H., *Poltergeist over England* (London, 1945).
PASPR = *Proceedings of the American Society for Psychical Research*.
PPA = *Proceedings of the Parapsychological Association*.
PSPR = *Proceedings of the Society for Psychical Research*.
PS = *Psychic Science*.
PSt = *Psychische Studien*.
Puls = Puls, —, *Spuk-Geschichten: der Spuk von Resau u.a.* (Berlin, 1889).
Remy = Remy, N., *Demonolatry* [1595], tr. M. Summers (London, 1930).
Robbins = Robbins, R. H., *The Encyclopedia of Witchcraft and Demonology* (London, 1959).
Roll = Roll, W. G., *The Poltergeist* (paper edn, New York, 1974).
Schrenck-Notzing = Schrenck-Notzing, A. von, *Gesammelte Aufsätze zur Parapsychologie* (Stuttgart, 1929).
Sinclar = Sinclar, G., *Satan's Invisible World Discovered* [1685] (Edinburgh, 1871).
Sinistrari = Sinistrari, L. M., *Demoniality* [written c. 1700], tr. M. Summers (London, n.d. [1927]).
Sitwell = Sitwell, S., *Poltergeists* (London, 1940).
Spicer = Spicer, H., *Sights and Sounds* (London, 1853).
SM = *Spiritual Magazine*.
Stead = Stead, W. T., *More Ghost Stories* (London, 1892).
Thurston = Thurston, H., *Ghosts and Poltergeists* (London, 1953).
Tizané = Tizané, E., *Sur la piste de l'homme inconnu* (Paris, 1951).
Williams = Williams, J. J., *Psychic Phenomena of Jamaica* (New York, 1934).

ZfP = *Zeitschrift für Parapsychologie*.

Where the title of a book is immediately followed by a date in square brackets, the date is that of the first edition of the book concerned as distinct from that of the edition which I have actually used. Sources which are given in square brackets are ones which I have not myself been able to consult.

1 Italy, Ravenna. AD 530. 1, 1(0.0950, 0.1494). *Acta Sanctorum* 27 Aug., p. 70; Krusch, B. (ed.), *Monumenta Germaniae Historica: Scriptores Rerum Merovingicarum* III (Hanover, 1896), p. 473; Thurston, pp. 187-8. 1, 1; 1 16 48.
2 Turkey (N.W.). About 609. 1, 1(0.0950, 0.1494). *Acta Sanctorum* Apr. 22nd, p. 58. 1, 1; 1 16 48.
3 Netherlands, Friesland. Before 738. 1, 1 (0.1534, 0.1879). Alcuin, *Vita Sancti Willibrordi* in Wattenbach, W., and Dümmler, E. (eds), *Monumenta Alcuiniana* (Berlin, 1873), p. 55; Thurston, p. 188. 1, 1; 1 19 28 42.
4 W. Germany, Kempten nr. Bingen. 856-8. 1, 2(0.2334, 0.2274). *Rudolfi Fuldenses Annales* in Pertz, G. H. (ed.), *Monumenta Germaniae Historica: Scriptorum Tomus I* (Stuttgart, 1963), p. 372; Lea I, p. 100. 2, 1; 1 7 16 21 23 28 43 48 49.
5 China. About 900. 1, 1(0.2026, 0.2708). Dingwall, E. J., *Ghosts and Spirits in the Ancient World* (London, 1930), pp. 63-4. 1, 1; 2 16 36 49 55.
6 Turkey, Istanbul. About 1100 (one night). 1, 1(0.0573, 0.1160). Owen, pp. 402-4. 1, 1; 1 6 9 16.
7 France, Le Mans. 1135-1144 (within). 2, 2(0.2430, 0.1957). Mabillon, J., *Vetera Analecta* (Paris, 1723), p. 326; Calmet I, pp. 284-5. 1, 1; 1 6 9 19 21 22 23 28 44 46 62.
8 England, Durham (vicinity). 1137-1149 (within). 1, 1(0.1111, 0.1671). *Surtees Society* 20, 1845, pp. 93-5. 1, 1; 1 6 9 16 23 63.
9 England, Orielton, Pembrokeshire. About 1184. 1, 1(0.1470, 0.1824). Giraldus Cambrensis, *Itinerarium Kambriae* [written about 1191] in J. F. Dimock (ed.) *Opera* (London, 1868), pp. 93-4; Thurston, p. 7. 1, 1; 1 16 23 36 43.
10 England, Dagworth, Suffolk. 1189-1199 (within). 1, 2(0.1454, 0.1348). Radulph de Coggeshale, *Chronicon Anglicanum*, ed. J. Stevenson (London, 1875), pp. 120-1; Thurston, p. 190. 1, 1; 1 19 23 24.
11 France, Paris? Early thirteenth century. 1, 2(0.1913, 0.1815). William of Auvergne, *De Universo* [written about 1225] in *Opera Omnia* (Orleans, 1674), p. 1030; Binsfeld, P., *Tractatus de Confessionibus* (Treves, 1621), pp. 92-3. 2, 1; 1 9 10 13 16 22 35 42.

12 France, Paris? Early thirteenth century. 1, 1(0.0760, 0.1453). William of Auvergne, *op. cit.*, p. 1030; Binsfeld, P., *op. cit.*, p. 93. 2, 1; 1 11 16.
13 France, Epinal. About 1212. 1, 1(0.2280, 0.2415). Calmet I, pp. 279–80. 1, 1; 1 19 23 33 36 44 46.
14 W. Germany, Stommeln, nr. Cologne. c. 1260–c. 1286. 3, 1(0.3818, 0.4202). Thurston, H., *Surprising Mystics* (London, 1955), pp. 1–26. 3, 2; 1 7 8 9 11 13 16 18 24 28 29 35 36 39 42 49 62.
15 France, Alais. 1323 (17 Dec.)–1324 (about Easter). 2, 2(0.1882, 0.0516). Gobius, J., *De Spiritu Gwidonis . . . satis horribilis historia* (Cologne, 1496); Thurston, pp. 53–60. 5, 3; 1 5 6 9 19 22 23 27 44 46.
16 France, Lagny. 1330. 1, 1(0.1393, 0.1420). Calmet I, pp. 282–3. 1, 1; 1 23 43.
17 W. Germany, Eistett, nr. Nuremberg. 1414–1418 (within; about a year). 4, 2(0.1882, 0.0516). Nider, J., *Formicarius* [1475; written about 1435] (Douai) 1602, pp. 344–5. 1, 1; 1 7 9 21 22 23 24.
18 W. Germany, Nuremberg. About 1425. 2, 2(0.1315, 0.0883). Nider, J., *op. cit.*, pp. 344–5. 1, 1; 1 9 22 39.
19 France, Poitiers. 1447. 1, 1(0.1099, 0.1717). Mamor, P., *Flagellum Maleficarum* [1490; written about 1465] in *Malleus Maleficarum* (Lyons, 1669) III, p. 144; Bodin, Book 3, f. 158^v. 1, 1; 1 16 19 48.
20 Location not given. About 1450. 2, 2(0.1261, 0.0973). A Spina, Alphonsus, *Fortalitium Fidei* [1467; written about 1459] (Lyons, 1511), f. 162^r–f. 162^v. 3, 1; 1 6 9 22 27.
21 France, Confolens. 1458. 1, 1(0.1575, 0.1596). Mamor, P., *op. cit.*, (see 19), pp. 144–5; Bodin, Book 3, f. 157^v, f. 164^v–f. 165^r. 1, 1; 1 23 44 46.
22 Italy, Milan. About 1464. 2, 2(0.1571, 0.1155). Cardan, J., *De Rerum Varietate* (Basle, 1557), pp. 661–2; Lang (*Dreams and Ghosts*), pp. 288–91. 1, 1; 1 9 15 21 61.
23 Italy, Rome. About 1500? 4, 2(0.1998, 0.0761). Alexander ab Alexandro, *Genialium Dierum* [1523] (Frankfort, 1594), p. 775. 3, 1; 1 9 15 17 21 22 23 24.
24 E. Germany, Wartburg. 1521. 2, 2(0.0965, 0.0794). Scheretzius, S., *Libellus Consolatorius de Spectris* (Wittemberg, 1621), B3^r–B4^r. 3, 1; 1 6 9 22.
25 France, Lyons. 1525 (late)–1526 (21 March). 5, 1(0.2721, 0.3050). See chapter 2. 4, 2; 1 6 8 9 11 12 21 23 24 42 43 44 46 48.
26 Switzerland, Schiltach. 1533 (April; one day). 1, 1(0.2033, 0.2543). Erasmus, D., *Opus Epistolarum* X, ed. H. M. Allen and H. W. Garrod (London, 1941), p. 275; Remy, pp. 134–5; Görres III, pp. 401–2. 2, 1; 1 6 11 13 23 28 42 44.

27 France, Orleans. 1534 (February). 2, 1(0.1575, 0.1699). Dufresnoy I, pp. 91–130; Wier (Weyer), J., *Histoires, disputes et discours* [1579] (Paris, 1885) II, pp. 139–43; Lavater, L., *De Spectris* [1570] (Geneva, 1580), pp. 35–9; Lang (*Cock Lane*), pp. 114–17; Lea II, pp. 519–20. 2, 1; 1 3 6 9 21 44 46.

28 E. Germany, Süptitz nr. Torgau. 1537–8 (at least a year). 1, 2(0.1183, 0.1047). Luther, M., *Table Talk*, ed. and tr. T. G. Tappert and H. T. Lehmann (Philadelphia, 1967), pp. 279–80; Scheretzius, S., *op. cit.* (see 24.), C5^r; Lea I, p. 420. 2, 1; 1 7 9 16 23.

29 Spain, Salamanca. About 1540. 1, 1(0.0985, 0.1894). Torquemada, A. de, *Jardin de Flores Curiosas* [1573] (Madrid, 1955), f. 130^v–f. 131^v; Eng. tr., *The Spanish Mandevile of Miracles* (London, 1600), f. 78^v–f. 79^v; Remy, p. 82. 3, 2; 1 5 6 16 56.

30 Italy, Loreto. About 1545? 2, 2(0.2075, 0.1429). Görres III, pp. 420–1. 2, 1; 1 21 22 24 39 44 48.

31 Peru, Pirsa, 1549 (some days). 1, 1(0.2375, 0.3442). C. R. Markham, ed., *The Travels of Pedro de Cieza de Leon* (Hakluyt Society, 1864), pp. 415–18; Lang, A. in Kirk, R., *The Secret Commonwealth* (Stirling, 1933), pp. 121–2. 1, 1; 2 6 8 9 10 12 14 16 24 30 42.

32 France, Toulouse, 1557. 1, 1(0.0684, 0.1479). Bodin, Book 3, f. 158^r–f. 158^v; Garinet, J., *Histoire de la magie en France* (Paris, 1818), pp. 123–4. 2, 1; 1 16.

33 France, Colombiers nr. Toul. About 1560. 1, 1(0.0921, 0.1479). Remy, p. 82. 2, 1; 1 16 28.

34 France, Auch. About 1563 (one day). 1, 1(0.0878, 0.1409). Remy, pp. 82–3. 3, 1; 1 6 9 16 54.

35 France, Colmar, Lorraine. About 1575 ('a long time'). 1, 1(0.0954, 0.1534). Remy, pp. 133–4. 2, 1; 1 8 9 16 28.

36 Italy, Bologna. 1579 ('some weeks'). 5, 1(0.1420, 0.2690). Menghi, G., *Compendio dell'arte essorcistica* (Bologna, 1582), pp. 513–14; Sinistrari, pp. xxxv–xxxvi. 2, 1; 1 6 11 12 16 36 39 48.

37 France, Tours. 1580? 2, 2(0.1054, 0.0909). Le Loyer, P., *Discours, et histoires des spectres* (Paris, 1605), pp. 659–79; Mackay, C., *Memoirs of Extraordinary Popular Delusions* (London, 1852) II, p. 221. 1, 1; 1 16 17 21 22.

38 Italy, Bologna. 1580. 5, 1(0.0744, 0.1982). Menghi, G., *op. cit.*, (see 36), pp. 514–16; Sinistrari, p. xxxvi. 2, 1; 1 6 11 12 16 17.

39 E. Germany, Tuttelstadt nr. Erfurt. 1581 (28 Feb.–28 Apr.). 3, 1(0.2158, 0.3171). See chapter 2; also Puls, pp. 114–18 (inaccurate). 5, 3; 1 5 6 8 9 16 17 20 39 40 50 60.

40 USSR, Riga. 1583. 1, 1(0.1532, 0.1890). Guazzo, p. 201; Del Rio, M., *Disquisitionum Magicarum* [1599] (Cologne, 1657), pp. 1117–18. 1, 1; 1 16 17 24 48 60.

41 W. Germany, Würzburg. 1583 (probably several weeks). 1, 1(0.1330, 0.1864). Guazzo, pp. 199–200. 1, 1; 1 16 17 48 57.
42 Italy, Trapani, Sicily. 1585 ('some months'). 1, 1(0.1414, 0.2150). Guazzo, pp. 202–203. 1, 1; 1 6 16 18 23 44 48.
43 Peru, location not given. 1590 (Aug.–Oct.). 1, 1(0.1523, 0.2187). Guazzo, pp. 68–70. 2, 1; 2 6 16 24 46.
44 England, N. Aston, nr. Banbury. 1591 (Nov. 19)–1592 (Easter). 3, 1(0.2631, 0.3024). See chapter 2. 5, 3; 1 5 6 8 9 16 19 20 22 25 27 28 35 44.
45 France, Bordeaux. About 1595. 4, 2(0.1930, 0.1414). Lancre, P. de, *L'incredulité et mescréance du sortilège* (Paris, 1622), pp. 817–18. 2, 1; 1 17 22 24 35 38.
46 France, Mâcon. 1612 (14 Sep.–22 Dec.). 3, 2(0.3704, 0.3364). Perreaud, F., *The Divell of Mascon* (3rd edn, Oxford, 1659); Thurston, pp. 39–50; Baxter, pp. 18–20. 4, 3; 1 6 8 9 16 21 22 23 24 29 33 35 39 40 43 44 53 56.
47 W. Germany, Oppenheim. 1620 (Nov.)–1622 (Jan.). 4, 2(0.2386, 0.1485). See chapter 8. 2, 2; 1 7 21 22 23 44 46 48.
48 France, Bonneval. 1625. 5, 1(0.1754, 0.2396). Dufresnoy I, pp. 167–77. 1, 1; 1 8 9 11 12 19 27 60.
49 Scotland, nr. Edinburgh. About 1635. 2, 2(0.1336, 0.0742). Baxter, pp. 85–7. 2, 1; 1 9 19 21 22.
50 W. Germany, Gottingen. 1636 (Jan.). 2, 2(0.1648, 0.1233). Horst VI, pp. 249–56. 6, 1; 1 3 5 6 9 21 22 23.
51 England, Bristol. About 1638. 2, 2(0.1176, 0.0761). Bovet, pp. 99–101. 1, 1; 1 9 17 22.
52 Scotland, Botarie, Strathbogie. 1644 (c. Feb.; 20 nights.). 1, 1(0.0839, 0.1442). *Extracts from the Presbytery Book of Strathbogie* (Aberdeen, 1843), pp. 50–51; Owen, p. 49. 4, 1; 1 6 9 16 47.
53 England, Plaistow, Essex. 1645. 3, 1(0.2822, 0.3270). *Strange and Fearfull Newes from Plaistoe* (London, 1645); Glanvill, Relation xx. 2, 3; 1 8 16 17 18 21 23 30 36 39 42 47 53.
54 England, Lutterworth. 1646 (Feb.; at least 3 weeks). 1, 1(0.0915, 0.1460). Baxter, p. 42. 2, 1; 1 8 16 23.
55 England, Woodstock. 1649 (16 Oct.–1 Nov.). 2, 2(0.2208, 0.2053). *The Just Devil of Woodstock* (London, 1660); repr. Ashton, pp. 28–46, and in Introduction to Scott's *Woodstock*; Hone, W. *The Every Day Book* (London, 1878) II, pp. 291–5; Aubrey, p. 84; Owen, pp. 33–45. 5, 3; 1 6 9 16 17 22 24 30 35 57 63.
56 E. Germany, Sebnitz nr. Dresden. 1654 (Mar.; several days). 5, 1(0.1639, 0.2569). Wilischius, J., *Sebnitzer Polter-Geist* (Dresden, 1654). 5, 1; 1 5 6 8 9 11 13 16 17 23 55.
57 Scotland, Glenluce, Galloway. 1654 (c. Nov.)–1656 (c. Sep.). 3, 1(0.4511, 0.4606). Sinclar, pp. 75–94; More, Relation iii;

Chambers, R., *Domestic Annals of Scotland* (London, 1861) II, pp. 228–32. 3, 3; 1 7 9 10 12 15 16 19 23 28 35 36 39 44 45 47 48 60 61.

58 Wales, Gower, Glamorgan. 1655. 4, 2(0.3032, 0.1867). Baxter, pp. 20–36. 2, 2; 1 9 21 22 23 24 39 42 51 57 63.

59 Poland, Torun (Thorn). 1655 (3 months). 1, 1(0.0779, 0.1798). Perty, M., *Blicke in das verborgene Leben des Menschengeistes* (Leipzig and Heidelberg, 1869), p. 122. 1, 1; 1 6 8 16 39.

60 England, Welton nr. Daventry. 1658 (about May). 1, 1(0.1443, 0.1978). Glanvill, Relation xxii. 3, 2; 1 6 16 21 32 35 47.

61 Wales, Blethvaugh, Radnor. 1659. 1, 1(0.1433, 0.1952). Glanvill, Advertisement to Relation xxiii. 2, 1; 1 16 18 19 23 39.

62 W. Germany, Maulbronn. 1659 (12 Aug.)–1660. 3, 1(0.2876, 0.2888). *Blätter* 5, 1834, pp. 142–7; Crowe II, p. 238. 1, 3; 1 5 8 9 16 17 18 22 24 25 28 35 38 40.

63 England, Brightling, Sussex. 1659 (7–15 Nov.). 5, 1(0.1709, 0.3097). Baxter, pp. 54–7; Mather, pp. 134–9. 5, 2; 1 3 6 8 9 11 12 14 16 28 47.

64 Sweden, Altuna, Upland. 1660 (24 Jan.–21 Feb.). 3, 1(0.2029, 0.2037). *SM* 6, 1865, pp. 108–9. 2, 2; 1 6 8 9 16 17 22 23 24 28 36 39.

65 Canada, Quebec. 1661 (some weeks). 5, 1(0.1641, 0.2191). Lambert, pp. 49–50. 2, 1; 1 6 11 12 16 22 24 47 49.

66 Ireland, Youghal, Cork. 1661 (Jan.–Mar.). 5, 1(0.2082, 0.3189). Glanvill, Relation vii. 5, 2; 1 6 11 12 16 19 24 39 41 42 47.

67 England, Maidenhead. 1661 (Aug.; 3 nights). 5, 2(0.2007, 0.1975). Glanvill, Relation xxiv; More, H., 'An Account of this Second Edition', in Glanvill, *op. cit.* 3, 3; 1 6 9 11 12 16 21 22 23 25 35 53.

68 England, N. Tidworth, Wilts. 1662 (Apr.)–1663 (c. Apr.). 3, 2(0.4794, 0.3869). See chapter 3. 5, 3; 1 7 9 16 17 18 22 23 24 25 27 35 39 40 42 44 47 53 62 63.

69 Hungary?, Kabsdorff. 1666 (July–Sep.). 2, 1(0.1622, 0.1850). Hauber III, pp. 541–53; Perty II, pp. 94–5. 3, 3; 1 6 9 16 17 18 22 50 57.

70 W. Germany, Aub. 1666 (Christmas)–1667 (Jan.). 1, 1(0.1152, 0.1534). Buchner, pp. 297–9. 2, 1; 1 6 8 9 16 21 24 48.

71 England, Kinton, Worcs. 1667 ('the latter end'). 2, 1(0.1441, 0.1471). Baxter, pp. 71–3. 2, 1; 1 6 8 9 16 21 24 48.

72 England, Burton, Herefordshire. 1669 (autumn; several months). 2, 2(0.2860, 0.2127). *The Daemon of Burton* (London, 1671); repr. Ashton, pp. 60–4. 1, 2; 1 9 15 17 19 21 22 25 33 47 59.

73 Scotland, Galashiels. About 1670. 5, 2(0.1569, 0.1348). Sinclar, pp. 200–2. 1, 1; 1 9 11 12 21 22 42.

74 Italy, Pavia. About 1670 ('a number of years'). 1, 1(0.1796, 0.2040). Sinistrari. pp. 14–21. 1, 2; 1 9 11 12 21 22 42.

APPENDIX TO PART I 371

75 Scotland, Keppoch, Ross and Cromarty. 1670 (8 days). 1, 1(0.0684, 0.1204). Crowe II, p. 235. 1, 1; 1 16.
76 England, London. 1674 (Mar. or Apr.; a few days). 1, 2(0.1757, 0.1659). *Strange and Wonderful News from London-Wall* (London, 1674). 5, 2; 1 19 22 36 48.
77 England, Lolworth, Cambs. 1676 (c. Feb.)–1677 (Oct.). 4, 2(0.1712, 0.0791). See chapter 3. 5, 2; 1 19 22 36 48.
78 England, Little Burton, Somerset. 3, 1(0.2317, 0.2323). Glanvill, Relation xxiii. 3, 3; 1 6 9 16 17 18 19 21 22 34 35 39 61.
79 Ireland, Dublin. 1678 ('about three months'). 5, 1(0.1235, 0.1743). Baxter, pp. 218–20. 2, 1; 1 6 9 11 12 21 48.
80 England, Little Minories, London. About 1679 (c. 6 weeks). 2, 2(0.1730, 0.1340). Glanvill, Advertisement to Relation xxiv. 2, 1; 1 6 21 22 23 44 46.
81 England, Leicestershire. 1679. 5, 1(0.1323, 0.1805). Ewen, C. L'Estrange, *Witchcraft and Demonianism* (London, 1933), p. 459. 2, 1; 1 3 11 12 21.
82 England, Leasingham, Lincs. 1679 (May) and 1680 (May–16 Oct.). 4, 2(0.2094, 0.1147). More, Relation v; Trollope, E., *Sleaford and the Wapentakes of Flaxwell and Aswardhurn* (London, 1872), pp. 266ff. 5, 3; 1 7 9 17 21 22 47 54.
83 USA, Newbury (Newburyport), Mass. 1679 (27 Nov.)–1680 (early summer?). 3, 2(0.4510, 0.4366). Mather, pp. 101–11; Burr, pp. 23–32; Coffin, J., *History of Newbury* (Boston, 1845), pp. 122–34. 5, 3; 1 3 6 8 9 16 17 19 20 21 22 23 24 35 39 40 41 42 47 57 61 62.
84 Scotland, Peaston, E. Lothian. About 1680 (winter; 'eight or nine weeks') 1, 1(0.1464, 0.2272). Sinclar, pp. 144–54. 2, 2; 1 6 9 10 12 16 18 24 46.
85 England, Ewell. 1681 (c. Oct.; a few days?). 5, 1(0.1513, 0.2598). Ewen, C. L'Estrange, *op. cit.* (see 81), pp. 363–4; *Strange and Wonderful News from Yowel in Surry* (London, 1681); repr. Ashton, pp. 64–8; *An Account of the Tryal and Examination of Joan Buts* (London, 1682). 5, 2; 1 6 11 12 16 19 24 39 47.
86 USA, Salmon Falls, Berwick, Maine. 1682 (June–at least Aug.). 1, 1(0.1682, 0.2018). Mather, pp. 116–18; Burr, pp. 37–38. 3, 2; 1 6 11 13 16 19 22 24 39.
87 USA, Portsmouth, N. H. 1682 (11 June–early Sep.). 3, 2(0.3127, 0.3063). [Chamberlain, R.] *Lithobolia* (London, 1698); Mather, pp. 114–16, 133; Burr, pp. 34–7, 58–77; Thurston, pp. 125–35. 5, 4; 1 6 8 9 16 17 18 19 21 22 23 24 29 32 47 59 61.
88 England, Spreyton, Devon. 1682 (Nov.)–1683 (Easter). 5, 1(0.2018, 0.3156). Bovet, pp. 107–13; Aubrey, pp. 142–8. 3, 3; 1 6 10 11 12 16 17 24 34 36 42.
89 USA, Hartford, Conn. 1683. 1, 1(0.1464, 0.2506). Mather, pp. 112–14. Burr, pp. 33–34. 3, 2; 1 6 8 9 10 13 16 18 28.

90 USA, Hadley, Mass. 1684 (winter). 2, 2(0.2330, 0.2109). Mather, C., *Memorable Providences, relating to Witchcrafts and Possessions* (Boston, 1689); Burr, pp. 131–4. 2, 1; 1 6 17 19 21 22 25 27 39 47.

91 USA, Boston. 1688 (summer)–1689 (Spring?). 5, 1(0.1940, 0.2925. Mather, C., *op cit.*; Burr, pp. 99–131. 5, 1; 1 6 8 9 11 12 39 41 42 47.

92 W. Germany, Döttingen. 1689. 2, 2(0.1436, 0.1054). Francisci, E., *Der Höllischer Proteus* (Nuremberg, 1708), pp. 1081–110); Görres III, pp. 389–90, 398–9. 5, 3; 1 19 22 24.

93 England, London. About 1690 (probably several years). 1, 1(0.2084, 0.2429). Baxter, pp. 60–2. 3, 1; 1 5 7 10 12 14 16 18 21.

94 E. Germany, Annaberg. 1691 (3 Aug.–3 Oct.). 3, 1(0.2560, 0.2925). Zobel, E., *Historische und theologische Vorstellung des abentheurlichen Gespenstes* (Leipzig, 1692); [Zobel E., *Declaratio apologetica oder Schutz-schaftliche und fernere Erklärung über das St. Annabergische Gespenster-historie* (Leipzig, 1695)]; *ZfP*, 1934, pp. 16–21; Buchner, pp. 323–6; Hauber III, pp. 343–8. 5, 3; 1 3 5 6 8 9 11 12 16 17 19 21 22 23 24 28 61.

95 USA, Boston. 1692 (summer)–1693 (at.least 16 Mar.). 5, 1(0.2328, 0.2448). Mather, C., *A Brand Pluck'd out of the Burning* [written 1693]; in Burr, pp. 259–87. 5, 1; 1 6 8 9 11 12 19 21 22 24 39 41 47.

96 USA, Boston. 1693 (10 Sep.–Oct.; over 5 weeks). 5, 1(0.2059, 0.2250). Calef, R., *More Wonders of the Invisible World* [1700] (Boston, 1828), pp. 17–42; Burr, pp. 307–23, 337–8. 6, 3; 1 6 11 12 22 24 25 39 41 42.

97 England, Cambridge. 1694 (about May; at least 2 weeks). 2, 1(0.0779, 0.0892). *Surtees Society* 54, 1870, pp. 39–42, 45; Owen, pp. 45–7. 2, 1; 1 6 9 16 22.

98 Scotland, Rerrick. 1695 (mid-Feb.–1 May). 3, 1(0.4744, 0.4841). See chapter 9. 6, 4; 1 6 9 16 17 18 19 21 23 24 27 28 29 33 39 40 42 44 49 55 60 61.

99 Italy, Naples. 1696 (4 May)–1697 (20 Mar.). 3, 1(0.6020, 0.6316). See chapter 9. 5, 3; 1 6 8 9 10 12 16 17 18 19 22 23 24 25 28 33 34 35 39 44 45 50 53 54 55 57 60 62.

100 Scotland, Bargarran, Renfrew. 1696 (Aug.)–1697 (Mar.). 5, 1(0.2014, 0.3072). *A History of the Witches of Renfrewshire* [1698] (Paisley, 1877). 5, 2; 1 6 8 9 11 12 16 23 25 28 41 42.

101 England, Bath (near). About 1700 (at least a week). 2, 2(0.1034, 0.0913). Beaumont, p. 312. 2, 1; 1 6 9 21 24.

102 W. Germany, Pfedelbach nr. Heilbronn. 1703–1708 (approx.). 3, 2(0.3026, 0.2974). Horst IV, pp. 245–59; *Blätter* 5, 1834, pp. 131–47. 3, 3; 1 7 9 10 11 13 16 17 19 22 25 36 39 62.

103 England, Butley nr. Glastonbury. About 1704 ('a long time'). 1,

APPENDIX TO PART I   373

1(0.1459, 0.2598). Beaumont, p. 306. 2, 1; 1 8 10 12 14 16 28.
104 Switzerland, Zürich. 1705 (Jan.). 1, 1(0.1567, 0.2503). Puls, p. 167. 1, 1; 1 3 6 10 13 16 55.
105 France, St Maur. 1706 (22 Mar.–Apr. sometime). 2, 2(0.2143, 0.1448). Dufresnoy II, pp. 73–127; Calmet II, pp. 264–97. 2, 2; 1 6 9 17 21 22 23 44 53 54.
106 Scotland, Annandale. 1707 (Aug.–Sep.). 5, 1(0.1746, 0.2095). Wodrow, R., *Analecta* (Edinburgh, 1842) I, pp. 95–7; Lang (*Cock Lane*), pp. 293–4. 2, 2; 1 6 8 9 11 12 14 16 21 22 24 42.
107 England, Canvey Island. 1709 (10–16 Sep.). 3, 1(0.2965, 0.3791). See chapter 11. 5, 4; 1 6 8 11 12 14 16 17 18 19 20 21 22 24 29 32 40.
108 N. Ireland, Island Magee. 1710 (Sep.)–1711 (Feb.). 1, 1(0.1740, 0.2150). Seymour, St. J., *Irish Witchcraft and Demonology* (Dublin, 1913), pp. 200–21; Robbins, pp. 329–30. 2, 3; 1 6 9 16 19 24 33 35 47.
109 W. Germany, Dortmund. 1713 (5 May–28 June). 1, 1(0.3024, 0.3831). Gerstmann, F. B., *Genaue und wahrhafftige Vorstellung des Gespenstes und Poltergeistes* (Leipzig and Osnabruck, 1714); Starmann, *Eigentlicher Bericht von der seltsamen und entsetzlichen Begebenheit* (Itzstein, 1714); Thurston, pp. 193–5; Puls, pp. 126–30. 6, 4; 1 6 8 16 18 19 20 23 24 33 36 56 61 62.
110 E. Germany, Diemnitz bei Halle. 1714 (Jan.; a few days). 5, 1(0.1187, 0.2653). Hauber III, pp. 734–48. 3, 3; 1 3 5 6 11 12 16 19.
111 England, Epworth, Lincs. 1716 (1 Dec.)–1717 (at least Mar.). 2, 2(0.2862, 0.1916). Wright, D., *The Epworth Phenomena* (London, 1917); Sitwell, pp. 157–88; Price, pp. 81–110; *PSPR* 17, 1903, pp. 316–21, 328–32, 333–6; *IJP* 2, No. 2, 1960, pp. 62–79; Stead, p. 78. 6, 4; 1 6 9 17 21 22 23 24 25 39 44 53 54.
112 Scotland, Kinross. 1718 (some weeks). 1, 1(0.1191, 0.2062). Sharpe, C. K., *A Historical Account of the Belief in Witchcraft in Scotland* (London, 1884), pp. 177–80. 3, 1; 1 8 16 17 19 36.
113 England, Cambridge. 1718 (May). 2, 2(0.1843, 0.1344). Price, pp. 113–20. 5, 2; 1 6 9 10 13 17 21 22 23.
114 W. Germany, Gröben, near Halle. 1718 (17–22 June, 29 July–8 Sep.). 1, 1(0.1505, 0.2316). Heinisch, J., *Das Zeugniss der reinen Wahrheit von den sonder- und wunderbaren Würckungen eines insgemein sogenanntan Kobolds* (Jena, 1723); Hennings, J. C. *Von Geistern und Geistersehern* (Leipzig, 1780), pp. 802–9; Eckhartshausen, K. von, *Sammlung der merkwürdigsten Visionen* (Munich, 1792), pp. 117–20; Puls, pp. 24–33; Thurston, pp. 36–7; *Magikon* I, 1840, pp. 311–16; *ZfP*, 1929, pp. 313–19.
115 E. Germany, Radewell bei Halle. 1719 (3 months). 2, 2(0.1610, 0.1570). Görres III, pp. 408–10; Perty II, pp. 82–3. 1, 2; 1 5 6 9 22 44 45.

APPENDIX TO PART I

116 Wales, Llangeler, Carms. 1719 (from 21 May; a few weeks?). 1, 1 (0.1478, 0.2396). [Lewis, D., *Golwg ar y Byd* (Carmarthen, 1725)] Davies, J. C., *Folk-Lore of West and Mid-Wales* (Aberystwyth, 1911), pp. 150–2. 1, 2; 1 6 8 9 16 17 20 28 52.

117 W. Germany, Riedlingen. 1720. 1, 1(0.1156, 0.1226). Buchner, pp. 301–2. 2, 1; 1 16 22 48.

118 England, London. About 1721–1724. 4, 2(0.2061, 0.1381). Beaumont, J., *Gleanings of Antiquities* (London, 1724) p. 202; Sargent, E., *Planchette* (Boston, 1869), p. 206. 2, 1; 1 7 11 13 21 22 27.

119 E. Germany, Sandfeldt. 1722 (26 Jan.–30 Mar.). 3, 1(0.4414, 0.5024). See chapter 6. 6, 4; 1 5 6 8 9 16 17 18 19 20 21 23 24 29 30 33 34 36 39 42 50 62.

120 Norway, Andenaes. 1722 (Aug.)–1723 (May). 1, 1(0.1282, 0.1361). Robbins, pp. 362–3. 1, 1; 1 6 16 22 23 57.

121 Spain, Madrid. About 1723. 2, 1(0.1237, 0.1284). Torres Villaroel, D. de, *The Remarkable Life of Don Diego*, tr. W. C. Atkinson (London, 1958), pp. 101–7. 3, 1; 1 6 9 17 21 57.

122 Italy, Monte Argentaro. 1725 (about)–1775 (about). 4, 2(0.2152, 0.1574). *The Life of the Blessed Paul of the Cross* (London, 1853) II, pp. 296–315. 1, 1; 1 7 10 13 16 21 22 24 39.

123 Netherlands, Tjomarum nr. Franecker. 1728 (at least 10 days). 5, 1(0.0870, 0.1611). Buchner, p. 303. 2, 1; 1 6 11 12 16 22.

124 Norway, Hellesø, Senjen. About 1730. 1, 1(0.1045, 0.1255). Robbins, p. 363. 1, 1; 1 16 21 53.

125 Poland, Warsaw. 1731 (Aug.; about a week). 1, 1(0.0971, 0.1060). Buchner, pp. 306–7. 2, 1; 1 6 16 22 23 24.

126 France, Amiens. 1732–1746. 4, 2(0.2872, 0.1448). See chapter 10. 3, 3; 1 7 9 15 17 21 22 23 27 38 39.

127 Sweden, Stockholm. 1732 (Jan.; a few weeks?). 1, 1(0.1391, 0.2459). Buchner, p. 307. 2, 1; 1 6 12 16 32 39 49.

128 England, Waltham nr. Melton Mowbray. 1732 (c. Oct.). 5, 1(0.1513, 0.2319). [Chambers, R., in] Home, D. D., *Incidents in my Life* (London, 1863), pp. 267–8. 1, 1; 1 5 6 11 12 21 39 44.

129 France, Toulouse. 1732 (about Dec.). 2, 2(0.1986, 0.1957). Chambers, R., *loc. cit.*, p. 268. 1, 1; 1 11 13 21 24 44 46.

130 England, Portishead. 1737 (Dec.)–1738 (Jan.). 5, 1(0.0907, 0.2187). *JSPR* 24, pp. 26–7. 2, 1; 1 3 6 11 12 16.

131 E. Germany, Saalfeld. 1738–1743. 1, 2(0.1351, 0.1203). Hennings, J. C., *Von Geistern und Geistersehern* (Leipzig, 1780), pp. 809–14. 2, 2; 1 5 7 21.

132 E. Germany, Schkeitbar, nr. Lützen. 1738 (17 June)–1739 (at least 2 Dec.). 4, 2(0.3829, 0.2970). *ZfP* 1931, pp. 212–15. 2, 2; 1 7 16 17 19 21 22 23 24 27 28 29 36 40 53 62.

133 W. Germany, Mulldorf nr. Bonn. 1740? 1, 1(0.1257, 0.1494).

Zingaropoli, F., *Case infestate dagli spiriti* (Naples, 1917), pp. 48–50. 2, 2; 1 11 16 22 49.

134 France, Walsche nr. Metz. 1740 (from 10 June; a few months?). 1, 1(0.1315, 0.2459). Calmet I, pp. 200–3. 3, 2; 1 6 8 16 18 33 59.

135 W. Germany, Unterzell nr. Würzburg. 1746 (late) 4, 2(0.1884, 0.1266). Horst I, pp. 205–11; Summers, M., *The Geography of Witchcraft* (London, 1927), pp. 504–16. 1, 1; 1 17 22 23 24 41.

136 W. Germany, Constance. 1746 (c. Dec.)–1747 (8 Feb.). 2, 1(0.1692, 0.2092). Calmet II, pp. 191–6. 3, 3; 1 6 8 9 16 21 23 39 42 50.

137 W. Germany, Wang, Oberbayern. 1748–1910. 4, 2(0.1971, 0.0757). Moser, pp. 213–35. 4, 3; 1 7 9 21 22 24 51.

138 E. Germany, Schwartzbach, Saxony. 1749 (from early July; 2 or 3 months). 5, 1(0.1919, 0.2873). [Fleischer, J. M., *Zuverlässige Nachricht von einem Gespenste* (Leipzig, 1750)]; *PSt* 22, 1895, pp. 289–300. 4, 3; 1 6 8 9 11 12 16 19 20 21 23 36 39.

139 Iceland, Hjalta-Stad. 1749–1750 (winter). 2, 1(0.1204, 0.1295). Lang (*Dreams and Ghosts*), pp. 246–9. 3, 2; 1 6 9 23 44.

140 E. Germany, Rathenau. 1750. 2, 2(0.1411, 0.0961). *Geister und Gespenster in einer Reiche von Erzählungen* (Basle, 1810) I, pp. 125–7. 1, 1; 1 4 9 22.

141 England, Smithfield, London. 1759 and 1762 (Jan.–Feb.). 4, 2(0.2071, 0.1470). [Goldsmith, O.], *The Mystery Revealed* (London, 1742 = 1762); Grant, D., *The Cock Lane Ghost* (London, 1965); Lang (*Cock Lane*), pp. 161–9; Price, pp. 121–8; *IJP* 4, 1962, pp. 71–87. 5, 3; 1 7 9 11 12 14 16 21 22 23 24.

142 E. Germany, Leipzig. 1760 (brief). 2, 1(0.1505, 0.1912). Buchner, pp. 313–14. 1, 1; 1 3 6 8 9 16 22 44 46.

143 England, Bristol. 1761 (13 Nov.)–1762 (19 Dec.). 3, 1(0.3738, 0.4151). See chapter 7; also Nicholls, J. F. and Taylor, J., *Bristol Past and Present* (Bristol, 1882), III, pp. 196–7; Evans, J., *A Chronological Outline of the History of Bristol* (Bristol, 1824). 6, 5; 1 5 7 8 9 11 12 16 17 18 19 21 23 24 39 43 44 45 47 52.

144 Italy, Lanzo nr. Turin. About 1762 (at least some months). 1, 1(0.2152, 0.2580). [Cavalli, A., *Delle apparizioni ed operazioni di spiriti* (Milan, 1765)]; Zingaropoli, F., *Case infestate dagli spiriti* (Naples, 1917), pp. 50–2; *JASPR* 67, 1973, pp. 403–4. 3, 2; 1 10 12 16 17 21 23 35 36 49.

145 Germany, Berlin or vicinity. 1765 (a few days). 2, 1(0.1270, 0.1358). Buchner, pp. 314–15. 5, 1; 1 6 9 23 40.

146 England, Hinton Ampner, Hants. 1765 (Jan.)–1771. 4, 2(0.2309, 0.0891). *JSPR* 6, 1893, pp. 52–74; Price, pp. 129–44. 5, 4; 1 5 7 9 15 21 22 23 24.

147 W. Germany, Dibbesdorf, Lower Saxony. 1767 (2 Dec.)–1768 (Mar.). 2, 1(0.1202, 0.1376). *Magikon* 5, 1853, pp. 288–92; Perty

376 APPENDIX TO PART I

II, pp. 86–7. 1, 2; 1 5 6 9 21 44.

148 England, Stockwell, Surrey. 1772 (6 and 7 Jan.). 5, 1(0.1723, 0.2873). See chapter 5. 5, 3; 1 6 8 9 11 13 16 17 18 30 32.

149 W. Germany, Hamburg. 1773 (June). 2, 1(0.1222, 0.1328). Buchner, pp. 315–16. 2, 1; 1 3 6 8 9 22.

150 N. Ireland, Newry, 1779 (Feb.)–1785 (at least June). 4, 2(0.2349, 0.1775). *Arminian Magazine* 9, 1786, pp. 660–2; Owen, pp. 20–1. 2, 1; 1 7 8 9 16 17 21 22 24 25 28 36.

151 N. Ireland, Co. Down. 1780 (Dec.). 1, 1(0.1216, 0.1868). *Arminian Magazine* 10, 1787, pp. 94–5, 147–8, 205–6. 2, 2; 1 5 16 19 35.

152 Scotland, Dumfries. About 1782. 1, 2(0.1259, 0.1099). Spicer, p. 30. 1, 1; 1 15 21.

153 USA, New Hackensack, N.J. About 1789. 5, 1(0.0967, 0.1706). Mahan, pp. 71–2; Spicer, pp. 31–2. 5, 2; 1 11 12 16 17 21.

154 Germany, location not given. 1789 (Dec.). 5, 1(0.1569, 0.2051). *Blätter* 8, 1837, pp. 157–66. 1, 1; 1 5 8 9 11 12 15 16 21 23.

155 Germany, location not given. 1794–1815. 4, 2(0.3241, 0.1619). *Blätter* 4, 1833, pp. 177–96. 3, 3; 1 5 7 9 15 17 21 22 23 24 25 27 53.

156 USA, Middleway, West Va. 1797. 5, 1(0.1752, 0.2051). Bayless, pp. 20–1. 1, 1; 1 11 12 16 22 24 36 48.

157 Scotland, Dunnottar, Kincardine. About 1800? 5, 1(0.1039, 0.2051). Scott, Sir W., *Letters on Demonology and Witchcraft* (2nd edn, London, 1831), pp. 367–8. 1, 1; 1 3 11 12 16.

158 England, Burrowdown, Northumberland. 1800 (Jan.). 1, 1(0.1012, 0.1446). Moor, pp. 74–7. 2, 2; 1 16 17 18 21.

159 England, Kent. Early nineteenth century (Feb.–June). 1, 1(0.1033, 0.1497). Moor, pp. 24–44. 2, 2; 1 6 58.

160 Poland, Slawensik (= Slawiecice now Ehrenforst), Silesia. 1806 (from late Nov. for some months). 2, 2(0.1226, 0.0976). Kerner, pp. 274–89; Crowe II, pp. 239–55; Sitwell, pp. 307–17; Perty II, pp. 106–8. 3, 3; 1 6 9 16 19 21 22 24.

161 Iceland, Garpsdal, 1807 (Nov.–at least 26 Dec.). 1, 1(0.1226, 0.1596). Lang (*Dreams and Ghosts*), pp. 249–253. 3, 2; 1 6 16 17 21 24 60.

162 England, Sampford Peverell nr. Tiverton. 1810 (c. Apr.)–1812. 3, 2(0.2270, 0.2094). Colton, C. C., *Sampford Ghost. A Plain and Authentic Narrative* (Tiverton, [1810]); Colton, C. C., *Sampford Ghost. Stubborn Facts against Vague Assertions* (Tiverton, 1810); Britten, pp. 92–4; Ingram, J. H., *The Haunted Houses and Family Traditions of Great Britain* (Second Series, London, 1884), pp. 226–33; Harper, C. G., *Haunted Houses* (London, 1924) pp. 132–8; Owen, pp. 56–9. 5, 3; 1 5 7 8 9 16 18 21 22 39 44 58.

163 W. Germany, Klefersulzbach, Württemberg. 1811–1841. 4,
2(0.3190, 0.1827). *Magikon* 2, 1842, pp. 1–17; Kerner, pp. 291–2;
Perty II, p. 105. 6, 3; 1 9 15 17 21 22 24 25 27 35 51 53.
164 Switzerland, Uffikon, Lucerne. 1814. 3, 2(0.2787, 0.2651). Moser,
pp. 303–9. 2, 2; 1 8 9 15 16 22 32 35 39 43 49 53.
165 W. Germany?, Schloss Schmiedefeld. 1815 (early). 2, 2(0.1293,
0.1273). Moser, pp. 297–9. 2, 2; 1 6 9 16 21 22 40.
166 USA, nr. Adams, Tennessee. 1817 (c. May)–1821, 1828 (Feb.–
Mar.). 3, 2(0.4219, 0.3858). [Ingram, M. V., *Authenticated
History of the Famous Bell Witch* (Clarksville, Tennessee,
1894)]; Bell, C. Bailey, *The Bell Witch: a Mysterious Spirit* (n.p.,
n.d. [1934]); Smith, S., *Prominent American Ghosts* (Cleveland,
Ohio, 1967), pp. 95–114; Carrington and Fodor, pp. 137–65. 4, 4;
1 5 7 8 9 11 12 16 19 21 22 23 24 27 35 36 39 43 45 61.
167 Austria, Munchhof nr. Voitsberg. 1818 (Oct.–c. Nov.). 1,
1(0.0960, 0.1776). Görres III, pp. 360–70; Thurston, pp. 27–32;
Perty II, pp. 104–5; Sargent, E., *Planchette* (Boston, 1869), pp.
209–13. 3, 3; 1 5 6 8 9 16 18 21.
168 W. Germany, Prevorst nr. Heilbronn. About 1824–1829. 3,
1(0.2705, 0.2771). Kerner; Podmore, F., *Modern Spiritualism*
(London, 1902), I. pp. 99–104. 4, 3; 1 7 8 9 11 13 14 16 17 18 21
24 26 53.
169 France, Ars-en-Dombes nr. Lyons. 1824–1856 (approx.). 4,
2(0.3277, 0.2499). Monnin, A., *The Curé of Ars*, tr. B.
Wolferstan (London, [1924]), pp. 182–201; Trochu, F., *The Curé
d'Ars*, tr. E. Graf (London, 1927), pp. 234–56; Ghéon, H., *The
Secret of the Curé d'Ars*, tr. F. J. Sheed (London, 1929), pp.
146–52; Bayless, pp. 189–92. 3, 2; 1 10 13 17 21 22 23 24 28 42 51
62.
170 Indonesia, Amboina. 1825. 1, 1(0.1451, 0.2495). *PSt* 8, 1881, pp.
5–12; Puls, pp. 16–24. 1, 1; 2 5 6 16 20.
171 England, Westminster. 1825 (Feb; 2½ hrs). 1, 1(0.1041, 0.1732).
Moor, pp. 59–63. 3, 2; 1 6 8 58.
172 England, Ewshott nr. Crondall, Hants. About 1826–1841. 4,
2(0.1745, 0.0635). Moor, pp. 112–33; Ingram, J. H., *The Haunted
Houses and Family Traditions of Great Britain* (Second Series,
London, 1884), pp. 124–37. 4, 3; 1 7 9 15 21 22.
173 Ireland, Kilmoran, Co. Clare. 1828 (5 Sep.)–c. 1834. 4, 2(0.3366,
0.2146). *SM* NS. 4, 1869, pp. 215–21. 3, 3; 1 7 9 15 16 21 22 23
27 35 38 39 44 57.
174 Canada, Belledoon (Baldoon), S. Ontario. 1829 (late)–1831
(summer). 3, 1(0.3507, 0.3663). MacDonald, N. T., *The
Belledoon Mysteries* [c. 1871] (Wallaceburg, Ontario, 1907);
Lambert, pp. 63–88. 4, 4; 1 7 8 9 16 17 18 19 20 22 28 40 47 49
56 60.

175 England, Chesterfield. About 1830 (more than a year). 1, 2(0.1419, 0.1366). Moor, pp. 45–59, 105. 2, 2; 1 7 58.
176 Java, Soemadang. 1831 (Jan.–Feb.; 16 days). 5,1(0.2443, 0.3993). *PSt* 8, 1881, pp. 5–12; Puls, pp. 7–24; Britten, pp. 344–6; [Baudisch, A., *Het Probleem van de 'Stille Kracht'* (Weltevreden, Java, 1926)]. 3, 2; 2 5 8 11 12 16 17 19 20 39 49.
177 W. Germany, Orlach, Württemberg. 1831 (Feb.)–1833 (5 Mar.). 5, 1(0.3059, 0.3446). Gehrts, H., *Das Mädchen von Orlach* (Stuttgart, 1966); Kerner, J., *Geschichten Besessener neuerer Zeit* (Karlsruhe, 1834) pp. 20–58; Watts, Anna M. H., *The Pioneers of the Spiritual Reformation* (London, 1883), pp. 89–105. 5, 3; 1 7 8 11 12 24 25 28 39 40 41 46.
178 W. Germany, Dünzling, Bavaria. About 1833 to about 1930. 4, 2(0.2447, 0.0839). Moser, pp. 242–50. 4, 2; 1 7 9 15 21 22 23 24 53.
179 USA, Woodbridge, N.J. 1834 (duration not clear). 5, 1(0.1369, 0.1886). Mahan, pp. 72–5; Spicer, pp. 43–5; Capron, E. W., *Modern Spiritualism* (Boston, 1855), pp. 26–9. 5, 3; 1 5 6 9 11 12 21 53.
180 Java, nr. Sukapure. 1834 (14 days). 1, 1(0.2150, 0.3182). As 176. 1, 2; 2 6 16 17 19 20 56 62.
181 England, Great Bealings, Suffolk. 1834 (2 Feb.–27 Mar.). 1, 1(0.1303, 0.1838). Moor, pp. 1–23, 55, 63–68, 77, 79, 111; Gould, R. T., *Enigmas* (2nd edn, London, 1946), pp. 95–105. 6, 4; 1 5 8 58.
182 England, Greenwich. 1834 (30 Sep.–5 Oct.). 1, 1(0.1173, 0.1596). Moor, pp. 71–4, 79–84, 87–91; Gould, *op. cit.*, pp. 101–2. 3, 3; 1 8 58.
183 England, Willington Quay, Northumberland. 1834 (c. end Oct.)–1847 (and later). 4, 2(0.3212, 0.1830). See chapter 10. 6, 4; 1 7 9 15 16 17 21 22 23 24 25 35 38 61.
184 Scotland, Edinburgh. 1835 (from Aug. or Sep.; at least several months). 5, 1(0.1878, 0.2283). Crowe II, pp. 255–8; Owen, R. D., *Footfalls on the Boundary of Another World* [1860] (London, 1899), pp. 181–2. 2, 2; 1 5 6 8 9 11 12 14 17 21 22 44.
185 France, Prunois-sur-Ablis, Rambouillet. 1835 (1 Oct.–c. Dec.). 2, 1(0.2179, 0.2224). Britten, pp. 80–1. 2, 2; 1 6 8 9 15 16 19 21 22 33 36 62.
186 England, Little Tew, Oxfordshire. 1838–9. 3, 2(0.3266, 0.3059). Hewlett, E., *Personal Recollections of the Little Tew Ghost* (London, 1854). 3, 3; 1 16 17 19 21 22 23 25 32 42 44 46 47 48.
187 Scotland, Baldarroch, Aberdeenshire. 1838 (from 5 Dec.). 5, 1(0.1057, 0.2411). Mackay, C., *Memoirs of Extraordinary Popular Delusions* (London, 1852) II, pp. 235–8; Owen, *op. cit.* (see 184), pp. 183–5. 2, 2; 1 3 6 11 12 16 19.

188 England, Devon. 1840s. 5, 1(0.1420, 0.2661). O'Neill, Hannah C., *Devonshire Idylls* (London, 1892), pp. 17–30. 1, 3; 1 8 11 12 14 16 17 47.
189 USA, Levant, Maine. About 1840? 2, 2(0.1942, 0.1244). Spicer, pp. 39–43. 1, 2; 1 5 9 17 21 22 27 35.
190 England, Sunderland. 1840 (Mar.–at least 22 June). 5, 1(0.2777, 0.2973). Clanny, W. R., *A Faithful Record of the Miraculous Case of Mary Jobson* (2nd edn, Newcastle-upon-Tyne, 1841). 4, 3; 1 6 8 11 12 14 21 22 24 30 41 53 55.
191 England, Clewer, nr. Windsor. 1841 (June). 2, 1(0.1127, 0.1255). Moor, pp. 99–104, 107–10. 3, 3; 1 5 8 9 21.
192 England, Chilwell, Notts. About 1843. 2, 2(0.1560, 0.1218). Mellors, R., *Attenborough, Chilwell and Toton* (Nottingham, 1919), pp. 25–8. 1, 2; 1 9 15 21 32.
193 USA, Ebensburg, Pa. 1844 (probably brief). 5, 1(0.1062, 0.2026). Wolfe, N. B., *Startling Facts in Modern Spiritualism* (2nd edn, Chicago, 1875), pp. 5–16. 3, 3; 1 11 12 16 47.
194 USA, Wrentham, Mass. 1844–9. 5, 1(0.1998, 0.2363). Hardinge, E., *Modern American Spiritualism* (New York, 1870), pp. 157–64. 2, 2; 1 5 7 11 12 17 19 21 41.
195 England?, location not given. 1844 (Sep.)–1848 (Sep.). 4, 2(0.3370, 0.1682). Spicer, H., *Facts and Fantasies* (London, 1853), pp. 75–101. 4, 3; 1 7 9 17 21 22 23 24 27 35 53 54 61.
196 England, St Pancras. 1846. 2, 2(0.1872, 0.0987). Osborn, A. W., *The Superphysical* (London, 1937), pp. 212–15; *JASPR* 66, 1972, pp. 243–6. 3, 2; 1 9 21 22 24 44 46.
197 France, Bouvigny, nr. La Perrière. 1846 (15 Jan.–10 Apr.). 5, 1(0.1297, 0.2642). Tanchou, S., *Enquête sur l'authenticité des phenomènes electriques d'Angelique Cottin* (Paris, 1846); Mahan, pp. 68–71; Podmore, F., *Modern Spiritualism* (London, 1902) I, pp. 41–3; De Mirville, pp. 371–80; Owen, pp. 100–2; Flammarion, C., *Mysterious Psychic Forces* (London, 1907), pp. 219–28; de Rochas, A., *L'Extériorisation de la motricité* (Paris, 1906), pp. 554–63. 5, 3; 1 3 6 8 9 11 12 16 17 32.
198 England, Bayswater, London. 1847 (Mar.). 5, 1(0.0822, 0.2158). Crowe II, pp. 224–6; De Mirville, pp. 368–70. 2, 2; 1 6 11 12 16 18.
199 USA, Hydesville, N. Y. 1848 (late Mar.–summer and beyond). 5, 1(0.2276, 0.2389). [Lewis, E. E.], *A Report of the Mysterious Noises* (Canandaigua, 1848); Capron, E. W. and Barron, H. D., *Explanation and History of the Mysterious Communion with Spirits* (Auburn, 1850); Capron, E. W., *Modern Spiritualism* (Boston, 1855); Brown, S., *The Heyday of Spiritualism* (New York, 1970), pp. 98–124. 6, 3; 1 5 7 8 9 11 12 15 21 44 46.
200 France, Guillonville, Orgères. 1848 (Dec.)–1849 (1 Mar.). 5,

1(0.2144, 0.3006). Bizouard, J., *Des rapports de l'homme avec le Démon* (Paris, 1863) IV, pp. 485–9; De Mirville, pp. 388–95. 5, 2; 1 6 10 12 15 17 19 48 53.

201 France, Paris. 1849 (Jan.–Feb.; at least 3 weeks). 1, 1(0.0573), 0.1160). Flammarion, pp. 71–2; De Mirville, pp. 381–4. 3, 2; 1 6 9 16.

202 England, Swanland, Hull. 1849 (probably spring; about 6 weeks). 1, 1 (0.0717, 0.1853). *PSPR* 7, 1892, pp. 384–94. 3, 4; 1 6 8 16 18.

203 England, Orton, Westmoreland. 1849 (17 Apr.–mid-May). 1, 1(0.1418, 0.2198). Thurston, pp. 106–15. 3, 2; 1 3 6 16 17 18 21 34.

204 France, St Quentin. 1849 (about Oct.–Dec.). 2, 1(0.1160, 0.1284). De Mirville, pp. 370–1. 2, 2; 1 6 8 9 16 21 22 32.

205 USA, Stratford, Conn. 1850 (10 Mar.–2 Oct.), 1851 (Mar.). 3, 1(0.5445, 0.5857). Elliott, C. W., *Mysteries, or, Glimpses of the Supernatural* (New York, 1852), pp. 171–211; Capron, E. W., *op. cit.* (see 199), pp. 132–71; Spicer, pp. 101–10; Brown, S., *op. cit.* (see 199), pp. 125–49; Carrington and Fodor, pp. 80–6. 5, 4; 1 7 8 9 10 11 12 16 17 18 19 21 23 24 28 32 33 36 39 42 43 44 46 52 55 61.

206 France, Cideville nr. Yerville. 1850 (26 Nov.)–1851 (15 Feb.). 3, 1(0.2680, 0.3446). *PSPR* 18, 1904, pp. 454–63; De Mirville, pp. 337–63; Owen, R. D., *op. cit.* (see 184), pp. 195–203. 6, 3; 1 6 10 12 16 17 18 21 24 25 26 39 43 44.

207 England, Aylesbury. 1851 (spring; a few weeks). 2, 1(0.1461, 0.1791). *SM* 3, 1862, pp. 326–9. 2, 2; 1 6 8 9 16 17 21 23 44 53.

208 England, Barby nr. Rugby. 1851 (Apr.)–1852 (c. Mar.?). Spicer, H., *Facts and Fantasies* (London, 1853), pp. 101–15. 4, 2; 1 6 9 21 22 23 24 27 46.

209 USA, Ashtabula Co., Ohio. 1851 (summer)–1853 (early?). 4, 2(0.2361, 0.1704). Hardinge, E., *op. cit.* (see 194), pp. 392–9. 4, 3; 1 7 9 11 13 16 17 21 22 24 44 46.

210 England, Peckham. 1852 or 3. 4, 2(0.2114, 0.1140). *PSPR* 10, 1894, pp. 346–9. 4, 3; 1 7 15 22 24 53.

211 W. Germany, Bergzabern, 1852 (1 Jan.–c. May). 5, 1(0.1765, 0.2723). *Magikon* 5, 1853, pp. 274–88; Perty II, pp. 87–8. 5, 3; 1 5 6 9 11 12 14 16 17 21 43 44.

212 Scotland, Pleaston (Peaston?), E. Lothian. 1852 (Aug.; not clear). 5, 1(0.1699, 0.2433). Spicer, pp. 51–3; Spicer, H., *Facts and Fantasies* (London, 1853), pp. 62–4. 2, 2; 1 6 11 12 14 21 44 47.

213 USSR, Liptsy, Ukraine. 1853 (Jan.–July). 1, 1(0.1109, 0.1978). Aksakoff, pp. 31–220; *PSPR* 12, 1897, pp. 319–22; Thurston, pp. 87–90. 6, 4; 1 6 8 9 16 28 49.

214 France, St Pol de Léon, Brittany. 1854–1859. 4, 2(0.1957, 0.1028). *JSPR* 3, 1887, pp. 105–6. 3, 2; 1 7 9 15 22 54.

215 England, Clifton Hampden nr. Oxford. 1854–1856, 1866–1867.

4, 2(0.2141, 0.1080). *JSPR* 2, 1886, pp. 385–402. 4, 4; 1 7 9 22 24 53 54.
216 Canada, nr. Charlottetown, Prince Edward Is. 1856–c. 1888. 4, 2(0.2050, 0.0917). *PSPR* 6, 1889, pp. 60–3. 3, 2; 1 7 9 22 23 24 46.
217 Switzerland, Stans, Nidwalden. 1860 (autumn), 1861 (summer), 1862 (15 Aug.–late Oct.). 4, 2(0.3928, 0.3018). See chapter 1. 6, 4; 1 7 16 17 18 21 22 23 24 26 27 34 53 55 60 61.
218 Ireland, Dublin. About 1860? 1, 2(0.1456, 0.1288). Seymour, St. J. D., and Neligan, H. L., *True Irish Ghost Stories* (Dublin, 1914), pp. 21–7. 1, 2; 1 16 21 23 24 35.
219 Trinidad. 1860–1880 (within). 1, 1(0.1519, 0.2114). Bell, H. J., *Obeah* (2nd edn, London, 1893), pp. 93–7. 2, 3; 2 6 9 15 16 19.
220 E. Germany, Lohme bei Kyritz. 1860 (Jan.–Feb.). 1, 1(0.0711, 0.1637). Hornung, D., *Neueste spiritualistische Mittheilungen* (Berlin, 1862), pp. 229–39; Puls, pp. 33–8. 4, 2; 1 5 6 8 9 16.
221 USA, Dory Hill, Gilpin Co., Colorado. 1861 (3–5 Dec.). 1, 1(0.1261, 0.2385). *Luce e Ombra* 67, 1967, pp. 233–40; Steiger, B., *Real Ghosts* (London, 1968), pp. 125–8. 3, 3; 1 6 8 16 19 33 48.
222 USSR, Taschlik nr. Jachnow. 1862 (Nov.)–1863 (c. June). 3, 1(0.2156, 0.2620). *PSt* 15, 1888, pp. 242–7; Puls, pp. 83–6. 3, 2; 1 6 8 9 16 17 19 21 23 35 36 43 44.
223 E. Germany, Oderwitz nr. Zittau. 1862 (before Christmas)–1864 (Feb.). 3, 2 (0.2725, 0.2640). Berthelen, K. A., *Die Klopf und Spukgeister zu Oderwitz* (Zittau, 1864); Moser, pp. 157–65; Daumer, G. F., *Das Reich des Wundersamen* (Regensburg, 1872), pp. 180–9. 5, 4; 1 5 7 8 9 11 12 14 16 17 18 21 22 23 24 55.
224 England, Bilsington, Romney Marsh. 1863 (c. Aug.). 5, 1(0.0752, 0.2217). *SM* 4, 1863, pp. 477–8. 2, 2; 1 6 8 11 12 16 17.
225 England, Tipton, Staffs. About 1863 (autumn). 1, 1(0.0581, 0.1394). *SM* 6, 1865, pp. 168–77. 3, 2; 1 6 8 9 16.
226 Scotland, Port Glasgow, Renfrew. 1864 (Apr.; about 2 weeks). 2, 1(0.1303, 0.1717). *Report on Spiritualism of the Committee of the London Dialectical Society* (London, 1871), pp. 260–3. 4, 3; 1 5 6 9 16 21 44 61.
227 England, location not given. About 1865 (from Feb.; a year). 4, 2(0.1745, 0.0635). Flammarion, pp. 140–9; *PSPR* 2, 1884, pp. 144–51. 3, 3; 1 7 9 15 21 22.
228 N. Ireland, Lenagh, Tyrone. 1865 (Feb.; a few days). 1, 1(0.0800, 0.1618). *SM* 6, 1865, pp. 329–30. 2, 2; 1 6 8 9 16 39.
229 England, Liverpool. 1865 (16 May–1 June, sporadically thereafter). 2, 1(0.2012, 0.2066). *SM* NS 1, 1866, pp. 257–62. 3, 3; 1 5 6 8 9 17 18 21 22 33 58.
230 France, Fives nr. Lille. 1865 (late June–early July). 1, 1(0.0661, 0.1497). Flammarion, pp. 84–6. 3, 2; 1 6 8 9 16 17.
231 USA, Plainview, Minnesota. 1865 (Sep.; 4 days). 2, 2(0.2681,

0.2328). *JASPR* 4, 1910, pp. 256–60. 3, 3; 1 6 9 17 19 21 22 43 44 45 57 61.

232 USA, Philadelphia. 1866 (from 1 Feb.; a few days). 1, 1(0.0818, 0.1776). Thurston, pp. 117–19. 4, 2; 1 6 8 9 16 17 18.

233 France, Normandy. 1867 (Oct.), 1875 (Oct.)–1876 (29 Jan.), 1876 (Aug. and Sep.). 4, 2(0.3692, 0.2647). See chapter 10. 5, 4; 1 7 9 15 16 17 19 21 22 23 30 33 35 50 53 54.

234 France, Labastide-Paumès, Haute-Garonne. 1867 (Apr.; about 2 weeks). 2,2(0.1135, 0.0757). Flammarion, pp. 149–53. 3, 2; 1 6 9 17 21 22.

235 USA, Boston. 1867 (3 July–12 Sep.). 1, 1(0.1020, 0.1802). See chapter 4. 6, 3; 1 6 8 16 17 21 58.

236 England, Thorney nr. Muchelney, Somerset. 1868 (Easter–Nov.). 2, 1(0.1294, 0.1820). *SM* NS3, 1868, pp. 423–4, 433–41, 478–9, 556. 5, 3; 1 6 8 9 16 17 21 35 58.

237 England, Hammersmith. About 1870–1883. 4, 2(0.2916, 0.1492). *PSPR* 3, 1885, pp. 115–17; *JSPR* 42, 1964, pp. 273–82. 3, 2; 1 7 9 22 23 24 27 35 51 53.

238 England, Brighton. 1870 (c. Apr.)–1871 (c. Mar.). 2, 2(0.2210, 0.1340). *JSPR* 3, 1887, pp. 115–20. 3, 3; 1 6 9 15 22 23 24 27 39.

239 USA, Buchanan, Va. 1870 (Nov.)–1871 (Feb.). 1, 1(0.1309, 0.1640). Thurston, pp. 122–4. 4, 2; 1 16 17 19 21 54.

240 USSR, nr. Orenburg. 1870 (14 Nov.)–1871 (about Mar.). 3, 1(0.3507, 0.3523). Aksakoff, pp. 221–316; *PSPR* 12, 1897, pp. 322–30. 5, 4; 1 5 6 8 9 11 13 16 17 21 22 24 27 28 35 44 45 47 61.

241 USA, Cumminsville, nr. Cincinnati? Late 1870. 5, 1(0.0942, 0.2411). *SM* NS 6, 1871, pp. 44–5. 2, 2; 1 6 8 11 12 14 16.

242 The Netherlands, The Hague. 1871. 1, 1(0.0560, 0.1574). *PSt* 8, 1881, pp. 5–12; Puls, pp. 16–24; *JASPR* 58, 1964, p. 111. 2, 2; 1 6 8 16.

243 England, Stepney Causeway, London. About 1871–about 1883. 4, 2(0.2376, 0.1470). *PSPR* 3, 1885, pp. 122–6. 4, 3; 1 7 8 9 15 16 21 22 24 51 61.

244 England, W. Brompton, London. 1871 (autumn)–1877. 4, 2(0.2281, 0.1329). *PSPR* 3, 1885, pp. 132–6. 3, 2; 1 7 9 11 12 21 22 23 24 58.

245 England, location not given. About 1872 (at least a year). 4, 2(0.2040, 0.0813). *PSPR* 2, 1884, pp. 144–51; Flammarion, pp. 140–9. 3, 3; 1 7 9 15 21 22 27.

246 India, Madras. 1872 or 1873. 1, 1(0.2709, 0.3207). Thurston, pp. 177–81. 3, 3; 2 9 16 19 33 39 47 58 62.

247 England?, location not given. 1873 (for about 4 years). 4, 2(0.1660, 0.0494). *PSPR* 2, 1884, pp. 141–4. 4, 3; 1 7 9 21 22 24.

248 England?, location not given. 1873 (Jan.)–1886. 4, 2(0.2503, 0.1348). *PSPR* 10, 1894, pp. 343–4. 3, 2; 1 7 9 17 22 24 27 53 61.

249 Ireland, Cookstown, Co. Tyrone. 1873 (c. spring)–1874 (c. autumn). 1, 1 (0.1668, 0.2077). *The Spiritualist*, 27 Nov., 1874, pp. 259–63; Thurston, pp. 5–6. 3, 2; 1 7 16 18 34 36.

250 England, S.E. coast. 1873 (19 June–18 Aug.). 4, 2(0.2756, 0.2417). Stead, pp. 71–6. 4, 3; 1 6 8 15 16 17 21 22 23 24 28 53 54 58.

251 USA, Oakland, Cal. 1874 (23–25 Apr., episodic till Aug.). 2, 2(0.2034, 0.1860). *PASPR* 7, 1913, pp. 193–425; Britten, pp. 519–29. 6, 4; 1 5 6 9 16 17 18 21 22 23 27 58.

252 USA, Milwaukee. 1874 (c. Aug.; several days). 5, 1(0.0822, 0.2158). Thurston, pp. 119–22. 4, 2; 1 6 11 12 16 18.

253 England, Lyme Regis. 1875 (Feb.)–1876 (Sep.). 4, 2(0.2447, 0.0839). *JSPR* 3, 1887, pp. 132–6. 4, 3; 1 7 9 15 21 22 23 24 53.

254 W. Germany, Nördlingen, Swabia. 1875 (22 May–18 Sep.). 2, 1(0.1437, 0.1442). *PSt* 51, 1924, pp. 333–43. 5, 3; 1 6 8 9 16 21 22 53 58.

255 Ireland, Kingstown, Co. Dublin. About 1876 (a few months). 5, 1(0.1633, 0.2455). Barrett, W. F., *On the Threshold of the Unseen* (3rd edn, London, 1918), pp. 37–43. 3, 3; 1 5 6 11 12 17 21 44 46.

256 W. Germany, Bavaria (location not given). 1876 (summer–autumn). 2, 2(0.1477, 0.1151). Perty, M., *Die sichtbare und die unsichtbare Welt* (Leipzig and Heidelberg, 1881), pp. 76–81. 3, 3; 1 6 9 16 17 21 22 23 51.

257 N. Ireland, Derrygonnelly, Fermanagh. 1877. 1, 1(0.1697, 0.2477). *PSPR* 25, 1911, pp. 390–5. 4, 3; 1 5 6 16 19 21 43 44 48.

258 England?, location not given. 1877–1882. 4, 2(0.3464, 0.2131). *JSPR* 2, 1885, pp. 136–41. 4, 3; 1 7 15 16 17 21 22 23 24 27 35 38 53 61.

259 Scotland, Strathtay, Perthshire. About 1878–1897 (6 May). 4, 2(0.3380, 0.1678). Goodrich-Freer, Ada, and John, Marquess of Bute, *The Alleged Haunting of B—— House* (new edn, London, 1900); Price, pp. 220–8. 7, 4; 1 7 9 15 17 21 22 23 24 25 35 38 53.

260 Ireland, Dublin. 1878–1894. 4, 2(0.1865, 0.0813). *JSPR* 7, 1896, pp. 335–9. 4, 3; 1 7 9 22 24 27.

261 Canada, Amherst, Nova Scotia. 1878 (Sep.)–1879 (Oct.). 3, 1(0.4521, 0.5112). Hubbell, W., *The Great Amherst Mystery* [1879] (London, 1888); Carrington, H., *Personal Experiences in Spiritualism* (London, n.d.), pp. 95–124; Sitwell, pp. 359–89; Lambert, pp. 89–105; *PASPR* 13, 1919, pp. 89–130. 5, 4; 1 5 7 8 9 11 12 14 16 17 18 19 21 23 25 28 30 35 39 40 43 44 46.

262 England, Cheltenham. 1880–1889 (at least). 4, 2(0.2305, 0.1548). *PSPR* 8, 1892, pp. 311–12; Collins, B. Abdy, *The Cheltenham Ghost* (London, 1948); MacKenzie, A., *Apparitions and Ghosts* (London, 1971), pp. 145–58.

263 St Lucia. About 1880 ('a day or two'). 5, 1(0.1775, 0.2763). Bell, H. J., *Obeah* (2nd edn, London, 1893), pp. 97–8. 2, 1; 2 8 11 12 30.
264 Ireland, location not given. 1880 (Aug.–Sep.) and 1881 (Aug.–Sep.). 4, 2(0.2088, 0.0787). *PSPR* 10, 1894, pp. 341–3. 3, 3; 1 7 9 15 22 23 24.
265 USSR, Leningrad. 1880 (Nov.–Dec.). 5, 1(0.1763, 0.2844). *PSt* 8, 1881, pp. 1–5; Puls, pp. 43–7. 3, 2; 1 6 11 12 16 19 21 30 34 40.
266 Czechoslovakia?, Klopotiva, Siebenbürg. 1880 (17–18 Nov.). 5, 1(0.2169, 0.3512). *PSt* 8, 1881, pp. 97–108; Puls, pp. 47–59. 5, 3; 1 5 6 8 11 12 16 18 19 20 22 29 49.
267 England, Bath. 1881 (Aug., and 'for some years'). 4, 2(0.2380, 0.1025). *JSPR* 5, 1892, pp. 305–8. 3, 3; 1 7 9 15 22 23 24 61.
268 Wales, location not given. 1881 (Sep.)–1884. 4, 2(0.2249, 0.0861). *JSPR* 2, 1885, pp. 133–5. 4, 2; 1 7 9 15 21 22 24 61.
269 England, Sheffield. 1882–1885, 1893 (Jan.)–1900 (Mar.). 4, 2(0.1957, 0.0624). *JSPR* 10, 1902, pp. 308–20; *JSPR* 11, 1903, pp. 25–36, 113–16. 4, 3; 1 7 9 15 21 22 24.
270 Italy, Turin. 1882 (5 Sep.)–1883 (about 8 months). 3, 1(0.2526, 0.2664). *Annals* 3, 1906, pp. 361–6. 4, 3; 1 6 8 9 16 18 22 23 27 30 39 42 58.
271 England, Southgate, London, 1882 (15 Sep.)–1884 (5 Apr.). 4, 2(0.2256, 0.1292). *PSPR* 5, 1889, pp. 476–85. 6, 4; 1 7 9 21 23 24 58 61.
272 England, Brighton. 1882 (Oct.)–1889 (June). 4, 2(0.3723, 0.1905). *PSPR* 6, 1889, pp. 255–69, 309–13. 7, 5; 1 7 9 15 17 21 22 23 24 27 51 53 54 58.
273 China, nr. Shin Tsai, E. Shantung. 1883. 1, 1(0.1812, 0.2851). Nevius, J. L., *Demon Possession* (London, 1897), pp. 401–6. 2, 1; 2 6 16 17 19 28 41.
274 England, Worksop. 1883 (20–21 Feb., and 1 Mar.–3 Mar.). 5, 1(0.1791, 0.3039). *JSPR* 1, 1884, pp. 199–212; *PSPR* 12, 1896, pp. 45–58; Lang, A., *The Making of Religion* (2nd edn, London, 1900), pp. 325–30; Sitwell, pp. 387–404. 6, 4; 1 6 8 9 11 12 16 17 18 53 57 58.
275 England, nr. Wem, Shrops. 1883 (31 Oct.–14 Nov.). 5, 1(0.1575, 0.3042). *JSPR* 1, 1884, pp. 19–26; *PSPR* 12, 1896, pp. 58–67; Sitwell, pp. 404–15. 5, 3; 1 3 5 6 8 9 11 12 16 28 42.
276 England, Norwich. 1883 (late)–1884 (Sep.). 2, 2(0.1511, 0.1166). *JSPR* 1, 1885, pp. 313–17.
277 England, Arundel, W. Sussex. 1884 (8–18 Feb.). 5, 1(0.1350, 0.2099). *JSPR* 1, 1884, pp. 57–62; *PSPR* 12, 1896, pp. 67–73. 5, 3; 1 6 11 12 16 17 21 24 54.
278 England, location not given. 1885 (8 Jan.)–1888 (Mar.). 4, 2(0.2548, 0.1158). *JSPR* 3, 1888, pp. 241–52, 322–30. 5, 4; 1 7 9 17 21 22 23 24 57 58.

279 Finland, Ylöjärvi. 1885 (12–27 Jan.). 3, 1(0.2346, 0.3435). See chapter 4. 6, 4; 1 5 6 8 9 11 12 14 16 17 18 19 21 23 34 40 53.
280 Switzerland, Bubendorf nr. Basel. 1886–1899 (about). 4, 2(0.2592, 0.1518). Moser, pp. 182–97. 3, 3; 1 7 9 15 16 21 22 24 28 57 61.
281 England, Borley, Essex. 1886–1946 (at least). 4, 2(0.4561, 0.3483). Price, H., *The Most Haunted House in England* (London, 1940); do., *The End of Borley Rectory* (London, 1946); Dingwall, E. J., Goldney, K. M. and Hall, T. H., *The Haunting of Borley Rectory* (London, 1956); *PSPR* 55, 1969, pp. 65–175; Tabori, P., and Underwood, P., *The Ghosts of Borley* (Newton Abbot, 1973). 7, 5; 1 7 8 9 15 16 18 19 21 22 23 24 27 35 39 51 54 55 58 63.
282 England, nr. Appleby, Westmoreland. 1887 (c. May–Sep.). 2, 2(0.1322, 0.1062). Price, pp. 204–12. 4, 3; 1 6 9 16 21 22 23 28.
283 England?, location not given. 1887 (23 Sep.–6 Nov.). 2, 1(0.1616, 0.2000). *PSPR* 7, 1891, pp. 160–73. 6, 4; 1 5 6 17 21 32 58.
284 England, Bramford nr. Stowmarket. 1887 (Nov.–Dec.). 5, 1(0.1536, 0.2257). *PSPR* 12, 1896, pp. 73–7. 5, 3; 1 3 6 9 10 11 12 16 17 21 24.
285 USSR, Silin nr. Gorki. 1888 (23 Sep.–1 Nov.). 5, 1(0.1878, 0.2114). Aksakoff, pp. 317–33. 4, 3; 1 9 11 12 16 21 23 44 46 53.
286 E. Germany, Resau (= Retzau?). 1888 (13–16 Nov., 6 Dec.). 3, 1(0.2109, 0.2539). *Der Spuk von Resau* (Berlin, 1889); Müller, E., *Enthüllung des Spukes von Resau* (Berlin, 1889); [Hellwig, A., *Okkultismus und Verbrechen* (Berlin, 1929)]; Puls, pp. 179–204; Thurston, pp. 90–4. 6, 4; 1 3 8 9 16 17 18 21 25 35 40.
287 France, Paris. 1888 (30 Nov.)–1889 (4 Feb.). 2, 2(0.1654, 0.1125). *PSPR* 7, 1891, pp. 193–8. 5, 3; 1 5 9 17 21 22 46.
288 England, Cambridge. 1889–1896 (at least). 4, 2(0.2770, 0.1155). *JSPR* 10, 1901, pp. 43–47. 4, 3; 1 7 9 15 21 22 23 24 57 61.
289 England?, location not given. 1889 (Jan.)–1891. 4, 2(0.1915, 0.1106). *PSPR* 10, 1894, pp. 344–6. 5, 3; 1 7 8 21 22 24 53.
290 Canada, Clarendon, nr. Shawville, Quebec. 1889 (Sep.–Nov.). 3, 1(0.3156, 0.3945). *Light* 9, 1889, pp. 620–3; *Light* 10, 1890, pp. 567–8; Thurston, pp. 162–71; Lambert, pp. 106–21. 5, 4; 1 5 6 8 9 16 17 18 19 23 24 28 37 44 45 47 55.
291 W. Germany, Swabia, location not given. About 1890–about 1900. 4, 2(0.2185, 0.1426). Moser, pp. 167–81. 4, 3; 1 7 8 9 15 16 22 23 24 30.
292 England, N., location not given. 1891 (5–13 Jan.). 1, 1(0.1538, 0.1982). Stead, pp. 79–80. 4, 3; 1 6 16 21 54 57 58.
293 Ireland, Waterford. 1892 (Jan.; 2 or 3 weeks). 1, 1(0.1321, 0.1497). *PSPR* 12, 1896, pp. 77–81. 6, 3; 1 3 16 17 21 23.
294 Java, Sitoebondo. 1892 (30 Nov. or 1 Dec.)–1893 (c. Feb.). 3, 1(0.2505, 0.4187). *JASPR* 67, 1973, pp. 391–406. 5, 3; 2 5 6 8 9 11 12 16 17 18 19 30 39 62.

295 W. Germany, Gossmandorf, Bavaria. 1893–1907 (about). 4, 2(0.2249, 0.1626). Moser, pp. 236–41. 3, 2; 1 15 16 19 21 22 23 27 51.

296 England, London, location not given. 1893 (late June)–1895 (Jan.). 3, 2(0.2839, 0.2532). *PSPR* 12, pp. 81–90. 5, 3; 1 8 9 16 19 21 22 24 30 37 54 55 62.

297 Britain, location not given. 1894–1896. 4, 2(0.3268, 0.1775). Goodrich-Freer, Ada, *Essays in Psychical Research* (London, 1899), pp. 55–64. 5, 3; 1 7 21 22 23 24 25 27 35 53 54.

298 England, Walton-on-Thames. 1894–1911 (at least). 4, 2(0.2484, 0.1214). Price, pp. 343–5. 3, 2; 1 7 8 9 15 17 21 22 23 24 39.

299 England, nr. Norwich. 1894 (May, up to; period uncertain). 4, 2(0.2253, 0.0802). *Borderland* 1, 1894, pp. 447–8. 5, 2; 1 7 9 15 21 22 24 27.

300 England, Durweston, Dorset. 1894 (13 Dec.)–1895 (about Mar.). 5, 1(0.2024, 0.3196). *PSPR* 12, 1896, pp. 90–5. 6, 4; 1 6 8 9 11 12 14 16 18 21 25 44 55 59.

301 Jamaica, location not given. 1895–1905 (within; a few nights). 1, 1(0.1598, 0.1985). Williams, pp. 11–13. 3, 1; 1 6 21 48.

302 Jamaica, location not given. 1895–1905 (within; one occasion only). 1, 1(0.1629, 0.2004). Williams, pp. 15–16. 2, 1; 2 6 21 41.

303 Jamaica, Alva Mission, Dry Harbour Mts. About 1895 (a few nights). 5, 1(0.1643, 0.2892). Williams, pp. 6–8. 3, 2; 2 6 9 11 12 16 18 56.

304 England, Ham, Berks. 1895 (Jan.–Feb.; c. 3 weeks). 5, 1(0.1398, 0.2815). *PSPR* 12, 1896, pp. 95–101. 6, 4; 1 3 5 6 11 12 16 17 40.

305 France, Objat, Corrèze. 1895 (mid-May–2 June). 5, 1(0.1614, 0.2833). Flammarion, pp. 118–26. 4, 3; 1 6 8 11 12 16 17 21 28 35 40.

306 France, Valence-en-Brie. 1896. 1, 1(0.1461, 0.1519). Flammarion, pp. 229–31. 2, 1; 1 17 23 32.

307 The Netherlands, Rotterdam. 1897 (Apr.–May; about a month). 1, 1(0.1251, 0.2183). *JASPR* 58, 1964, pp. 112–13. 2, 2; 1 5 6 16 20 62.

308 India, Ooty. 1897 (20 Apr.–4 May). 5, 1(0.1593, 0.2499). *Borderland* 4, 1897, pp. 261–2; Flammarion, pp. 296–301. 5, 3; 1 5 6 9 11 12 13 16 24 41.

309 England, Tick Fen, Hunts. 1897 (26 Apr.–8 May). 5, 1(0.1365, 0.1956). *Borderland* 4, 1897, pp. 259–260. 5, 2; 1 5 6 9 11 12 13 21.

310 England, Blackburn. 1899 (about Feb.)–1919. 4, 2(0.1857, 0.0902). Bennett, E., *Apparitions and Haunted Houses* (London, 1939), pp. 304–8. 4, 3; 1 7 9 22 24 58.

311 W. Germany, Cronheim. 1899 (up to June; apparently some months). 3, 1(0.2773, 0.3626). *PSt* 52, 1925, pp. 31–7. 3, 3; 1 3 6 8 9 11 12 16 17 18 20 21 22 28 29 39 55.

312 England, City of London. 1899 (c. July)–1901 (after Feb.).
3, 1(0.2435, 0.2811). Thurston, pp. 96–105. 5, 3; 1 7 8 16 18 19
21 43 44 50 53.
313 Italy, Turin. 1900 (16 Nov.–7 Dec.). 3, 1(0.1379, 0.2539).
Lombroso, C., *Richerche sui fenomeni ipnotici e spiritici* (Turin,
1909, pp. 246–9; Eng. tr., *After Death–What?* (London, 1909),
pp. 273–9; *Annals* 3, 1906, pp. 367–70. 5, 3; 1 5 6 8 9 16 17 18 19
32.
314 Central Africa, location not given. Early twentieth century?
1, 1(0.1488, 0.2169). De Vesme, C., *History of Experimental
Spiritualism* (London, 1931) I, pp. 142–3. 3, 1; 2 8 15 16.
315 France, Monneville, Oise. Early twentieth century? 2, 1(0.2274,
0.2712). Thurston, pp. 175–7. 3, 3; 1 6 9 10 12 17 21 43 44 45 47.
316 S. Africa, Boshof. 1901 (3 nights). 2, 2(0.1459, 0.1403). Carrington, H., *Psychic Oddities* (London, 1952), pp. 160–2. 3, 2; 2 6
9 22.
317 England, Midlands, location not given. 1901 (c. Apr.)–1913
(June). 4, 2(0.5064, 0.3486). *JSPR* 16, 1914, pp. 274–97. 5, 4;
1 7 9 15 16 17 21 22 23 24 25 27 38 40 50 51 54 57 61 63.
318 USA, Newburyport, Mass. 1901 (1 Oct.), 1903 (late Sep.), 1904
(Nov. 29th). 4, 2(0.1758, 0.0768). Carrington, H., *The problems of
Psychical Research* (London, 1914); do., *Psychic Oddities*
(London, 1952), pp. 162–9. 4, 3; 1 7 9 21 22 51.
319 W. Germany, Gerolstein. 1901 (4 Dec.)–1902 (20 Feb.). 3,
1(0.4237, 0.4532). *PSPR* 18, 1904, pp. 464–80. 4, 3; 1 3 8 9 11 12
17 19 21 24 28 33 35 38 44 47 53 59 60.
320 W. Germany, Bavaria, location not given. 1902–1927. 4, 2(0.3210,
0.1697). *ZfP*, 1927, pp. 83–9. 3, 3; 1 7 9 15 17 21 22 23 25 27 58
61.
321 England, Cambridge. 1903–1959. 4, 2(0.2307, 0.1184). *JSPR* 46,
1972, pp. 109–23. 5, 3; 1 7 9 15 16 21 22 24 25 35.
322 Sumatra, location not clear. 1903 (Sep.; one night). 1, 1(0.1791,
0.2653). *JSPR* 12, 1905, pp. 260–6, 278–84, 294–7, 328–332;
Sitwell, pp. 380–386. 3, 4; 2 6 9 16 18 20 29.
323 Sweden, S., location not given. 1904 (9 May)–1905 (at least Jan.).
2, 2(0.2432, 0.2131). *Annals* 2, 1905, pp. 143–80. 5, 4; 1 6 9 11 13
14 21 22 27 44 46.
324 England, Upholland nr. Wigan. 1904 (c. July–mid-Sep.). 1,
1(0.1387, 0.1960). *JSPR* 12, 1905, pp. 124–37. 6, 3; 1 6 16 18 21
27 60.
325 England, nr. Minster, Kent. 1905 (at least)–c. 1965. 4, 2(0.1957,
0.0624). *JSPR* 44, 1967, pp. 131–49. 4, 3; 1 7 9 15 21 22 24.
326 Britain, location not given. About 1905, 1907 (Dec.), 1908 (Nov.).
1, 2(0.1693, 0.1570). *Light* 29, 1909, pp. 603, 616–17. 3, 3; 1 7 8 9
16 22 28 33.

327 England, nr. Grimsby, Lincs. 1905 (Jan.). 1, 1(0.1070, 0.1897). *JSPR* 12, 1905, pp. 137–42. 5, 3; 1 6 16 28 40.
328 England, Tackley, Oxford. 1905 (Apr.)–1908 (Feb.). 4, 2(0.3515, 0.2436). See chapter 10. 6, 4; 1 7 15 16 17 21 22 24 27 35 38 48 53 57.
329 S. Africa, Transvaal? 1906 (from; for at least 10 years). 4, 2(0.2799, 0.1934). Du Plessis, pp. 33–8. 3, 2; 2 7 9 15 17 22 53 54.
330 France, Neuville. 1906 (June–July). 5, 1(0.1494, 0.2617). *Annales* 16, 1906, pp. 523–7. 5, 2; 1 6 8 9 10 12 16 17 25 40.
331 India, Calcutta. 1906 (c. July). 1, 1(0.1538, 0.2415). *Light* 26, 1906, p. 389. 2, 1; 2 6 16 28 35.
332 Austria, Vienna. 1906 (July–Aug.). 1, 1(0.1600, 0.2940). *JSPR* 13, 1907, pp. 66–79. 1 5 8 10 12 16 17 18 30.
333 Canada, Windsor, Nova Scotia. 1906 (Oct.)–1907 (Feb.). 1, 1(0.1385, 0.2473). *PASPR* 1, 1907, pp. 431–519; Carrington, H., *Personal Experiences in Spiritualism* (London, n.d.), pp. 3–19. 6, 4; 1 3 5 6 8 16 17 19 23.
334 Scotland, Glasgow? 1907 (13 Aug.)–1908 (23 Jan.). 2, 1(0.2319, 0.3330). *JSPR* 13, 1908, pp. 194–7. 5, 3; 1 6 8 9 16 17 21 22 33 35 44 61 63.
335 England, location not given. 1907 (Sep.–Oct.). 2, 2(0.1556, 0.0909). *JSPR* 13, 1907, pp. 156–8. 6, 3; 1 6 9 21 22 24 58.
336 Iceland, location not clear. 1907 (Dec.). 1, 1(0.1653, 0.2539). *L'état actuel des recherches psychiques d'après les travaux du IIème Congrès International tenu à Varsovie en 1923* (Paris, 1925), pp. 148–68; *PS* 4, 1925, pp. 90-111; Thurston, pp. 8–10. 6, 4; 1 6 10 13 16 17 42 46.
337 Italy, Ancona. 1907 (Dec.)–1908 (Jan.). 1, 1(0.1435, 0.1758). *Annals* 7, 1908, pp. 110–12. 5, 2; 1 16 17 21 30 31.
338 USA, New York. 1907 (11 Dec.)–1909 (May). 3, 1(0.2080, 0.2521). Carrington, H., *The Problems of Psychical Research* (London, 1914), pp. 298–315; do., *Psychic Oddities* (London, 1952), pp. 170–82. 3, 3; 1 7 8 9 11 13 16 17 18 19 21 33.
339 Madagascar, Ambatolampy nr. Miarinarivo. 1909 (July–Aug.). 1, 1(0.1888, 0.2631). Rusillon, H., *Un culte dynastique* (Paris, 1912), pp. 51–5; *PSPR* 38, 1927, pp. 213–14. 2, 2; 2 6 16 19 24 44 46.
340 USA, Portland, Oregon. 1909 (28 Oct., 20 Nov.). 5, 1(0.2080, 0.3556). *JASPR* 4, 1910, pp. 465–524, 561–636. 6, 4; 1 3 5 6 8 10 12 14 16 17 18 21 60.
341 Portugal, Comeada, Coïmbra. 1909 (early Oct.). 2, 2(0.2687, 0.2296). Flammarion, pp. 159–168; *Annales* 20, 1910, pp. 90–2. 3, 3; 1 6 9 15 16 22 23 26 39 53 54 57.
342 USA, Dale, Georgia. 1909 (Dec.). 1, 1(0.1422, 0.2103). *Occult Review* 13, 1911. pp. 276–9; *PSPR* 25, 1911, pp. 404–6; Sitwell, pp. 353–355. 5, 3; 1 6 8 16 17 18 19 22 53.

343 Tanzania, location not given. 1910–1914 (within?). 1, 1(0.1911, 0.2899). See chapter 2. 3, 1; 2 6 8 15 16 48 60.
344 S. Africa, location not given. About 1910? (several years?). 4, 2(0.2577, 0.2164). Du Plessis, pp. 39–44. 3, 2; 2 7 9 16 17 18 22 24 35 39.
345 Ireland, Enniscorthy, Co. Wexford. 1910 (7 July–29 July). 2, 2(0.1656, 0.1244). *PSPR* 25, 1911, pp. 380–90; Sitwell, pp. 330–40. 6, 3; 1 6 9 17 21 22 35 42.
346 England, London, location not given. 1911 (Sep.–Oct.). 2, 1(0.1705, 0.1941). *JSPR* 15, 1912, pp. 225–240. 6, 4; 1 3 5 6 9 21 44 46.
347 France, location not given. 1912 (Oct. or Nov.; a few days). 5, 1(0.0835, 0.1842). Flammarion, pp. 197–9. 3, 2; 1 6 11 12 16 17 21.
348 Rumania, location not given. 1913–1914. 1, 1(0.2196, 0.3428). Carrington and Fodor, pp. 87–91. 5, 2; 1 3 5 6 10 13 16 18 19 44 46.
349 N. Ireland, Coonian nr. Brookborough, Co. Fermanagh. 1913–1941 (at least a year). 4, 2(0.2828, 0.1927). Leslie, S., *Shane Leslie's Ghost Book* (London, 1955), pp. 40–8. 3, 3; 1 7 9 11 12 15 21 22 23 33 35 44.
350 Switzerland, location not given. 1913 (July)–1915. 4, 2(0.1448, 0.0505). Moser, pp. 278–82. 3, 2; 1 7 9 21 22.
351 Belgium, Marcinelle nr. Charleroi. 1913 (30 Jan.–2 Feb.). 5, 1(0.1092, 0.2499). Flammarion, pp. 278–80; *Annales* 23, 1913, pp. 152–3; Bozzano, E., *Die Spukphänomene* (Bamberg, 1930), pp. 193–6. 5, 2; 1 5 8 11 12 16 18.
352 France, Fougères-sur-Bièvre, nr. Blois. 1913 (27 Dec.)–1914 (Feb.). 5, 1(0.1847, 0.2528). Flammarion, pp. 193–7. 2, 2; 1 5 6 10 12 17 21 35 60.
353 England, S., location not given. About 1914–1946. 4, 2(0.2065, 0.1500) *JSPR* 34, 1947, pp. 132–5. 5, 2; 1 7 9 16 22 26 27 57.
354 England, Worcestershire. 1914 (c. Mar.–Aug.). 2, 2(0.2795, 0.2164). *JSPR* 17, 1915, pp. 34–42. 5, 3; 1 6 9 11 13 22 23 24 27 35 39 61.
355 Switzerland, Molignon nr. Sion. 1914 (18–27 Apr.) 1, 1(0.1348, 0.2506). Flammarion, pp. 301–3. 5, 2; 1 6 10 12 14 16 47.
356 France, Vodable, Auvergne. 1914 (7 Sep.–24 Sep., 17–18 Dec.). 2, 1(0.1183, 0.1611). Flammarion, pp. 128–32; *Revue metapsychique* 1, 1921, pp. 472–4. 3, 3; 1 6 9 16 17 19 21 58.
357 England, location not given. 1915 (6–13 March). 5, 1(0,1791, 0.1846). *JSPR* 17, 1915, pp. 85–95. 5, 3; 1 6 9 11 12 13 14 17 21 22.
358 Austria, Lading. 1916–1918 (about). 3, 1(0.2958, 0.3604). *ZfP*, 1932, pp. 97–101. 2, 3; 1 5 7 10 11 12 16 17 18 21 35 39 44 46 53.

359 W. Germany, Grosserlach nr. Sulzbach. 1916 (30 Apr.–mid-May). 3, 1(0.2684, 0.2943). *PSt* 43, 1916, pp. 295–300, 343–65; Lambert, R., *Spuk, Gespenster und Apportphänomene* (Berlin, 1923), pp. 50–9. 5, 3; 1 6 8 9 16 17 18 22 24 25 32 40 56 60.

360 Ireland, location not given. 1916 (about Nov.). 1, 1(0.0843, 0.1648). Thurston, pp. 172–5. 3, 2; 1 6 16 49.

361 New York, location not given. 1917 (Sep.; several weeks). 1, 1(0.1057, 0.1754). Carrington, H., *The Invisible World* (London, n.d.), pp. 75–80. 3, 3; 1 3 5 16.

362 England, Cheriton nr. Folkestone. 1917 (late Oct.–Nov.). 1, 1(0.1340, 0.2532). *JSPR* 18, 1918, pp. 155–82, 196–8. 6, 4; 1 3 6 8 16 17 18 57.

363 England, Plumstead, London. 1918 (up to; several years). 4, 2(0.1745, 0.0635). Leslie, S., *Shane Leslie's Ghost Book* (London, 1955), pp. 48–52. 3, 2; 1 7 9 15 21 22.

364 USA, Montclair, N.J. 1918 (c. 10 Apr.)–1925 (at least). 3, 2(0.2486, 0.2131). Prince, W. F., *The Psychic in the House* (Boston, 1926). 7, 5; 1 5 7 8 9 11 13 14 17 21 22 44.

365 France, Cherbourg. 1918 (26–28 Apr.). 2, 2(0.1056, 0.0653). Flammarion, pp. 169–74, 176–7, 6, 3; 1 6 9 21 22.

366 Basutoland, location not given. 1918 (Oct. or later; one night). 2, 2(0.2104, 0.1801). Du Plessis, pp. 26–32. 3, 2; 2 6 9 21 22 25 47.

367 Switzerland, Berne, location not given. 1919 (a day or two). 2, 2(0.1376, 0.0943). Moser, pp. 293–5. 2, 2; 1 9 22 40.

368 India, Suri, W. Bengal. 1919 (about 2 months). 1, 1(0.2732, 0.3853). *JASPR* 66, 1972, pp. 235–40. 3, 3; 2 6 10 12 16 19 23 44 46 48 52.

369 The Netherlands, Amsterdam. 1919 (Apr.–May; 10 days or more). 1, 1(0.0843, 0.1501). *JASPR* 58, 1964, p. 117. 4, 2; 1 5 8 9 16.

370 England, Swanton Novers, Norfolk. 1919 (8 Aug.–8 Sep.). 5, 1(0.1389, 0.2606). *JSPR* 19, 1919, pp. 95–9. 5, 2; 1 3 6 8 11 12 30.

371 England, location not given. 1920s? 4, 2(0.2847, 0.1879). Price, pp. 337–43. 4, 3; 1 7 8 9 16 21 22 23 24 29 53 54 58.

372 India, Poona. About 1920, and 1923–1930 (about Oct.). 3, 1(0.3967, 0.4496). See chapter 6. 6, 4; 2 7 8 9 10 12 16 17 18 19 20 21 24 39 42 44 46 50.

373 India, Nidamangalam, Tanjore. 1920 (3–19 Mar.). 3, 1(0.3431, 0.4085). Thurston, pp. 61–79. 5, 3; 2 6 8 9 16 19 23 24 28 39 44 45 46 47 48.

374 E. Germany, Hopfgarten nr. Weimar. 1921 (14 Feb.–28 Feb.). 5, 1(0.1901, 0.2334). See chapter 4. 6, 3; 1 5 9 11 13 14 16 17 21 55.

375 Hungary, Kecskemét, nr. Budapest. 1921 (29–31 July, 13 Nov.). 1, 1(0.1136, 0.2539). *PSt* 49, 1922, pp. 84–9. 5, 3; 1 6 8 10 12 16 17 28.

APPENDIX TO PART I 391

376 S. Africa, Blaauwvlei, Cape Prov. 1921 (Sep.–Oct.; 2 months).
2, 1(0.1655, 0.2018). Du Plessis, pp. 13–16. 2, 3; 2 6 9 17 51.
377 France, Ardèche district. 1921 (early Sep.)–1922 (c. Jan.). 1,
1(0989, 0.2165). Flammarion, pp. 76–81. 5, 3; 1 6 8 16 18 20.
378 Austria, Lieserbrücke, Kärnten. 1921 (24 Nov.)–1922 (31 Jan.).
3, 1(0.3554, 0.3982). Schrenck-Notzing, pp. 283–302; *PS* 1, 1922–
3, pp. 272–87, 306–30; Thurston, pp. 32–6. 6, 4; 1 5 8 9 11 12 16
17 18 19 20 21 22 27 31 32 35 39.
379 W. Germany, Wildberg, nr. Stuttgart. 1921 (late; 10 days).
5, 1(0.1340, 0.1820). Lambert, R., *op. cit.* (see 359), pp. 46–9.
4, 2; 1 6 8 9 11 12 16 17 21 22 53.
380 Canada, Caledonia Mills nr. Antigonish, N.S. 1922 (Jan.–Feb.).
2, 2(0.1789, 0.1444). *JASPR* 16, 1922, pp. 421–41; Lambert,
pp. 122–31. 6, 3; 1 6 9 21 22 28 39 40.
381 Ukraine, Brody. 1922 (3 Nov.–17 Dec.). 3, 1(0.2627, 0.3560).
PSt 50, 1923, pp. 465–74, 502–15. 5, 4; 1 5 6 9 10 12 16 17 19 21
43 44 46 49 55.
382 S. Africa, Gt. Marico Station. 1923 (a few weeks?). 1, 1(0.1057,
0.2176). Du Plessis, pp. 22–6. 2, 1; 2 6 8 16.
383 Scotland, Penkaet Castle nr. Haddington. 1923–1947 (at least).
4, 2(0.3561, 0.1953). *JASPR* 41, 1947, pp. 171–80; *Experimental
Metaphysics* 2, 1947, pp. 140–8. 5, 2; 1 7 9 17 21 22 23 24 27 32 35
44 53 61.
384 N. Vietnam, Phat-Diem. 1924–1925. 1, 1(0.2433, 0.2745). Bayless,
pp. 171–2. 1, 1; 2 10 12 16 22 23 41 48.
385 England, Yorks., location not given. 1924 (Aug.)–1925 (5 June).
3, 1(0.2608, 0.3703). *PS* 4, 1925, pp. 182–205; Hankey, M.,
J. Hewat McKenzie (London, 1963), pp. 116–24. 5, 4; 1 5 6 8 9
11 13 14 16 17 18 19 21 33 35 36.
386 England, London, location not given. 1924 (Xmas)–1925 (Feb.).
2, 2(0.1685, 0.1567). *JSPR* 23, 1925, pp. 83–8. 6, 3; 1 4 6 16 21 22
23 26.
387 Buhai, Rumania. 1925 (Feb.)–1927 (May). 3, 1(0.3668, 0.4008).
See chapter 7. 7, 5; 1 3 4 7 8 9 11 12 16 18 19 22 23 28 30 39 40 47.
388 Austria, Güssing. 1925 (Sep.–Dec., sporadically for 2 or 3 years
thereafter). 3, 1(0.2064, 0.2319). Schrenck-Notzing, pp. 389–401.
6, 3; 1 7 8 9 11 12 16 17 19 22 42 53.
389 W. Germany, Peissenberg. 1925 (Oct.–Nov.). 5, 1(0.1497, 0.2444).
Schrenck-Notzing, pp. 303–9; *JASPR* 58, 1964, pp. 118–19. 5, 3;
1 6 8 9 11 12 16 19 21 53 61.
390 Sumatra, Padang. About 1926–1927. 1, 1(0.2412, 0.2418). *ZfP*,
1927, pp. 634–5. 2, 1; 2 7 16 17 19 22 28 62.
391 The Netherlands, the Hague. 1926 (Oct.)–1927 (Apr.). 5,
1(0.0923, 0.2261). *JASPR* 58, 1964, pp. 119–20. 4, 2; 1 6 8 9 11 12
16 17 19.

392 Greece. Missolongi. 1926 (Dec.)–1927 (Jan.; 15 days). 1, 1(0.0841, 0.1982). *ZfP*, 1927, pp. 413–15. 3, 2; 1 6 8 9 10 12 16.
393 W. Germany, Munich. 1927 (Jan.; a few days). 5, 1(0.2406, 0.3622). Schrenck-Notzing, pp. 310–26. 5, 4; 1 3 5 6 11 12 14 16 18 21 29 53 58.
394 Czechoslovakia, Kotterbach. 1927 (July; several days). 1, 1(0.1841, 0.3340). Schrenck-Notzing, pp. 326–35; *JASPR* 58, 1964, pp. 120–1. 6, 4; 1 5 6 8 9 10 12 16 18 19 20 29.
395 Czechoslovakia, Kosten-Steinhügel. 1927 (Aug.–Nov.). 1, 1(0.0690, 0.1816). Schrenck-Notzing, pp. 343–4. 4, 2; 1 5 6 8 16.
396 Czechoslovakia, Bratislava. 1927 (11–13 Aug.). 1, 1(0.1249, 0.2752). Thurston, pp. 6–7. 2, 2; 1 6 8 10 12 16 18 20.
397 Czechoslovakia, Nikolsburg, nr. Brno. 1927 (Oct.)–1928 (at least summer). 3, 1(0.5200, 0.5659). Schrenck-Notzing, pp. 335–43, 344–78. 6, 4; 1 5 8 9 11 12 16 17 18 19 21 22 25 30 31 32 34 35 36 39 42 44 52 53 54.
398 England, Sussex, location not given. 1927 (Oct.–Nov.). 1, 1(0.1270, 0.1857). Garrett, Eileen J., *Many Voices* (London, 1969), pp. 77–80. 2, 2; 1 6 10 12 16 22 35.
399 England, Battersea, London. 1927 (Dec.)–1928 (late Jan.). 1, 1(0.1103, 0.2088). Price, pp. 229–39; *JSPR* 24, 1928, pp. 285–6. 5, 3; 1 3 5 6 8 16 17 21.
400 England, London S.W. 1928 (Mar.–c. Sep.). 2, 1(0.1734, 0.1787). *PS* 7, 1928, pp. 235–41. 5, 3; 1 6 9 16 18 21 23 24 44 46.
401 W. Germany, Upper Bavaria, location not given. 1928 (autumn; a few months?). 1, 2(0.1529, 0.0876). Moser, pp. 263–70. 3, 2; 1 6 9 21 22 23 35.
402 Ireland, Co. Cork, location not given. 1928 (Sep.)–1929 (Jan.). 1, 1(0.2439, 0.2738). Thurston, pp. 181–6. 5, 2; 1 6 16 21 24 25 35 36 39 47 55.
403 Germany, Charlottenburg, Berlin. 1929 (9 Jan.–end Apr.). 3, 2(0.4194, 0.3918). See chapter 8. 6, 4; 1 5 6 8 9 16 17 21 22 23 24 34 35 39 44 46 52 53 55 57 58.
404 Austria, Eggenberg, Graz. 1929 (25 Oct.–early Dec.). 3, 1(0.4585, 0.4661). *ZfP*, 1931, pp. 107–23; *Transactions of the Fourth International Congress for Psychical Research* (London, 1930), pp. 54–62. 5, 3; 1 5 8 9 11 13 16 17 18 19 20 21 22 24 26 27 29 32 34 44 46 55.
405 France, location not given. 1929 (Dec.)–1930 (Jan.; 3 or 4 weeks). 5, 1(0.0965, 0.2349). Tizané, pp. 28–33. 5, 3; 1 6 8 11 12 16 61.
406 France, Seyssuel nr. Lyons. About 1930 (c. 2 weeks). 5, 1(0.1624, 0.2532). *JASPR* 25, 1931, pp. 24–9. 4, 3; 1 6 8 9 11 12 35 39 47.
407 S. Africa, Cape Town. About 1930 (one day). 1, 1(0.1690, 0.2932). Du Plessis, pp. 55–7. 2, 1; 2 6 8 16 18 44 46.
408 India, Pilibhit. 1930 (some years). 1, 1(0.1713, 0.1934). Taillepied,

APPENDIX TO PART I 393

N., *A Treatise of Ghosts* tr. M. Summers (London, n.d.). p. 215. 1, 1; 2 7 8 9 16 19 21.

409 England?, location not given. 1930–1936. 4, 2(0.2162, 0.0999). *JSPR* 29, 1936, pp. 239–43. 5, 3; 1 7 9 17 22 23 24 61.

410 USA, Cape Cod. 1930s (summer of one year). 2, 2(0.1353, 0.0958). *Harper's Magazine* 169, 1934, pp. 733–41; Stevens W. O., *Unbidden Guests* (London, 1949), pp. 64–71. 3, 3; 1 6 9 21 22 31.

411 W. Germany, Oppau. 1930 (9 Oct.)–1931 (late Feb.). 5, 1(0.1715, 0.2697). *ZfP* 1931, pp. 321–36. 5, 3; 1 6 7 8 9 11 12 16 44 46 55.

412 Jamaica, Roehampton. 1931 (May–c. July). 5, 1(0.2059, 0.3251). Williams, pp. 220–34. 2, 3; 2 6 8 9 11 12 16 17 20 24 56.

413 E. Germany, Leipzig. 1931 (4 Sep.–20 Nov.). 2, 2(0.1841, 0.1233). *ZfP*, 1932, pp. 59–62. 3, 2; 1 6 9 21 22 23 26 46.

414 Poland, Stettin. 1931 (Jan.)–1933. 4, 2(0.4416, 0.2926). *ZfP*, 1933, pp. 500–10, 540–9. 5, 3; 1 7 9 15 16 17 19 21 22 23 24 25 27 30 35 44 51 53 61.

415 Austria, Vöst nr. Peuerbach. 1932 (26 Jan.–5 Feb.). 4, 2(0.2787, 0.1626). *ZfP*, 1932, pp. 342–6. 4, 3; 1 5 9 21 22 23 24 27 44 46 53.

416 France, Ain, location not given. 1932–1933 (about a year?). 4, 2(0.1855, 0.1199). *Revue Metapsychique* 17, 1936, pp. 87–93. 3, 2; 1 7 19 21 22 40.

417 Germany, Berlin. 1934 (c. Oct.; a few weeks). 3, 1(0.1480, 0.2272). Moser, pp. 283–9. 3, 3; 1 6 8 9 16 18 19 21 30 39.

418 Grenada. 1934 (17 Sep.)–1935 (14 Jan.). 1, 1(0.2288, 0.3185). Thurston, pp. 136–42. 4, 3; 2 5 6 8 9 16 17 24 28 47 55.

419 Spain, Zaragoza. 1934 (Nov.–Dec.). 5, 1(0.1295, 0.2015). Carrington and Fodor, pp. 101–9. 2, 2; 1 6 11 12 23 44.

420 Norway, Toten. About 1935. 5, 1(0.1567, 0.2257). *JASPR* 29, 1935, pp. 149–50. 3, 2; 1 6 7 8 11 12 14 17 21.

421 France, location not given. 1935 (a few days). 5, 1(0.1321, 0.2183). Tizané, pp. 35–8. 5, 2; 1 3 5 6 11 12 21.

422 Canada, Burgess Township, nr. Perth. 1935 (Jan.; about 2 weeks). 2, 1 (0.1061, 0.1361). Lambert, pp. 140–2. 2, 2; 1 6 9 34.

423 India, Cuddapah, Madras. 1935 (c. Apr.). 1, 1(0.1932, 0.3053). *Light* 35, 1935, p. 267. 1, 1; 2 6 10 13 16 18 28.

424 England, Chelsea. 1937 (a few weeks). 5, 1(0.1080, 0.1497). Fodor, N., *The Haunted Mind* (New York, 1959), pp. 74–7; *JASPR* 31, 1937, p. 189. 3, 2; 1 11 12 21.

425 S. Africa, Lansdowne nr. Cape Town. 1937 (July; at least several days). 1, 1(0.2688, 0.3167). Du Plessis, pp. 17–22. 3, 2; 2 6 10 13 16 18 28.

426 Mauritius, 1937 (21–22 Sep.). 5, 1(0.1327, 0.2995). Carrington and Fodor, pp. 92–6. 3, 3; 2 6 8 11 12 16 18.

427 England, Thornton Heath, London. 1938 (Feb.–June). 5, 1(0.1859, 0.2840). *JASPR* 32, 1938, pp. 152–60; Carrington and

Fodor, pp. 110–36; Fodor, N., *The Haunted Mind* (New York, 1959), pp. 79–92; do., *On the Trail of the Poltergeist* (New York, 1958). 7, 5; 1 3 5 8 9 11 13 16 19 32.

428 England, Chelsea. 1938 (c. Apr.–c. Dec.). 2, 2(0.1951, 0.1570). Fodor, N., *The Haunted Mind* (New York, 1959), pp. 92–7; *JASPR* 33, 1939, pp. 54–7. 3, 2; 1 11 13 15 19 21 22.

429 Scotland, Fifeshire, location not given. About 1939–1942. 3, 1(0.2290, 0.2352). Price, pp. 240–6; *PS* 21, 1942, pp. 88–92. 2, 3; 1 7 8 9 15 16 17 19 27 28 35.

430 France, location not given. 1940 (30 Sep.–6 Nov.). 3, 1(0.2398, 0.3707). *Annales de médecine legale et de criminologie* 31, 1951, pp. 67–78. 4, 3; 1 5 6 8 9 11 12 16 17 18 21 30 36 39 44 46.

431 England, Malvern. 1942 (early Jan.–c. end Mar.). 1, 1(0.1480, 0.2914). *Experimental Metaphysics* 2, 1947, pp. 59–63; *JSPR* 33, 1946, pp. 265–7. 5, 4; 1 5 6 8 11 13 16 18 49.

432 England, Sunderland. 1942 (Feb.–Nov.). 5, 1(0.1622, 0.2066). Price, pp. 354–8. 3, 3; 1 6 8 11 12 15 22 35.

433 USA, Los Angeles. 1942 (Dec.)–1943. 5, 1(0.1020, 0.1835). Bayless, pp. 153–6. 2, 2; 1 6 11 12 16 19 22.

434 England, Durham. 1943–1946. 4, 2(0.1762, 0.0809). *JSPR* 34, 1947, pp. 71–4. 5, 3; 1 4 7 9 21 22.

435 England, location not given. 1943 (Jan.–Sep.). 2, 2(0.2812, 0.2220). *JSPR* 33, 1943, pp. 34–40. 5, 2; 1 6 9 21 22 27 31 35 38 60 63.

436 France, location not given. 1943 (Nov.). 5, 1(0.0915, 0.2422). Tizané, pp. 46ff. 5, 3; 1 3 6 8 11 12 16.

437 Canada, nr. Halifax, Nova Scotia. 1943 (24 Dec.)–1944 (8 Jan.). 5, 1(0.1575, 0.2591). Lambert, pp. 144–6. 1, 2; 1 6 8 11 12 16 17 21 24 31 39.

438 England, location not given. 1944 (Aug.)–1946 (Feb.). 3, 1(0.2750, 0.3182). *JSPR* 33, 1946, pp. 224–230. 6, 5; 1 3 5 7 10 12 16 17 19 22 28 44 55.

439 W. Germany, Lauter (Chiemsee), Bavaria. 1946 (Sep.–Dec.). 5, 1(0.1569, 0.2547). [Schrey, C., *Die Wahrheit über den Spuk am Chiemsee* (Wiesbaden, 1950)]; *JASPR* 58, 1964, pp. 122–3. 3, 2; 1 6 11 12 13 19 62.

440 England, N., location not given. 1947 (Apr.)–1948 (Jan.). 2, 2(0.1465, 0.1091). *JSPR* 34, 1948, pp. 294–300. 5, 3; 1 6 9 22 24 60.

441 England, Frimley, Surrey. 1947 (Apr.)–1948 (Aug.). 4, 2(0.1654, 0.0776). *JSPR* 35, 1949, pp. 56–60, 91–2. 5, 3; 1 7 9 15 22.

442 W. Germany, Vachendorf, Bavaria. 1948. 5, 1(0.1439, 0.2473). Bender, pp. 46–7; *PPA* 6, 1969, pp. 87–8. 5, 2; 1 6 9 11 12 16 19 31 54.

443 USA, Washington, D.C. 1949 (Jan.–Apr.). 1, 1(0.1616, 0.2250).

Parapsychology Bulletin, Aug. 1949, pp. 2–3. 5, 3; 1 6 10 12 16 17 22 35 48.

444 Java, Surabaja. 1950 (about 6 weeks). 1, 1(0.1639, 0.2774). [*Tijdschrift voor Parapsychologie* 21, 1953, pp. 3–22]; *Parapsychology Bulletin* no. 34, 1954, pp. 1–3; *JASPR* 67, 1973, p. 401. 3, 2; 2 5 6 16 18 56.

445 France, location not given. 1950 (Apr.; a few days). 1, 1(0.1154, 0.1890). Tizané, pp. 162–6. 5, 3; 1 6 8 19 35.

446 Canada, Chilliwack, B.C. 1951 (Oct.)–1952 (several months). 5, 1(0.0915, 0.2037). Lambert, pp. 147–9. 5, 2; 1 5 6 8 9 11 12 16 21.

447 England, Runcorn, Cheshire. 1952 (11 Aug.–13 Dec.). 1, 1(0.1140, 0.1916). Braddock, J., *Haunted Houses* (London, 1956), pp. 198–202. 3, 2; 1 6 16 26 40.

448 England, Runcorn, Cheshire. 1952 (Aug.–Oct.). 1, 1(0.1723, 0.2866). Dingwall, E. J., and Hall, T. H., *Four Modern Ghosts* (London, 1958), pp. 68–85; Braddock, J., *Haunted Houses* (London, 1956), pp. 192–9. 4, 3; 1 5 6 9 10 12 16 17 18 35 36.

449 W. Germany, Neudorf, Baden. 1952 (9 Oct.–10 Nov.). 1, 1(0.1682, 0.3042). *PPA* 6, 1969, pp. 88–91; Bender, pp. 49–50; *Tomorrow* no. 3, 1953, pp. 34–44; *Luce e Ombra* 60, 1960, pp. 407–16. 6, 3; 1 6 10 12 16 18 19 20 29.

450 USA, Los Angeles? 1953–1961 (14 May). 4, 2(0.2498, 0.1166). Bayless, pp. 138–46. 6, 4; 1 7 9 15 21 22 23 38 39.

451 Scotland, Ardachie, Inverness. 1953 (17–23 Aug.). 2, 2(0.1884, 0.1470). *JSPR* 38, 1955, pp. 159–72. 6, 5; 1 6 11 13 15 21 22 24.

452 Malaya, Kuala Kangsar. About 1955? 2, 1(0.0989, 0.1075). *Daily Telegraph Magazine* no. 168, Dec. 22nd, 1967, pp. 25–6. 3, 2; 1 6 9 23.

453 England, Selby, Yorks. 1955 (Nov.)–1956 (Jan.). 2, 2(0.1620, 0.1615). Dingwall, E. J., and Hall, T. H., *Four Modern Ghosts* (London, 1958), pp. 86–101. 5, 2; 1 4 6 9 11 13 22.

454 England, Tydd St Mary nr. Wisbech. 1957 (Aug.–Nov.). 2, 2(0.1980, 0.1604). See chapter 16; also *JSPR* 40, 1960, pp. 343–58; A. MacKenzie, *Frontiers of the Unknown* (London, 1968), pp. 184–205. 7, 5; 1 5 6 9 16 17 21 22 23 24 44 46.

455 USA, Seaford, Long Island. 1958 (3 Feb.–c. mid-Mar.). 3, 1(0.1581, 0.2763). Roll, pp. 12–23; *JASPR* 52, 1958, pp. 72, 108–13; *Journal of Parapsychology* 22, 1958, pp. 79–124; *JASPR* 62, 1968, pp. 262–308. 6, 4; 1 5 6 8 9 10 12 16 17 18 21 32.

456 England, London, location not given. 1960–1970 (?within). 2, 2(0.1467, 0.0824). Petitpierre, R., *Exorcizing Devils* (London, 1976), pp. 79–83. 2, 2; 1 17 21 22 23.

457 USA, Baltimore, Md. 1960 (14 Jan.–9 Feb.). 1, 1(0.1360, 0.2661). Fodor, N., *Between Two Worlds* (West Nyack, 1964), pp. 145–

52; Steiger, B., *Real Ghosts* (London, 1968), pp. 130–3. 2, 2;
1 6 8 9 10 12 16 17 18 32.
458 USA, Lynwood, Cal. 1960 (Sep.), 1, 1(0.0692, 0.1438). Bayless, pp. 55–61. 5, 3; 1 8 16.
459 Brazil, Brasilia. 1960 (night of 18–19 Sep.). 1, 1(0.0843, 0.1350). Playfair, pp. 260–3. 2, 2; 1 6 9 16 53.
460 Scotland, Sauchie, Clackmannanshire. 1960 (22 Nov.)–1961(Mar.). 5, 1(0.1323, 0.1827). See chapter 4. 6, 4; 1 6 8 9 11 12 16 17 21 22 35 39.
461 USA, Newark, N.J. 1961 (6 May–Sep.). 1, 1(0.1567, 0.2488). Roll, pp. 39–50; *JASPR* 63, 1969, pp. 123–74. 5, 5; 1 3 5 9 10 12 16 17 19.
462 USA, Indianapolis. 1962 (10 Mar.)–1963 (Feb.). 1, 1(0.1560, 0.2338). Roll, pp. 51–63; *JASPR* 64, 1970, pp. 66–99. 6, 5; 1 3 5 6 8 9 16 21 34 39.
463 USA, Big Bear City, San Bernadino, Cal. 1962 (June–c. Nov.). 1, 1(0.1160, 0.2217). Bayless, pp. 44–53; *Luce e Ombra* 62, 1962, pp. 241–5. 5, 3; 1 5 6 8 9 16 18 29.
464 USA, Clayton, N.C. 1962 (early June–15 July). 5, 1(0.1305, 0.2011). Roll, pp. 64–79. 5, 4; 1 5 6 9 11 12 27.
465 USA, Cedar Rapids, Iowa. 1962 (16 Aug.). 1, 1(0.0560, 0.1574). Bayless, pp. 38–42. 4, 2; 1 6 8 16.
466 New Zealand, Wellington. 1963 (Mar.). 2, 1(0.1453, 0.2708). Bayless, pp. 33–4, 180–1. 2, 2; 2 5 6 8 16 48.
467 USA, Lawrence, Mass. 1963 (c. Oct.–Nov.). 1, 1(0.1156, 0.1765). Bayless, pp. 87–95. 4, 2; 1 5 6 30.
468 Iceland, Saurar. 1964 (18 Mar.–mid-Apr.). 1, 1(0.1080, 0.1218). Roll, pp. 80–4. 1 6 8 9 16 17 22 24.
469 England, London, location not given. 1964 (Jan.)–1974 (June–sporadic). 1, 2(0.2222, 0.1916). *JSPR* 43, 1965, pp. 11–20; *JSPR* 45, 1969, pp. 149–61; *JSPR* 48, 1976, pp. 293–8. 5, 4; 1 7 11 13 14 16 18 21 22 23.
470 Philippines, Tabing Ilog, Luzon. 1964 (Oct.–Nov.). 5, 1(0.1078, 0.1996). Bayless, pp. 151–3. 4, 2; 2 6 8 9 16.
471 England, Ealing, London. 1965–1966. 4, 2(0.3351, 0.2844). Branston, B., *Beyond Belief* (London, 1974), pp. 52–149. 5, 4; 1 5 7 9 16 18 22 24 30 31 39 51 53 63.
472 W. Germany, Bremen. 1965 (June)–1967 (c. July). 1, 1(0.1888, 0.2617). *PPA* 6, 1969, pp. 91–3; *PPA* 5, 1968, pp. 37–8; Bender, pp. 50–2. 4, 2; 1 5 7 10 12 14 16 32.
473 England, Cambridge. 1966 (20 Feb.–c. Sep.). 1, 1(0.1400, 0.1960). Pike, J. A., *The Other Side* (London, 1969). 3, 2; 1 16 28 39 46.
474 USA, Miami. 1966 (mid-Dec.)–1967 (c. Feb.). 1, 1(0.1501, 0.2536). See chapter 5. 8, 5; 1 5 7 8 10 12 16 18.
475 India, Degaon, Maharasthra. About 1967. 1, 1(0.1398, 0.2213).

JASPR 66, 1972, pp. 240–3. 3, 2; 1 11 13 16 18 44.
476 Brazil, São Paulo. About 1967–1973. 3, 2(0.2656, 0.2647). Playfair, pp. 263–74. 5, 3; 1 5 7 8 9 17 19 21 28 30 48 53.
477 USA, Philadelphia. 1967 (June)–1968 (Aug.; at least). 4, 2(0.1357, 0.0924). *Theta* no. 23, 1968, pp. 2–3. 5, 2; 1 7 16 22 24.
478 England, E. Midlands, location not given. 1967 (5 June)–1969 (Apr.; phenomena after Aug. 1967 doubtful). 2, 1(0.1839, 0.2172). See chapter 14. 8, 5; 1 5 6 9 10 12 17 21 23 60.
479 W. Germany, Rosenheim, Bavaria. 1967 (Nov.)–1968. 5, 1(0.1594, 0.2921). Bender, pp. 52–60; Bender, H., in Beloff, J. (ed.), *New Directions in Parapsychology* (London, 1974), pp. 131–4; *PPA* 5, 1968, pp. 31–5; *PPA* 6, 1969, pp. 93–5; *Zeitschrift für Parapsychologie und Grenzgebiete der Psychologie* 11, 1968, pp. 104–12. 8, 3; 1 5 8 11 12 16 17 31 32.
480 Canada, Scarborough, Toronto. 1968–1971 (about). 4, 2(0.1670, 0.0527). *New Horizons* 1, 1972, pp. 35–9. 5, 3; 1 7 9 21 22 23.
481 England, Askern nr. Doncaster. 1968 (1 Apr.–May). 2, 2(0.1575, 0.1544). *JSPR* 45, 1970, pp. 325–53. 5, 2; 1 5 6 16 17 21 22 24 51.
482 USA, Olive Hill, Kentucky. 1968 (mid-Nov.–late Dec.?). 3, 1(0.2237, 0.2499). Roll, pp. 134–42; *PPA* 6, 1969, pp. 57–8; *Research in Parapsychology 1973* (Metuchen, N.J., 1974), pp. 64–7. 5, 4; 1 5 6 9 10 12 16 17 18 21 22 24 46 48.
483 W. Germany, Nicklheim, Bavaria. 1968 (Nov.)–1969. 1, 1(0.2146, 0.2433). Bender, pp. 61–4; *PPA* 6, 1969, pp. 95–9. 5, 2; 1 3 5 17 19 21 29 33.
484 Paraguay, Ponta Porã. 1969–1973. 1, 1(0.2325, 0.2844). Playfair, pp. 253–7. 5, 3; 1 5 7 16 17 19 28 29 39 42.
485 Brazil, Suzano. 1970 (May). 5, 1(0.1715, 0.2778). Playfair, pp. 257–60. 4, 3; 1 5 6 8 9 11 12 16 21 27 28 48.
486 W. Germany, Pursruck. 1970 (Nov.)–1971 (Aug.). 5, 1(0.1356, 0.1842). Bender, H., in Beloff, J. (ed.), *op. cit.* (see 479), pp. 135–8. 8, 4; 1 3 5 6 9 11 12 16 21 22.
487 England, Midlands, location not given. 1971–1972. 5, 1(0.3253, 0.3842). *Research in Parapsychology, 1972* (Metuchen, N.J., 1973), pp. 17–19. 4, 2; 1 5 7 11 12 14 16 18 24 25 31 45 46 53.
488 USA, Pittsburgh. 1971 (c. July)–1972 (22 Apr.). 2, 2(0.1897, 0.1856). See chapter 18. 6, 5; 1 6 8 9 16 17 22 23 24 26 31.
489 USA, S., location not given. 1971 (2 Dec.)–1972 (early Jan.). 2, 1(0.1189, 0.1622). *JASPR* 68, 1974, pp. 1–33; *Research in Parapsychology 1972* (Metuchen, N.J., 1973), pp. 70–2. 5, 5; 1 6 10 12 16 17 21 22.
490 Switzerland, location not given. 1972 (Jan.–June). 1, 1(0.1829, 0.2969). *Metapsichica* 28, 1973, pp. 78–80. 5, 2; 1 6 10 12 16 17 19 31 39 53.

491 USA, New Jersey, location not given. 1972 (early)–1974. 1, 1(0.2086, 0.2202). *Theta* no. 39–40, 1974, pp. 17–18. 5, 3; 1 5 7 17 19 54 55.
492 Brazil, São Paulo. 1972 (7–c.28 July). 5,1(0.1620, 0.2991), Playfair, pp. 248–51. 5, 2; 1 5 6 8 9 11 12 16 18 19 23 48.
493 Brazil, Sorocaba. 1972 (18 July, for some weeks). 5, 1(0.0973, 0.2319). Playfair, pp. 251–3. 5, 2; 1 5 6 8 11 12 16 17 21.
494 W. Germany, Scherfede, Westphalia. 1972 (Sep–Dec.). 5, 1(0.1297, 0.2360). Bender, H., in Beloff, J. (ed.), *op. cit.* (see 479), pp. 138–41. 4, 2; 1 5 6 8 9 11 12 30.
495 USA, Los Angeles. 1972 (Nov.)–1973 (Feb.). 3, 1(0.3035, 0.3461). *JSPR* 47, 1974, pp. 438–45. 5, 3; 1 5 6 8 9 16 19 22 26 31 34 39 48 51 53.
496 USA, Maryland, location not given. 1973 (Mar.)–1974 (Feb.). 1, 1(0.1363, 0.1666). *Theta* no. 42, 1974, pp. 1–3. 5, 3; 1 6 16 22 26 31.
497 USA, Bronx, New York. 1974 (9 Feb.–c. Apr.). 5, 1(0.0903, 0.2279). *Research in Parapsychology 1974* (Metuchen, N.J., 1975), pp. 139–43. 5, 3; 1 5 6 8 9 11 12 16 17.
498 USA, location not given. 1974 (19 July)–1975. 1, 1(0.1416, 0.1684). *Research in Parapsychology 1975* (Metuchen, N.J., 1976), pp. 115–20. 5, 4; 1 5 9 10 13 16 21.
499 USA, location not given. 1974 (9 Oct.–c. Nov.). 5, 1(0.1973, 0.2929). *Research in Parapsychology 1975* (Metuchen, N.J., 1976), pp. 109–15. 6, 3; 1 3 5 6 8 9 11 12 16 17 21 23 39 61.
500 Italy, Rome. 1975 (19 Apr.–2 May). 1, 1(0.0820, 0.2161). *Metapsichica* 30, 1976, pp. 48–54. 5, 2; 1 6 8 10 12 16.

Index of cases
(The Appendix is not indexed)

Adams (1817–21), 159, 171, 330
Alais (1324), 144
Alsace (1865–9), 173
Amherst (1878–9), 174, 240, 247, 342
Amiens (1732–46), 181, 331
Andover (1970s), 27, 341
Annaberg (1691), 40
Annandale (1707), 65
Appleby (1887), 220, 256
Ardachie (1957), 239, 356
Argentaro, Monte (1725–75), 173
Ars-en-Dombes (1824–56), 117, 173
Auberire, Canton de (1816), 65

Bargarran (1696), 65, 126–7, 172
Bath, near (1963), 301–7
Belledoon (1829–31), 331
Bergzabern (1852), 341
Bologna (1580), 19
Borley (1886–1946), 134
Boston (1692–3), 65, 111
Boston (1693), 111
Boston (1867), 68–71, 174, 247, 341
Bratislava (1927), 34
Bremen (1965), 341
Brightling (1659), 65
Brighton (1882–9), 186–95, 206–7
Bristol (1761–2), 111, 118–26, 144, 172, 173, 175, 240
Buhai (1925–7), 127–42, 240, 247, 341, 342, 353

Cambridge (1718), 246
Cambridge (1966), 144
Cambridgeshire (1957), 249–50
Canvey Island (1709), 211–19, 240
Charlottenburg (1929), 148–57, 240, 343, 360
Chelmsford (1579), 42
Cheltenham (1880–9), 178–9
Cherbourg (1918), 356
Cheriton (1917), 247
Cideville (1850–1), 111
Cieurac (1926), 65
Clairefontaine (1846), 65
Clarendon (1889), 98, 171, 240, 356

Cork (1928), 65
Coullons (1850), 173
Cronheim (1899), 246
Cumminsville (1870), 65

Devonshire (1840s), 65
Dibbesdorf (1767–8), 330
Dijon, near (1838–40), 65
Dortmund (1713), 40
Döttingen (1689), 111
Durweston (1893–4), 109, 215–16

Earling (1928), 173, 174–5
East Midlands (1967), 263–78
Eggenberg (1929), 258, 321, 356
England (c. 1920), 247
Epworth (1716), 111, 202, 208, 238, 239, 246, 356
Ewell (1681), 42, 65

Fewston (1621–2), 124–6
Fougères (1913), 331
France (1940), 247, 353

Georgetown (1949), 173, 174–5
Germany (1789), 42
Germany, Kloster N—— g (1794–1815), 181–2
Gerolstein (1901), 65
Glasgow (1907), 239, 356
Glasgow (1974–5), 361
Glenluce (1654), 65, 172
Grenoble (1907), 342
Gröben (1718), 40, 41, 247
Grosserlach (1916), 111
Guillonville (1848), 220, 353
Güssing (1925), 321

Hinton Ampner (1765–71), 181
Hopfgarten (1921), 68, 76–9, 340
Hydesville (1848), 26, 144, 321

Iletski (1870), 325, 356
Indianapolis (1962), 326, 341

Kabsdorff (1666), 64–5
Kecskemet (1921), 331

Kempten (856–8), 171
Kingstown (1876), 342
Klefersulzbach (1811–41), 182–3
Klopotiva (1880), 34
Kosten-Steinhügel (1927), 116
Kuala Kangsar (c. 1955), 144

Lading (1916), 353
Lagny (1210), 144
Lancashire (1968), 278–82
Leipzig (1931), 144, 356
Little Minories (1679), 145
Lolworth (1676–7), 42, 65
London, City of (1901), 356
Lyons (1525–6), 23–7, 145

Mâcon (1612), 43, 170, 240, 356
Madras (1872), 356
Malvern (1942), 261
Maryland (1973–4), 283
Mauritius (1937), 247
Miami (1966–7), 19, 88–94, 247, 260, 325–6, 327, 341
Midlands (1971–2), 99
Molignon (1914), 65, 174
Monneville (early twentieth century), 65
Montclair (1918–25), 220–2
Munchhof (1818), 247, 325
Munich (1927), 328

Naples (1696–7), 111, 161–70, 172, 240
Neudorf (1952), 341
Newark (1961), 155, 326, 341
New Bedford (1974–5), 223
Newbury (1679), 42, 62–4, 111, 172
New Jersey (1972–4), 210
New York (1907), 311
New York, Bronx (1974), 341
Nicklheim (1968–9), 258, 322
Nidamangalam (1920), 111, 356
Nikolsburg (1927), 342, 356
Normandy (1867), 199–202, 204, 207, 238, 283
North Aston (1591–2), 32–8, 240
Nottingham (1597), 172
Nottingham (1971–2), 284–94
Nottingham, near (1972), 345–9, 354
Nottingham, near (1977), 307–11

Oakland (1874), 209–10, 239, 247, 331
Oberbayern (1928), 145
Oderwitz (1862–4), 111, 356
Olive Hill (1968), 247, 327
Ooty (1897), 111
Oppenheim (1620–2), 146–8
Orenburg (1870), 328–9
Orielton (1184), 353

Paris (1888), 240, 311, 356
Pfedelbach (1703–8), 118
Philadelphia (1866), 247
Pittsburgh (1971), 239, 356–9
Pleaston (1852), 65
Ponta Porã (1969–73), 246, 353
Poona (1920), 100–15, 144, 240, 353, 355
Portland, Oregon (1909), 331
Portsmouth, N.H. (1682), 62, 64, 356
Pursruck (1970), 65

Ravenna (530), 22
Rerrick (1695), 167–70, 240, 356
Resau (1888), 42
Roehampton, Jamaica (1931), 34
Rome (1975), 341
Rosenheim (1967–8), 88, 94–7, 174, 258, 341

St Maur (1706), 246
St Pancras (1846), 144, 145
St Petersburg (1880), 321
Sampford Peverell (1810–12), 211, 238, 240
Sandfeldt (1722), 40, 99–115, 240, 246, 355
Sauchie (1960–1), 68, 79–83, 246, 263, 340, 341
Scarborough, Ont. (1968–71), 205
Schkeitbar (1738–9), 246
Schwartzbach (1749), 353
Seaford (1958), 325, 326
Seyssuel (1930), 65, 341
Sheffield (1882–5), 256
Siebenburg (1880), 321
Sitoebondo (1892–3), 19
Slawensik (1806), 238, 239, 247
Soemedang (1831), 34
Spreyton (1682–3), 110
Stans (1860–2), 5–18, 208, 238, 325
Stockwell (1772), 19, 85–8
Stommeln (1260–88), 117, 118, 121, 173, 356
Stratford, Conn. (1850), 240, 356
Strathtay (1878–98), 246
Sumatra (1903), 34
Suri (1919), 111
Sussex (1927), 344–5

INDEX 401

T——, Chateau de, *see* Normandy (1867)
Tackley (1905–8), 183–6, 197, 246
Tanzania (1910–14?), 31–2
Tedworth, *see* Tidworth
Thorn (Torun) (1655), 42
Thorney (1868), 332
Tidworth, North (1662–3), 42, 43–62, 98, 170–1, 208, 238, 240, 246, 331, 356
Töttelstedt (Tuttelstadt) (1581), 27–31
Tydd St Mary (1957), 239, 256, 312–18, 356

USA (1971), 341
USA (1974), 247, 260
USA (1975), 340–1

Vöst (1932), 145

West Brompton (1871–7), 223
Willington (1834–47), 195–9, 202, 204, 207, 238, 246, 283
Windsor, Nova Scotia (1906–7), 244
Woodstock (1649), 43, 239, 246
Worcestershire (1914), 223, 239
Worksop (1883), 247
Württemberg (1844), 173

Ylöjärvi (1885), 19, 68, 71–6, 84, 240
Youghal (1661), 65, 111

Index of names
(The Appendix is not indexed)

Acres, M., 211
Alder, Mary, 36
Alphonsus de (a) Spina, 180
Anders, Margarethe, 151–2
Apollonius of Tyana, 22
Ashton, J., 44
Aubrey, J., 60
Ayliffe, Col., 45

Bartlett, F. C., 254–5
Baxter, R., 43
Bell, Mr, 217
Beloff, J., 95
Bender, H., 94–7, 258, 319
Bennett, Sir E., 261
Birck, H., 147–8
Blackburn, D., 192
Blair, R., 135
Branston, B., 80
Brayley, J., 87
Brewka, Marthe, 151–2
Brooks, H., 90
Brooks, R., 335
Brotherton, J. M., 313–15
Bruck, Dr, 137
Buckman, L., 110
Burdick, D. S., 325–7

Caesarius of Arles, St, 22
Calmet, A., 146–7
Campbell, Virginia, and family, 80–3, 84, 246
Carr, Jane, 197–8
Carrick, Mary, 68–71, 83, 84
Cawley, Sir W., 45
Chamberlain, R., 64
Chamberlaine, Sir T., 52
Chambers, R., 167–8
Charles II, 59–60
Chaundry, B., 184
Chesterfield, Lord, 59
Christina of Stommeln, Blessed, 117, 121
Churchill, T., 36
Clancy, Julia, 261
Clarke, Ella, 273–5

Clarke, T. B., 209
'Connolly, B.', and family, 264–78
Cooper, Mrs, 217
Cope, J. I., 59
Cope, Mr, 37
Cragg, J., 47, 59
'Cramer, E.', and family, 356–9
Crandon, Stella, 321
Crawford, W. J., 322–3
Creed, W., 44, 45
Crowe, Catherine, 85, 195
Curtis, R., 42, 65

Daly, A. A., 211
Dariex, Dr, 200
Davidson, Mary, 196, 197–8
Davidson, R., 196
Davison, C., 332
Dawson, W. O., 188–9
Decremps, H., 245
Defoe, D., 159, 211
Degenkolbe, W., 78–9
Del Rio, M., 3, 5
Dingwall, E. J., 32, 330–1
Dowse, W., 59
Doyle, Sir A. Conan, 146
Drury, W., 45–6, 48, 50, 58–9, 62
Dufresnoy, N. Lenglet, 23
Dumba, M., 138
Dunckelman, H. J., and family, 99–115
Durbin, H., 118–24, 245, 247

Edwards, Violet, 307, 310–11, 345–8
Eerole, E., 73
Eleazar, 22
Elgart, N., 29
Evans, J., 123
Ewen, C. L'Estrange, 59

Fairfax, E., and family, 124–6
Falmouth, Lord, 59
Farrell, J. K., 297
Fi(e)ck, C., 105
Flammarion, C., 199
Fletcher, I., 244

INDEX

Fowler, R., 87
Fulman, W., 44

Galisio, D., 164, 165
Galisio, P., 164, 165
Garrett, Eileen, 344-5
Geller, U., 323
Gerould, G. H., 19
Gerstmann, F., 40
Gilby, Clara, 187-91, 206-7
Giles, E., 33, 34
Giles, Molly and Dobby, and family, 119-26
Glanvill, J., 44, 45, 55-8, 60-2
Golding, Mrs, 85-7
Goligher, Kathleen, 322
Greer, D. S., 254, 257, 259
Gresham, Mr, 86
Grollée, Anthoinette de, 24-7
Grönfors, G., 73-4
Grunewald, F., 127, 129-31, 327
Gurney, E., 186, 190, 192

Hackenberg, Frau, 156
Haenell, H. G., 99-115
Hahn, W., 133-4, 136
Hall, T. H., 192, 330-1
Hardwick, W. W., 135
Hasted, J. B., 329-30
Heinisch, J., 41
Hellèn, G., 73, 74
'Henry, P.', and family, 356-9
Herbert, B., 324
Hickes, R., 35
Hillebrandt, Pfarrer, 150, 151
Hoffman, R., 136, 138
Holden, Anne, 190-1, 207
Hone, W., 85, 87
Howitt, W., 22
Hyslop, J. H., 209

J., Mr and Mrs, and family, 284-94
James, Mrs, 217
Jenkins, J. D., 101
Joines, W. T., 325-7
Joller, M., and family, 5-18
Jones, Hannah, 64
Joseph of Copertino, St, 67
Josephus, F., 22
'Julie', 307-11

Karger, F., 95, 96
Kaye, Lucie, 135
Keil, H. H. J., 324
Kerner, J., 181
Ketkar, D., and family, 100-15

King, W., 36
Klein, K., 127, 129-30, 132
Kohn, Miss H., 101-15
Körber, Dr, 137
Körner, J., 27-31
Kröner, W., 136-7, 138
Kruswicki, Frau, 156
Kruswicki, Herr, 150
Kulagina, Nelya, 323-4
Kulovesi, Y., 72

Lamb, C., 263-76
Lambert, G. W., 330-7
Lang, A., 23, 63
Latimer, J., 119
Laubheim, A., 90
Lavater, L., 181
Law, R., 167
Lea, H. C., 158
Lee, E., and family, 32-8
Lehman, F., 41
Le Loyer, P., 181
Leslie, Sir S., 159
Lewis, Ruth, 276
Lindell, Amanda, 75
Lindell, Sexton, 74-5
Lindholm, K., 75
Lindroos, Emma, 72-5, 83, 84
Livy, 22
'Liz', 307-11
Logan, Dr W., 79, 80, 81-2
Logan, Mrs, 82
Lord, Mr, 211, 214-18
Lund, T. W., 79, 80-1, 82, 83

M., Mr and Mrs, 294-301
Macarescu, 128-9
McConnell, R. A., 356
Macfarlane, A., 33
McHarg, J. F., 99, 361
Malcolm, J. P., 85
Mann, T., 197
Map, W., 158
Marshall, J., 254
Martin, E., 71-6
Martin, Eva, 72-6
Martin, Mary, 86
Mathews, F. M., 223
Maton, W., 44, 53, 59
Measey, Joan, 34, 36-7
Mihai, 130, 328
Miller, of Barwick, 50
Möller, L., 107
Mompesson, J., and family, 43-62, 65
Montalembert, A. de, 23-7

More, H., 60-1
Morice, J., 199, 200, 202
Möricke, Pfarrer, 182-3
Morris, Miss L., 187-91
Morse, E., 63-4
Morse, W., 63
Moser, F., 5, 14
Moss, Mary, 213-18
Murray, D. J., 313-15, 335

Neugarten, Dr, 152, 154
Newman, Mr, 109, 215-16
Nicolson, Marjorie H., 44
Nisbet, W. H., 79, 81-2
Norton, R., 42, 65
Notestein, W., 33

Osborne, H., 335, 336
Ostafi, N., 128-9
Owen, A. R. G., 43, 79, 175, 341

Page, D., and family, 312-18
Pain, J., 86
Pain, Mary, 86-7
Palmer, E. Clepham, 135
Palmer, W. M., 42
Pappe, Frieda, 76-8
Parry, F., 44, 53
Paul, St, of the Cross, 173
Pepys, R., 42
Pepys, S., 59
Pfeil, Police Commissioner, 79
Philostratus, 22
Pierce, H. W., 356-9
Pinetti, G., 245
Pleydell, Mr, 53
Podmore, F., 186, 253-4, 255-6
Pollard, Nurse, 199
Popham, H. M., 303-7
Powell, C., 63
Pratt, J. G., 89-93, 260-1, 324
Price, H., 43, 44, 85, 87-8, 101, 134-5, 138, 141, 168, 184
Prince, Theodosia, 221-2
Prince, W. F., 220-2
Procter, E., 195, 199
Procter, Elizabeth, 195, 197, 199
Procter, J., 195-9, 204, 206
Punala, Helene, 75

Raumburger, J., 29
Regulski, Lucie, and family, 149-57
Rhine, J. B., 320
Richard, C. K., 181
Richardson, J., 198

Richardson, M. A., 199
Robert-Houdin, J. E., 245
Robinson, Ann, 85-7
Rogo, D. Scott, 173-5
Roll, W. G., 89-94, 247, 325-9, 340-1
Rosenburg, R., 210
Rosenbusch, H., 138-40
Roughton, D., 346

Sauerbrey, E., 76-9
Sauerbrey, Minna, 76-9, 83, 84
Sch., Annemarie, 96-7
Schawer, T., 28
Schiel, H., and family, 27-31
Schmidt, Dr, 152, 153
Schrenck-Notzing, A. von, 72, 76, 79, 137, 328
Schröder, C., 129
Schschapoff, Mr, 328-9
Schultz, H. H., 105
Schuppart, Prof., 118
Schwab, Dr, 152, 154
Setnik, V., 129
Sharpe, Ada M., 183-6, 197, 206
Sharpe, C. K., 167
Sharpe, Florence M., 184
Shaw, Christian, 126-7
Shotter, J. D., 266-8, 272
Sinclar, G., 167
Sitwell, S., 44, 200
Smagge, J., 211-18
Smith, G. A., 188-9, 191-5, 206-7
Smith, Susy, 89, 93
Solfvin, G. F., 223, 340-1
Somers, W., 172
Squillante, *maestro*, 161-2, 163, 164
Stead, W. T., 195
Stephenson, C. J., 278-82
Stephenson, G. M., 272
Stern, W., 255
Stevenson, I., 254, 256, 350-2
Stewart, Margaret, 79, 80, 81, 82, 83
Stiles, J., 63-4
Stüve, F., 103, 107
Sünner, P., 148-57

Taillepied, N., 181
Taylor, J., 323-4
Telfair, A., 167-8, 170
Telieux, Alis de, 24-7
Teodorescu, J., 128
Teschener, P., 28
Thirring, H., 138
Thurston, H., 101, 111-12, 117, 144
Thyraeus, P., 179, 181

Paperbacks also available from White Crow Books

Elsa Barker—*Letters from a Living Dead Man*
ISBN 978-1-907355-83-7

Elsa Barker—*War Letters from the Living Dead Man*
ISBN 978-1-907355-85-1

Elsa Barker—*Last Letters from the Living Dead Man*
ISBN 978-1-907355-87-5

Richard Maurice Bucke—*Cosmic Consciousness*
ISBN 978-1-907355-10-3

Arthur Conan Doyle—*The Edge of the Unknown*
ISBN 978-1-907355-14-1

Arthur Conan Doyle—*The New Revelation*
ISBN 978-1-907355-12-7

Arthur Conan Doyle—*The Vital Message*
ISBN 978-1-907355-13-4

Arthur Conan Doyle with Simon Parke—*Conversations with Arthur Conan Doyle*
ISBN 978-1-907355-80-6

Meister Eckhart with Simon Parke—*Conversations with Meister Eckhart*
ISBN 978-1-907355-18-9

D. D. Home—*Incidents in my Life Part 1*
ISBN 978-1-907355-15-8

Mme. Dunglas Home; edited, with an Introduction, by Sir Arthur Conan Doyle—*D. D. Home: His Life and Mission*
ISBN 978-1-907355-16-5

Edward C. Randall—*Frontiers of the Afterlife*
ISBN 978-1-907355-30-1

Rebecca Ruter Springer—*Intra Muros: My Dream of Heaven*
ISBN 978-1-907355-11-0

Leo Tolstoy, edited by Simon Parke—*Forbidden Words*
ISBN 978-1-907355-00-4

Leo Tolstoy—*A Confession*
ISBN 978-1-907355-24-0

Leo Tolstoy—*The Gospel in Brief*
ISBN 978-1-907355-22-6

Leo Tolstoy—*The Kingdom of God is Within You*
ISBN 978-1-907355-27-1

Leo Tolstoy—*My Religion: What I Believe*
ISBN 978-1-907355-23-3

Leo Tolstoy—*On Life*
ISBN 978-1-907355-91-2

Leo Tolstoy—*Twenty-three Tales*
ISBN 978-1-907355-29-5

Leo Tolstoy—*What is Religion and other writings*
ISBN 978-1-907355-28-8

Leo Tolstoy—*Work While Ye Have the Light*
ISBN 978-1-907355-26-4

Leo Tolstoy—*The Death of Ivan Ilyich*
ISBN 978-1-907661-10-5

Leo Tolstoy—*Resurrection*
ISBN 978-1-907661-09-9

Leo Tolstoy with Simon Parke—*Conversations with Tolstoy*
ISBN 978-1-907355-25-7

Howard Williams with an Introduction by Leo Tolstoy—*The Ethics of Diet: An Anthology of Vegetarian Thought*
ISBN 978-1-907355-21-9

Vincent Van Gogh with Simon Parke—*Conversations with Van Gogh*
ISBN 978-1-907355-95-0

Wolfgang Amadeus Mozart with Simon Parke—*Conversations with Mozart*
ISBN 978-1-907661-38-9

Jesus of Nazareth with Simon Parke—*Conversations with Jesus of Nazareth*
ISBN 978-1-907661-41-9

Thomas à Kempis with Simon Parke—*The Imitation of Christ*
ISBN 978-1-907661-58-7

Julian of Norwich with Simon Parke—*Revelations of Divine Love*
ISBN 978-1-907661-88-4

Allan Kardec—*The Spirits Book*
ISBN 978-1-907355-98-1

Allan Kardec—*The Book on Mediums*
ISBN 978-1-907661-75-4

Emanuel Swedenborg—*Heaven and Hell*
ISBN 978-1-907661-55-6

P.D. Ouspensky—*Tertium Organum: The Third Canon of Thought*
ISBN 978-1-907661-47-1

Dwight Goddard—*A Buddhist Bible*
ISBN 978-1-907661-44-0

Michael Tymn—*The Afterlife Revealed*
ISBN 978-1-970661-90-7

Michael Tymn—*Transcending the Titanic: Beyond Death's Door*
ISBN 978-1-908733-02-3

Guy L. Playfair—*If This Be Magic*
ISBN 978-1-907661-84-6

Guy L. Playfair—*The Flying Cow*
ISBN 978-1-907661-94-5

Guy L. Playfair—*This House is Haunted*
ISBN 978-1-907661-78-5

Carl Wickland, M.D.—*Thirty Years Among the Dead*
ISBN 978-1-907661-72-3

John E. Mack—*Passport to the Cosmos*
ISBN 978-1-907661-81-5

Peter & Elizabeth Fenwick—*The Truth in the Light*
ISBN 978-1-908733-08-5

Erlendur Haraldsson—*Modern Miracles*
ISBN 978-1-908733-25-2

Erlendur Haraldsson—*At the Hour of Death*
ISBN 978-1-908733-27-6

Erlendur Haraldsson—*The Departed Among the Living*
ISBN 978-1-908733-29-0

Brian Inglis—*Science and Parascience*
ISBN 978-1-908733-18-4

Brian Inglis—*Natural and Supernatural: A History of the Paranormal*
ISBN 978-1-908733-20-7

Ernest Holmes—*The Science of Mind*
ISBN 978-1-908733-10-8

Victor & Wendy Zammit —*A Lawyer Presents the Evidence For the Afterlife*
ISBN 978-1-908733-22-1

Casper S. Yost—*Patience Worth: A Psychic Mystery*
ISBN 978-1-908733-06-1

William Usborne Moore—*Glimpses of the Next State*
ISBN 978-1-907661-01-3

William Usborne Moore—*The Voices*
ISBN 978-1-908733-04-7

John W. White—*The Highest State of Consciousness*
ISBN 978-1-908733-31-3

Stafford Betty—*The Imprisoned Splendor*
ISBN 978-1-907661-98-3

Paul Pearsall, Ph.D. —*Super Joy*
ISBN 978-1-908733-16-0

All titles available as eBooks, and selected titles available in Hardback and Audiobook formats from www.whitecrowbooks.com

www.ingramcontent.com/pod-product-compliance
Lightning Source LLC
Chambersburg PA
CBHW031418150426
43191CB00006B/317